MW00335246

Pogrom in Gujarat

Figure 1: Frontispiece. Indistinction

Pogrom in Gujarat

HINDU NATIONALISM AND ANTI-MUSLIM
VIOLENCE IN INDIA

Parvis Ghassem-Fachandi

PRINCETON UNIVERSITY PRESS

Princeton and Oxford

Copyright © 2012 by Princeton University Press
Published by Princeton University Press,
41 William Street, Princeton, New Jersey 08540
In the United Kingdom: Princeton University Press,
6 Oxford Street, Woodstock, Oxfordshire OX20 1TW

PRESS.PRINCETON.EDU

All Rights Reserved

Library of Congress Cataloging-in-Publication Data

Ghassem-Fachandi, Parvis.
   Pogrom in Gujarat : Hindu nationalism and anti-
Muslim violence in India / Parvis Ghassem-Fachandi.
      p.   cm.
   Includes bibliographical references and index.
ISBN 978-0-691-15176-2 (hardcover : alk. paper) —
ISBN 978-0-691-15177-9 (pbk. : alk. paper)
   1. Gujarat Riots, India, 2002. 2. Pogroms—India—
Gujarat. 3. Ethnic conflict—India—Gujarat.
4. Muslims—Violence against—India—Gujarat.
I. Title.
   DS485.G88G48   2012
   954'.750531—dc23   2011026167

British Library Cataloging-in-Publication Data is
available

This book has been composed in Minion

Printed on acid-free paper. ∞

Printed in the United States of America

10 9 8 7 6 5 4 3 2 1

Contents

Figures

Pogrom in Gujarat

Introduction

Pogrom in Gujarat is a study of an anti-Muslim pogrom in Gujarat, India, that began on February 28, 2002, and lasted for three days—approximately seventy-two hours. Officials rationalized the violence as a reaction—*pratikriya*—to the aggression of its victims. In the city of Ahmedabad and in Gujarat's central provinces, a state of exception ruled for approximately three weeks. Several mass killings were followed over a few months by many instances of violence on a lesser scale. Muslim homes and religious structures were desecrated and destroyed; Muslim commercial establishments were boycotted. Countless flyers circulated, appealing to Hindus to awake to the essence of who they were—and many did. For weeks on end, a curfew was put into effect in select areas of Ahmedabad and other cities. When it was over, 150,000 individuals had been driven from their homes and more than 1,000 people lay dead, the majority of whom were Muslims.[1] Many Muslims understand the pogrom to have lasted much longer than three days and, instead, still today insist it lasted anywhere from six weeks to three months. Central Gujarat did not return to normalcy until spring 2003, which coincided with my departure from the scene after eighteen months of ethnographic fieldwork. Despite its severity and some singular aspects of its organization, the pogrom resembled similar events experienced by previous generations in Ahmedabad and elsewhere at the end of the 1960s, 1980s, and the 1990s (RCR; Sheth and Menon 1986; Spodek 1989; Nandy et al. 1995: 104–107, 110–123; Breman 2003: 253–262; 2004: 221–231; Shani 2007: 77–132, 156–188; Kumar 2009: 80–215).

A pogrom is an event driven by words and images, as much by the associations and invocations that precede it as by those that accompany it. The enactment of the Gujarat pogrom followed a script collectively shared on the streets and in media representations. In the chapters that follow, I examine the forms of complicity that the pogrom demanded and the quotidian understandings it engendered. While many of these understandings seem to be recurrent instances of collective violence, I focus only on events of 2002 and seek to unravel the specific cultural and psychological processes of individual and collective identification that were then prevalent in central Gujarat. The extant literature about the pogrom, I will argue, insufficiently understands and inadequately takes into account these processes.

While I had completed an ethnographic study in a Gujarati village by the mid-1990s, I began field research in urban Ahmedabad in 1999. At that time, most residents of the city I spoke to insisted that this thing called "politics" was ultimately responsible for past outbreaks of violence in the city. By politics (*rajkaran*), reckoning with the causes and purposes of power, they meant the inherently corrupt and profoundly immoral political theater of all violent altercations. By contrast, following the pogrom in 2002, many non-Muslim residents explained the violence as an extralegal collective punishment of a recalcitrant Muslim minority by the Hindu majority, conceived of as "the people." By 2009, while some Hindu-identified residents continued to hold this view, others had softened their stand. Many acknowledged Muslim victimization but nonetheless insisted that events in 2002 had been overblown in the national and international media, giving the state a bad name.

By 2009, many Muslim residents I knew, though still holding to an understanding of themselves as the primary victims of the pogrom, were no longer eager to hold any political party, civic institution, or individual accountable for the violence. Some even preferred the Bharatiya Janata Party (BJP)—which has been in rule this entire time—outright above the Congress Party because, in the words of one interlocutor, "They will stab you from the front not from the back." Such a cynical apprehension of the mechanics of political representation is nothing new in the state and, some argue, had already obtained in the 1990s (G. Shah 2003b: 231).

Many Muslims also acknowledged the state government's successes for bringing economic development in the intervening years to Gujarat, which it has subsequently made central to its legitimation. Many still agreed that the events in 2002 had been "politics," which means to say that the ruling political party had instigated the pogrom in order to counter a downward trend in support, as it had lost the state's *gram panchayat* elections in 2001 and then the assembly by-elections in early 2002. But by 2009, the rule of the BJP in the state had stabilized, and Muslims were secure—for a while. Accordingly, although the pogrom had been part of a timely political calculation, many people claimed that because it was ultimately predictable, they could at least reckon with it.

In these understandings, a cyclical pattern of violence with a recurrent rationalization is apparent. The way of least resistance is the relegation of all violence to an amorphous "politics", the common denominator with which all—Hindu or Muslim, Dalit or Vaniya—will agree. Speaking transparently about past experiences with violence risks summoning a past that still vividly lurks in the present. Such interpretations elide the more disturbing realization that not only do political parties manipulate constituencies for electoral gain, but people themselves become complicit in this by inhabiting representations, participating in acts and thoughts that have effects beyond the mere political calculations of those who organize for violence. The political machinations of the pogrom reveal only half of the story.

The other half is the focus of this study. How was the chief minister of Gujarat able to mobilize city residents psychologically for violent action while, at the same time, extricating the political from the event? How were vernacular print media successful in deploying phantasmal material despite city residents' profound experiences with earlier rounds of violence? How did specific members of lower and middle classes inhabit these representations, and how did their identifications relate to local practices of nonviolence, sacrifice, and disgust? How do contemporary forms of identification relate to the state's most famous figure, Mahatma Gandhi? How is violence anchored in the urban hardware of a city whose spatial configuration is profoundly scarred by violent experiences? And, last, what is the peculiar logic of inclusive exclusion as it revolves around the inherent instability of the categories "Hindu" and "Muslim" evoked in the pogrom?

HINDU NATIONALISM AND GUJARAT

While Gujarat has traditionally been and is still today one of India's most prosperous states, urban areas such as Ahmedabad have been the scenes for flashes of serious communal conflagrations for a very long time. After Indian Independence in 1947 and the formation of the state of Gujarat in 1960, Ahmedabad, its largest city, emerged as "one of the most violent prone urban areas in all of India" (Varshney 2002: 220). In Ahmedabad, collective violence is indeed endemic.[2]

Recurrent events of what is frequently called "ethnic" or "communal" violence in modern India bring to the fore complex problems inherited from the various empires that have refigured the South Asian continent. Hence recent territorial displacements and population movements often remind historians of the familiar themes that form the detritus of modern South Asian history: Orientalism, colonialism, partition, war, nationalism, social movements, ethnic and religious conflict, and global networks of trade and brutality of every imaginable sort. Academics from political science and sociology have largely focused on issues and ailments such as environmental exploitation, labor migration, communalism, the nuclear threat, and the contradictory effects of democratization and new state formation.

These macro themes certainly are not to be neglected. The anthropological contribution here, however, is to show how their significance is inflected locally by the experiences of more immediate and intimate concerns, such as upward mobility, ambivalence towards a symbolic father, marriage and sexuality, culinary practices and dietary disinvestments, the disappearance and transformation of traditional styles of worship, and the experience of social stigma in urban space. As my research places strong emphasis on ethnographic exposition, for reasons I will explain below, experiences are situated in multiple geopolitical and temporal scales.

Gujarat is unique within India. The state harbors a strong regional identity, which culminated in the establishment of a separate territorial entity in 1960 (Yagnik and Sheth 2005: 226–228; Ibrahim 2009: 13–31). It is today also known as the "laboratory of Hindutva" with a self-chosen role of vanguard for India as a whole. The term *Hindutva*—Hindu-ness (literally, the essence of the Hindu)—is commonly translated as "Hindu nationalism." Hindutva has become a reference point for political articulation in Gujarat at least since the late 1980s and early 1990s, but its activity in the state reaches much further back (G. Shah 1993: esp. 196; A. M. Shah 2002b).

Hindu nationalism initially emerged before Independence in western India as an upper-caste ideology with universal scope. It held an ambiguous relationship to traditional Hindu worldviews and practices as well as to the West. While it opposed British colonialism, it simultaneously sought to emulate the West and was in favor of rapid modernization (Jaffrelot 1996 [1993]: 11–79; Hansen 1999: 79–80). Mahatma Gandhi, the recognized symbolic father of modern India, epitomized an oppositional relationship both to Western modernity and to Hindu nationalism. He was, indeed, assassinated in 1948 by a Hindu nationalist, an identification that Gandhi referred to as placing them among "the moderns." Although he considered himself an orthodox Hindu, Gandhi rejected this form of nationalism because it channeled colonial subjugation as a form of mawkish innocence to authorizing violent expression, which he vehemently opposed (Bhatt 2001: 83).

Promulgated most succinctly by the revolutionary nationalist Vinayak Damodar Savarkar in the 1920s, Hindutva ideology ascribed a notion of nationhood to Aryan and non-Aryan peoples on the subcontinent. These peoples would form a single Hindu nation (*hindu rashtra*) that included members of diverse castes and religious communities such as Jains, Buddhists, and Sikhs, while excluding Muslims and Christians (Savarkar 2005 [1928]: 113). Influenced by European writers such as the English evolutionist sociologist Herbert Spencer, the German Romantic philosopher Friedrich Schlegel, the French race theorist Arthur Comte de

Gobineau, and the Italian revolutionary nationalist Giuseppe Mazzini, Savarkar proposed definitions of Hindu-ness based on territory, race, culture (understood as civilization—*sanskruti*), and strong affective ties (Bhatt 2001: 79–94).

In Savarkar's influential formulations there is an important omission: religion. Although he found it important to emphasize an inclusive Hindu identity in order to encompass the many sectarian traditions that constituted the category "Hinduism," he programmatically passed over *particular* traditions—differences, which, many argue, are the essential defining feature of Indian cultural traditions—in favor of nonreligious, affective, territorial, and racial belongings. While Savarkar demoted religion and belief with one stroke, as Bhatt (2001: 85) has written, he curiously reintroduced the concept in order to exclude Muslims and Christians from a definition of national belonging. This contradictory tension in Savarkar's writing was never resolved, and it remains essential for contemporary followers of Hindutva in Gujarat or elsewhere.

Curiously, Savarkar mentions three Muslim communities that have special ties to Gujarat: the Bohra, the Memon, and the Khoja. For Savarkar, notwithstanding that the practices of these communities are examples of the mutual imbrication of local cultures with Hindu society, he uses them as argumentative linchpins to drive home their nonmembership in the Hindu nation (Savarkar 2005 [1928]: 98, 101–102, 115). This line of argument can still be heard today. There is, on the one hand, a clear acknowledgment, especially by Hindu nationalists in the state, that Gujarati Muslims are influenced by local cultural styles and segmented into many diverse communities. On the other hand, Hindu nationalists' constant barrage of accusations nonetheless targets an indigestible core that renders Muslims external to the state, and by extension, to India. This study examines this core, which renders an internally divided minority simultaneously unified and external.

In addition, Savarkar's formulation of Hindutva inscribed notions of fatherland (*pitrabhumi*) and "Holyland" (*punyabhumi*) that became territorially and culturally defined (Andersen and Damle 1987: 33–34). The notion of fatherland was coupled with the simultaneous notion of motherland (*matrubhumi*), the former associated with paternal descent and the latter with place of birth (Savarkar 2005 [1928]: 110). Although Muslims and Christians relate to India as their country of birth as well as the country of descent, they could never understand it as their "Holyland," the country of origin of their religious traditions (Bhatt 2001: 94–99).

For Muslims or Christians, the coincidence of birth, descent, and civilization with an Indian "Holyland" was not possible. Due to this fact, whatever they shared with Hindus in common culture, they would always be divided in their love for the mother country (Savarkar 2005

[1928]: 113). An Oedipal theme can be identified here, an implicit assumption that without divine origins, one risks betrayal of the country. Addressing Indian Muslims, Savarkar suggests:

> Ye, who by race, by blood, by culture, by nationality possess almost all the essentials of Hindutva and had been forcibly snatched out of our ancestral home by the hand of violence—ye, have only to render wholehearted love to our common Mother and recognize her not only as Fatherland (*Pitribhu*) but even as a Holyland (*punyabhu*); and ye would be most welcome to the Hindu fold. (Ibid.: 115)

There is here a strong need to define an origin that remains unscathed and undivided. Directing attention elsewhere, even if only in part or temporarily, betrays the perfection of that wholeness. Only if all is rendered to the "common Mother"—descent, birth, and belief—can there be a unity between father, mother, and divinity that promises the absence of division. That said, Hindu nationalism is not simply about cultural homogeneity, though it seems to privilege this, but, as in Savarkar's formulations, it is about father, mother, deity—a congruity between unstable elements that risk becoming unhinged from one another.

ORGANIZING UNITY

Notwithstanding its elite ideology, Hindu nationalism quickly understood the need to unify diverse segments of Indian society by, for example, including untouchables as "true" Hindus (Andersen and Damle 1987: 28–29; Zavos 2000: 87–98). Social division was seen as one of the causes for Hindu ineffectualness, a constitutional cowardice when opposing enemies in the present and in the past: the colonial humiliation by a handful of British foreigners, the losses through religious conversion or clashes, and the waves of invading armies that were seen as having penetrated into the subcontinent for millennia.

In the 1920s, several organizations, among them the Hindu Mahasabha and the Rashtriya Swayamsevak Sangh (Organization of National Volunteers, or RSS), experimented with political ideologies and organizational models that have since become constitutive for the practices of Hindu nationalism. This period saw the sustained anticolonial mass mobilization of the Indian National Congress under the leadership of Mahatma Gandhi, who promulgated a complex set of nonviolent methodologies in order to wrench national Independence from the British (Spodek 1971). During this formative period, also, Hindu-Muslim violence flared up all over India, although the particular groups, castes, and communities involved showed much regional variation. Founded by Keshav Baliram

Hedgewar in 1925 and later continued by Madhav Sadashi Golwalkar, the RSS initially portrayed itself successfully as an organization that protected Hindus during communal violence, a claim it also later made during Partition (Zavos 2000: 186–187).

The first RSS *shakha* (branch) in Gujarat began its activities in 1938 (Andersen and Damle 1987: 38).[3] Banned for approximately one year in 1948 for its alleged involvement in the assassination of Mahatma Gandhi, the organization was acquitted in 1949 and resumed its activities nationwide. Over the years, many other organizations began to be formed that owe their origin to the RSS. They specialize in various activities such as the Vishva Hindu Parishad (World Hindu Council, or VHP), founded in 1964 as a cultural and religious branch of the RSS, and its militant youth wing, the Bajrang Dal, founded in 1984. As civic institutions with an extremist anti-Muslim rhetoric, both played a paramount role in the 2002 violence. Realizing the increasing importance of a public political face, in early 1950 the RSS launched the Jan Sangh, a political party whose aim was the establishment of a Hindu nation with a human touch (Hansen 1999: 84–86). Initially unsuccessful, its appeal nonetheless rose markedly in Gujarat in the 1960s (Kumar 2009: 91).

During the crises of governance in the 1970s, the Jan Sangh began changing its electoral strategy by addressing landless laborers, small peasants, urban working classes, students, and small entrepreneurs (Andersen and Damle 1987: 182–186). Background for these changes were conflicts over reservation—that is, policies of protective discrimination (affirmative action)—for lower and backward classes. At the end of the 1970s, an electoral strategy pursued by Congress-I called the KHAM formula promulgated a caste configuration consisting of a combination of Kshatriya (large cluster of castes), Harijan (Dalit groups), Adivasi (tribal groups), and Muslims, thus displacing elites—Brahmins, Vaniyas, and especially the Patidars (Patels)—from access to political power in Gujarat (Sanghavi 2010: 488).

In 1985, the Congress Party won the Gujarat assembly elections through this strategy. While the conflict over reservation and the new electoral formula had successfully displaced traditional elites from political power in the state, tensions culminated in the 1985 violence in Ahmedabad. Curiously, however, although it was spurred by an agitation against state policies over reservation, after a month the violence against Dalits turned anti-Muslim (Sheth and Menon 1986). As Shani (2007: 105) has argued in a detailed case study, the 1985 violence was an expression of how caste cleavages then began providing the backdrop for "an all-Hindu communal consolidation," a strategy that finally began to bear fruit. The conjunction of these two types of structural tension—upper versus lower castes and classes as well as Hindu versus Muslim—came to the fore in the Gujarat pogrom of 2002 without in any way resolving these issues for the future.

In 1980, the Jan Sangh was renamed the Bharatiya Janata Party. After growing anti-BJP feeling among Dalits because of the party's earlier anti-reservation stance, the VHP reversed the oppositional trend by including Dalits as well as Adivasi in cultural-awakening programs (Nandy et al. 1995: 103–105). Dalit youth in Ahmedabad were recruited into the Bajrang Dal and put in charge of organizing neighborhood festivals and meetings (G. Shah 2006: 83). In the tribal belt of Gujarat, the VHP and other Hindu organizations inaugurated programs to oppose Christian conversion and to "Gujaratize" and "Hinduize" tribal groups, including attempts at social assimilation (Lobo and Das 2006: 90, 118–120). The division of labor between the organizational work of the RSS, the grassroots work of the VHP, the violent labor of the Bajrang Dal, and the political work of the BJP has become a routine strategy today. No comparable institutional framework exists for Muslims in Gujarat.

The late 1980s also saw the first beginnings of the Ramjanmabhumi movement for the installation of a Hindu temple dedicated to the epic god Ram in the town of Ayodhya, Uttar Pradesh, on the site of a former mosque. This campaign, which pitted Hindus and Muslims against one another nationwide, is the most successful Hindu nationalist campaign to date. It was designed to unify social categories as Hindus in order to counter the splintering forces that the conflict over reservation had unleashed. The mosque was finally destroyed by an organized mob in December 1992, triggering serious reverberations throughout India.

In 1995, the BJP became the strongest political force in Gujarat, developing into the state's most successful champion of Hindu nationalism. In 1998, the BJP also emerged as strongest political party in the Lok Sabha in Delhi. During the period 1998 to 2004, the state government of Gujarat was in the unique position to share a political agenda with influential members of the central government coalition in New Delhi, which had formed the National Democratic Alliance (NDA). One of the long-term successes of the backroom travails by the RSS in this period was the infiltration of government, administration, and the police forces in the state (Bunsha 2006: 36, 57–65).

In sum, as a political project in Gujarat today, Hindutva presents formidable possibilities. It offers an interpretation of Hinduism that unites upper and lower caste and class groups as "Hindus," a historical subject threatened by Islam and Christianity. In this way, it provides a historical rapprochement for untouchability by displacing and channeling antagonism into nationalist registers. It portrays Hindus as victims of an aggression that demands a response. Although Hindu nationalist rhetoric drives the rejection of Muslims, its regional implementation relies on local specificities connected to meanings and identifications peculiar to the state.

POGROM AND COMPLICITY

A pogrom, as I am construing it, is a communal sacrifice, a cleansing device to make a portion of one's own society into sacrificial victims. It requires logistical planning and preparation, and its successful execution relies on support from the state apparatus, including the police and criminal actors, but also on spontaneous and vicarious forms of participation by groups or sets of ordinary citizens in active and passive capacities. Specific targets have to be located and marked, resistances be overcome through intimidation and propaganda, and regional, national, and international registers be invoked.

In this, a pogrom is easy to distinguish from a riot. It is not a serendipitous event but a planned one, characterized by a specific kind of collective consciousness that makes forms of complicity possible. A pronounced blurring of boundaries between state, movement, and people is characteristic of fascist mobilizations everywhere (Marcuse 2007 [1947]: 92–111). Following the work of Kakar (1995: 51), Brass (2003: 30–34, esp. 32), and Das (2007: 205–211), the question is how the planning and spontaneous action become linked in the collective understanding of events *by those in whose name the violence is perpetrated.*

Pogroms entail not only acquiescence to acts of violence but also are followed by psychological denials. Participants who partake in the emotional rage that is mobilized by key actors and organizations often share a profound belief in their own innocence during the events and are therefore later incapable or unwilling to support legal retribution and redress, resulting in moral impunity for the perpetrators. During the events, the explanation of karmic reaction—a generalized "angry Hindu" wreaking vengeance against the phantasmagoric figure of the Muslim—was paramount.

Hindu residents of Ahmedabad at the time of the pogrom explained to me that in their view, the Modi government obviously had no other choice than to allow the eruption to take its course. Otherwise, it would have been dealing in "politics." If such explanations obfuscate the agency of political and civic actors, they also inscribe the people as the collective agent of violence in the realization of their potential. Even relatively uninvolved members of a majority community are cast into supportive roles by compelling them to engage in defensive postures and, later, elaborate denials. In this way, pogroms exhibit a marked tendency to produce their own rationalizations: the psychological and symbolic inscription becomes "explanation" for division afterwards.

All these forms of complicity rely on means that scholars of Eastern European pogroms, such as Jan Gross (2001: xv), call the "institutionalization of resentment." Collective mobilization of resentment cannot be created ex nihilo but must resonate with local, intimate themes already in place. The slippage between a mythical violence rendered legitimate during its unfolding while denigrated as "politics" afterwards was possible through the work of an elaborate array of stereotypes that configure the Muslim locally. In contemporary Gujarat, the specific elements that serve as the basis for forms of resentment are linked to a sacrificial logic.

For me as a German national only three generations removed from the Holocaust and the Second World War, violent collective phenomena such as pogroms carry a peculiar resonance. Nazi crimes included orchestrated pogroms that were long a part of European history. Yet, still today, many aspects of the National Socialist policy that were successfully deployed to cleanse Europe of its Jews seem to defy explanation. The fact that many ordinary Germans affirmed, in various direct and indirect ways, the Nazi government's racist policies and genocidal practices continues to puzzle scholars.

Analysis of Nazi crimes has given much attention to forms of complicity and has developed concepts such as *Schreibtischtäter*, which depicts bureaucratic complicity in sitting at one's office desk and attending to (minor) state functions while other state employees engage in mass murder. Such concepts have entered everyday speech in the German language. Likewise, much analysis has focused on the relation of anti-Semitic notions in traditional folklore and identifications to active and passive toleration for persecution of one's neighbors (Grunberger and Dessuant 2000 [1997]: 460–480). Today in Germany, there is widespread agreement that responsibility rests not only with those actively giving or passively executing orders but also with residents who remained silent or inactive. Several generations of postwar Germans have worked hard to overcome collective resistance to acknowledging forms of agency in acquiescent roles.

This is not the case in Gujarat. For me, the single most disturbing experience during the violence in Gujarat was not the complicity of politicians and orchestrations of large parts of the state machinery but the psychological *Gleichschaltung* (coordination) of "ordinary" Gujaratis with whom I was acquainted. There are many reasons for the often temporary inability to distance oneself emotionally and intellectually from the revengeful rhetoric of violence during its unfolding. But complicity and disavowal were too pervasive to be ignored. As Hannah Arendt pointed out, in 1933 when Hitler came to power in Germany, many of her friends fell prey to their own intellectual fabrications—"*Sie gingen Ihren eigenen Einfällen in die Falle*" (They fell into the trap of their own ideas).[4] I describe and investigate some of these traps in Ahmedabad, the ways individuals personally invested emotions in ideas and political events and found reasons for their legitimacy.

Pogrom, Sacrifice, and Ahimsa

There are also parallels between WWII German complicity and contemporary Gujarati complicity related to the logic of sacrifice. The ideology of National Socialism was based on appeals to notions of collective victimhood and sacrifice (both rendered as *Opfer*) applied to the people (*Volk*), who, if properly led by the *Führer*, could by default never be defeated (Geyer 2002). Conceptions of "the people" lie at the foundation of notions of sovereignty of all modern political systems, totalitarian and democratic alike. As Lefort (1986: 292–306) has stressed, the totalitarian impulse toward unity was a response to problems within democratic political form itself, in which division is overcome through an invocation of the People-as-One. In contemporary India—a postcolonial society and the world's largest democracy—arriving at a united people requires a rearticulation of the relationship of victim to sacrifice.

In classic anthropological literature, sacrifice is understood as a structural principle of rites of initiation, rituals that regenerate and transform the social, and it is understood as a means to displace aggressive impulses onto scapegoats (cf. W. Smith 1889: 244–324; Frazer 1960 [1890]: 348–386; Hubert and Mauss 1964 [1899]; Durkheim 1995 [1912]; 330–354; Evans-Pritchard 1956: 197–286). Its symbolic technologies include expiation and incorporation, consecration and profanation, as well as substitution and mimesis. All sacrificial procedures compel some form of loss—at its most extreme, physical death, which is then recuperated by reconstituting a new entity or by marking a new beginning.

Sacrifice belongs to a general theory of economy and exchange, as both Simmel (1989 [1900]: 55–92) and Bataille (1992 [1949]: 45–77; 1991: 43–61) have insisted. It is an act of regenerative expenditure involving destruction and abnegation as well as its inverse, an act of production and symbolic appropriation. The loss in sacrifice, the expenditure accrued, has the objective of accessing some form of value, permanence, transcendence, or recovery of a lost vitality (Bloch 1992: 24–45). This insight is especially pertinent when the constitution of a loss compels killing. When regeneration is understood as an act of annihilation, sacrifice can become a means for the ritual control of death, or its failure, which, if unacknowledged, can wreak havoc and lead to terrible consequences (Siegel 2006: 1–26).

Sacrificial violence in India is closely linked to the doctrine of ahimsa (nonviolence), initially not an ethic of nonviolence but a protective technique against the effects of the necessary violence in ritual—namely, the ritual of sacrifice. The meanings of ahimsa have continually shifted through three millennia. With roots in the Vedic sacrificial complex, ahimsa became an ethical ideal for behavior only with the emergence of a doctrine of renunciation, which implied a transformation and departure from, and even a severe critique of, ancient Brahmin ritualism (Alsdorf 1962; Schmidt 1968; Heesterman 1984; 1993: 34–34, 79–83; Biardeau 1989 [1981]: 30–32; Gonda 1959: 95–117; Fuller 1992: 57–82; Vidal, Tarabout, and Meyer 2003 [1994]: 11–26, 85–104).

During the Gujarat pogrom, people invoked the symbolic technologies of killing and sacrifice metaphorically, and they enacted them in situ on three interconnected levels. First, the imagery and vocabulary of sacrifice became a main referent in print-media representations, in forms of violent action, and in talk on the streets. This alone is nothing unusual, for all modern nationalist rhetoric relies on sacrificial invocations and imageries (Anderson 1991: 11; Marvin and Ingle 1999: 63–97; Eghigian and Berg 2002). India poses no exception to this fact (Jaffrelot 2003 [1994]). What is specific to India, however, and this is the second level, is that the identification of ethnic and religious differences between Hindus and Muslims was primarily established through reference to diet and styles of worship, further appealing to the domains of animal slaughter and religious sacrifice. In the cultural history of Gujarat, these levels are intimately connected to notions of ahimsa. Third, political and civic actors treated the pogrom as a reactive ritual mechanism—*pratikriya*, a form of automatic sacrificial retribution.

AGGREGATION, STEREOTYPE, AND AFFECT

In a national register, "Hindus" and "Muslims" tend to be understood as categories of population. Yet the divisions within and between respective religious communities, and the way citizens apprehend these divisions in quotidian life, still play out on the level not of society (*Gesellschaft*) but of community (*Gemeinschaft*). Gujaratis are aware that terms like "Hindu" and "Muslim" are synthetic. These categories relate only abstractly to their lived realities. There is not one Muslim community in Gujarat but many, as there are many diverse Hindu, Jain, Dalit (Harijan), and Adivasi (tribal) communities. A complex pattern of differentiations and symbolic gradations of status and attribute structure this agglomeration of groups.

The kind of social struggles that many subaltern communities face are often about the meaning of and legitimate membership in abstract aggregate categories of population. A specific Gujarati subaltern community might struggle to be recognized as a full Muslim community, while the same holds true for communities in relationship to the Hindu category.

Furthermore, socioeconomic class and individual difference always inflect local considerations, the latter frequently in direct opposition to group dynamics. Thus it is not uncommon to find amicable relations between neighbors despite massive mobilization and propaganda at higher levels of abstract membership in opposed aggregate categories.

Aggregate categories tend to eviscerate empirical differences while creating new orders that focus and reconfigure these. In times of violence and generalized anxiety, this erasure is particularly palpable and constitutes political power for those able to manipulate these categories. The emptier and more abstract a category, the more vociferously it can be inhabited—or projected—in order to garner the substance it lacks. In Gujarat, Hindutva, which literally means the "essence of the Hindu," serves the purpose of aggregation.

Residents of Ahmedabad sometimes say *"mane hindutva ave chhe"* or *"mane hindutva thai chhe,"* which loosely translates as "Hindutva rises up in me" or "Hindutva is happening to me." They locate a visceral sentiment or affect, which can spontaneously arise in them, as an authentic expression of Hindu-ness. Here, it describes an awakening of something sleeping deep within the subject—a surging essence that can be brought to the surface—Hindutva organizes and shapes this amorphous surge into an aggregate political subject and thus holds the key to contemporary mass politics in the state.

Once Hindu is invoked as essence, pregnant emotionally but emptied of much content, the figure of the Muslim may arouse a phantasmagoria of fear, anger, visceral abhorrence, and particularly disgust. Much fear appears to come from the imagined trope of the Muslim as criminal and terrorist in alignment with the archenemy Pakistan. Such a figure calls for heightened security measures, including delegation of violent labor to nongovernmental organizations like the VHP, the RSS, or the Bajrang Dal. More momentous, however, is the figure of the Muslim as carrier of revulsion and abjection, which frames experiences that index traditional practices of untouchability in the contemporary imagination.

Stereotypes based on clichés are relatively enduring symbolic forms that can be studied in space and time. Their present sociopolitical mobilization through "awakening" gives them a spontaneous thrust and direction that has been underestimated in analyses of violence in India. The pervasiveness of the image of awakening as well as the experience of becoming present to an essence has much to do with the mythical unity that aggregate identity concepts such as "Hindu" can invoke by ideally bridging class, caste, religious, and sectarian separation. It appears to overcome social division and allows for the idea of a unified Hindu people to emerge as a sovereign entity and historical subject. In a democratic polity governed by the rule of law, however, legal provisions guarantee protection of minorities against the tyranny of the majority. They are supposed to regulate and even control agonistic popular expressions of unity.

Such limitations may, in turn, lead to defiance and resistance to law. Such defiance is an integral strategy employed by many Hindutva leaders. In 2002, Chief Minister Narendra Modi himself did everything he could to affirm the legitimacy of the tide against the Muslim minority. At the level of the street, circulating stereotypes filled out the emptiness of this mobilized, politicized "Hindu," who had become present to himself with materials that invoke cultural forms conceived of as "traditional," in both vernacular idioms and conceptions of ritual purity.

In the context of the pogrom, stereotyping of the familiar neighborhood Muslim was important in order to confirm stigmatizations that were often at odds with empirical reality. Yet stereotypes are always generative and creative. As Herzfeld (1992: 71–97, esp. 72) has argued, they render intimate the abstraction of otherness, which constitutes an important signature of nationalist identification.

This study examines the relation of Hindu stereotypes of Muslims to the consumption and production of meat in concrete quotidian practices and conceptions of diet and worship: meat eating, vegetarianism, and the rejection of animal sacrifice. While the origin and operation of these stereotypes is diverse, during the pogrom they became unified and effective to produce a collective imaginary. This relation carries the power to arouse the affect of disgust and can produce the most pronounced sentiments of moral indignation including even physical experiences of nausea and collapse. Disgust for a substance and, by extension, for those associated with it does not, however, engender stable representations; on the contrary, it collapses distinctions and culminates in intimate experiences and proximity to the subject of stigmatization.

In this way, individual Gujaratis participated in the violence in ways that made it hard for them to later maintain emotional distance from these events. This fact had momentous consequences in the political developments in the state. References in the media, in everyday conversations, and among political actors to meat consumption, butchering, and bodily mutilation played a major role in Gujarati imaginaries leading to and accompanying the pogrom.

The middle to lower classes maintain a routine division of labor to Hindu nationalist organizations. Even when financially supported, organizations such as RSS, VHP, and Bajrang Dal are often derided and viewed with skeptic detachment in calm times. But it is through the sophisticated institutional scaffolding of these organizations that the *krodh hindu*–the angry Hindu—emerges on stage to allow individual residents to realize the possibilities of a belligerent nationalist posture (Makawana

2002: 11–17). Anger is mustered most easily through narratives of betrayal employing the rival sibling Pakistan. To be sure, this line of association may seem overly simplistic, but national divisions are minutely projected into many city areas through designations such as "mini-Pakistan" and "mini-Hindustan."

At the same time, Gujarat is the birthplace of Mahatma Gandhi and strongly self-identified with the doctrine of ahimsa (nonviolence), which he deployed so effectively in the fight for Indian Independence from the British. Despite Gandhi's current unpopularity in Gujarat, it is wrong to assume that his particular interpretation of ahimsa has simply been discarded. The levels of reception are more nuanced. Many people in Gujarat cannot avoid being addressed by ahimsa's lofty ethical claims, and the figure of Gandhi himself remained a contentious reference point even at the height of violence. Loyalty to Hindutva, and the reaction it calls for, however, appears at odds with the address of ahimsa. It is through ahimsa in its many forms that a relay between nationalist ideology and regional pride is constructed.

The contradictory nature of this identification, an ego ideal sated by identification with ahimsa and a political project pregnant with resentment against minorities, broke to the surface, with particular virulence, in the pogrom. Even after its successful engineering, a bedazzled middle class, hesitating while evidently in awe about their own extra-legal possibilities, continued to insist on the nonviolent credentials of their province. This work takes these assertions seriously and, following the spirit of work by Lobo and Das (2006: 41–62), Pandey (2006: 13), and Kumar (2009: 37), places these issues of self-identification at the center of analysis.[5]

Understanding the paradox of how ahimsa, understood as a doctrine of nonviolence, becomes implicated in the production of the very violence it renounces is the central puzzle of the Gujarat pogrom. How is the address of ahimsa reconciled with aggressive nationalist posturing? How are traditional forms of inner-worldly renunciation transformed, specifically informing vegetarian dietary practices, under contemporary demands for political mobilization and ethnic-religious identification?

AHIMSA, VULNERABILITY, AND ANGER

The doctrine of ahimsa is more than a salient ideal in Gujarat. It is also a concrete practice, closely associated with forms of traditional worship and diet, specifically vegetarianism and the rejection of animal blood sacrifice.[6] The ongoing disappearance of animal blood sacrifice is an all-India phenomenon (Fuller 1992: 83–105). Distinctive in Gujarat, however, is how the consolidation of high-caste political dominance makes ahimsa, cow protection, and vegetarianism difficult to distinguish conceptually. The influential merchant communities of Jains and Hindu Vaishnavas (Vaniya), as well as dominant groups like the Patel community, think of themselves as vegetarian, on the face of it, as do all other dominant Hindu sects and movements largely financed by them, such as the Swaminarayan *sampradaya* (A. M. Shah and Shroff 1958; Pocock 1973: 41–80, 81, 122–157, 164–171; Tambs-Lyche 1997: 224–232).

The opposition to animal sacrifice is attested for a long time in the region. Already in the twelfth century, the Caulukya dynasty patronized Jain elites who played a paramount role in their unwavering opposition to royal sacrifices. With the decline of Caulukyas, the royal Shaiva cult, which included animal sacrifices diminished, while the influence of Vaishnava worship styles grew. Shakta practices nonetheless continued among pastoralists and other groups apparently for a long time (Sheikh 2010: 115, 129–184). Medieval Gujarat was characterized by the complex interaction between merchants and rulers, the latter of whom were mostly from pastoral background and propitiated Mother Goddesses with animal sacrifices. In the sixteenth century, claims to ahimsa feature supremely in Vaishnava conversion of pastoral communities to vegetarianism and abolition of animal blood sacrifice in the context of Mother Goddess worship (Clémentin-Ojha 2003 [1994]: 127–142). It seems, however, that these practices even then continued to coexist with those considered nonviolent in Gujarat (ibid.: 140).

The complementary cultural styles between traders and pastoralists and their religious institutions have partly survived into the present (Tambs-Lyche 1997: 224–255, 96–120). The conversion of Goddesses to vegetarianism instead of the patronizing of temples through caste and clan associations is an ongoing process in the regional integration of Gujarat state (Ibrahim 2009: 163–175; Sheikh 2010: 84–99; Tambs-Lyche 2010: 109–111). By the nineteenth century, Alexander Forbes (1924 [1878]: 324) mentioned ritual animal sacrifices in at the shrine of Ambaji Mata, nowadays Gujarat's patron Goddess. Such allusions are today unfathomable. Proper Gujarati-ness in the present is defined by the inheritance of an unambiguous vegetarian ethos from a Hindu past.

Mahatma Gandhi pointedly described the severity of the vegetarian atmosphere during his childhood in the late nineteenth century: "The opposition to and abhorrence of meat eating that existed in Gujarat among the Jains and Vaishnavas were to be seen nowhere else in India or outside in such strength" (1927: 18). In the following years, in organizing the struggle for independence from colonial rule, Gandhi appealed to ahimsa as a political method for grassroots mobilization (Spodek 1971: 361–372; 1989: 765–795; Bondurant 1988 [1958]: 23–29, 105–145).

Much of Gandhi's political success was predicated on the upwardly mobile Patel segment among his Gujarati followers, with whom he shared a strong vegetarian ethos.

The trend towards "unequivocal vegetarianism" (Pocock 1973: 81) among the Patel and other groups in Gujarat, and the abolition of all blood sacrifice, is pervasively documented in the ethnographic literature of the region (Westphal-Hellbusch and Westphal 1976a: 176; 1976b: 88–89, 175–179; Goody 1982: 114–127, esp. 124; Hardiman 1995 [1987]: 18–67; Randeria 1989: 183; A. M. Shah 2002b: 59–66; Basu 2004b: 19; Ghassem-Fachandi 2008: 120–125; Ibrahim 2009: 163–181; Simpson 2008: 91–111).

The new twist in this development, however, is the clever and systematic politicization of vegetarianism in the context of Hindu nationalist activities that are often more astute and culturally attentive than they are credited for. Vegetarianism as an "ahimsa austerity" (Bayly 2001 [1999]: 218) enters into the psychologically very complex relation between communities mediated by the aggregates "Hindu" and "Muslim" along with the "Indian nation." It is complex because this relation does not simply imply a dietary stigma attached to Muslims but adumbrates the historical distinction between merchant and warrior communities as well as between upper and lower castes, Hindu and non-Hindu. Throughout South Asia in the last half century, such transformations of social distinctions of class and caste into national oppositions have been accompanied by comparable transformations in personhood. This study analyzes only the contemporary manifestation of these transformations.[7]

Several ethnographers in Gujarat and adjacent states have pointed out that the opposition between vegetarianism and nonvegetarianism did not spell automatic conflict in the past—nor does it do so automatically today. Forms of value relativity, modern practices of consumption, caste complementarity, and a division of roles secured a working relationship in many contexts between strictly vegetarian communities and those that did not hold to such views or follow such practices (Pocock 1973: 81–93; Babb 2004: 225–235). Yet the reductive inscription of "ahimsa austerity" into the depths of Gujarati cultural history suggests that a sense of vulnerability underlies contemporary assertions of regional pride.

The answer to this vulnerability is the angry Hindu. The *krodh hindu* in Gujarat stands in a relation to the common stereotype of the weak effeminate Gujarati Hindu, who propounds ahimsa (nonviolence), misconceived not only as a cultural quality of traditional society but as the very cause for passivity of the common citizen in the present. The binary between weak vegetarian and brazen meat-eating Hindu became exacerbated during the colonial encounter (Nandy 1998b: 1–63). In their administrative classificatory practices in the nineteenth century, British officials picked up such differences and pragmatically distinguished between so-called martial races and nonmartial groups—a distinction that continues to have collective psychological effects in the present.

Today the pronounced feeling of emasculation among former colonial subjects has much to do with this transformation of precolonial conversion to the colonial and modern emphasis on martial prowess and masculinity. A glorious Gujarati past suffused with ahimsa brings forth the angry Hindu, who becomes, for many, the answer to the nonviolent Hindu's castration. According to this logic, adherence to a position of nonviolent renunciation renders the acts of the Hindu as historical subject ineffectual. The same argument is made when trying to explain how the state of Gujarat could have fallen so easily to the onslaught of Islam in the early medieval period.

An early example for how nonviolence is translated into Gujarati regional vulnerability can be found in a standard work of Gujarati historiography published shortly after the founding of the new state. M. R. Majumdar, in his *Cultural History of Gujarat*, remarks in a footnote: "Jainism with its insistence on non-violence, and Buddhism, with its clarion-call to renunciation, combined to create an atmosphere in which patriotism and the martial virtues withered and dropped—naturally" (1965: 106,n. 30). This view concurs with Savarkar's (2005 [1928]: 18–24) exhortations on ancient Indian history more than forty years earlier. When elaborating on the fall of Buddhism, Savarkar expounded on the deleterious effect that "Buddhistic power" had on ancient India, including on its "national virility" (ibid.: 18). Against the political influence and vibrancy of Gandhi's anticolonial methodologies, Savarkar painted an ancient Buddhism filled with enlightened unconcern and "mealy-mouthed formulas of Ahimsa" (ibid.: 19). Ahimsa, together with Buddhist universalism, was an "opiate" that eventually spelled catastrophe allowing sin and crime, as well as foreign invasion, to penetrate the vulnerable nation.

The Hindu awoken in anger takes charge of his or her own destiny by either individually assuming the right to mete out violence, or alternatively, through varied forms of complicity and delegation to authority (Bourdieu 1991: 203–219). There exists today a profound blurring between the excessive expenditure of consumption and the excess of violence that, in the pogrom, became metaphorically linked. Examining the collective mobilization for the pogrom as a diagnostic event allows us to catch a glimpse of the mythical unity that religious nationalism tries to invoke by referencing its absence as a Hindu lack that needs to be overcome (Hansen 1999: 77–83). In what follows, I will argue that the affect of disgust for meat is an expression of this sensitivity that has become conceived as indicator of the quality of nonviolence itself. Disgust, moreover, while immediately invoking notions of purity and pollution, allows for a new form of identification with the doctrine of nonviolence. In this way, nonviolent renunciation whose essence is disgust becomes itself an integral aspect of the legitimization of violence against Muslims.

MEAT AND DISGUST

In Gujarat, meat is not an indifferent substance, but one much alive through a plethora of meanings that inform an array of unique behaviors and reactions. The powerful capacity of meat to signify has been recorded by ethnographers of South Asia in diverse settings (Osella and Osella 2008). The quotidian classification of communities on the basis of vegetarian and nonvegetarian food habits is perhaps the most obvious and immediate expression of this fact. What different communities consume is a common subject of discussion and of much chatter, sometimes benign and sometimes not. I have witnessed and participated in such discussions many times. In urban contexts throughout South Asia this salience is connected to particular shifts from caste-based to class-based socialities without canceling the sociological importance of the former (for Kathmandu, e.g. Liechty 2005: esp. 3).

Besides chatter, idioms, gestures, and facial mimics reference meat consumption. Villagers in rural areas of central Gujarat often substitute a typical cutting gesture with a hand when alluding to the act of procuring, butchering, and eating meat while refraining from uttering these acts in speech. Vegetarianism is a widespread dietary practice not merely among upper-caste Hindus but among lower orders, too (Goody 1982: 114–127; Westphal-Hellbusch and Westphal 1976a: 176; 1976b: 88–89, 175–179). It can include Muslim saints (*Pir*) of local shrines, who are sometimes hailed as vegetarian and celibate by their followers, including Hindu communities (Ghassem-Fachandi 2008: 120–126).

In sum, meat is a highly communicative substance in Gujarat connected to a vast array of practices and conceptions that await ethnographic inquiry in diverse settings. It is an overdetermined substance, powerful precisely because it enters into multiple relationships between and among members and sections of society that are exactly *not* Muslim. The Muslim minority community as carrier of disgust for meat is not simply a stable traditional stereotype, part of a series of symbolic and metaphorical contents. Rather the identification of the Muslim meat-eater is a form of *practical expiation*, insofar as the figure of the Muslim comes to stand for all those vices that many are incapable of renouncing on the one hand, and that are associated with meat consumption on the other. Muslims are made to stand openly for what many others do anyway more clandestinely, or find various alternative contexts to engage in. In this moral economy of food substances, disgust is a defense against the appeal of lurking transgressive possibilities that meat signifies, and the disgusted reaction is habitually portrayed as a form of religious authenticity and dietary innocuousness.

The development towards vegetarian food ethics and nonviolent worship practice remains fundamentally fraught with inconsistencies. On the one hand, vegetarianism becomes challenged and at times eclipsed by modern forms of consumption in urban restaurants and food stalls. Moreover, blood sacrifices reappear or continue as more or less secret and criminal practice in many places in Gujarat. Its salience has only become more pronounced, either as "magical superstition"—anachronistic remnants of a misunderstood ritual past—or in communal provocations between Hindus and Muslims. Questions of slaughter and carnivorous diet dominate stereotypes and accusations against minorities, especially Muslims. Hindutva ideology, in turn, has dismissed the moral basis of strict vegetarianism, ahimsa, which it has held responsible for Hindu weakness in the past and in the present. On the other hand, vegetarianism skillfully buttresses a discourse of pronounced stigmatization of Muslims in the state inclusive of the aforementioned allusions. The application of an artificially ritualistic and nationalist language by organizations propounding Hindutva owes much of its appeal to sacrificial registers.

It is tempting to see discontinuities between concepts such as ahimsa and vegetarian practices, modern meat consumption and notions of animal sacrifice, ancient ritual forms and Hindu nationalist rituals, Vaishnava and Jaina conceptions, and so on. A focus on such discontinuities risks missing, however, what this study is at pains to elucidate: namely, how disparate units of thought and practice can become part of a collective imaginary whose expression remains opaque to a logic of scholarly investigation that stresses continuity or discontinuity in the systematic arrangement of the objects of study. When employed during a pogrom, and combined with other elements, these units are not easily made congruent with an ideal scholarly coherence. Taking this limitation seriously carries important methodological implications to which I will turn now.

METHOD

This study differs from a history, or a political science or sociological account, in that it is the work of an ethnographer who was also witness to the violent events under investigation. By "witness" I do not mean to say that because of proximity I know things better, and with "ethnographer" I do not wish to invoke a superior epistemology to other forms of knowing. My intent here is to stress the particularity of intersubjective insight generated by long-term field research. The intellectual questions in this study are profoundly inflected by the way I was made to participate in the pogrom as an event, its quotidian representations, smells, images, and sounds. Certainly such participation can also limit insight by leaving me too intimately entangled in my own experience of the pogrom.

During the numbing weeks of violence, I lived with two young men, both Hindus and complicit in different ways in the events. My discussions with them and their peers were important for refining many of the insights that I present in this study. At the same time, I interacted daily with a wide array of city residents of middle- to lower-middle-class background, some of whom I met accidentally while exploring neighborhoods and some of whom I met through my association with three institutions of higher education: Gujarat University, Gujarat Vidhyapit, and M. S. Baroda University. In the middle stage of fieldwork, acting on the urgent advice of friends and neighbors (my name identified me as Muslim), I moved to a Muslim area of the city, where I lived in a housing society for another seven months.

Although I discussed events with a wide range of people over the years, my insights during my field stays came mostly from serendipitous encounters that congealed into closer and long-term personal relationships. I had not prepared for this contingency beforehand. In this book I have selected for illustration exemplary cases of perspectives on and into the Gujarat pogrom; they do not create a rounded, closed, and finished narrative. Instead they are, in part, intended to unsettle top-down paradigms of thinking about this particular violence, and hopefully, for violence in India more generally. I found glaring confirmation of an old ethnographic suspicion, namely that more intimate relationships allow for unguarded statements, and the unique opportunity to revisit such statements later on. It is through interpersonal dynamics that I came to take seriously what I consider to be unconscious material—spontaneous statements, confusing locutions, slips of the tongue, unexpected jokes, dreamlike stories—which is usually successfully censored in the exchanges of formal interviews.

During the height of the violence, and for a long time afterwards, not all interlocutors were comfortable with my questions, and they deployed diverse strategies when confronted with more or less subtle queries. Many made a distinction between information that should be openly relayed and other forms of communication with me that had no place in official narratives. A few interlocutors went so far as to literally perform as a different persona in a discussion, without making explicit why they were doing this. I interpreted such moments as attempts to please my demand for engagement and yet dodge the pressure for disclosure or judgment, which I inevitably came to represent. What the recorder and the notebook demanded was performed with a sly conspiratorial smile, which could be disclaimed afterwards when the interview was finished and an even more momentous discussion began. It was as if the formal relay of information could be mediated, and the truth told, through a shift in registers.

The authority of this study, then, rests largely on classic participant observation, living intimately with the people studied, refined by event analysis, where the pogrom is used as a diagnostic occasion, inclusive of the media analysis with which it is inextricably linked. In the field, I also conducted narrative and focused thematic interviews, and I collected life histories as well as written accounts of the same events by local actors and other academics both during and after research. I used these written accounts primarily to corroborate, fill in, or delimit my own observations.

I used a notebook, tape, and mini-disk recorder selectively, whenever practical and interlocutors felt comfortable with the use. During the chaotic months of violence and the tense atmosphere in its immediate aftermath, life-history work and my attempts to shine a light on the present through inquiries into the biographical past grounded to a halt. Discussions of the past drifted unalterably into present events. Nonetheless, some biographic material has been included in the present analysis.

Insights about the pogrom are linked to a description and analysis of urban space in Ahmedabad, Gujarat's largest city and the main stage of the violence. Drawing out these connections adds insight to further fields of inquiry: how the city is undergoing fast and profound changes, and how the spatial experience of the city in the period 2001–2003 points to oscillations between intimacy and separation in both material and ideational domains. Through a complicated array of sensitive areas, bridges, roadside temples, permanent police posts, and magical remainders of expiation rituals at traffic intersections and plazas, the urban landscape participated in the experience of division. As I lived in five different residences over the course of several periods of fieldwork, my own residential experiences index some of the varied social geographies of violence.

Finally, this study draws on only part of my broader research; it focuses mainly on the perpetrators or those identifying with them and not on the victims of the pogrom. This focus is the result of a decision made in the course of my analysis after the events, namely that my theoretical and empirical contribution about the nature of the pogrom, sacrifice, and ahimsa would be greater if I narrowed it to complicity rather than also included the loss of agency of the victims.

Symmetry and Secondary Revision

Epistemologically, this study tries to remain true to the ethnographic encounters from which it draws its primary insights, and in this does not try to account for the particular forms of violence in Gujarat with a general explanatory model or theory of violence. Instead, what it tries to achieve is an arrest of perception of the pogrom by drawing attention to some singular instances of violence and complicity where a deeper instead of a more general understanding seems promising.

The diverse approaches of historians, political scientists, anthropologists, sociologists, activists, and legal experts have contributed to a growing literature on Gujarat that now offers specific explanations of many phenomena related to the pogrom: political advances of the BJP, Hindu activism, governance failure, electoral violence, Gujarati pride and subnationalism, the surge of Hindu nationalist ideology, the dynamics of gender and sexuality, global financing of ethnic violence, and class struggle. This study, by contrast, is ethnographically limited in space and time, necessarily partial in the sense of being written from a particular perspective, and inherently incomplete by initial design. What this approach hopes to avoid is the compulsion to make the widely diverse and inassimilable responses that I witnessed in the field retroactively fit the questions that I initially asked. To avoid secondary revision of this sort means that I am apprehensive of establishing too exact a symmetry between question and answer, that is, I am wary of what often goes by the name of "explanation."

That said, I am neither dismissive at attempts to explain, nor immune to the argumentative appeal of an explanation. But I am critical of interpretative closures *where an important question is laid to rest by a seemingly comprehensive answer*. The perspective of ethnographic fieldwork very rarely allows for a form of closure that pretends to have gotten to the bottom of things (Geertz 1973: 29). Instead, the answers it finds most often splinter the discursive demand that engendered the initial set of questions in the first place. Thus, instead of rendering particularities into the generalities of recognizable causality, it might be better to defer the desire to explain and risk a detour through *Verstehen* (understanding) in the tradition of Georg Simmel (1972 [1918]: 77–99, esp. 98) or the Weberian tradition followed by Clifford Geertz (1973: 15). Both placed, in different ways, emphasis on the act of fashioning an understanding and thus stressed the creativity in the act of interpretation. Anthropological accounts that derive their insights from field experiences allow for such a detour. I elaborate in more detail in the last chapter where that approach leaves me in relation to other interpretations of the Gujarat pogrom and alternative events.

There are at least two reasons for this disclaimer—one disciplinary and methodological, the other personal and existential—that are moreover inextricably linked. I want to outline them briefly here. An ethnographer engaged in the sort of field research I engaged in cannot pretend to be a technician of the empirical. There is no prefigured scientific casuistry of life during a pogrom that I could have applied to organize this inquiry. I did not and likely could not have anticipated the data I collected beforehand; nor do these data necessarily allow easy integration into meta-narratives of, for example, India, violence, and postcolonialism that are readily available. The more closely one listens to a speaker, the more difficult it is to construct elegant plausibility structures that satisfy the demand for representation and replication in which colleagues of other disciplines can recognize themselves or feel affirmed in their own arduous approaches. Instead of identifying this lack of congruence as a form of defect, I suggest that consideration of insights beyond what is assimilable to meta-narratives and commentaries is ultimately valuable. I see the productive role of anthropology among the disciplines precisely to the degree that it resists taming ethnographic insights to retrofit and conform to knowledge projects of other disciplines. I want to avoid the currently very common practice of relegating ethnography to a position of anecdotal supplement authorizing larger theoretical-historical claims (Borneman and Hammoudi 2009: 1–24)

Interdisciplinarity is not automatically or necessarily a sign of epistemological maturity. It often enough expresses a lack of understanding about what a particular discipline and its method might actually allow for. Thus I prefer an ethnographic focus not out of epistemological rigidity, especially since it concerns the unpredictability of field research, but rather because it provides a possibility to acknowledge a reality that remained surprising and indifferent to my academic understandings and my bias toward coherence. It goes without saying that such an approach can never allow itself to renounce reflexivity and a concern for what it does not grasp.

But while it is one thing to assert reflexivity theoretically, it is another to provide it practically. In my view, reflexivity is not achieved by abstractly invoking theories that critique the metaphysics of presence, the discursive production of scientific objects, the nexus of knowledge and power, or any other such assertions, as profound and legitimate as they may be. Foregrounding them risks drowning reflexivity in mere academic posture. Instead, the most significant reflexive gesture for an ethnographic author consists in providing a description for which one must assume responsibility. This description must be such that others can follow, appropriate, reinterpret, or disagree with it. In short, true reflexivity is achieved through the confrontation with the critical reader, who completes the text and has the opportunity to disagree with the author's production. Reflexivity is thus a relation that occurs between an author, a reader, and a text, not reducible to declarations of intent in an introduction.

Even if I were not an anthropologist with an ethnographic agenda, I would find it difficult to remain silent about the Gujarat pogrom. During the darkest days of the pogrom I was not simply a researcher but a trembling witness and puzzled bystander, a participant in events that far surpassed any professional preparation or expectation. The fact that I cannot provide but an intervention into the analysis of the pogrom has much to do with the severity of the events experienced in 2002. Ethnography seen in this light does more than produce authoritative knowledge about an object of study, be it "culture" or a historical event such as a pogrom. It includes within its descriptions a suspicion about the process of secondary revision that certain types of knowledge production implicitly encourage.

It does this by systematically privileging considerations of intelligibility deeply at odds with the realities of social phenomena and subjective experiences in question—especially that of violent events. I am wary here because the desire to comprehensively explain can indicate both a premature impulse towards intellectual closure on the one hand and the provision of a blueprint for possible instrumental engineering on the other. Sometimes it might be preferable to steer towards but never to arrive at a comprehensive picture. I, for one, have made peace with that admittedly frustrating fact.

DESCRIPTION

If we eschew certain forms of explanation due to epistemological considerations and privilege *Verstehen*, where does this leave us in relation to description? Describing violence—scenes, acts, and imaginations—is a difficult task. The more an author takes seriously what and how a particular violent act speaks, the more he or she risks sliding into a form of pornography. Dealing too closely with varied forms of destruction can have the contaminating effect of damaging the author's moral integrity in the eyes of the reader. Evocative material collected during violent events remains redolent when recorded and written up in an account, and again when presented to an audience. Observing violence is equally precarious. Especially in the context of collective violence, the crowd frequently understands itself to be on stage, and individuals perform part of their actions for that audience: bystanders, reporters, the occasional ethnographer. I would hope that the more reflexive consideration of violent acts and their representation in this book might mitigate some of these problems (Ghassem-Fachandi 2009: 1–14).

In the hollow media discourses on ethnic conflict in India, as well as in some scholarly writings, violence is examined merely for its cause and outcome: who is responsible, how many killed, how much destroyed? The accomplishments of violent exploits are then related to political gain and *voilà*—there we have an explanation of violence. The violent act itself, including its idiomatic expressions and imaginations, especially at the moment it is meted out, remains unexplored, as if it were self-explanatory. Violent acts and thoughts, however, have structure, intent, and form. Conceptualized as cleansing pollution, purifying spaces, desecrating bodies, or profaning objects, such acts can articulate content that is meaningfully related to perceived qualities of groups that are assaulted in ritual dramas (Davis 1973: esp. 59–63). Preceded by anticipation, projection, and hallucinations that provide blueprints for enactment, they are followed by narratives, images, or memories that keep the deeds alive.

Finally, although this book focuses on Hindu Gujaratis, I invested an equal amount of research on Muslims. In my experience, Muslims in Gujarat think and act in most respects like other Gujaratis. I have, therefore, no reason whatsoever to conclude that they are less prone to violence or that the same social and psychological dynamics that led to massive violent mobilization among Hindus are absent among Muslims. However, this book deals with an empirical event in which Muslims were the explicit targets. Muslims in Gujarat did not call the shots in 2002, nor do they today. The event here is a pogrom, and the focus is on those in whose name the violence was perpetrated. That, in this case, is the aggregate category of the Hindu people or the Hindu nation, and my interest is primarily to account for and understand the social facts of an empirical event.

Identifying cultural motivations in people's conceptions and violent actions, as I do, does not mean I attribute some form of causality to "culture" or that I displace agency onto religious or symbolic forms. My assumptions are that actors are never fully conscious of their own motivations and that actions are always socially informed, influenced by schemas of which actors likely cannot make themselves aware. I begin, therefore, with what people utter unself-consciously, what they read, what movies they see, and how they act during the actual violence. As initial statements and behaviors tend to be puzzling, many analysts ignore or dismiss them and instead move immediately to a more abstract level of analysis, or they focus solely on the public statements of political actors without attempting to understand what people perceive and apprehend. It is my experience that within a couple of years of the violence, many local actors themselves tend to deny their own statements made or actions during the pogrom. Accounting for such disavowal after the fact can lead to a deeper understanding of the motivations during the initial violence.

Along these lines, I am also not arguing that vegetarianism itself, as an ideology or set of cultural practices, causes ethnic violence, or that a tradition of sacrifice, for that matter, or a doctrine of nonviolence makes a people act more or less aggressively. But if actors invoke meat eating, use sacrificial vocabulary, and invoke nonviolence, the analyst must take their statements seriously—minimally as explicit forms of rationalization allowing other things to remain unstated. A decade ago, Jonathan Spencer (1990b) pointed to a homology between nationalist thought and the discipline of anthropology, as both are in the business of interpreting cultural expression. Our response to this unsettling affinity cannot be to reject the culture concept or to ignore its local appeal. Such a response is, in fact, irresponsible, as it conveniently absolves the anthropologist from owning his or her own disciplinary history, distancing instead of assuming responsibility.

To be attentive to what people say, what they choose to reveal or inadvertently omit, and how they experience an event demands attentiveness to things that cover much more than what actors are able or willing to express in word or deed. The analysis of identification, affect, and emotion and of the content of idioms and opinions must include the consideration of that which remains unspoken, of that which goes without saying, or of that which remains unconscious—often enough not only to the native but also to the ethnographer him- or herself.

First Encounter

My first travel to India in late 1995 brought me to a village in north Gujarat where, for approximately four months, I explored interactions and exchanges between living Muslim saints at a shrine and their devotees and followers—including many Hindus (Ghassem-Fachandi 2008). Despite all apparent concord between diverse categories of village residents, primarily Hindus and Muslims, I experienced an occurrence that foreshadowed much of what I was to encounter in years to come. At the time I did not entirely grasp the significance of this episode.

One day I was told to avoid a local pond that had dried out, just a mile outside the village in which I lived. A ghost was present there, and it would be dangerous to encounter the wrathful spirit. Then, a young Hindu man from a neighboring village took me aside and, as if to convince me that not rearward superstition but real events were at work, explained that a few years earlier an unmarried Hindu woman had been raped and killed by a Muslim man in that village. Consequently, the entire Muslim community of that village was forced to relocate to a nearby town. The young man even took me to his village and showed me the ruins. Meanwhile, the angry spirit of the murdered woman continued to haunt the local pond—the alleged site of the crime.

When other villagers discovered that this young man had related the incident to me unsolicited, they severely reprimanded him. The religious authorities of the village I lived in, Hindu and Muslim alike, went out of their way to cast doubt on the young man's character. They said he was corrupt and had a loose morality. They advised me not to trust anything he said. From then on, it proved impossible for me to meet him without the risk of affronting my hosts, who forbade me from visiting the abandoned and destroyed Muslim houses of the neighboring village. Intimidated by these severe reactions, and not wanting to cause the man any further tribulation, I put this event out of my mind.

And yet it came back. I can see now that the village authorities tried to prevent a curious foreigner from causing unintended trouble by stirring up a sensitive subject. Their reaction was a defense against my perhaps overly inquisitive and insensitive advances. But the incident also reveals a more general uncertainty pervading such intimate local issues. Though out of my mind temporarily, the incident had not been relegated to the past, it had not disappeared or been forgotten with the departure of the Muslims of the neighboring village or with mine from the field site. Villagers were afraid, and legitimately so, that the whole matter could blow up at any moment, all over again. Something had not been resolved, and the female ghost was the immaterial proof of an enduring presence.

Eight years after my initial encounter, I spoke with some of the Muslims involved and came to appreciate the precarious status of this incident. They denied the crime and blamed the family of the girl for the murder. She was killed, they claimed, because she had had an amorous affair with a local Muslim boy—not a unique occurrence in Gujarat. What in one version of the story had been an act of intercommunal rape and murder had, in another version, metamorphosed into a case of intrafamilial honor killing. Whatever occurred between the two ill-fated individuals, the incident adumbrates the intricate nature of a wounded relationship. I will return to this episode in chapter 2.

In both versions, the woman stands at the center of all deliberations, yet without any voice. In fact, as a murder victim, she finds herself completely bereft of any agency. As she is a ghost, her presence is merely spectral. Her predicament is caused by a problem of desire, either by her unacceptable inclination or by an unwanted desire for her. While her desire for a Muslim man is unpalatable, so is the desire of a Muslim man for a Hindu woman.

This incident exemplifies how communal conflict in India creates women as spectral, which on the one hand places them at the apex of sacred things but on the other hand dispossesses them of any agency. Communication, the exchange of facts and perspectives, has become splintered and continuously risks reentering discourse as rumor, fomenting the violence that I was attempting to understand. Accusations, whatever their initial truth, are often indistinguishable from mere suspicions and, when circulated, frequently resemble superstitions. I will say more about this in the pages to come.

During the pogrom of 2002, this particular village remained peaceful. When things threatened to get out of hand, the local Hindu swami and the local Muslim pir acted promptly and performed collectively a *bhumi puja* (a worship ritual of the earth) in the main village square. The religious authorities thus obligated the residents to keep the peace. Such strategies to resist the temptation of violence can be found in other parts of Gujarat, too. And yet, unfortunately, they frequently fail.

CHAPTER 1

"Why do you leave? Fight for us!"

INCIDENT IN GODHRA

THE GUJARAT POGROM BEGAN ON FEBRUARY 28, 2002, but in local understandings it was set in motion the previous day at a railway station in the midsized town of Godhra in the Panchmahals district of eastern Gujarat. In the early morning hours of February 27, a tightly packed Sabarmati Express reached the station four hours behind schedule. Godhra is the administrative headquarters of the district, located near the railway junction connecting the large cosmopolitan centers New Delhi in the north and Mumbai in the west. The overcrowded train included many Hindu pilgrims on their way back from the temple town of Ayodhya in north India. They had ventured there to offer *karseva* (worship through service) in active support for the building of a Hindu temple at the site of a sixteenth-century Muslim mosque, the Babri Masjid, that had been destroyed by a violent crowd in 1992. Ayodhya had since become a center of political turmoil in India. The mobilization leading up to the destruction of this Muslim structure, and its long aftermath, is one of the most significant political events in post-Independence India, inciting widespread communal violence all over the country, including in Ahmedabad and elsewhere in the state of Gujarat.[1]

The Vishva Hindu Parishad (VHP), or World Hindu Council, an association for the protection of Hindus and the furtherance of Hindu culture and civilization, had for some time organized such groups of agitated travelers, which included many extremists armed with tridents (*trishul*), the sharp tip of a three-pronged lance and symbol of the deity Shiva and the Mother Goddess. Aided by the Bajrang Dal, its militant youth wing, the VHP planned a *shila puja*, a worship ritual (also called a *mahayagna*, a grand sacrifice), in which bricks for temple construction in Ayodhya would be consecrated. With the BJP in power in the state and at the center in New Delhi, the previous years had witnessed an unprecedented activity of Hindu organizations mobilizing for Hindutva in various forms. The campaigns had been mainly geared towards Dalits and Adivasi groups in the state and inscribed a stark opposition towards Christians and Muslims (QET: 41–44; Kumar 2009: 181–194).

Although the town had been calm for almost a decade, skirmishes erupted within minutes of the train's arrival. On the railway platform, Muslim vendors had set up their shops to take advantage of the heavier than usual travel. Young Hindu men who had purchased items from the vendors refused to pay for what they consumed. According to some eyewitnesses a Muslim woman was molested and there was the attempt to drag her into one of the bogies. The travelers then chanted slogans and taunted the vendors, pulling on their beards and forcing them to say "*Jay Shri Ram*" ("Hail Lord Ram"). Such scuffles had been reported for several days wherever *karsevaks* (activists for temple construction) passed through.[2] In a communally sensitive state such as Gujarat, these acts of humiliation amount to forms of extreme provocation.

A few minutes later, after leaving the station, the train halted to let passengers who had been left behind board. Then again, just moments later, the train mysteriously stopped a second time, a kilometer away from the station. After being heavily stoned by residents of the nearby slum of Signal Falia, home to the Muslim Ghanchi community situated along the tracks, fifty-nine passengers of coach S6 were killed when two bogies (railway wagons) of the train ignited in a raging, ghastly fire, trapping its victims (Punwani 2002a: 3–35; 2002b: 45–74; Bunsha 2006: 110–121; Nussbaum 2007: 17–20).

There are competing versions as to how exactly the fire started in the train bogies. While the Nanavati commission of inquiry (NCI) instated soon after the Gujarat pogrom and completed in 2008 declared that the fire in the train bogies was a premeditated act by Muslim conspirators, the Banerjee commission instated in 2004 questioned the theory of premeditation and called the incident an accident. The latter commission had been ruled illegal by the Gujarat High Court in 2006. Both commissions of inquiry are regularly derided as "politically motivated" by respective opposing political constituencies. Uncertainties surrounding the incident remain.

BRACING FOR IMPACT

In the late afternoon of February 27, 2002, after the Godhra incident, the atmosphere on Ahmedabad's streets was nervous and tense. I met my friend Ranjitbhai for an early dinner at Regal, a well-established local vegetarian restaurant frequented by lawyers, businessmen, doctors, and other professionals. Ranjit, a Dalit who hailed from a nearby village, enjoyed meeting with me in places with a more prosperous clientele. It allowed him, a first-generation college professor, to participate in a world that still seemed somewhat odd to him. As usual, he greeted me warmly.

The establishment was situated on Ashram Road in west Ahmedabad, a few meters away from City Gold, a new entertainment complex with a first-floor restaurant called Cinemasala and various cinemas. In a few days, the city's elites expected the fabulous new opening of a McDonald's outlet on the ground floor; Pizza Hut had entered the city a year earlier on CG Road.

Regal suddenly looked humble with its washed-out colors and single-room charm next to the pompous City Gold complex that had inaugurated a new self-confident entertainment and consumer culture in Ahmedabad. In Regal, I heard people talking about the opening of the fast-food giant next door. Then the discussions veered towards another issue: the burning of human beings in Godhra. Restaurant guests began borrowing cell phones and contacting relatives in the old city. Were they together with other people, they asked. Were they with someone trustworthy? Which route would be the safest for driving their scooters home in case the atmosphere turned sour in Ahmedabad? People were sober and composed while anticipating various possible scenarios.

The immediate effect of a communal incident for residents of Ahmedabad is to calibrate all behavior with caution. Everyone speaks and acts more carefully, avoiding certain areas of the city, or certain topics, and generally preparing for all eventualities. I knew a husband who withdrew cash from a bank, housewives who procured extra provisions of milk and vegetables or medicine from a pharmacy for mothers-in-law, a trusted neighbor who fetched someone else's children along with her own early from a school. This is a general characteristic of many places in India where communal conflict is endemic and, hence, where violence is continually anticipated (Brass 2003: 357, esp. n. 2).

Normal life is suspended, and before the event emerges, time is filled with perceptive thoughts about what might be incumbent. It is not uncommon to witness a Hindu advising his Muslim colleague how to navigate in their respective residential areas in order to dodge danger—or vice versa. Residents claim to be acquainted with the nature of their own neighborhoods and thus dutifully advise colleagues how to pass through it safely. Close friends might even insist on accompanying each other, exchanging friendly gifts of protection by risking their own well-being in the process.

On this evening, I was astonished that everyone seemed to know what to do. The city was bracing itself for another possible round of violence. No one panicked or disturbed the uneasy calm. People moved swiftly and showed determination. Many made plans to move to a safer location for whatever might be in store. Although Godhra had been peaceful for a while, residents of Ahmedabad were acutely aware of its bad reputation. This notoriety had developed at least since Partition. Many Muslims in Godhra belong to the poor Ghanchi community—former converts who had supported the Muslim League in pre-Independence days. They live adjacent to the migrant Hindu Sindhi community who had entered the town as refugees from the late 1940s onwards. The two communities share an abject status in Gujarat and have often been pitted against one another in serious disturbances. In the early 1980s, members of the Muslim Ghanchi community burned to death a Sindhi family during one such clash.[3]

While treading cautiously, most residents in Ahmedabad did not expect a pogrom. They had recently lived through a traumatic earthquake in January 2001, and they were accustomed to repetitive bouts of communal violence, which took place only in select city areas. The last bout of violence had occurred during the short but highly televised Kargil War against Pakistani military advances in Kashmir in 1999. This led to a jingoistic atmosphere in Ahmedabad. At that time, a series of mysterious stabbing incidents were reported in the city. Most were attributed to pairs of men on scooters. A rumor circulated that the blades in the knives used were prepared with a chemical ointment numbing the inflicted wound and making the victim realize the injury only when it was already too late for medical help. Victims would then bleed to death without becoming aware of it—a silent secret death akin to sorcery. For a few weeks, the city's traffic police had thus interdicted pillion riding. Though I was stunned at the time by the paranoid undertone of these productions, I did not follow them up.

While Ranjit and I discussed the incident in Godhra, a freelance press reporter and photographer with excellent credentials overheard us, and politely asked if he could join the conversation. The owner of Regal, too, left his elevated position behind the cash register to sit with us and participate in the discussion. Then came two Muslims, an employee from the kitchen and his cousin, who had just arrived with his scooter to take his relative safely home after work. Stabbing could best be avoided if one did not ride alone. And yet two Muslims on a scooter inevitably looked suspicious to the police. What to do? Both lived in the predominantly Muslim neighborhood of Jamalpur in the old city. The employee's family did not want him to ride the bus that night. Public buses, too, are typical targets in times of communal violence, because everyone guesses the identities of passengers by the routes they take and the areas they pass through.

The owner of the restaurant and the press reporter, both Hindus, left no doubt that the aggressive pilgrims—referred to as *karsevaks* (temple construction activists)—returning from Ayodhya were looking for trouble, because "They always do." The Muslims nodded in serious silence. Godhra was purposefully chosen, they told me, as it was a town where divisions between Hindus and Muslims were replicated within the Muslim community (*kom*). Whenever Muslims were divided among themselves, I was told, they could not make peace with the Hindus. And Muslims in Gujarat are usually divided. The journalist laughed and said, "It is like 'divide and rule'"—a common reference in Gujarat which draws attention to the fact that communal politics appear to be an avatar of British colonial politics. That just a handful of "Britishers" were able to rule and control the entire Motherland puzzled many Gujaratis and seemed embarrassing for contemporary sensibilities, Hindu and Muslim alike.

The scene was familiar to me: the two Hindus—the restaurant owner and the journalist—spoke for and about Muslims without feeling awkward that the two shy young Muslim men remained silent. They were neither addressed nor asked to speak for themselves—a typical experience of an on-the-job hierarchy. The person of higher standing speaks for the subordinates while those spoken for simply keep quiet. No one seems to find this structure uncomfortable.

Ranjit and I finished our vegetarian meal and drove on his motorcycle over the bridge to the east side of the river to Lucky's Chai Walla, one of the most popular teashops in the city. Usually Ranjit does not drink tea immediately after dinner, because it was a "Muslim custom," he told me. Hindus drink tea before dinner, Muslims after taking food. Situated opposite the picturesque Siddi Sayyad Ni Jali, a sixteenth-century mosque, Lucky's is uniquely integrated into its surroundings. A rare tree was equipped with a bench for sitting, and several decorated graves are within the shop's compound, making the tea experience akin to the experience at a Muslim shrine. It was the first time the owner of the teashop recognized me through a friendly nod. Waiters handed me the obligatory glass of water that inaugurated the thick tea brew. Muslims and Hindus of all colors and shapes mingled freely and talked about Godhra.

The *chai* (tea) here is known for its delicious fatty unadulterated milk and the buttered buns that come with it. Men sat on two long light blue wooden benches facing one another and drank tea. Most customers came from the surrounding areas of Khanpur and Mirzapur, others had come from farther away. There was heated debate but no angry talk or accusations. Why had not more policemen been stationed at Godhra railway station? Why were the *karsevaks* allowed to descend en masse from the train at the station? Why was the train four hours late? Why did the Muslim attackers only target a few bogies and not the entire train? People discussed intensely the incident, its possible significance and employment in the service of political and civic actors. After this evening, Lucky's remained closed for many weeks. A relaxed interaction in public that remained unconcerned about the religious identity of the speaker became the exception for months.

Ranjit left for the night. He had to drive all the way to his home village on the outskirts of northern Ahmedabad. He was relieved to drive home. I continued on foot alone on Relief Road, the old city's central causeway stretching from Lal Darwaja to Kalupur railway station. At the station, I bought a new round of newspapers, then circled back again through parts of the inner city, passing areas such as Kalupur and Dariapur—both known as "sensitive" localities in which communal violence is likely to erupt. As I walked back home, I sensed something palpably transforming the city.

As the sun set, people filled the streets, talking and clustering at corners. Residents seemed vigilant and looked at me suspiciously when I strayed off the main road entering empty side alleys where public space disperses quickly into vulnerable, intimate space. They wanted to be sure that I was not a local but simply an oblivious, wandering tourist. They asked, "Hallo! Hallo! Mumbai? Delhi? Which hotel?" For now, no one asked my name or religious affiliation, though this was to change radically in the following weeks. Gradually, Relief Road became filled with police vans and jeeps, but I did not see the usual BSF (Border Security Force) or RAF (Rapid Action Force) that takes charge of the streets when there is potential for urban violence.

There was now a tangible avoidance of mixing by members of various communities. In the Muslim section of Dariapur, area people gathered around mosques and teashops. At one shop I was told that, *Inshallah (God willing)*, nothing would come of this terrible accident (*akasmat*). After all, it was a local problem, because Godhra has been known to be communally tense. I retorted that Ahmedabad, too, the largest city in Gujarat, was known to be a rather volatile place. A bearded man wearing a Muslim skullcap introduced himself as Amir and explained that Bajap (vernacular for BJP, or the Bharatiya Janata Party) cannot let violence erupt. "They would like to, but they can't," he smiled. "If violence were to erupt that would mean they would lose the next election. No party can survive on communal violence."

I passed into the Hindu section of Dariapur, a few houses farther away. People were watching reports of the Godhra incident on TVs at street shops. The camera zoomed in on charred bodies, analyzing surfaces and guiding curious eyes; people reacted with many ahhhs and ohhhs, and they listened attentively to claims of premeditation. When I asked what will happen next, the man standing on my right told me *"tofan, ladai kar she"* (they will make mischief, battle). I asked who exactly will begin *ladai*. Realizing from my accent that I was not a native Gujarati, and after a short hesitation, he told me stridently, as if that was well understood, "protektor of Hindu!"

BANDH IN AHMEDABAD

The following morning, on February 28, the VHP, backed by the ruling BJP, declared a *bandh*—literally, a standstill, closure, strike. An event in the making, the Gujarat pogrom, then officially began. I woke up to an early morning that had hardly cooled from the searing heat of the previous day. Living in a two-bedroom apartment in Naranpura, a middle-class Hindu neighborhood in west Ahmedabad, I shared the lodgings with two roommates, Bharat and Pratab. That day, Bharat had planned for me to accompany him to work to meet his new boss at Ambedkar University. He had just begun a new job as a lecturer.

His colleague Mahesh dropped by to pick us up. He introduced himself to me with, "Hello, I am Brahmin. One should not drive alone today." We departed on two motorbikes, Mahesh riding his Suzuki and Bharat his fancy Hero Honda, with me riding pillion behind him. Within a kilometer we encountered backed-up vehicles and traffic pandemonium. Bharat turned his head and pronounced dramatically, "R-S-S", the acronym for Rashtriya Swayamsevak Sangh, the Hindu nationalist organization. Youths with orange headbands had positioned themselves strategically on street corners and traffic islands shouting *"Vande Mataram!"* ("Hail to the Motherland!"). Orange headbands usually indicate the VHP, while RSS members wear khaki shorts, but for Bharat there was absolutely no distinction between the two Hindu organizations.

Mimicking motions of the notorious traffic police who were absent on this day, the young men were whistling orders to commuters to return home instead of going to work. They had constructed roadblocks by lighting bonfires with furniture from ransacked shops . They were thin, wore shabby clothes, and did not display the usual characteristics of the Hindu middle class.

Nonetheless, in an inversion of normal hierarchies they displayed great self-confidence and visibly enjoyed what they were doing by raising their arms and shouting. Stuck in a thick traffic jam, I saw absurd scenes pass in front of my eyes as if in a film: young men in T-shirts, appearing adolescent to me, were ordering around professional businessmen in fancy cars. No one argued, no one disobeyed. Bharat cautioned me not to meet the young men's gazes, because that could be dangerous. They could do anything today. "Anything," I was told. Bharat was particularly concerned for his motorbike. Bikes were routinely used for bonfires on such occasions.

I asked for an explanation from the driver of a two-wheeler, wedged in and coughing, in traffic next to us, but he just shrugged helplessly. Another driver laughed and said in English, "Welcome to India!" We finally reached the university. "There will be no work today," we were told. I was offered tea, a prelude to a lengthy and meandering discussion. I told Bharat that I did not want to waste much time. I wanted to leave for the inner city. People cautioned me to stay, however, warning that things would be getting worse by the minute. Phones rang incessantly.

On our return, not far from Circuit House, we passed a large refrigerator in the middle of the road, now smashed and abandoned. Fences, too, and vehicles, especially cars, were damaged. Bharat pointed to a large blot of blood on the road near the Calico Textile Museum beneath an underpass. There were no policemen in sight. In fact we hadn't seen a single one all morning. At another corner lay the insides of a car; the steering wheel, seats, and styrofoam were ripped out and scattered on the cement. Many small fires lined the streets, and people stood armed in clusters around them. Bharat, visibly shaken, picked up speed. Nonetheless, he insisted on visiting a popular temple for the Hindu god Hanuman located in a nearby military camp in the north of the city.

Then, not wanting to accompany me any farther, he dropped me off in the middle of Shubash Chandra Bose Bridge—a neutral space stretching over the dry Sabarmati riverbed separating the two halves of the city. I initially turned around, went back to the west shore and walked carefully south to Mahatma Gandhi Bridge—an area I was more familiar with. Gandhi made me feel safer than Bose. The entrance to Gandhi Bridge, which leads over the river into Shahpur area, was provisionally closed.

Orange-colored plastic cubes were supposed to block the entry to vehicular traffic, but some had been tipped over. Stones were placed in the way. The bridge had suddenly become a barrier. Several men in plain clothes talked loudly to the two-wheelers as they approached, wildly gesticulating and directing them away from the bridge. At first, I thought there were no policemen around, but then I perceived a single officer standing at the corner. He looked uninvolved.

A cluster of scooters made noises, their drivers pondering whether or not to cross the long, wide bridge. The two-wheelers roared their engines indecisively as they languished at the bridge's entrance. I asked some people what was going on, and they shouted back that I should go home. They told me everything was closed (*bandh*). I saw a couple of vehicles moving to and from the other side of the bridge, despite warnings not to cross over. Its usual flow of traffic arrested, the bridge was no longer a point of access but one of confinement—the moment when violence erupts in Ahmedabad.

I walked all the way to the middle of the bridge, wondering whether I should cross. Smoke was rising from fires in the east. It appeared as inverted pyramids, thin at the bottom but spreading over the sky to cover the diverse areas of the walled city. Something in the historic city was burning, or did the fires lie beyond it? With my camera, I took a last picture of the old city and then, almost instinctually, stuffed the camera deep into my bag. In Berlin, my hometown, taking pictures of street actors during their yearly clashes with the police on May First was the surest way to get beaten up—even if they wore masks. Uncomfortable with my visibility in the middle of the bridge, I picked up my pace and walked over it directly into Shahpur.

Contagion in Shahpur

Within a few city blocks, I found myself in the middle of peculiar scenes. I quickly passed one, then two, then three, then four cars that had been upended and set on fire, vigorously burning. Shops were ransacked, the street full of dust and smoke. On one corner, in the safety of the charred ruins of a white Ambassador car, two policemen sat on a metal case, probably a box for cold drinks. Facing the bridge with their backs to the rampage behind them, they smoked in silence. About twenty-five cows, large for a cluster of cows, lingered around them, and the policemen seemed intent on guarding them. They ignored me.

I walked farther up the road. People were on a rampage against all cars and scooters. Men ran back and forth. I saw no Muslims, and in this sense I was reminded of the new city to the west, the wealthier half of the city, where I had taken up residence. Muslims, who make up a large part of the population of the eastern city, had disappeared from sight, into areas where they were in the majority and thus safe. What was yesterday a "mixed area" had now become a "border area" as members of the respective residential minority had chosen to move temporarily to safer locations. A "mini-Pakistan" immediately adjacent to Hindustan is how the locals conceived of it.

The cows, too, were herded into safe corners and were guarded there. Farther ahead, a crowd jubilantly attacked an unoccupied car. They successfully overturned the car and set the tires aflame in a jolly fire. Running feet, burning cars and scooters, jubilant noises. I was among many moving bodies.

I passed a pan shop, supposedly closed but surrounded by many onlookers who watched the action in a seemingly relaxed manner. The shutters were down but the shop did offer pan—betel leaf rolls with areca nut—and cigarettes for a higher price than usual, typical conduct during curfew in the city. The greater risk undertaken by the shop owner to sell goods despite the imposed *bandh* translated into higher prices for the gawking customer. People gathered around, chewed juicy pan, spat, and watched. A man who seemed to be the shop owner waved at me and greeted me with a smile. As they looked at me, people wiggled their heads in unison in the customary affirmative manner. They talked about me, but I did not understand what they were saying.

I was afraid to draw too much attention, but I wiggled my head in response. I noticed to my right a group of about ten policemen with water jugs, their rifles leisurely leaning against a brick wall. Some stood, others sat on blue plastic garden chairs under an open tent that protected them from the blazing sun. They silently watched the "car killers," about fifty to a hundred youngsters acting out their infantile aggressions. I positioned myself next to the police, just to be safe. Children brought implements—stones, bricks, plates, and iron rods—for the rioting adolescents. One policeman looked intently at me but remained completely silent. Perhaps he felt ashamed. I am often addressed at public events, perceived as a foreign guest, but this time they said nothing to me.

The last car still untouched was flipped over and set on fire, detonating a noiseless explosion and a short panic in the crowd. About twenty youths suddenly scurried away from the upended car as a burning liquid seeping from it quickly followed them. The lower edge of the trousers of one youth caught fire, and he tried, first calmly but increasingly frantically, to quench the dancing flames while moving away from the car. People around him tried to help put out the fire and ultimately succeeded, though I could see that his lower leg was badly burned. Large reddish spots speckled the tan skin of his leg. He limped away, and some people went with him. The policemen began discussing what we had just seen. They commented on the fact that the car caught fire in an unexpectedly strong explosion. How foolish it was, they said, for untrained people to light the tank of a car without knowing how much fuel was in it.

In a building nearby, what seemed to be children were throwing stones at another building. No one stopped them. I wanted to cross the street and move closer to the buildings from which stones were thrown, but people started shouting at me as soon as I approached the street. Their attention took me by surprise, as I thought I was now successfully submerged into the other spectators in the crowd. One young man wearing a long red T-shirt and holding a metal rod in his hand immediately moved towards me. He said, almost politely, "You better go," gesturing towards Gandhi Bridge. It was clear that he did not think I belonged there. I tried to rejoin the policemen, who continued staring in absolute silence. Strange policemen, I thought, as they did not even tell me to leave.

Finally a middle-aged, clean-shaven and well-dressed civilian man appeared, holding a cell phone. He acted with authority and, speaking only Hindi, unambiguously ordered me to leave. His demeanor and clothing made me think that he was definitely as out of place in this part of the city as I was. He shouted to the youngsters to lead me away, but I indicated I'd rather leave alone. To my surprise, the rioting youths were more courteous than he was, and they did not accompany me. I passed the people at the pan shop who were smiling and again wiggling their heads. "*Saru chhe ne?*" (How is everything?)[4] I circled back and turned around the left corner, passing the two smoking policemen again in order to reach a place from which to better see what the crowd was throwing stones at. I addressed them, and they said, "All the city is like this now." They did not tell me to go home but instead offered me a *bidi* (Indian-type cigarette). They pointed to a dense labyrinth of lanes and said, "Inside there, it is even worse," referring to the old city center, the bowels of Ahmedabad. The policemen seemed resigned. Only in hindsight today do I realize the frustration and humiliation that many policemen must have felt, as they had been given unambiguous orders not to intervene in the violent street action unfolding in front of their eyes.

I entered another square in front of Shahpur Darwaja on Ring Road where an even larger audience without apparent police presence observed the attacking mob. The Ring Road was once a fortified wall, protecting the old city from forgotten enemies. Today, with the wall demolished, air can circulate into the old city's dry lanes. The city is now instead divided by a complex array of invisible walls between resident communities. Three shops were already burning and the immense fire could be felt from the other side of the street. Nearby a street temple had also caught fire, and the white paint slowly peeled, curled, and turned dark. A god was burning, but no one paid attention. Had Muslims set fire to this small temple, the vernacular newspapers would have reported it in colorful letters the next day. But there was no foul cry, and it was ignored as minor side effect in the *passage à l'acte*. Sitting on scooters and bicycles on the road, a silent audience of perhaps fifteen to twenty people stared at the rampaging crowd. Some sat on newspapers placed on the pavement, others on their scarves, protecting their pants or skirts from stains. One man told us, "They are all insured." I asked if that is true, and he said, "Yes, of course, they will all get money. They all left."

From all sides, people were throwing stones at two compounds in front of us, from the roofs of adjacent houses, from the street, from behind a large tree decorated with hundreds of Hindu flags, which suggested there was another temple nearby. I asked if there were any Muslims inside the other target compound. A man caught me by the arm to say, "There, that is a Muslim building." Another man said, "They already left last night." Those throwing stones were enthusiastic and excited, but there was no anger in the rioting crowd. I expected to see anger, but I saw only fun.

A newspaper seller arrived with his bicycle. I bought one, sat with the others, and began skimming it. The thin Gujarati-language paper *Western Times* boldly announced the latest events: "In the city people are rioting." It carried the headline "Frightened, Burning Gujarat" (Bhadake Baltu Gujarat) and spelled out in great detail all the areas, districts, and subdistricts of the city as well as locales throughout central Gujarat where violence had broken out and curfews had been imposed. It said the entire Shahpur area, where we were sitting, was under curfew, too. But here we were, sitting on the street, and people were rioting right in front of us in sight of an inactive police. Many people bought a paper (less than five cents each) and the seller made a good business. Turning our faces away from the heat of the burning shops, we started to read. No one seemed to find this moment extraordinary.

The newsprint was hard to read in places because of its cheap quality. Words were smudged or parts were missing where the paper had been folded or crinkled. Almost half of the entire first page of the *Western Times* carried advertisements: a mouth freshener, Must Vahar, for "clean breath and lovely mood"; miraculous Ayurvedic capsules called Big Body that promised more bodily strength with only one capsule a day by increasing appetite and weight while simultaneously lessening physical fatigue ("*Bhuk vadhare, vajan vadhare, thak bhagade*"). An ad for Breast Cream and Only-me Spray by Synthico Exports for multiple erections depicted a rare erotic scene of a man on top of a woman in a suggestive pose ("*jetli uttejna tetlij maja varamvar*"). On the paper's fourth and final page there was even an ad for the Gujarat Police and Military Store framed by a gun and a rifle on each side. It advertised its merchandise explicitly for self-defense and as a symbol or ensign ("*svarakshan ane nishan mate*"). After a pious introduction ("Jay Ramapir"), it offered air pistols and air guns for 600 to 3,400 rupees (US$12–$70). In brackets it said, "no license required" ("*lisens ni jarur nathi*").

I was astonished how the ads so unashamedly accompanied the ongoing events. I asked a man sitting next to me to read the paper with me; he had just bought a paper himself. He pointed to the burning shops in front of us and told me in a flat tone, "This is what is happening." He meant, no need to read the newspaper because you can see in front of you what is happening. But then, I wondered, why had he even bought a newspaper? Besides ads, the paper showed black-and-white photos of charred bodies in the burned-out coach S6 of the Sabarmati Express. The front page and the last page also showed "riot scenes," policemen, and burning houses. But there were no rioting people in the pictures. The streets were completely empty, as if everybody had already left the scene when the photographs were taken. The empty places depicted in the newspaper were hence framed like typical crime scenes, suggesting in their emptiness that things had happened. Strange, I thought, as I watched the streets filled with rioters in front of me even though the published pictures of those very streets omitted the people. While the action was being committed right in front of my eyes, the *Western Times* showed empty scenes devoid of perpetrators.

Beside me, a young man wearing blue jeans and an American sweatshirt sat on his scooter and silently stared at the burning shops. Through a hand gesture, he asked to see the paper I had just bought. We talked. He spoke Gujarati mixed and inflected with English words. His name was Rajan. He was a college student at a university in the other side of the city. He talked of Ayodhya. "They will build a temple there," he said, "even though the Muslims are against it." I asked why the shops were attacked. "They are from the Musalmans," he said, and added dispassionately, "Muslims have attacked Hindus in Godhra. That's why these shops are being burnt. They have taken our women." His manner was detached, unemotional, and he seemed to be merely mouthing words and slogans. I asked why shop owners in Ahmedabad were responsible for the attacks on Hindus in Godhra. In lieu of an answer, he simply took my hand and said, "Come, you want to see? Come on, I'll show you."

Leading me by the hand, he got off his scooter and briskly walked toward the burning shops where agitated youths stood and threw stones. We passed the heat of two burned-out shops in a little alleyway. Standing between the shops, the heat from the still-glowing fires was so great that I had to cover my eyes despite my spectacles. He joined the others and started throwing stones. Firing one after the other, he quickened his assault. But the stones were not directed to what was left of the shops. They landed behind a high white wall along a small road. I assumed there were people there, but if so, they made no noise; there was no response. I felt embarrassed and somewhat ashamed, standing amidst people attacking a Muslim structure of worship. Rajan wanted me to throw stones too, but I simply turned around and left. I did not know what to do. I did not know what to say.

I had unself-consciously hesitated for a small instant, caught between wanting to please his unexpected call to participate, and my resistance to it. In retrospect, it seemed as if, after seeing the newspaper photos, the young man had put himself into the picture, into the scenes without people of the newspaper. He looked at the empty rioting scenes and then took my hand in order to put us both into the picture. The *Western Times* not only informed readers of what was happening, but by showing empty crime scenes the paper encouraged residents to fill and complete the pictures, to take part.

Confused, I walked back and positioned myself on a traffic island next to a blind and bearded old man who was squatting silently, seemingly protected from view by another closed pan shop. It is not uncommon to see single men, or cows or dogs, sitting somewhat indiscernibly on a traffic divider or street corner as if merged with the city's hardware. Men like him eat, sleep, and die on this pavement. They are treated like unheard noise, barely visible disturbances that escape the powerful religious and political logics of Ahmedabad. For a moment, I was tempted to ask him if he happened to be a Muslim, but I abstained so as not to frighten him in case he was. Behind us stood the Shahpur Darwaja Gate and its mosque, guarded by two policemen whose presence I had missed before. They, too, had bought a newspaper from the seller, again, to read about what they were looking at. It made sense that the crowd would not attack the structure they were guarding as behind the Shahpur Gate lay a Muslim-majority residential area. The Muslims of Shahpur would certainly try to retaliate if someone was to assail their safe zone. I wondered for a moment why the police were guarding what was not being attacked.

The blind man wore thick glasses, and it appeared that he did not hear well either. I suddenly grasped his vulnerability. He was crouched next to a huge block of ice covered with jute sheets, which provided some protection from the heat. In front of us we witnessed the looting of three new shops on Ring Road at Maiya Fateh Ni Chali. From the outside, there was nothing to suggest that these were Muslim shops. But in the crowd there were leaders, or men of the moment, who rushed to specific shops and gave signals with their hands for the others to come. They were secure and self-confident. They wore neither masks nor helmets.

The crowd managed to break open a beverage shop. Happily shouting at their accomplishment, they drank the soft drinks as if they had earned them following a hard day's work. They smashed the empty bottles on the pavement. One boy opened a bottle with his teeth, knowing full well that we were all looking at him. He was on stage. In front of us was a small garage shop called Nutan Tyres. The men gesticulated and seemed to know the shop. They broke open the door with a loud bang and many "Arrrayyyss." They used stones and steel lances to smash the locks of the shutters. The blind man squatting next to me asked me which shop it was. I told him "Nutan Tyres." I had to shout several times "Nutan Tyres, Nu-u-ta-a-n Ty-y-y-res!" until he got it. He nodded as if he understood it was a "Muslim" shop. It was clear the shops had been handpicked. The crowd selected precisely this shop, a Muslim shop, and not the shop to the right or to the left. Someone offered me a *bidi* but, ironically, we had no match despite all the fire in front of us. The old man showed no emotion, no discomfort, no fear or anger toward the attacking youth or the targeted Muslim community. He was waiting out the violence, as he would a passing storm.

The shops were looted, but the goods taken from them were not kept. The very first thing removed from Nutan Tyres was a scooter, probably parked inside the shop as precaution. With great ceremony several men dragged it out and set it on fire. Then one young man brought out a small stereo, a kind of ghetto blaster. Aside from vehicles, these objects were the most sought after by the young and poor working class. To my amazement, he immediately smashed the machine on the pavement and kept slamming it down with large circular movements to make sure it was completely destroyed. Others picked up several of the parts and smashed them again and again.

Next, a big red phone was brought out and joyfully demolished, repeatedly thrown to the ground until unrecognizable. Another man brought out a large mirror and victoriously slammed it on the pavement. He stepped on the glass shards with his thin sandals, startling me as I thought he might injure his feet. But he was prudent enough and not at all in a hurry. I saw no anger, just excitement. The idea seemed to be to make the goods splatter in all directions. No one kept anything. The acts were about destruction in a dramatic fashion.

If the looting and destruction were merely a performance, then who was the audience? Answering this question made me uncomfortable. For it was not only for us, the bystanders, to whom the rioters performed. Behind us on the other side of Shahpur Gate lay a predominantly Muslim area, which was not being attacked. In other words, the audience included nearby Muslims, especially those who had left the previous day for safer grounds—neighbors who rubbed shoulders with the attackers on a daily basis. That's why the objects were not kept. To keep them would have meant that the Muslim neighbor might recognize and claim the items later, when life was back to normal. Instead the goods were ostentatiously destroyed, and this destruction communicated sovereignty over someone else's belongings and property.

The small violent crowd finally left and disappeared in an alley in the direction of Jayantilal Punjalal Marg. Their attention turned elsewhere. A tribal woman, or perhaps a member of the Vagri community, stood in front of the ransacked Nutan Tyres shop and viewed in fascination the debris of things she could hardly ever herself afford. Suddenly the burning scooter made a loud bang. A policeman approached the startled women and scolded her for standing so close to the smoldering vehicle. He told her to move on. This little scene stood out, because the policeman was sincere about her safety even though the context of his care was so absurd. An armored police van appeared, and we all had to run for cover as it shot water and tear gas chaotically in all directions. Still wondering why the police targeted us, the spectators, instead of the armed bands of rioting youth, I tried to avoid rubbing the tear gas in my eyes.

I ended up in a Vagri *mohallah* (small residential neighborhood) with narrow lanes and masses of people pushing in. There we rested. Some women were closing their shutters and shops as we all moved away from the spreading tear gas. Men and women were distributing ice water to temper the heat and help with the tear gas's effects. People stared at me. Suddenly I felt out of place. Without much ado they showed me the way out, roughly, and with hubris. I tried to exit the narrow lane quickly, but outside three women, whom I identified as Vagri by the interesting collection of dots on their faces and decorations on hands and feet approached and stopped me. One said, "Do not leave, why do you leave, fight for us!" They addressed me jokingly, as if openly flirting. They asked where I came from and what I was doing here. I am German, I said, but I live in Naranpura. After some discussion, and with the usual amazement that I actually did speak Gujarati, they agreed that I should leave. They smiled mockingly, and before they let me go they commanded me to say "Jay Sitaram" ("Hail Sita and Ram," in respect of the two protagonists of the classic Indian epic *Ramayan*).

I hurried back over Gandhi Bridge into west Ahmedabad, wary of a police van behind me. My eyes were still watering and hurting from the tear gas. Two boys stopped me and introduced themselves. We had "lots of fun," they said, expecting I would agree. One told me that I should take him to "this Jarmany of yours," where he could study German. He planned to settle for good in Bangalore, a city famed for its wealth, job opportunities, cleanliness, and other modern amenities. Both showed no fear and seemed aloof from all that was happening around us. I asked them why no one was afraid. Isn't this supposed to be a riot? Where were the Muslims?

They told me that Muslims were hopelessly outnumbered. There would be stabbings soon, they added, and the police would fire real bullets at some point in the future to stop the rioting. But today, there was no real danger. I asked why all this was necessary. The older of the two said, "This is what we do here once a year." They did not mention the Godhra incident of the previous day, nor the Ayodhya agitation. Seeing that I was taken aback by these answers, one told me that Muslims had abducted "Hindu girls" in Godhra. I looked at him and could say nothing. He stressed that they were "very pretty girls," as if that would make a case of abduction worse.

•   •   •

The walk back home to Naranpura in the late afternoon on that first day of pogrom, February 28, 2002, was deceptively idyllic. I noticed how my pace slowed down while I was trying to assemble the pictures in my head. I controlled my breathing, letting the impressions do their work in me. The part of the city where I was living was devoid of its usual noise and dust. One could actually enjoy these trees, the singing of these birds, and even the hot climate. I caught myself in the perversion of the situation.

To my surprise, I was not alone. In parts of Naranpura and Ambawadi, in the western areas of the city, I saw married couples sitting on their garden swings (*hitchko*), enjoying the calmness of the day. They were unperturbed and had no interest talking with someone about what he had seen, the disturbing things across the bridge. The usual curiosity towards all foreigners seemed short-circuited. Members of families swung and wanted to be left alone. The *bandh*, which in the east of the city freed laborers from work to engage in violence, translated in the west into an atmosphere of bourgeois leisure, a cultivated ignorance, where one could enjoy a day off with the accomplishments of a middle-class life.

Ambawadi and Naranpura are posh districts considered "good areas." Residents appreciate that they are absolutely safe from Muslims, as none are around, while members of lower classes who are able to live or work there simply praise what they refer to as "full faciliti," that is, the availability of jobs, water, electricity, and public services. This quality is made possible through the financial clout of the *savarna*, communities of the Gujarati middle class consisting mainly of upper castes like Vaniya, Brahmin, and Patidar (Patel). The typical "no Muslims around" means that Muslims are not present in any way as a community, even if occasional middle-class Muslim families had found their way into an apartment here and there. The consequence of this invisibility of Muslims as a community is that there are no mixed or border areas, which defines the overall area as "safe." The relaxed atmosphere in Naranpura subsequently changed when agent provocateurs started spreading false rumors of impending Muslim counterattacks on these areas.

For the time being, the mood was calm indifference. I might have ignored these curious garden swings had I not, on that first day of pogrom violence, passed an entire series of fancy homes where residents swayed back and forth under the afternoon sun in their front gardens. The swing is a symbol of royalty in Gujarat and also the pride of every middle-class apartment or house. It is the symbol of Krishna, the deity, who is ritually swung back and forth in worship during the festival of Janmashtami, which celebrates Bal Krishna, the god incarnated as a perky young child lying in a swinging cradle. In popular *bhajans* (devotional songs) of the immensely popular goddess Amba Mata, she too is frequently depicted sitting on a swing. Swings are not only used in gardens but also in multistory apartment houses. Each family has a swing in the stairways right behind the entrance door grills. I often see elderly married couples swinging in middle-class homes, enjoying the cool breeze in the late evening.

On this day, too, as if narcotized by their own cluelessness, or perhaps soothing some nervousness, the comfortable residents swung indifferently back-and-forth to the repetitive squeaking sound of metal joints amidst an unusual silence. This picture, and the accompanying sound, has remained with me.

Phallic Women and Poisonous Lizards

I spent the evening at home with my two roommates, Bharat and Pratab, discussing the events. Bharat asked me what I had seen during the day. He inquired specifically about the neighborhood lane in which I had found refuge from the tear gas of the police. After I told him about my encounter with members of the Vagri community, Bharat made an appalled face and commented that they were considered a low caste (*halka loko*).[5] Bharat considers himself something better than these Vagri, because his community is a member of the Naroda branch of the Rajput and claims Kshatriya status.

Many Gujaratis—Hindu, Muslim, and Jain alike—speak with contempt about the Vagri community, who are believed to indulge in "dirty practices" such as meat eating, alcohol consumption, and animal sacrifice or killing. The discourse of urban residents in Ahmedabad about Vagris is vaguely reminiscent to similar productions among an older generation of Germans about Sinti and Roma communities from Eastern Europe.

The traditional hunting practices of Vagris—using nets to catch wild birds and other undomesticated animals—are looked down upon, and their food is not considered proper fare for *shuddh* Gujaratis (proper Gujaratis). In the moral economy of the city, their civilized standing is often doubted and frequently their poor residential quarters are in immediate proximity to poor Muslim residential neighborhoods.

Vagri women are known for their beauty and fatal seductive powers and also are frequently accused of using magical spells. Since in Ahmedabad many sell vegetables from street carts in middle-class areas, male residents of these areas excite one another with cautionary tales about the consequence of amorous affairs with attractive Vagri women. Late every night one can see these women rolling their carts over the bridges back from west Ahmedabad to the cheaper quarters in East Ahmedabad.

I asked Bharat why he thought the Vagri community participated in attacking Muslim neighborhoods, since they seem to share with Muslims an undesirable status in the city. Instead of answering, Bharat smiled and told me a saying about Vagris: "*Gho marvani tay, tyare Vagri vadhe jai*" (Once the poisonous lizard is killed, then the Vagris move on). The participation of large parts of the Vagri community in the anti-Muslim violence in many quarters in Ahmedabad astonished even experienced Hindu nationalist hardliners and shocked many local peace activists.[6]

Later that evening, Pratab received a phone call from a relative from his home village in the province of Mehsana. His voice turned frenetic during the conversation. The family member informed him that in the morning, while Bharat and I had been sipping tea with the registrar at Ambedkar University, a group of burqa-clad Muslim women had swiftly entered the central bazaar in the nearby town of Mandal. The market vendors curiously took notice of the women, who were shrouded completely in black, but no one could see their faces.

When they reached the center of the market area, the women suddenly threw off their coverings and pulled out massive swords from under their long robes. They started to beat the Hindus all the while shouting "*Allahu Akbar!*" (Allah is great!). The Hindu vendors quickly fled into their shops and closed the doors firmly to escape the bloody butchery (*katleam*). The event had provoked a major uprising in Mandal, the relative on the phone claimed. Pratab, visibly exasperated by the account, underscored that the concealed weapons had been extra sharpened beforehand in order to cut Hindus.

Initially, I tried to joke about Pratab's story of panic, but he explained to me exactly what he imagined: Muslims were now sacrificing Hindus. He used a Gujarati causative verbal construction, "*dharave chee*," to make this point, which literally means, "to make an offering." It is often used to mean to feed or increase a God or a person, to satisfy and endow with.[7] Muslims were feeding blood to their deity, their religion, which gave credence to the claim that Hindus can now expect anything of them. It is important to note how and in what precise terms Pratab imagines the obligation of Muslims to kill Hindus, because it reversely explains the Hindu obligation to kill Muslims, although he did not say so explicitly.

While Pratab and I talked, Bharat dialed the number of one of the few phones in his home village, which was relatively near Pratab's. His relatives informed him that they had not heard this particular "news item" yet, and that the village was absolutely peaceful. They were, in any case, prepared to meet all eventualities, since they had gathered several old country-rifles from a nearby temple. Bharat, unimpressed by my skepticism, lectured me that in Mandal, a town with a small Muslim majority, Hindus were made to suffer like those in the walled city of Ahmedabad. There, Muslims were oppressing Hindus systematically.

This was just one of a series of such rumors that I heard in the weeks and months to come. Bharat and Pratab took each one seriously without fail. The fact that almost all of these stories turned out to be nonsense did not make an impression on them. The rumor's falsity left no mark. The point was, they explained, that the accusations *could have been true.* What to me seemed exaggerated and bordering on the absurd appeared ultimately realistic to them. That the enemy was planning and scheming new, inventive ways to score against Hindus seemed certain; the possibility that women were used to accomplish this seemed plausible at least if not ingenious. The force of these rumors subsided only after many months and not by disproof but by a change of the general paranoid climate in the state. By then, Bharat and Pratab had simply lost interest in such stories.

Although less familiar with the realities on the ground in Mandal than Pratab and Bharat, I nonetheless could not bring myself to believe this overly dramatic story. To me, the image of veiled women concealing extra sharp swords, throwing off their garments, and running after Hindu merchants simply seemed ridiculous. The insistence on taking at face value such imaginative productions, or at least on entertaining their strong probability, more than anything else describes the conspiratorial atmosphere in Ahmedabad. To me, it seemed exaggerated right from the start. How was it, then, that Pratab and Bharat took these stories at face value? How was it that their proximity to local ways did not allow them to perceive the odd gestalt of such stories? This question goes to the heart of the matter—the collective and psychological nature of communal conflict in Gujarat. For now, I must defer that question and a possible answer. Instead, I want to return to the image of the burqa (*burkho* in Gujarati), and the varied possibilities lurking beneath it, which seem important in the material of the rumored story.

The sight of a woman veiled, shrouded, or cloaked is a quotidian experience in Gujarat, where not only Muslim women but also women of other communities frequently veil in their own respective ways—be it in the presence of deities or religious authorities or in front of their husband's elder brother, the natal men of the villages into which they entered through marriage, or strange men in traffic. Common criminals, too, are habitually believed to disguise themselves as veiled Muslim women when they commit crimes. If the Muslim burqa can hide weapons and criminals, other female covering practices can seem equally suspect.

Young female college students in the city, for example, will often carefully shield their faces with colorful scarves while in sluggish commuter traffic. Once I asked a group of garrulous female college students why they covered their faces and was told that besides filtering out dust, heat, and the sun, the scarf also protected them from aggressive male gazes.

The problem with the urban male gaze was that if eyes met by accident and interlocked, many a young man felt addressed and would behave in an emboldened fashion—often to the dismay of young independent women. Veiling protected these women against what is locally referred to as "eve-teasing," an intrusive sexually charged behavior by men toward women, part of a larger aggressive gender configuration of urban space. Female college students wore a cloth covering as one might wear sunglasses. It allowed them the freedom to gaze at the outside world without risking unwanted and annoying attention. Many times the swathe did not have the desired effect, and men approached them improperly anyway.

A male college professor in Baroda offered a different opinion that surprised me at the time. Young college women, he explained, chose to cover up because they do not want to be recognized when they engage in illicit relations with boys, or when the women work as prostitutes. In other words, the veiling of women in general is suggestive and allows suspicion to become insinuation. If a woman veils, she might try to retain control over whom she interacts with and on what basis. Yet, once she subtracts herself from public visual exchange by covering up, she risks fomenting the space for projection: she must be hiding something, preferably something exciting or illicit, as the above example suggests. In this particular scheme of visual spatial control, the Muslim veil simply becomes the most extreme possibility for imaginative projection.

In the imaginative frame of the rumored Mandal story above, the Muslim veil becomes infused with its dark and tempting possibilities—sex and violence, which are feared yet also convey excitement. During times of curfew in tense city areas, Muslim women are believed to smuggle under their robes the typical assortment of weaponry regularly used for urban street violence, like acid bulbs, stones, guns, swords, and knives. This might be the case. Yet no one ever explained to me how members of Hindu communities are able to smuggle the urban arsenal of weapons past the police checkpoints, if only ingenious Muslim veils can successfully hide them. Nevertheless, in the Mandal rumor related by Pratab, women not only carried weapons but also made use of them, suddenly and terrifyingly.

The immense power of the veil to attract all kinds of projections can lead to other more astonishing and puzzling interpretations than the above one. Many Muslim women in Ahmedabad started veiling particularly fervently after the Gujarat pogrom, whenever they moved outside of their immediate residential area. As we shall see there were incidents of mass rape of Muslim women during the violence, a fact well known in Ahmedabad, as they occur frequently in events of mass violence (Kumar 2009: 80–217). But as much as residents acknowledged incidences of rape at the time, many of the same people today will deny not only that the incidences occurred but, more importantly, that they ever personally affirmed them.[8] Muslim women will usually claim that by a more vehement veiling practice, they stress their Muslim identity by setting themselves apart from majority Hindu society. To me, in turn, it seemed also as if they implicitly wanted to reverse the atmosphere of general sexual accessibility created during the violence.

Bharat, perceiving this shift, however, did not interpret this as a collective act of distancing by the Muslim community from the rest of society, which had severely harmed them. Instead, he interpreted it as an expression of individual female shame. I came to understand this unfamiliar view better after I accompanied him to his home village weeks after the pogrom. There we discussed his personal understanding of the veiling practices of Hindu women.

In Bharat's home village in Mahesana, married Rajput women from neighboring villages are obliged to cast down part of their garment (*palav*) over their faces in front of all natal men. This is a common sight in rural Gujarat, underscoring the agonistic elements of alliance in the context of village exogamy and postmarital residence, which are normally patrilocal. Unmarried daughters, or natal women who occasionally return for a visit to their home village, are not obliged to veil in such a manner in front of their male relatives and neighbors. This practice is particularly ubiquitous during village festivals where every woman who married into the village is thus publicly marked as "stranger" and affinal relative. The veiling practice is called *laj*, a word simultaneously connoting shame, honor, and modesty as well as deference (cf. GED). Women inhabitants not native to the village veil their faces—*laj kadhe chhe*—in front of native men by covering their faces with a part of their saris, which is called *palav*.

Bharat interprets this practice with a decisive twist: Women who have married into his home village cannot show their faces because they have been shamed. The physical boundary that was crossed through exogamous marriage remains fraught with sexual connotations and possibilities—its scandal is not entirely tamed. The veiling practice expressed a putative sexual availability of married women to all natal men through a habitual taboo. Bharat is not shy about looking at veiled Hindu women in his village—his modesty is not at stake. It is the women who have to avert his gaze. In Bharat's male understanding, the women have entered into the sphere of his sexual possibilities.

The casting down of *laj* expresses a pronounced hierarchy for Bharat between women who are lower and those denizens who are clearly superior, which includes all natal men of the village. In this sense, marital ties are humiliating ties. They carry the shame of having crossed a boundary, the limits of *atak* (family and surname, but also hindrance, obstruction, stoppage). Even his own mother lets *laj* down whenever his paternal grandfather (*dada*) appears, he added.

Bharat used this logic of *laj*, a veiling practice of Hindu women, and his understanding of it, to clarify the Muslim burqa. Veiled Muslim women are "stolen women," he explained, stolen by the Muslims, seduced and then forcibly married, which is to say, converted. For Bharat, as for most Gujaratis, marriage and conversion are synonymous. Religion (*dharma*) is not simply a matter of individual belief (*manyata*) or practice; it is also always about group membership, which more than philosophical or spiritual orientation compels forms of social organization: marriage and commensality.

Thus Muslim women hide their faces out of shame the same way, in Bharat's understanding, as affinal women in his home village hide their faces from natal village men. They are ashamed to have been made Muslim men's wives because all of them are really converted Hindu women (*sharam*, shame; also blot or stigma). For Bharat, this humiliation remains pertinent even many generations after having "converted."[9] Confounding laj with burqa, Bharat obfuscates both, the former is an ubiquitous, routine behavior, frequently practiced also by Muslim women in front of their older male affinal relatives. Laj follows an all-Indian logic in various local ways and is part of a general patriarchal configuration of marriage and kinship.

The burqa in the Mandal rumor hid the individual identities of the women while marking them at the same time as Muslim. Their invisibility makes the veiled women somewhat mysterious; their visibility signifies them as Muslim, a perfect incarnation of an abstract aggregate category. Muslim women, however, also signify loss for Bharat, since they are converted Hindus. Bharat does not identify these women clearly and unambiguously as members of a different community, but rather registers them only as a "Hindu loss." In his consciousness, they are unable to assume a clear-cut Muslim origin. Instead, they assumed a prior origin, a female origin, or more precisely: they became *females without an origin*.

The female as free-floating signifier is, of course, the assimilable female par excellence—the one without a name who can be claimed by all communities and all individuals. That a veiled Muslim woman signifies this prosthetic origin makes her the physical space where the enemy communities routinely intersect and interface. The interface is first and foremost a female and, by virtue of that fact, encompasses sectarian or religious division. Veiled Muslim women are ghosts in that they seem to float, having no faces and obscured origins. Their real origin lies in the matrimonial dialogue among men and the triangulation of desire among them (Das

2006: 18–38).[10] The spectrality of women as the product of competing male desire becomes expressed indirectly with reference to supernatural figures, and I will have to say more about this in the next chapter.

In general, Bharat does not feel harmed as a man by the presence of women who are not of his community. But through positing the prosthetic origin of Muslim women, he established his own claim to and over them, and only then are they absent. This narcissist wound, in which he is strongly invested, is what made him a follower of Hindutva. For him, these women *could have been Hindu*, which is to say they could have been *his*. This claim is curious because he did not consider all Hindu women of marriageable age necessarily proper marital choices for himself (even if he might fantasize about some of them). He still respects the rules of caste endogamy—if weaker now than for previous generations. Someone like Bharat affirmed such traditions on the face of it without fail. To him, marriage rules are fundamentally boundaries and limitations of decency and modesty (*maryada*), which constitute the foundation of Hindu culture and civilization.

Yet the category "Muslim" unsettles this thought. He imagines Muslim women as "his" because he insists that their origin is obscured. Muslim women are "missing" for Hindu men. They are not forbidden by *dharma* (here: law, order), because they were illegitimately stolen through conversion anyway (*dharmaparivartan*, as he called it). It is through the aggregate identity category "Muslim" that they became "stolen," and thus theoretically they are open to him or, by extension, to all Hindu men. The notion that women, whether Hindu or Muslim, first and foremost belong to themselves does not feature in these deliberations. In this way, at least for Bharat, every Muslim woman becomes a sign of Hindu loss, a male loss. The imagined Muslim male's enjoyment of her is a theft of a possible enjoyment by the Hindu male (Žižek 1993: 200–205).

The imagining of burqa-clad Muslim women, who in broad daylight bring out their phalluses in order to terrorize nonviolent Hindu male vendors, is suggestive in yet another way. As in the case of the newspaper reportage discussed in the next chapter, the evocativeness of such overblown images relies on common clichés, but also on unconscious fears. Muslim women are often imagined both as shamed, submissive victims of male Muslim aggression and as fearless, oversexed matrons who produce too many babies and routinely prepare meat dishes unperturbed by the sight and smell of blood. Although these two representations seem contradictory, they are in fact complementary. While the former allows Muslim women to remain sexually desirable (and thus ultimately conquerable), the latter expresses a profound fear of castration. The very object upon which men have erected their masculinity and claim to want to protect has become the agent of their emasculation.

KILLING INDISCRIMINATELY

The night after the pogrom began, I became restless after my roommates went to bed. I left my apartment for a local pan shop that I frequented, at a street corner where two-wheelers usually met for chewing pan and political debate. Nearby was also a vegetarian sandwich stand where youths met at night for colas. I wanted to hear more about the day's events, as I could not wait to read the newspapers in the morning. Three blocks from my apartment I realized that not just my immediate neighborhood but the entire area was deadly silent.

At the Naranpura railway crossing, I ran into two youngsters who were smoking and asked them where I could find an open pan shop. They were visibly startled to see me on the street. One boy, slightly overweight with a clean shirt neatly tucked in, was clearly a member of the area's resident middle-class; the other, scrawny, dark, and shorter, definitely was not: his T-shirt was dirty and untucked, his hair was cut poorly, and he looked unkempt. They both smelled heavily of alcohol. Quite an odd pair, I thought, in a city obsessed with social boundaries.

The skinny one responded, in a bossy and impolite tone, that I should not be out here. This was not a night to walk around. But I live here, I said, astonished by his aggressive tone. He pointed his flat hand in a typical gesture, warning me: "Do not promenade around here like this!" He added in English, "No woalking!" The middle-class boy remained silent. It was at my own risk, the skinny boy continued, and repeated in English, "et yaar oawn riks."

I responded, "I am just on my way to a *panwala* [small tobacco and *pan* shop]. Isn't this, after all, Naranpura, a safe area?"

"No!" he retorted, and mumbled in Gujarati to his friend something about what a fool I was. "Everything is closed now. Everything."

At a loss for words, I helplessly pointed to his cigarette and, seeing my gesture, he handed me his lit one. The gesture surprised me, as Gujaratis usually do not share used cigarettes with strangers. I wanted to hand it back after a drag but he indicated I should keep it, which I did not expect either. He repeated that I should go home. I might get hurt. There were people all over who stab, kill, and attack indiscriminately. His unexpected patience with me countered his initially bossy and unfriendly behavior. I sensed some sincere concern for my safety, which paradoxically produced fear in me.

His words rang in my ears as I hurried back home. I had the impression that when he said, "They kill indiscriminately," he meant, "We kill indiscriminately." It was a personal warning. Later, I learned that on the first day of violence, 235 Muslims had been killed in central Gujarat, 176 in Ahmedabad alone.

CONCLUSION

The way violence erupted in Ahmedabad was similar to other such events in the past. The Godhra incident became the occasion to declare a *bandh* for the following days supported by all the main institutions of civil society and by political parties. The *bandh* call facilitated logistical preparation and psychological mobilization of various kinds. It allowed a large part of a poor and despondent city population, who work as daily wage earners and can ordinarily ill afford to abstain from work or skip income, to engage in street activities.

However, there is a major complication in the way the temporal frame unfolded. During the entire day of February 27, residents of the city did not immediately fall into agonistic thoughts and acts typical of Muslim and Hindu aggregation. Instead, they were bracing themselves for events that they knew were surely to follow; but what then followed went beyond their initial expectations. Many residents initially seemed undecided, and I witnessed open discussion, anticipation, and palpable uneasiness in forms of neighborhood interaction. Despite the severe psychological and collective productions that characterized the city on February 28 and the following days, the roles were not yet cast on the 27th, and identification with violence not inevitable. How is that possible?

The social and moral foundation of this interaction, the fact that residents did not immediately address one another as possible occasions of death, would be eclipsed to a shocking extent in the days to come. The violence that then followed was "expected and yet [took] everyone by surprise" (Kakar 1995: 51). There is thus an important element missing in the description above, which passes too quickly from a bracing for to an acting out of violence. Apparently, into the liminal phase that suspended routine life, a third element entered. In the next chapter, I will examine this disparity by considering the severe accounts given in the vernacular print media and the official framing of the Godhra incident by political actors.

Some of the themes in the descriptions above already gesture to elements that will be further explored in the following chapters: a permissive and carnivalesque atmosphere of fun and joy on the street in relation to a purported sense of anger; a cultivated and aloof distancing from the unfolding events by the middle class; the utter abdication of civic order and the visible passivity of the state police; invocations of sacrifice as idiom for killing; the discernment of an uncanny presence in sensitive city space; and imaginative material that mainly concerned sexual fantasies about women.

Finally, the invocation of anonymous Muslim women carrying phallic swords and victimizing Hindu men bespeaks more than a mere gender-ing of violence. It expresses a fear of castration, and an attack in the maternal register. Women are the objects of matrimonial communication between men, but as they are the ultimate objects of male desire, possessing them indicates having the phallus. If an attack is imagined in the guise of women, there is then a tacit recognition that it is really Muslim women who defeat Hindu men. The defeat consists in the fact that their potential availability to Hindus is turned into stable Muslim belonging. Stable Muslim belonging becomes Hindu loss. Thus, in the timeless space of the unconscious, Muslim women remain the living proof of Hindu male castration. When they attack, it is the object of desire that attacks, or, to put it another way, the woman *is* the phallus. Possessing them means having won the battle, even if they have to be reduced to dead corpses first.

CHAPTER 2

Word and Image

FROM INCIDENT TO EVENT

ON FEBRUARY 27, 2002, several hours after the Godhra incident, the chief minister of Gujarat, Narendra Modi, insisted against the explicit advice of the local district collector, Jayanthi Ravi, that the charred bodies of the train victims be transported in a motorcade to Sola Hospital in Ahmedabad. Modi also allowed ample time for the press to take detailed photographs of the corpses recovered from the burned-out coach. The images then appeared in the evening news, and a day later in many local newspapers, as bundles of charred bodies wrapped in linen.

In the evening, Chief Minister Modi proclaimed on TV, not without a certain pathos in his voice, that the Godhra incident was a "preplanned attack," explicitly contradicting the collector's statement released just a few hours earlier, also on TV, which had described the incident not as preplanned but as an "accident" (Setalvad 2005:102). Senior members of the central government in New Delhi echoed Modi's words, speculating that the "foreign hand" of the infamous Pakistani intelligence services (ISI) was involved. At the time, however, no investigation had been completed; nor do we today, nine years later, understand fully what happened in the morning hours of that fateful day at the Godhra railway station.[1]

The next morning, on February 28, Modi alleged that no ordinary group could have committed such a "cowardly act." The Godhra incident was, he argued, "not a communal incident" caused by long-standing hostility between two communities but a "one-sided collective violent act of terrorism from one community."[2] This authoritative gloss immediately circulated on the airwaves of radio and TV and in the print medium of newspapers.

Modi hit a particular nerve with this formulation, which initially seemed less imbalanced than the constant barrage of commentary from speakers of the VHP (Vishva Hindu Parishad, or World Hindu Council).

In the local logic, the claim that the Godhra incident was not "communal," and not committed by any ordinary group, appeared contradictory. For a moment, the formulation suggested that the chief minister might try to thwart the attempt to divide communities along religious and ethnic lines and instead make a general condemnation of a criminal act by extraordinary violent players. But, quite ingeniously, he did the opposite.

First, Modi further communalized the moment in the very act of saying that the Godhra incident was not a communal incident—"*komi ghatna nathi*"—by adding "*ek komnu ek tarafi samuhik hinsanu trasvadi krutya.*" Instead of being "communal," he deemed the incident to be the "one-sided collective violent act of terrorism from one community." In other words, he said the incident was not communal (*komi*) but originated nonetheless from one community (*ek komnu ek tarafi*), which had unilaterally targeted the other.

Second, Modi used a form of the word "terrorism" (*trasvad*) to qualify the incident. The predictably recurrent communal clashes in Gujarat, whether religious or caste motivated, are usually referred to by a series of possible terms: the English-derived term *riots* (in plural), *himsa* (violence), *dhamal* (disorder, commotion), *ramkan* (riot, trouble, destruction), *ladai* (battle, war, quarrel), *humlo* (attack, assault), *hullad* (disturbance, tumult, mischief, riot, brawl), or *tofan* (tumult, mischief, battle).[3] Accordingly, leading vernacular newspapers frequently used *tofan* to refer to communal violence and described the pogrom violence that began the following day as *tofan*, but they rarely used this term for the Godhra incident.[4]

Media representations of Godhra stand in sharp contrast to how residents in Ahmedabad initially talked about the incident. Throughout February 27, which I spent in several locations in Ahmedabad discussing the burning of the train, interlocutors understood the incident in Godhra to be the serious expression of an ongoing violent exchange as reflected in repetitive communal clashes. It would be wrong to assume that Gujaratis take recurring incidences of *tofan* lightly. However, the term related to something many urban Gujaratis were familiar with and for which there existed routine responses.

Narendra Modi never varied, however, in his declaration that the incident was not routine but an example of international terrorism. Two days after Godhra, on March 1, while houses all over Gujarat were burning, he proclaimed that the "black deed" of Godhra showed "how collective terrorism could take an organized form." The whole world, he claimed, had condemned this "organized terrorist act."[5] In asserting an international significance for the incident, he was suggesting a belated equivalence between Godhra and the massacre of 9/11 half a year earlier in the United States. The tendency of the media or of academics to place communal events in India into a larger international frame of analysis has a longer history dating back to the late 1980s (Ludden 2006 [1996]: 3–4; Shah 2006: 80–82).

Modi defined the Godhra incident, as Bush did 9/11, as an attack not on one group but on the whole world. Unlike Bush, however, he unambiguously implicated *all* local minority Muslim communities, who have long been subjected to established patterns of stigmatization and prejudice. Thus, when Modi called the Godhra incident an act of "collective terrorism," he effectively blended the register of international terrorism with communalism, which signified long-standing fault lines deeply entrenched in central Gujarat. The threat was, in other words, not old but something emergent and new.[6] Terrorism, in this view, was just an intensification of communalism. As if to back the chief minister, one vernacular newspaper described the town of Godhra hyperbolically as the state's "communal center of sacrificial fires."[7] Hindu residents, it reported, claimed that "terrorists" from across the border in Pakistan had been living in the Gujarati town for a very long time.

The superseding of local communal history with international threat, a fusion of the intimate with the distant, was an ingenious move, as it summoned the specter of a sort of *unheimlicher* terrorism that dispelled any attempt to recognize something familiar in the incident. What residents in Ahmedabad had always known to be "communalism" was now suddenly "terrorism." The already common dislike for the neighborhood Muslim became the basis for a new suspicion. When Gujaratis looked at Godhra, they recognized a recurrent problem—communal clashes—and yet they were being told that they did not grasp what they were seeing: international terrorism.

What first and foremost defines the Gujarat pogrom is this shift in perspective. The Godhra incident was spun as an experience outside ordinary logic. The blurring of internal and external threat positioned the local neighborhood Muslim at the center of a long-standing and deeply psychological conflict with neighboring Pakistan, a country whose origin reaches into the traumatic breakup of British colonial India. By contrast, many Hindu residents in the city did not use such plot narratives to make sense of recurrent communal clashes in the city in years before. This shift implied seeing Godhra as the West saw 9/11. Consequently, what followed it had to be equally extraordinary to participants and victims alike.

COMPLICITY

With the advent of the "international terrorist," the usual strategies of moderate middle-class Gujaratis to attribute recurring incidences of communal violence to specific "criminals" (*goondas*) and "anti-social elements" (*asamajik tatvo*) were no longer effective. Although these formulations had always been hollow in themselves, the inability to apply them facilitated a disintegration of the psychological defenses that might have resisted the massive anti-Muslim propaganda that was to follow. It set the stage for widespread complicity and collective mobilization through a shift in the symbolic location of imminent danger.

The familiar narratives of underworld dons, who engaged in the business of contraband liquor were connected to corrupt local politicians and the police while fomenting clashes between Hindus and Muslims—or, alternatively, the frequent conflicts between cow-protection organizations and Muslim butchers—were implicitly dismissed. With a few authoritative sentences, Modi had transformed the "criminal" and "antisocial" into the "terrorist" and the "antinational."[8] Through this gesture, a symbolic parity was achieved with places that most Gujaratis identify as preferred destinations for immigration: India now faced the same threat as the United States, Australia, or Britain—the West in general.

The equation of communal violence with terrorism allowed for a pogrom to emerge, laden with sacrificial terminology and unifying Hindus in new ways. In a practical sense, a pogrom is a violent social technology, a cleansing device that makes into sacrificial victim a portion of one's own society. It requires both organization and the complicity of large parts of mainstream society. Although Gujaratis may hold religious stereotypes, these views do not translate automatically into participation or acquiescence, nor do they explain why people might resist accountability after the ebbing of violence. Complicity had to be induced through a particular employment of the logic of exception, excessive language, and permissive transgression.

On March 2, three days into the pogrom, the chief minister described what was unfolding: "Every action has an equal and opposite reaction."[9] The ongoing pogrom violence was *svabhavik pratikriya*, a "natural reaction" to the Godhra incident. His logic was consistent with that of many Hindu organizations, like the VHP, as well as major vernacular newspapers that had criticized the inability of politicians to protect the people (understood as the Hindu people). Many Gujaratis subsequently repeated to me this logic of "reaction" by employing words such as *pratikriya*.

Pratikriya means reaction, counteraction, or remedy. What inaugurates it, *kriya* (act, deed), is a term originally belonging to the domain of ritual practice, used in religious ceremonies and funerary rites. *Pratikriya* follows automatically from *kriya*: *kriya* is defined as an act that demands an automatic remedy, or *pratikriya*.[10] If Muslims collectively were waging "jihad" in India, then Hindus should mobilize their "Vedic" defenses by means of *pratikriya*. If apprehended as ritual technology or mechanism, such repeated invocations of *pratikriya* contributed not insignificantly to the perception of inevitability of violence by people who had deep reservations about the use of violence and could not easily bring themselves to fully approve of its deployment. Modi's rhetorical domestication of violent reaction became the general rationalization for the pogrom.

In my work with residents of Hindu neighborhoods and with members of minority Muslim communities, most people were initially reluctant to engage in this rhetorical excess. Nor did many expect such a massive collective response to the Godhra incident. The atmosphere immediately after the Godhra incident was rather one of cautious anticipation, as depicted in the last chapter. Few people initially attributed any world-historical significance to the admittedly shocking incident or perceived it as an expression of international Islamic terrorism. Despite the urban brutalities of the past, the fault lines for the pogrom were yet to be drawn.

To be sure, people were certain that the tragic incident in Godhra was ominous; it would engender some sinister consequences, like riots, ritualized stone throwing, and deadly stabbings in tense city areas as in years before. Still they were surprised at the enormity of what began the day after.[11] Slowly, in the accounts of both the victims and the perpetrators of the violence, the contingency and ambiguity of these initial perceptions has been erased. Once the violence was in full swing, its meaning became a retroactive collective *pratikriya*.

Ambivalent sentiments, with their actual origin in the intimate nature of communal relations in central Gujarat, had to be mobilized into a much-invoked "Hindu anger" (*hindu krodh*). Under the pressure for collective identification, and spurred on by Modi's articulations, Hindus integrated the Godhra incident into an event après coup: the Godhra *hatyakand* (Godhra massacre) as causal prelude to the organized violence of the pogrom with its own massacres.

In the following weeks, Hindu residents of Ahmedabad, some of whom had never been militant or extremist, found it difficult to distance themselves emotionally from the violence unleashed around them, let alone protect their fellow Muslim citizens. What was being perpetrated in their name required their complicity. The Muslims were to be punished, collectively, irrespective of each individual's actual involvement in, or agreement with, the Godhra incident. Inhabiting the language and logic of the Sangh Parivar, many Gujaratis were resigned to *karvu j pade*, which roughly means, "It had to be done."[12]

It was in this way that the Godhra incident became an event that cast a long shadow into the future. For Muslims as well as Hindus in Gujarat, the Godhra incident became a point of psychological and collective orientation: Muslims were confirmed to be second-class citizens in a state that did not appreciate their presence; Hindu residents defensively recited the official line, "This is not a communal issue—this is about terrorism."

By linking the Godhra incident to the pogrom that followed, Modi managed to derive maximum political benefit from the incident and won every subsequent election. How did he obtain the complicity, and later electoral support, of large parts of mainstream society, of people who normally are not unwary of or naive about the political uses of religion, however deep communal prejudices have been internalized?

Complicity in the pogrom was obtained, I am arguing, first by legitimating violent "reaction" as an extralegal necessity to fight terrorism, second by disallowing any individual distancing from the Godhra incident, and third by creating unity in mandating identification with the figure of the Hindu as quintessential victim. Once the violence of reaction was successfully unleashed, it became difficult to back off its excessive rhetoric without admitting individual error, guilt, and participation. The following analysis of media coverage helps to elucidate complicity and collective mobilization. As will become apparent, the imaginaries evoked in word and image relied on local and national themes that are both part of the intimate experiences and the psychohistorical heritage of Partition.

NEWS COVERAGE

The print news coverage on February 28, 2002, the first day of the Gujarat pogrom, deserves particularly close attention, for it brings into play an imaginary grid that motivated, justified, and made sense of the "reaction" that followed the Godhra incident. Of particular importance are rumors of the abduction of young women, an unusually evocative terminology for killing, the circulation of images of corpses whose identities remained unstated, and visual imagery drawn directly from the widely viewed 2001 feature film *Gadar Ek Prem Katha*, which provided a screen memory of, and for, Partition.

It is common to blame various electronic media for creating and spreading rumors and false information, for playing sinister roles in violent contexts. While this is perhaps true and vital to reiterate, my intention here is to enter into a different sort of analysis. In the pogrom, the print media operated as a relay for larger collective processes of imagination, inscription, and identification. To enter into these processes and grasp some of the elemental themes in the very forms in which they initially circulated requires that we scrutinize their stories and look at their published pictures.

Media representations of the violence and their reception by a willing audience suggest the enactment of a script that preceded the events and changed its substance only in the details. The pogrom was an acting out of an imaginary script whose elements had special salience in the Gujarati context. This script appealed to sacrificial and culinary imagery that referenced ritual conceptions of sacrifice, the doctrine of nonviolence, practices of vegetarianism, the abduction of women, and Partition. As informed by this script, the pogrom violence was motivated not merely by an "initial" violent attack—the burning of Hindu pilgrims in Godhra—but by a mimetic desire that preceded the Godhra incident and provided a rationale for the enactment of violence. Psychological mobilization in this context means making manifest a latent content.

The media representations selected in this chapter—print news, photographic images, and the deployment of a feature film—should not be mistaken for "causes" of violence. They are to be understood, rather, as a symbolic repository to imagine violence. This analysis is largely of the receptions of selective media reports, not a comprehensive or comparative account of coverage during the Gujarat pogrom. It seeks to understand what media on the streets were being read, seen, and later referenced in discussions and interviews to form an imaginary of the violence as it unfolded.[13]

I will focus mainly on *Sandesh*, a Gujarati vernacular newspaper, and *The Times of India*, a national English-language newspaper, with some material from other newspapers such as *Gujarat Samachar*.[14] These newspapers are analyzed paradigmatically, that is, with a particular focus on recurrent themes and terms, as well as on how these imply one another. The paradigmatic quality of the text is visible in links and gaps between articles from one particular newspaper, between editions of the same newspaper, as well as between articles from different newspapers. What a local edition of *The Times of India* reports is never completely unrelated to what is reported in local editions of *Sandesh* or *Gujarat Samachar* on the same day, or vice versa.

There is another level, more intricate and complicated, that relates vernacular to English-language newspapers: quotidian language practices. Although many residents in Ahmedabad are not fluent in English, they nonetheless inhabit a world that is inundated with English terms as well as English speakers. It is not uncommon to find words and thoughts expressed in English considered unspeakable in Gujarati.

A college student conversant in English might have no qualms saying aloud the vilest curses in English while falling silent rather than expressing the equivalent in Gujarati, Hindi, or Urdu. This inability can be visceral, the contrition real, not simply a matter of surface politeness. Not only is there a fear of the consequences of someone overhearing, but more significantly, the person in question cannot herself bear to hear or speak similar words in the more intimate vernacular. In other words, the weight of meaning seems heavier and the effects of the curse stronger and more severe in the mother tongue.

Some subject matters are emphasized in English or Hindi, rather than Gujarati, which for most residents renders them less intimate and more national, international, modern, secular, or scientific. Generally, strategies of language use become expressive of intent, rhetoric, and affect, not necessarily entirely conscious to the speaker, reader, or listener.

Methodologically, to simply read newspapers interpretatively, especially if the rationality of this procedure is merely statistical analysis, is of limited utility (cf. Varshney 2002). Instead one has to suppose a relationship of supplementarity and complementarity between the papers, in which one paper reports what the other paper omits and vice versa. Such a method attempts to read the newspapers from the perspective of the consumer, that is, from the way content of several papers was experienced by the reader.

How is the Gujarati reader called upon to participate in the news accounts and how does this interpellation predispose one to a particular understanding of unfolding events? *Sandesh*, *Gujarat Samachar*, and *The Times of India* were the preferred dailies of the diverse circle of interlocutors, friends, and acquaintances with whom I interacted regularly.

Empirically on the street or between neighbors in residential colonies, each printed version of a newspaper is not only read, or the images viewed, by a single purchaser but passed around to, in my estimate, many other readers. The content of news reports is often transported through chatter, like rumor. By this feat, the *Sandesh* reader can be keenly aware of what is written in *The Times* even if not competent in English or vice versa.

Invisible Women

On the front page of *Sandesh*, on February 28, 2002, situated in a central box (below Modi's assertion that the Godhra incident was not a communal incident), is a short but very significant report titled, "Religiously zealous mob abducts 10–15 Hindu girls out of train bogies."[15] The common compound verb *uthavi javu* means literally "to pick up and walk away, to steal." The verb is also often used for marital elopement, that is, "to run away (with a woman)"—a phenomenon not uncommon in a society where such acts frequently result in honor killings and serious intercommunity trouble.

After the title, the box reports that "Only one kilometer from Godhra station where *karsevaks* of Sabarmati Express along with women and children were attacked in a demonic collective massacre by a religiously zealous crowd, 10–15 Hindu young women (girls, *yuvatio*) were abducted from the bogies. . . ."[16] The sentence brings into play the word *pishachi*, in its adjectival form meaning "ghost-like," "demonic," or "devilish." As a noun, the term means "she-demon" or "female ghost." Taking this meaning into consideration, another possible translation might be "during the massacre, *karsevaks* of Sabarmati Express were attacked by a group of evil ghosts as part of a religiously zealous crowd."

The text continues to report that in the town of Godhra, people talked about the collective massacre and the abduction of the girls. Those travelers that had escaped this inhuman slaughter added to the evidence of the incident through chatter (*vatchit*, conversation). The anonymous author claims that as long as the police did not find out who these girls were and how many were taken, the atmosphere in Godhra would remain tense. These girls were unloaded alive by the mob from a compartment of the train and saved from the fire only in order to entrap them (*sapdai gai*, ensnared). They had no possibility of resisting their capture, the article reports. The local VHP in charge, Kaushik Patel, the report continues, openly confirmed the accusation that Hindu girls had been abducted (*uthavi javai chhe*). No one knew the abducted girl's whereabouts.

Another article on page 16, under the pictures of traumatized victims of the Godhra incident with bandages and crying kin (most of them female), presents an "eyewitness account" by a *karsevak* from Bapunagar, a highly sensitive area in East Ahmedabad. The article claims that during the preplanned attack, eight to ten women were forcefully snatched away by a mob, referred to as *shaytano* (devils) in the title.[17]

The article is subtitled, "Mob dragged away 8–10 women into slum hutments" (*jhupadapatti*). The text claims that a group of women were shouting for help but that no one came to help them. The article continues that the VHP informed *Sandesh* that when the train was still on the platform in Godhra, the Ram devotees started incantations of "Jay Shri Ram," which turned the atmosphere sour and spread excitement. Only one kilometer after the train had left the station, the perpetrators pulled the emergency chain. Once the train had stopped, more attackers appeared out of the surrounding areas, an estimated 2,000 to 2,500 "devils" in the form of a mob (*shaytano tolana svarupma*). The attackers started throwing stones at the train.

Finally, in another adjacent box, a family from Amraivadi that included three women is described as having been made into "martyrs" (*shahidi*). In the title, they are described as having been made into "sacrificial offerings to beasts" (*tran mahilao hevaniyatno bhog bani*, literally, "three women made into a beast's sacrifice").[18]

These texts highlight the magical quality of rumor as that which can never be contradicted because it could always be true. The most urgent question is the whereabouts of the allegedly abducted women. The articles admit that the "evidence" that women were abducted in the first place is given by *vatchit* (talk, chatter). This talk is that of surviving travelers and people in the town of Godhra. Some *karsevaks*, or other travelers, were, it seems, worried that women were abducted. Yet, the article offers no clue as to why and how this suspicion was sustained and confirmed as if fact. There were no firsthand witnesses to the abduction, and the newspaper cites no evidence other than chatter to support the claim. Who else besides VHP activists told the reporters, for instance, that people were missing? The police were unable to report how many women were abducted, who they were, and where they might be. The VHP functionary Kaushik Patel also knew nothing specific about the young women, though he nonetheless complained about their live "abduction."

Another form of "evidence" is given by the *karsevak* on the paper's last page (page 16). The "slum hutments" (*jhupadapatti*) are the residential areas around the Godhra railway station of the underprivileged and abject Ghanchi Muslim community who are collectively accused of attacking the train and held responsible for the entire incident. The *karsevak* heard women crying out for help and made the statement, "no help ever came to them." But he did not know who they were, either.

To be sure, there must have been confusion and chaos among the survivors regarding who had escaped the fire and who was still on the train. But in the *Sandesh* reportage, the momentary suspicion that there were surviving victims was transformed into a firm plot. As the police were largely silent, VHP members took charge of the situation and managed the subsequent emplotment of missing women into a tale of abduction.

The story quickly took on several lives. No policeman came forth to caution that accounts of the missing were based solely on speculative talk. Nor did newspapers try to substantiate or disperse the claims of abduction. Thus it remained in the realm of the possible that some women had been saved from the fire intentionally in order for a "religiously zealous crowd" to abduct them. There was one other instance of alleged abduction not mentioned by the newspaper. During the altercations on the railway platform, a Muslim women accused a *ramsevak* (devotee of Ram) of attempting to drag her toward the halted train. The Nanavati commission of inquiry ruled her testimony to be unconvincing (NCI: 48–50).

The invisible women present an emerging narrative, a tale told not on the basis of evidence but revolving around its lack. The very absence of knowledge about the identity and whereabouts of these women made possible the belief in their abduction. They were "missing." An absence makes possible a claim to presence of women, but only in order to claim their absence via abduction. It is *they* who must have taken them.

We still do not know how, precisely, the fire started inside the bogies and who was responsible for it. But we do know that no women had ever been abducted from the bogies of the Sabarmati Express and dragged alive into Muslim slum hutments (Varadarajan 2002: 271–304; Bunsha 2006: 205–214). The abductions were merely a rumor spread either intentionally in the confusion of the moment or in order to sell newspapers that took on the form of a collective fantasy. In *Sandesh*, these fantasies were given the stamp of truth and distributed as "information" in homes throughout Gujarat.

Since the abducted women were never present, or rather were present only in their absence, they functioned like ghosts. Ghosts have the quality of invisibility, but the abducted women were both present and invisible on several levels. For one, women had disappeared because no one saw them or knew their addresses, while people nonetheless assumed these particular women existed and that they had been abducted. For another, there is the claim in *Sandesh* that the *pishachi* perpetrators kidnapped women. Kidnappers who carry the quality of invisible female beings were said to have kidnapped women who then disappear and are "missing." The article in *Sandesh* presents the confusing tale of women who disappeared, based on the evidence that no one has seen them. And then there are the abductors, the devilish and ghost-like attackers who are referenced through the term *pishachi*, which can also denote female supernatural beings that are often said to cannibalize their prey.

This confusion did not escape the anonymous author of the short article because at the end of the text, in the last line of the report, after using *pishachi*, the author suddenly deploys the term *narpishacho*. By adding the prefix *nar-* to the ghostly perpetrators, the author indicates that it was really male ghosts who abducted the female victims. Why render the ghosts explicitly male? The specification appears to be an afterthought, once the article was nearly complete. The author needed to make sure that the readers would distinguish the devilish attackers from the disappeared victims, the former supposed to be male and the latter female. It should be understood that these *pishachi* attackers who so inhumanly abducted the girls were really "male ghosts" (that is, demons, narpishacho). Why did the author not simply use the word *narpishach* throughout the entire text in the first place?

To use instead of *narpishacho* the term *pishach*, which could be male, or neuter (that is, neither male nor female gender), might have weakened the insinuation of a sexual motive to the abductors, an allusion that the entire article is trying to summon. The *nar* in *narpishacho* can communicate the ghost's gender without any ambiguity, whereas the term *pishach* could not. In other articles, the term *shaytan* (devil) is employed, a term that is unambiguously masculine. But why, then, not use the compound word *narpishacho* or alternative terms such as *shaytan* throughout this entire text? Why did the author need to qualify the attackers with the term *pishachi*? Why not avoid the later term altogether for clarity's sake?

As a noun, the term *pishachi* (she-demon) does more than merely reference the generalized idea of a specter. The *pishachi* is a well-known supernatural figure in rural Gujarat usually associated with unmarried women who became victims of sexual crime. Killed before marriage and childbirth, a *pishachi* is a young woman whose unnatural death at an early age causes her to return as an angry spirit. The traditional *pishachi* haunts wells and fields to the dismay of village residents. Villagers fear these angry spirits; stuck between the worlds of the living and the dead, they sometimes make secret blood offerings to appease their anger. Hence, it was no coincidence that the word used for the abducted victims in the articles above was *yuvatio*, which literally means "girls," indicating unambiguously their status as unmarried young women.

The cause of the unnatural death of a young woman is frequently narrated in rural contexts as an accident (*akasmat*), such as "She fell into the well." Uttered more as an appeasement than as explanation, such stories frequently conceal instances of rape or illicit love affairs and subsequent honor killings that carry the dangers of caste and communal strife locally. There is something inherently circular about such accounts. For example, it may be claimed that the woman that committed suicide was attacked by a ghost and pushed into the well. Her unnatural death, which causes her spectral return to haunt the well, is itself explained through a supernatural attack by ghosts dwelling at the same site. Angry spirits are the product of former forgotten illegitimate love affairs, desperation, or, alternatively, of sexual crimes.

I know of a particular example, which I briefly mentioned in the introduction. A female ghost was said to haunt part of a dried-up pond (*talav*) between two adjacent villages in Banaskantha, northern Gujarat, for several years to the dismay of many rural residents. I spent several months in one of the villages in the winter of 1995–1996 and was told to avoid the area around the pond especially at night. Some villagers claimed to see her in the dark; others disagreed since they believed one could never actually "see" a ghost. Villagers explained to me that this ghost was the spirit of an unmarried young Hindu woman of the neighboring village that had been raped and killed at the pond by a young Muslim man of that same village.

They maintained that the woman was killed before being able to mother a child, which explained the spirit's fierceness. The entire Muslim community of the village consequently left, most settling in the nearby town, leaving behind a series of empty abandoned houses (Sheth 1998: 115). In a narrative reversal that is typical for such local conflicts, Muslims in the nearby town claimed instead that the young woman's family had killed her after it was revealed that she had an affair with a local Muslim boy. My interest in the story at the time created an uncomfortable stir, and I did not inquire further into the sensitive matter, as I was a first-time guest.

In other words, the *pishachi* are themselves "invisible women"—victims of an accident, misfortune, or a crime who have gone missing. They return to haunt the living for the injustice they had to suffer. Every *pishachi* evokes an incident that cannot be laid to rest and therefore haunts those left behind. In using the term *pishachi to* refer to the Muslim attackers of Signal Falia, *Sandesh* is evoking sexual crimes. *Pishach* are the "spiritual embodiment" of a man's vice (Briggs 1920: 132), frequently represented by female supernatural entities: spirits of women violently killed before their time—that is, before their female sexuality could become tamed in marriage and childbirth.

We can see here a fertile ground for imagining the Godhra incident discursively as an amalgamation of terrorism with the more intimate theme of gender and the ambiguous emotional attitude towards female sexuality. The uncontrollable sexuality of women and the excessive sexuality of Muslims both pose formidable threats. Most importantly, however, the *pishachi* invoke in a spectral way the traumatic experiences of Partition, which included the live abduction and later repatriation of women across national borders (Das 2007: 18–37). Additionally, implicitly expressed is the widespread middle-class fear of the slum as a site of excess: sexual, violent, loud, poverty-ridden, wasteful, and festive. Rape and the sexual violation of women are central to the imaginary script employed in the pogrom of 2002.

The curious passage from adjective to noun, the ambiguity between female *pishachi* and male *narpishacho*, in the article mentioned above is an example of what Freud (1996 [1900]: 482–500) called secondary elaboration. In this process, latent thought content is manipulated and revised, rendered overly coherent and unified, to make it fit an acceptable narrative. The sexual associations invoked by the figure of female ghosts manifest in the form of a common prejudice: the fear of Muslim predatory behavior with respect to Hindu women. Underlying this relatively common stereotype is the much more significant fear of uncontrollable female sexuality. In this way, rational thought is enlisted by the unconscious to impose its own ends (Weber 2000[1982]: 40–49, esp. 43). The enduring quality of this widespread accusation, which, as we shall see, is furthermore substantiated through a dietary logic, is predicated on this latent content that has less to do with Muslims or their culinary preferences than with the sexuality of women as such.

For something to be missing, it first had to have been in its proper place. The women of whom the articles speak never were present, and yet they nonetheless became inscribed as lost. They are figures *qui manque à place,* spectral products of the triangulation of desire between Muslim men, Hindu men, and the unmarked category "woman." It is through the attribution of obscured origin that she becomes the relay between them. Furthermore, it is through secondary elaboration that the anxiety about women is revised and the figure of the Muslim becomes inserted as cause for a peculiar lack.

The reportage in *The Times of India* on February 28 differed from *Sandesh* in that the English-language newspaper was more careful to identify sources. Articles are less often written in an editorial style and frequently give the names of authors. Hence some measure of accountability was executed in its coverage. While *Sandesh* claimed a national and international significance to the incident, *The Times*, although itself a national newspaper, did not. It questioned whether the Godhra incident was provoked by the behavior of VHP members, although it did not elaborate the point. It also suggested that the town of Godhra was marked by sectarian divisions within the Muslim community, alluding to other social dynamics that might have lain behind the incident.

A report called "Survivors seethe with rage, mourn the dead" describes attacks on female *karsevaks* traveling on the Sabarmati Express.[19] It quotes sixty-five-year-old victim Devika Luhana: "[T]hey will all go to hell for this act of malice." Another victim, Sushma Shukla, tells the Times News Network (TNN), "[I]n our culture, women are respected and not attacked with swords and acid. We should not take this lying down." Other women *karsevaks* in the background are described as shouting, "No sacrifice should go in vain" (*koi kurbani khali na jaye*). The term used for sacrifice here is *kurbani*, a word invoking blood sacrifice during the Muslim festival of Bakri-Id. Heta Patel, a member of Durga Vahini, the women's wing of the Bajrang Dal, states, "They stormed inside the women's bogie, and before we could react they set the entire bogie on fire. Some of us managed to escape, but a number of our sisters got trapped. . . . [I]t was horrifying."

Heta Patel's statement describes the image of violence against women and how women got trapped in the fire. Curiously, however, *The Times* reportage did not feature the live abduction of Hindu girls. On another page of the newspaper, VHP unit joint secretary Kaushik Mehta points to the "blatant slaughter of cows in Bharuch" despite a slaughter ban, referring to an incident just a few days earlier.[20] Mehta also informed the newspaper that "We will keep on building the Ram temple but a tradition of sacrifice will have to be started."[21] Notably, the Hindi sentence remained untranslated in the English-language paper: The term for sacrifice is *balidan*, which relates to a blood sacrifice invoking the violence of ritual animal killing. The VHP called a *bandh* and all Hindus were told to remain indoors on Thursday "as a mark of respect to the departed souls."[22]

Much like *Sandesh*, the *Times* derived its information by interviewing officials of Hindu organizations and victims of the train incident, but no Muslim resident or other eyewitness of Godhra was asked to give a statement. This is all the more puzzling in that the English-language paper failed to report so serious an accusation as the abduction of live Hindu girls. Instead there is a substitution of cows for Hindu girls: in *Sandesh*, the VHP functionary Kaushik Patel alluded to missing women; in *The Times,* the VHP official Kaushik Mehta alluded to the illegal slaughter of cows. The accusation of abduction of women in *Sandesh* becomes the complaint about cow slaughter in *The Times*.

Did the interviewees change their story when talking to journalists from a different newspaper, like *The Times*? Or was it an editorial decision of *The Times* to simply ignore the accusation of abduction and instead focus on cow slaughter? Would it then not have been adequate to inform the readers that the accusation of abduction in the vernacular newspapers was doubtful in the first place?

Leaving aside the possibility that these two VHP officials, who share the first name "Kaushik," might be one and the same person, the two versions relate paradigmatically to one another in a peculiar substitution. Cows are sacrificed and/or women are abducted. *Sandesh* printed accusations that were omitted in *The Times* and vice versa. One newspaper's claim is internal to the other paper's omission. This supplementary logic presents the precise form in which most interlocutors on the street understood the allegations: Muslims consume our women the same way they consume our cows, uncontrollably and for the sake of mere pleasure.

The other large vernacular paper, *Gujarat Samachar*, also carried on its front page an article titled "3–4 young girls have been kidnapped." Again the report gave neither the names of the missing nor any other details. Again, there was no need to cross check with officials or railway police. The lack of certitude of information is supplemented by more insinuation on page 10 of the paper, where the aforementioned VHP leader Kaushik Patel is quoted as saying that ten girls were kidnapped. On page 2, an eyewitness is quoted, "Young girls from Amraiwadi traveling with us are lost." It was unclear whether the girls were lost to the fire or to the Muslim abductors (PUCL, p. 142).

The spectral tale of invisible women has a much larger significance than either the confusion between "missing women" and "female ghosts" who are really "male demons" abducting "Hindu girls" who then return to haunt as *pishachi*, or the peculiar substitution of cows for women. Instead its significance lies in the total effects these invocative transformations had on the streets of Ahmedabad that day.

Throughout the entire day of February 28, 2002, a day of terrible violence in Ahmedabad, especially against Muslim women, I was told repeatedly about abducted girls, Hindu women who were assumed to have been there. When I asked young men why they were throwing stones into Muslim shops, one explanation was that these young women (*yuvatio*), as reported in *Sandesh* and *Gujarat Samachar*, were nowhere to be seen, because they had been abducted from the bogies, were probably raped, and then killed and hacked into pieces. "Where do you think they are?" I was repeatedly asked. The logic that fueled this anxiety started with the perception that women were missing because they were no longer there, as reported in vernacular papers. That they were no longer there, in turn, was proof that they had gone missing: an argument of perfect circularity from which there was no exit.

Especially young men elaborated the point that the missing girls had been used for *enjoi* and then simply cast away and killed. They used the expression "*enjoi*"—pronounced like the English word "enjoy" with a phonetic emphasis on the first syllable—as an idiom for rape, looting, and destruction of Muslim bodies and property. The popularization of the word, to my knowledge, was enhanced by the very successful Coke commercial "Enjoy, Enjoy!" that entered India some time in the 1990s. *Enjoi* here, is a typical syntactical mixture of Gujarati and English as in "*enjoi leva mate*" (in order to enjoy), a linguistic practice common among many urban residents and often referred to as "Gujarezi" (Gujarati and *angrezi*, that is, English).

Enjoi rationalizes a free afternoon or evening at the movie theater or food court, or denotes sexual relations for the sake of pleasure—licit and illicit, marital and premarital, prostitution, and rape as well as homosexuality. As the pleasure of *enjoi* is always for no particular reason, it implies a wasteful expenditure. The excess inverts the ideals of renunciation popular with local religious and nationalist leaders, revealing the strong ambivalence in contemporary consumption. In shadowing the Gujarati verb *bhogavavu* ("to enjoy, to use" as well as "to suffer, to undergo") and *bhog* (the victim of a sacrifice), it is a synonym to express a wasteful consumption. Accompanying the violence by invoking the logic of sacrifice and expenditure, the term forms a key concept in the collective imaginary of the 2002 pogrom.

Whereas the fight between notoriously aggressive Hindu *karsevaks* on their way back from the temple town of Ayodhya and the infamous Ghanchi Muslims of Godhra made perfect sense to many Gujaratis, the abduction of young Hindu women entered a much more severe register. Abduction of women evoked an imagery of wasteful sacrificial expenditure, of *enjoi*, by accessing secret sexual fantasies.

Retaliation seemed necessary to many residents because the abduction of innocent Hindu girls was the most heinous of crimes. Motivating the tale of these missing women, these female ghosts, was outrage over the idea that Muslim ghetto dwellers of Signal Falia had the audacity to abduct women for sexual pleasures. Through the process of secondary revision, the *pishachi*, terrifying female ghosts who in the end turn out to be male ghosts (*narpishacho*), inscribe the theme of an uncontrollable sexuality onto the Ghanchi Muslims of Godhra and, by extension, to Muslims all over central Gujarat. The anger on the street, directed against a putative "joy," itself appropriated the form of joy and fun.

In addition to orally transmitted rumors, similar stories were reported from other editions of the same papers by several fact-finding commissions. Some of these stories went even further by claiming that the mutilated bodies of two murdered girls were actually found in towns and areas throughout the state. Here, the unanswered question of the whereabouts of the missing women is answered by "bodies found." The *Concerned Citizens Tribunal* translates:

> Vadodara, Thursday: News about the dead bodies of two girls, abducted from the bogies during the attack on the Sabarmati express yesterday, found in a mutilated and terribly disfigured form near a pond in Kalol, has added fuel to the already volatile situation of tension, not only in Panchmahal, but in the whole state. In an act of inhumanity that would make even a devil weep, both girls had their breasts cut off. It is evident from the dead bodies that the victims had been repeatedly raped. There is speculation that the girls might have died because of gross sexual abuse. (CCT II: 133, translation theirs)

Communalism Combat reprinted a longer version of the same article from *Sandesh*. I add only the missing lines of their translation:

> The police, however, have kept quiet and have not spoken about the sensitive event. On account of that, various speculations during an already tense situation are like adding ghee to the fire. According to the talk heard during the night one more dead body of a girl, also in a terribly mutilated form, had been found. After being raped and mutilated, the body of the woman was set on fire with petrol. Is there no limit to the lust? (GG: 127, translation theirs)

In this version, a third body was found. Moreover, the treatment of these women was so barbaric that the police chose to remain silent in order not to cause even more tension. What the police allegedly did not want to speak about to avoid more tension, *Sandesh* simply reports without qualms. Here, also, the newspaper did not even have to bother to crosscheck information because the police anyway "kept quiet," which becomes not a reason for caution but for convenient affirmation. The silence of the police becomes the sign of unspeakable crimes about which the English-language press gives no factual details. *Sandesh*, as a local Indian idiom would put it, "adds ghee to the fire." Indeed, *Sandesh* and *Gujarat Samachar* repeatedly use the term *homavavu*, an expression for offering oblations into the fire, to describe the ongoing violence.

Testimonies from fact-finding reports have reported variations of the same tale in several villages in Panchmahal, an area with a large tribal population. There, Adivasi women were allegedly abducted for pleasure by Muslim men and then raped in a local Islamic school (*madrasa*), or in another version, in a local mosque (*masjid*). One investigative report concluded that these spin-off stories assumed the "proportions of folklore" (TSS: 10–12). There was something structural and recurrent about these rumors in which familiar associations inhered. Even if circulated and transmitted by flawed newspapers reportage and VHP propaganda, their real origin lie outside and beyond their point of departure: in the fantasies and imaginations of the people participating in them.

It is for this reason that these accounts testify to the operation of an imaginary grid. Although the police eventually found all of these rumors to be entirely baseless, their efficacy did not rest in their veracity. Particularly during the first three days of violence in central Gujarat, the tale of the invisible women expressed sexual fantasies that were mimetically constructed. What is imagined will be acted out, not on invisible women, but on actual Muslim women, who will be in turn made to be "invisible." The evidence of raped and mutilated female Muslim bodies will also be systematically destroyed with a disturbing technological sophistication. For many surviving Muslim family members, it proved later nearly impossible to claim compensation because the killed were still "missing."

Equally disturbing in this tale of the invisible women is its obvious historical referent, Partition and the birth pangs of the two enemy nations, India and Pakistan. The expression of collective fantasies about consumption of abducted women—be they lustfully cannibalized by ghosts, sexually used for *enjoi* by enemy neighbors, or ingested as mother cows—strikes a familiar cord in India, returning with an astonishing circularity and substitutability in subsequent rounds of communal violence. In sum, whereas Modi's discourse mobilized an emergent new threat, international terrorism, vernacular and English-language media additionally related more familiar and intimate themes that employed gender, cow slaughter (or beef eating), and Partition.

SACRIFICIAL SCRIPT

A second element of the imaginary grid is the use of unusual sacrificial verbiage. It is impossible to ascertain the original source of the linguistic incitements reiterated by the media and mirrored and supplemented on the streets in the first few days of violence. Moreover, sacrificial imagery has been repeatedly deployed in the context of post-Independence communal violence in India (Chandra 1996: esp. 84; van der Veer 1997: 197–198; Davis 2006 [1996]; Hansen 2008: 1–14). Most recently, Hindu nationalist organizations—like the VHP, the RSS, and the Bajrang Dal—have been at the helm in deploying sacrificial language to invoke the register of war and national sacrifice: *yagna* (sacrifice), *mahayagna* (great sacrifice), *balidan* (blood offering or oblation, animal sacrifice), *kurbani* (animal sacrifice).

Chief Minister Narendra Modi referred to the ongoing pogrom violence as a legitimate *pratikriya*, a term derived from the domain of ritual action. Young men in the streets referred to abducted women as used for *enjoi*, adumbrating the Gujarati verb *bhogavavu*. The newspaper *Sandesh* surpassed these usages by supplementing them with diverse other terms—such as *homaya* (ghee oblation into fire), *hutashan* (sacrificial fire), *holi* (ceremonial bonfire), and *katleam* (slaughter)—with visual imagery that could shock and fascinate at the same time. The consequence of this lustful expenditure in its newspaper language is that people were not only depicted as "burned alive" (*jivta salgavaya*) but also as "roasted" (*bhujai marya hata*), not only killed but also "ensnared by devils" (*sapdai gai* and *shaytano*) and "sacrificed as food offerings" (*bhog bani*) to "beasts" (*hevaniyato*) in a communally sensitive town like Godhra, which is referred to as the "communal center of sacrificial fires" (*komi hutashanio nu kendra*).[23]

Not only political leaders but also city residents widely used such terminology during the unfolding of events. In addition to sacrificial imagery and terminologies, many residents in Ahmedabad turned to dietary and culinary metaphors, which had the effect of stigmatizing Muslims. References to excessive meat eating and butchering among Muslims, or to their insatiable sexual appetite for Hindu girls, appeared to be part of an almost automatic fantasy script (cf. Lobo and Das 2006: 54).

On the streets itself, I heard goods looted from Muslim shops referred to as "gifts of the gods" (*prasad*, or the remains after *puja*-worship that are consumed); mutilated female bodies were "spent" and "used" as in sacrifice (*khapi jay chhe*), or they were "offered up" (*dharave chhe*); killing was expressed in metaphors such as sacrifice (*kurbani*); a series of terms were used that are employed by local Muslim butchers for animal slaughter (*katleam*; *katal karvu*).

At work in the use of such words is a formidable contagion of sacrificial logic: to be burned alive (*jivta jalavi devani*) becomes, on the following day, to be offered as a sacrifice into fire (*homaya*) or, on the next day, into the fire of violence (*hinsa ni holi*)—Holi also being the name of the popular spring festival. The *holi* is a bonfire of that which is held in public contempt; idiomatically, the term also means "scapegoat." Several dictionaries give evidence to what Stallybrass and White (1986: 171–190) aptly termed "carnival debris" when the entries offer indications of an older form of the festival: "a riot, an affray; a petty warfare between villagers; terrifying the enemy by shouts and gestures" (GED). Women are not only killed but also offered as *bhog*, a term that simultaneously references suffering as well as enjoyment, meaning "victim" or "an object of enjoyment" as well as "a suffering" (cf. GCD, GED, GUCD, and TMGED). On the streets, these women are imagined as consumed for pleasure (*enjoi leva mate*), and all killing becomes a form of devouring, a spectacle for imagining lustful ingestion.

This usage indicates a great expenditure in language, a celebration in words and images taken from an inverse register of renunciatory logic. The words and images invoke usually forbidden associations like causing pain and suffering in worship (animal blood sacrifice), dismembering bodies (meat butchering), slaughtering cows (beef consumption), and consuming women (rape) as well as indirect associations to cannibalism ("roasted bodies"). Yet, what was forbidden and taboo was also scripted. The sacrificial terminology makes comprehensible the evocations of forbidden imagery, and listeners participate in image, word, and moving picture in their own way to make the picture cohere. Residents of Ahmedabad appropriated and appealed to this script during the pogrom, as it helped them objectify a particular part of society that is intimately connected with the stigmatized activities thus invoked.

PHOTOGRAPHIC IMAGERY

A third element of the imaginary grid, alongside the talk of abducted women and the sacrificial verbiage in vernacular newspapers and in dietary accusations on the street, concerns the circulation of dramatic photographic imagery of burned corpses. The evidence for missing women who were raped and brutalized suddenly appeared as the mutilated corpses in the photographic imagery that circulated. However, there was a sharp distinction in the published visual material between *The Times of India* and vernacular papers such as *Sandesh* and *Gujarat Samachar*. While *The Times* showed restraint, *Sandesh* especially offered excessively brutal imagery.

Explicit reference to sacrifice accompanied the many pictures of wounded women with bandages and bloodstains starting from February 28, 2002. *Sandesh* consistently reproduced the horrifying images of "roasted" bodies lying on top of each other in a hospital.[24] On March 2, the front page of *Sandesh*, where all images had become spectacles,

FIGURE 2: *Sandesh*, March 2, 2002, front page

flaunted a ghastly color picture of several charred corpses. While some of my Hindu interlocutors were certain the photo depicted a brutalized Hindu woman, a victim of Godhra, the title seemed to suggest Muslim victims of the ongoing pogrom violence. It showed a part of the corpse of a woman and several parts of charred corpses of children around her fused by fire into each other, as if welded together, with the title, "Without stop two hundred were sacrificed in violence."[25] The children seem to belong to the woman.

The woman wears a white tag around her wrist indicating that the photographer did not take this picture spontaneously. This was no photographic catch. Instead the operator of the camera left nothing to the imagination, nothing to remain secret about how a murdered, charred body looks. The picture has no interest in suggesting what its object used to be, but is a detailed study of what it has become: a mass of burned flesh.

While most Godhra victims were depicted wrapped in linen a few days earlier, these bodies are naked and not veiled. Ethnic or religious identity is again trumped by gender. The picture's pornographic display awakens in the viewer a sort of interest and fascination that one encounters in children when they dissect live insects or experiment with the neighbor's cat. Although its exhibitionist excess is disgusting, there remains a strange attraction as repulsion is mingled with fascination. In this way, the picture creates disgust but not empathy, because the depicted object allows little possibility for identification. The production of disgust, as we shall see in chapters 4 and 5, is a key element of Hindutva identification and mobilization for the pogrom.

As Roland Barthes has elaborated in his reflections on photography (1982), the photographic image brings alive the death of the referent, the human victims in this case. This picture does not capture the death of a woman with her children, because the victims are obviously already dead. Rather, in the act of signification, it brings alive the deadness, the burned-ness of the victims, and thus, paradoxically, resurrects what is already dead. It desires, in other words, to eternalize not life but death—a terrible death at that. In a way the picture speaks and says: "Look here, this is how it looks when they are burned alive." The image mortifies a dead woman with children by fixating them in an agonizing pose, which can now be consumed by us, the spectators.

For a limited duration early in the pogrom, such spectacles of burned bodies eclipsed the logic of sectarian division, because in the absence of reference to the particular identities of the victims, no one really knew for sure whose charred remains were actually depicted in the photos. Were these still the Godhra victims or already the victims of the ensuing "riot"? Were these Hindu or Muslim corpses? The same imagery could depict different religious identities. One consequence of the ambiguity of the victim is that the photographic image is therein reduced to its denotative signification, stripped of all secondary connotative association and distinction. Once in circulation, every group could appropriate the images for its own purposes and consume its exhibitionist excess, underscoring an atmosphere of exception and the unfolding of extraordinary events.

There is another aspect of the picture peculiar to local sensitivities. In Gujarat, this picture quite literally allows and even encourages the viewer to visually consume charred bodies. Many Gujaratis consider seeing to be an extension of touching. Seeing death—be it blood, dead flesh, or roasted meat—is often understood as having an adverse effect on one's mental state. Outside of ritual contexts such as funerary rites, for which there exist ritual precautions, it can pollute and permanently corrupt a person or place.

The pornographic permissiveness of the picture not only reveals a perverse form of sexuality, but it also encourages the gazing at roasted corpses. In this, it also inscribes a cannibalistic desire, which is not uncommon in other violent contexts (Feldman 2002: 241–245; Patterson 1998: 198–202). This aspect of the picture appeals to the connotative, not the denotative, level of the picture's signification. It is intimately connected to local forms of abstention from meat and the avoidance of the sight of death. It is on the connotative level, argues Barthes (1982 [1980]: 25–30), that cultural and historical information is revealed for the interpretation of what is seen.

The uncertainty of religious identity goes hand in hand with the general atmosphere of excess and consumption, where opposing communities appropriate simultaneously the dramatic language and imagery of death. As Varadarajan (2002: 274) has rightly pointed out, in a pogrom the careful avoidance of identification of victims obfuscates the murderous *Realpolitik* on the street. While an ambiguous imagery of corpses circulated in the media, it was almost exclusively Muslims in their neighborhoods who were singled out for gratuitous attacks. In short, the excessive violence in the photographic imagery reinforced the circulation of rumors of abduction and the deployment of sacrificial language and dietary stigma, producing collective hallucinatory effects that both further incited and legitimated violence on the streets.

Other forms of visual consumption of violent imagery from DVDs and videocassettes circulated secretly in Ahmedabad and were viewed by entire families or groups of neighbors for weeks to come. I was asked to attend one such viewing of a seventy-five-minute-long DVD by a well-to-do Muslim middle-class family. All family members, women and men, along with neighbors, watched the video together; it depicted without sound or voice-over an endless series of charred corpses, the remains of victims of the Naroda Patiya massacre, carried by aid workers wearing Muslim caps (*topi*) from one compound to another. Body after body, filmed by an amateur camera; the little white tags on their feet kept falling off as the flesh dissipated. The images reminded me of the publicly circulating images of the Godhra carnage in the newspaper from just a day earlier. Once the video began playing, it became impossible to shut it off despite the unbearable, repetitive sight of the brutalized victims. It was as if the viewers owed to the victims this last "viewing."

It seemed as if the Muslim acquaintances with whom I watched the video still could not believe this had actually happened to them. They were still in the process of assuring themselves of something. I was invited to a second Muslim screening in Juhapura, to a larger audience, but I politely excused myself. I had reached my limit. Many Muslims in Ahmedabad handled such video material with great secrecy. I told an academic friend about these videos, coincidentally a Hindu by birth and usually of a rather sober nature. He shocked me by expressing his suspicion that the bodies depicted might actually be "secretly killed Hindu victims" used by Muslims conspiring to create "false evidence." For him, these visual materials were potential evidence for the missing Hindu victims used for anti-Hindu propaganda by scheming Muslims. Again, one group's evidence for harm is cause for the other group's confirmation of suspicion: a fundamental instability is at work about the status of victim and perpetrator.

Rumor and News

During the pogrom, both Hindus and Muslims read *Sandesh* at illegally opened teashops in the old city during curfew, surrounded by police vans. When I asked a group of Muslims why they inspected a paper filled with distortions about them, I was told that not all information in *Sandesh* was wrong, and that journalists and writers, too, are victims of rumors (*afvao*), so I should not make the newspaper solely responsible. Despite *Sandesh*'s clear partisanship and tendency to spin all news items into quasi editorials, its content also appealed to Muslim readers. Especially in narratives about evocative experiences, such as those that concern secret sexual and violent fantasies, Muslims and Hindus alike appeared to share a similar desire to peruse and gape. A tale's evocativeness seemed to be its own fuel, and the story—never quite told in full— became complete only in the act of reading and gawking.

Such newspaper content is akin to rumor in that every reader can participate in the fantasy that is summoned up. The real fuel of the rumor is neither its referent in the real nor the desire of the reader for information but the experience of collective participation in, and imagination of, the fantasy expressed by a news story and its accompanying pictures. Rumor derives its power from the fact that it accesses a level of consciousness in which everyone can participate, even those skeptical of the rumor's content. Negating the rumor's veracity has no effect on its successful circulation. It does not have to be believed to be effective but must be sufficiently evocative in order to stick to memory and be further communicated. Initiating a series of associations that enable the emergence of collective fantasies, rumor provides satisfaction for a desire to imagine tabooed and forbidden things. The very skepticism that might lead someone to share the rumor with someone else, in order to see what that person has to say, propels it forward. Thus rumor can fulfill its function even against the will of its carrier, that is, to be distributed further and to be communicated to others. It does this by way of its anonymity (it seems to have no origin) and transitivity based on the relative malleability of its content that secures its immense circulatory force (Guha 1999 [1983]: 259–262).

That is also the reason why the incredible accusations of abducted women suddenly just disappeared and interest waned, despite the absence of correction or further information about the initial insinuations.

Once the content of the rumor is de-cathected, there remains no interest in what it is that aroused so much passion weeks earlier and legitimized violent reactions and verbal incitements. By the same feat, the formulaic and repetitive nature of the implicit accusations seems to suggest a substitutable target: the "Muslim" today, the member of a lower caste yesterday, perhaps a tribal member tomorrow.

What then is the source of rumor? Its real source is a collective libidinal economy that normally lies dormant. Once this libidinal energy is expended, the rumor simply disappears. The obsession with rumor soon turns into disinterest. It reappears when re-cathected collectively in the next round of violence.[26]

THE MOVING IMAGE

On June 15, 2001, the film *Gadar, Ek Prem Katha*, directed by Anil Sharma (2001), was released and had a popular run in Gujarati theaters. Due to the excitement in the audiences with whom I had seen the film several times in the city of Varodara that year, I had already taken cognizance of the movie six months before the pogrom began. This movie about a romance across religious boundaries led to much communal posturing in Gujarat while not necessarily in other parts in India. That its protagonist was not a representative Hindu, but a Panjabi actor playing a Sikh, did not seem to matter.

Yet, as I will demonstrate below, the imagery from this movie formed one central referent in print media accounts, serving not merely to obfuscate and enlarge what happened in Godhra but also to summon the specter of Partition, the more ghostlike because of the combination of historical remoteness, psychological proximity, and the fact that for a generation of young residents in central Gujarat, there is no direct experience of Partition. The deployment of the imagery of this movie in print references compels a brief account of a few scenes of the movie. Again, it is important to understand that *Gadar* is no cause for violence, not even for the memory of Partition, but *the occasion for the emergence of something that in general remains latent*. There might be other instances and occasions that allow for such an interpretation that I have missed.

Gadar is a Panjabi story of love between Sakina, a pretty Muslim aristocratic girl played by the Gujarati actress Amisha Patel, and Tara Singh, a Sikh truck driver played by the Panjabi muscleman Sunny Deol (whom Gujaratis often refer to simply as "big body").[27] The movie begins with violent scenes of Partition, flashes back to when Sakina and Tara initially met at a Christian convent school, then further unfolds in post-Independence time. Tara is depicted as a simple but honest rural Jat who is made fun of by young girls at the convent, including Sakina. After Sakina allows him to sing a Panjabi folk song at an annual convent function to the initial dismay of the Christian teachers, Tara secretly falls in love with her but never reveals his feelings.

During Partition, Tara's family is betrayed by the newly formed Pakistani government and has to flee Lahore, now in Pakistan, to Amritsar, now India, where Tara awaits them at the train station. Before venturing on the dangerous journey, Tara's father gives his two unmarried daughters little paper folders with poison so that they may take their own lives before anyone might take their honor (that is, rape them). The overcrowded train at the Pipla station has only eight bogies for 10,000 passengers. When masses of people try to board the train, it is attacked by an armed Muslim mob shouting "*Allahu Akbar!*" A young bearded Muslim with a bloodstained *kurta* (Indian male chemise), black *topi* (cap), and a sword in his hand, shouts, "Butcher and kill the old and the children. Pick up the Hindus. Do not leave anyone alive!"

The Muslims, armed with swords, attack the hapless victims in the overcrowded train, killing the men and raping the women before killing them also. While defending his family in the narrow compartment, Tara's father is killed by a stroke of the sword. Tara's mother manages to stab one of the attackers with a small knife while defending her daughters. In the last scene, a man begins the rape of one the daughters, over her agonized screams, after she was unable to swallow the poison that her father had given her. Then the scene breaks off abruptly.

"In this way the dead corpses of Hindus and Sikhs from different parts of Pakistan were sent to Hindustan," explains the narrator in a dramatic voice. The train carrying hundreds of slain Sikh and Hindu bodies arrives at Amritsar railway station at night. Bloody corpses are bizarrely hanging out of windows or lying on top of the train. In one shot a barely recognizable cadaver is shown. At the train station, relatives who had been waiting for the slain passengers are reduced to eerie silence. The reddened eyes of the movie's hero Tara Singh—realizing that his sisters, father, and mother were all brutally murdered—capture an Urdu message scribbled in dripping blood on the train, translated into Hindi subtitled for the movie audience: "Hindustanis learn killing from us."

The movie plays an important role in the *Sandesh* news coverage on February 28, 2002, especially the dramatic scenes that I have described above. An article titled "Is the ISI implicated in the attack on Sabarmati Express?"[28] underscored Modi's statements from the front page informing Gujaratis about the danger that lies ahead. The article bluntly claims that no one doubts that the Godhra attack indeed was "preplanned" and that Pakistani involvement was very likely. The article then asserts that the attack method (*dhab*) the killers of Godhra used was inspired by the movie *Gadar*. The article continues with a historical comparison: the difference between the train massacres at the time of Partition and the one in Godhra was simply that the trains in 1947 arrived with bodies soaked in blood (*lohithi lathpath lasho jova malti*), whereas the corpses arriving on February 27, 2002, were bloody and also strongly charred. Godhra had been selected for an attack because minority areas surrounded the railway station on all four sides, permitting a quick escape of the perpetrators after the deed.

As I read *Sandesh* that day, I had already lived an entire year in Gujarat and had had many conversations about communal violence and Partition with residents. No one had ever mentioned the "bodies soaked in blood" of Partition before, let alone those depicted in the Bollywood movies that young men watched with gusto. In central Gujarat, Partition violence was most directly experienced by an older generation of the migrant Sindhi community; mainstream Gujaratis had largely been spared the ordeal.

Reference to the movie *Gadar* and Partition reappears on page 16, in an article titled "Memories of the slaughter during Hindustan's division emerge."[29] The article argues that the incidents in Godhra reminded an older generation of the time of "breaking" of Hindustan. In exactly the same way trains were sent from what was suddenly Pakistan full of slaughtered Hindus (*katleam karine*). A younger generation, the article asserts, knows this from the movie *Gadar*. While in the past, Hindus were considered *kafir* (unbelievers, infidels) by extremist Muslims, the situation would be different today, because Indian politicians (that is, secular politicians) were treating Hindus like unbelievers. In sum, the article asserts that both old and young are reminded of brutal imagery attributed to Partition, the former directly via the Godhra incident, the later indirectly via the movie *Gadar*.

The writer asserts that such barbarities as witnessed during Partition—when "heaps of corpses of Hindus were piled up in the trains" and "mountain of girl's corpses" were sent from Pakistan—were firmly established. Moreover, these Hindu victims in the trains were not only coming from Pakistan. Hindus were not only killed by Muslims in the newly formed Pakistan, but also by Muslims who had chosen to remain in India. It is time, the article continues, to ask politicians what "they" are doing here in Hindustan. The article closes by accusing politicians of inaction in not revealing the "power brokers" (*satani dalali*) while the people are demanding a hero, a *virnayak*, like the hero Tara Singh from the movie *Gadar*.

On page 2 of the same issue of *Sandesh*, there is a short article with the dramatic title, "In the moment of crisis the driver of the train was hijacked with swords . . . !!"[30] Again the movie becomes internal to a description of experiences in Godhra. Rajendra Shah, a leader in Dholka, is quoted as saying that the shameless attack in Godhra will be avenged in equal terms and that this time the Hindu population will be organized. Survivors Manoj Patel, Mina Rajput, and others are quoted as saying that, "For us, this is a new birth." The *ramsevaks* (devotees of Ram) explain, "What we have experienced we will never be able to forget."[31] They affirm that it was a spectacle such as they had seen and dreaded in the *Gadar* film.[32]

"We have seen and experienced with our own eyes" (*te najare joya— anubhavya che*), the article continues. This can also be translated as "We have experienced that which we had seen with our own eyes." The compound verb *najare jovu* means to have a personal look, to see with one's own eyes. "Brandishing swords openly," the description continues, "a mob came, and from the neighboring carriage four young women were abducted."

Although the title suggests that the train driver was "hijacked" (*haijek karayo*) by a crowd armed with swords, this is never substantiated or explained in the article. The real driver of the Sabarmati Express train at Godhra station was never "hijacked," if that word is understood literally. Instead, he was told not to come down from the engine or he and his assistant would be cut into pieces (NCI: 67). He did not mention that the persons who uttered those threats were carrying swords. Nor is it entirely clear if or how many Muslims of Signal Falia in Godhra were actually brandishing swords. In fact, most reports describe them as throwing stones, carrying sticks, or throwing burning rags, and it is unlikely that many ever entered the train as the bogies were shut from the inside. One of the initial puzzles for the investigative commissions was how to square the "eyewitness" accounts of VHP activists that a mob of two thousand Muslims attacked the train with the facts that only two bogies of a long train were burned and that many people who managed to escape the fire were exposed to a huge Muslim killing mob but miraculously survived.

Yet, although the described scene of the driver being hijacked never happened, it is cursorily stated once in the title and once in the text. "[T]he driver of the train was hijacked with swords. . . ." The word "vision" (*drashyo*) has to be understood literally here. The *drashyo* that was *seen* was the re-envisioning of the *movie scenes* of *Gadar*. In the movie, the train is attacked (*haijek*) and piles of bloody corpses are depicted hanging out of bogie windows. In it Muslims are also brandishing swords when entering train compartments and slashing hapless victims. It is as if the Godhra victims here remember what they experienced in the scenes from the movie *Gadar*. The driver and his assistant indeed were threatened with harm if they did not stay on the engine, but it seems that the idea of "haijek" and "swords" had to be added in order to dramatize the scene. In other words, the movie became integral to the experience of Godhra by lending concrete form to something more amorphous. At the very least, the unguarded reference to *Gadar* confirms that the movie *about* Partition has become part of the imaginary script *of* a real incident in Godhra and thus is integral to the Gujarat pogrom that followed.

Since several other articles in this issue of *Sandesh* describe the details of Godhra, it is likely that the primary function of the article on page 2 is to invoke and reinforce the pictures of the movie. It serves the purpose of dramatizing what we already know from page 1: that Hindu women were abducted. The article does not provide any new information but simply returns to the insinuations about the abduction of young Hindu girls, this time citing the "leader of Dholka," who is never identified as a VHP leader, although he is precisely that. The VHP leader claims he saw four girls being abducted.

In sum, all articles examined here communicate the same picture, though in different arrangements. The texts always use the same experiences: survivors who all happen to be *ramsevaks* and *karsevaks* are questioned; in the absence of words to express the terror, they describe their horrific experiences by reference to the movie *Gadar*. The train scenes of the movie are repeatedly brought together with the idea of abduction of girls from the train in Godhra, invoking the specter of Partition.

The last, short article from page 2 is noteworthy for actually saying what it does: "We have experienced that which we had seen with our own eyes" (*te najare joya—anubhavya chhe*). In other words, that which could be seen in the movie *Gadar* was now experienced in Godhra. In this way, the commercial movie *Gadar* serves as an imaginative script for the Godhra incident. The imaginative labor one can witness here has the effect, and the intent, of mobilizing the specter of Partition and an imagery that many Gujaratis actually have experienced by seeing the movie *Gadar* a few months earlier.[33]

In 2001, the release of the movie *Gadar Ek Prem Katha* had led to serious trouble in several Indian cities, including Gandhinagar, Ahmedabad, and Varodara in Gujarat, where I watched the movie several times. During a night screening of the movie in Ahmedabad, a cinema and some vehicles were set on fire in a Muslim area.

The minister of state for home affairs at the time, Haren Pandya, appealed to the people not to disrupt the screening of a "nationalist film." Gujarat's social welfare minister, Fakirbhai Vaghela, opined in a letter to the then chief minister, Keshubhai Patel, that enemy intelligence must be behind the disturbances in Gujarat and elsewhere because "No Indian national can have any objection against the film presented in a passionate way to imbibe the spirit of nationalism. It must be the work of anti-national elements guided by the Pakistan spy agency, the Inter-Services Intelligence (ISI)." In New Delhi, the Shiv Sena, another Hindu nationalist organization, launched a campaign against the opposition to the movie and "demanded an immediate ban on outfits involved in violent protests" against the release of *Gadar*.[34]

The movie could not have gotten better recommendations, and all screenings I attended in Varodara were sold out and uncomfortably exuberant. There was already trouble due to the usual practice of selling more tickets than there were places to sit, and some agitated visitors got angry. During one steamy evening screening, when the character Tara Singh shouts "Hindustan Zindaband" three times in a climactic scene , young men in the theater went wild. Youngsters broke two folding chairs in the theater when they jumped up and down on them. *Gadar* had become the rallying cry for those young Hindu men whose own experience and vocabulary were insufficient to imagine the coming of a Hindu *rashtra* (Hindu nation, Hindu rule). In Gujarat, the main hero of the movie came to stand for the strong, self-assertive new Hindu in general.

As with all successful Bollywood soundtracks, young men and children could recite by heart not only the songs and especially specific dialogues. But unlike other movies, such as, for example *Lagaan*, *Gadar* became popular because it performed the historical division between Hindus and Muslims while offering an imagined resolution that was desired. During religious festivals like Ganesh Chaturthi (Ganapati Virsarjan) or marriage functions, its music and dialogues were played in neighborhoods, as is done with many successful Bollywood films. When I visited an artfully constructed *pandal* (an installation similar to the Nativity scenes displayed in Catholic countries during Christmas time) in the old city of Baroda in 2001, the entire train scene between Lahore and Amritsar from the movie was carefully depicted under the title "Partition."

The *pandal* was introduced to me by a group of proud youngsters, while the movie dialogues were blasted from loudspeakers the size of little file cabinets. During the same festival in 2002, within the confines of the same neighborhood and by the same *mandal* (neighborhood association), one *pandal* referred to the Godhra incident by depicting the burning Sabarmati Express, despite the explicit prohibition by the police against referencing the Godhra incident.[35] Again, through the mediation of a Bollywood film, Partition had become Godhra, and Godhra evoked Partition.

An astonishing frequency of references to *Gadar*—in street conversations and print media—accompanied the Godhra incident. Indeed, almost immediately in the heads of young Gujaratis, the movie seemed to have

FIGURE 3: Reading *Western Times*

become the major referent for imagining the nature of Hindu-Muslim relations. People referred to the movie during interviews and discussions. During endless curfew hours in 2002, I heard its music and dialogues also broadcast into Muslim neighborhoods from adjacent Hindu areas of Ahmedabad, especially from Vejalpur into the suburban Juhapura. During the 2002 election campaign, Narendra Modi's Gaurav Yatra employed tunes from *Gadar* as BJP election songs with altered lyrics; at the Hindu Pat Padsahi Yatra, a propaganda campaign launched by the VHP late in 2002 parallel to Modi's campaign, replicas of the burning Sabarmati Express in Godhra were displayed.[36]

There is another chilling example of the effect that the movie had on at least one of the attackers at the site of one massacre during the pogrom in the outskirts of Ahmedabad. Echoing one of the early movie scenes of *Gadar*, when Tara reads at Amritsar train station "Hindustanis learn killing from us" written in blood on one of the bogie's doors, an attacker at Naroda Gam wrote in Gujarati with chalk on the metal door of a destroyed Muslim house: "Muslims learn arson from us."

CONCLUSION

This chapter has demonstrated that a paradigmatic structure emerged in the news coverage of February 28, 2002, and the following days, in which the depth of a story is constructed not through certainty of fact or evidence but through allusion and accumulated suggestion. One article lends depth to another. The same story is told in different versions, even in the very same newspaper, and the weight of accountability is displaced to somewhere else—for example, to the experience of fright evoked by watching scenes of the commercial feature film *Gadar*. One person's suggestion is supplemented by another person's opinion that, in turn, is appended to another person's insinuation, resulting in a tale without closure told repeatedly.

The different versions of missing women are structural transformations of one another. In *Sandesh*, "10–15 girls" abducted by a mob on page 1 become girls "hijacked" by men with swords on page 2, then "sacrificial offerings to beasts" and "8–10 women snatched away by devils" on page 16, or "dead bodies of two girls with breasts cut off in Kalol" in another edition of the same newspaper. The version becomes "3–4 kidnapped girls" in *Gujarat Samachar*, "our sisters got trapped" in *The Times of India*, and Adivasi women raped in a mosque in some of the versions circulating on the street or in tribal areas of the state. Ultimately, the transformative possibilities even allow for the substitution of "cows" for "women" in *The Times of India*, when it mentions "blatant slaughter of cows in Bharuch" in lieu of the accusation of abducted women. One forbidden object of affinity is replaced with another forbidden object of ingestion.

Most newspapers in Gujarat refrain from referring to communities explicitly as Muslim or Hindu during violent conflagrations. Through the absence of any minority voice in the reports, *Sandesh* is presenting a "spectral Muslim," which haunts the entire paper for weeks to come. Once the Muslim is "spectral," that is absent and present at the same time, this figure does not have to be addressed, asked, or dealt with as an actual entity. The terms used for the "spectral Muslim" beget a fantastic character. Instead of "Muslim," *Sandesh* substitutes "aroused demons" or "ghosts," "satans," "beasts," "antisocial elements," and "terrorists" who—helped by the demonic activities of the ISI—play their sinister game openly (*khullo khel khelay chhe*) while all India is on "red alert."

The word imagery throughout *Sandesh* is generally one of sacrifice, blood, revenge, and martyrdom. While pretending to describe violence, the paper is actually mobilizing for it through word suggestions and evocations. The uncontrollable sexual urges of Muslims are expressed in abduction and rape, and enhanced by an excessive imagery of bodily mutilation invoking severing, cutting, burning, and butchering—activities that Muslim butchers are stereotypically identified with. We see the overlapping of three discrete themes, the fear of terrorism (the ISI, or Pakistani intelligence services), traditional ritual practices and butchering, and the register of the supernatural. Additionally, references to the specter of Partition abound and are inflected with stories of abducted women, with the commercial Bollywood movie *Gadar* underscoring the spectral quality of the undigested event.[37]

By proclaiming the Godhra incident to be a sort of "collective terrorism," Modi confirmed what the VHP had been claiming for many years. The VHP, in turn, promised swift action while accusing political leaders of being too complacent. *Sandesh*, too, repeatedly hinted at politicians and the police as being indifferent and incompetent. These pronouncements of exception and emergency culminated in a call for a cinematographic solution, as personified by Tara Singh, the *virnayak* (he-man), the virile hero of the movie *Gadar*. Tara's virility is not merely predicated on his marvelous ability to catch a sword stroke with his bare hands or beat up dozens of armed opponents with his bare fists.

More importantly, his virility is assured because the sophisticated Sakina offers herself freely to him in love after he rescues her from a violent mob wanting to have their way with her. Sakina offers Tara more than any coercion could ever achieve. Here, the Muslim woman as symbol of lack becomes the hero's reward. The loss that is defined by her unavailability, enhanced in the movie by Sakina's aristocratic background, is recompensed by her eventual submission due to her circumstances, which while tragic at the same time allow her to fall in love with Tara. She indeed becomes completely his. The price Sakina has to pay for restoring Tara's phallic integrity is not the loss of her personal Islamic faith, which poses no problem for Tara, but a change of her relationship to her own natal family, namely her father, who is Tara's main competitor for her attention and love.

Sakina now must show allegiance to her husband, her son, and thus her father-in-law's patriliny. The movie celebrates how Sakina proves this loyalty to her husband despite sincere emotions towards her natal family—classic adumbrations of epic themes. Hence, in the movie, the Muslim woman's obscure origin, oscillating dangerously between two religions, two families, and two countries, becomes fixed only by her renunciation of the name of the father, which betrays not only a Muslim but, moreover, a different national origin. In the end, however, even Sakina's renunciation of her natal family becomes reversed and culminates in a hurried happy ending.

The most objectionable scene of the movie for Muslims in Gujarat unfolds when Tara applies his blood to Sakina's forehead, making her spontaneously into a *Sikhni*, a Sikh woman. I was astonished how offended Muslims in Gujarat were of this scene, which they took to be a form of ritual anointing, a consecration of a daughter for the sacrifice of marriage to a Sikh. Most of my Muslim interlocutors stubbornly dismissed the narrative logic of the scene, which after all, is supposed to save Sakina from a terrible predicament: gang rape and possible death. They defensively insisted that, among all others, *this* particular scene was an intended affront against Islam. This despite the fact, that in the movie Tara does not force Sakina to become a Sikh nor his wife. It is she who decides, after further tribulations and under the false assumption that her family was killed, that she should become his wife. It is then that she eventually falls in love with him. In the offending scene, Tara simply saved Sakina from mental and bodily harm.

Must I suppose that my interlocutors would have preferred her death, similar to the one suggested by Tara's father who offered poison to his daughters in one of the movie's early scenes? Whence cometh this willingness to sacrifice one's own children, that is, to prefer filmic death above honor or marriage? If the death of one's daughters is indeed preferable to their marriage to an enemy, then women enter fully into the sacrificial circulation of death. What is so unacceptable about the aforementioned filmic scene is that it allows the spontaneous incorporation of desirable Sakina, and hence access to the other group's women, in the name of her "well-being" given the general desire to take advantage of her vulnerability.

Tara's uncontrolled outbreaks of "just wrath," exemplified in the movie through his dubbed hysterical scream, is a perfect template of identification for a young generation of underprivileged and upwardly aspiring youngsters motivated toward extralegal violent acts by organizations such as the Bajrang Dal, which runs semi-military training camps all over the state. The identification with the hero's wrath allowed the release from inhibitions to act out violence. Once the just wrath of the ordinary man is aroused, *Gadar* teaches its viewers, his revenge is as terrible as Tara Singh's.

The next chapter takes a closer look at actual events at sites of massacres during the pogrom, as there were simultaneous attacks in diverse locations in Ahmedabad and across central Gujarat. The violent acts committed have a form and structure that follow a sacrificial logic. The descriptions in the next chapter rely mainly on fact-finding and police reports, as well as some anonymous First Information Reports (FIRs). The accounts of eyewitnesses to other scenes and of other published works supplement my own account from the previous chapter. I also give short accounts of visits to two of the sites of massacres shortly after the killing.

CHAPTER 3

The Gujarat Pogrom

IN THE FIRST FEW DAYS, the epicenter of the Gujarat pogrom was not in the old city, where I had ventured expecting to witness "communal violence" at one of the traditional trouble spots, such as Shahpur Darwaja. The scenes were short of anything like a "riot," but rather a festival of sorts by one community in the absence of the other, while the police guarded cows, smoked *bidis*, and read the newspaper accounts about what unfolded in front of them. In other parts of the city, however, from the early morning hours to the late afternoon, Muslim residential areas such as Gulbarg Society and Naroda Patiya were hammered by waves of attacks by armed killers, while spectator crowds and sometimes even the police looked on or participated. It is to these deadly sites that I now turn.

It is important to remember that I was not an eyewitness to any of these events. Nor are the details of these massacres completely captured in fact-finding or police reports to date. Given the accusations of systematic attempts to obfuscate, delay, and derail the investigative and judicial process, and the complex political infighting in Gujarat, the accounts of these massacres remain incomplete. If prior altercations are any indication, it is highly likely that they will remain so for good. The significance of these sites as evidence for premeditation and logistical planning of the pogrom, however, is undeniable. Part of this chapter describes in more detail the murderous events at one particular site, Gulbarg Society, based on independent fact-finding, scholarly, and investigative reports.

While not a witness, I was nonetheless a resident of Ahmedabad at the time. I was thus a participant in the circulation of accounts of massacres and, like most people there, came to know about them through vernacular and English-language newspapers and through talk and chatter on the street. Residents today will sometimes deny knowledge of the most gruesome events at specific sites in the city during the pogrom, but gossip about the events traveled with the speed of wind throughout Gujarat at the time. What later caused consternation and denial was narrated with triumphant fascination for roughly three weeks. Names such as Gulbarg and Naroda became epithets with a deadly ring. Even in villages in Kachchh, and in northern Gujarat, these names circulated. When I visited North Gujarat in March 2002, I was intently asked about events at those sites. It was certainly next to impossible to live in Ahmedabad in March and April of 2002 and not have heard about Gulbarg Society or Naroda Patiya, both of which became synonymous with excess far surpassing most "normal" narratives of communal violence.

During the initial phases of the pogrom, the worst organized violence occurred in places where Muslim residents were hopelessly outnumbered or where Muslim migrant communities from outside the state had settled and were not well connected to local Muslim networks. After the first few days of violence, a pattern became visible: the highest number of killings took place in Meghaninagar, Naroda, Odhav, Amraiwad, Bapunagar and Gomptipur, all areas far beyond the old city (also called the walled city) situated at the fringes of east Ahmedabad.

These locations have in common that they lie at the periphery of Ahmedabad and are characterized by dusty and decrepit industrial settlements, segregated living arrangements, a large population of daily wage earners, and gross civic neglect. After the progressive closure of textile mills beginning in the late 1970s, most of these workers had been forced into unskilled labor in the informal sector (Breman 2004: 143–148). Many residents are immigrants, most are from lower-caste and -class backgrounds, and a substantial number are Muslim. Arranged in a crescent around the old city, the residential landscapes in which these communities dwell are marked by the geographic and psychological craters caused by rapid industrialization in the second half of the nineteenth century and followed by deindustrialization in the late twentieth century. For most residents of east Ahmedabad, the situation has been one of prolonged economic precariousness.

The government becomes internal to these areas in the exact same way as local criminals do. The difference between what is legal and what is not, what is feasible and what is not, is dependent on access to local henchmen (often referred to as *dada*) supported by political strongmen. Residents in Shah Alam, Behrampura, or Gomtipur have colorful stories to tell of assassinations, arrests, encounter killings, or murderous rivalries. They know these strongmen by name and can point out their residences—unusually luxurious dwellings in the midst of dust and civic neglect. These bizarre palaces have fences and guards positioned around them. In apartments, the opulence is marked by flat-screen TVs and translucent crystal glass tables. Local strongmen regularly give feasts for the poor and thus secure their goodwill.

The police, too, are a dubious force in these areas, notorious for their transgressions, while politicians can be seen visiting in clean white cars flashing blue lights to garner votes during election times. They offer bribes, give speeches, and buy tea for residents (many urban poor live on sweet tea for days). Confronted by this intertwined network of dangerous urban players—high-ranking police officials, criminal leaders, and politicians—civic engagement by local residents is largely absent or ineffectual. Only rarely do higher-up housing societies with better-off Muslim residents show interest in community matters. Most civic engagement is reduced to entrepreneurial matters, and the middle-class sense of responsibility to reduce widespread destitution can only be described as abysmal. In times of violence, I have witnessed many of these families quickly shift to alternative living arrangements in Bombay, Dubai, or elsewhere without much ado.

These neighborhoods and their vicinities have never been exactly peaceful in any reasonable sense of that word.[1] Postindustrial landscapes such as Naroda have been subject to large- and small-scale violent bouts of every imaginable sort in almost every decade since the 1969 violence, when the city witnessed its first massive post-Independence altercation. Since at least the 1980s, it has also been a rallying ground for the VHP and later the Bajrang Dal, who together with slumlords have become major players in the local economy of influence and competition (Kumar 2009: 116–122). Scuffles, altercations, and clashes arise between residents, spurred by competition over business transactions or locations, parking spaces, electricity and water connections, or love affairs and marriages between girls and boys of different religious or community backgrounds. Whenever such problems occur there is the possibility that petty activists from these Hindu organizations insert themselves into the exchanges. While on the surface they seem to mediate between parties that are routinely at variance, they often enough exacerbate conflict by inscribing the logic of aggregate bounded communities into the matter.

Drug addiction is quite frequent, especially to a combination of country-made liquor and brown sugar, a crude form of the opiate heroin; and domestic violence also. The spatial arrangements are such that while communities often are segregated, they nonetheless have intimate contact with one another by sharing the local landscape markers such as tea shops and temple platforms. In fact, given these parameters, it is legitimate to wonder conversely how so many residents manage to resist the temptation to violently act out. Despite these conditions, however, I have witnessed many an act of kindness and civility between neighbors who bravely try to resist the general tide of indifference. Given the precariousness of life in such spaces, it is remarkable that many residents are able to maintain a balanced conduct in daily neighborhood interactions. It is in these neighborhoods that one can find the true and unsung heroes of the city.

The most momentous source of violence, however, is the fact that these areas have become the domain of Hindu nationalist organizations, which again stepped up activities significantly in the late 1990s during the Ramjanmabhumi movement. A veritable laboratory in a laboratory, the complicated shadowy nexus between local strongmen, a "bribe-eating" police force, and people living in abject poverty allows for fabulous social experiments in how a generalized destitution can be transformed into systematic resentment against a Muslim neighbor.

In the Naroda Patiya neighborhood, for example, during the Kargil War in 1999, a series of small-time Muslim bakeries were set on fire in order to forcibly evict their proprietors and allow Hindus to take over the "lucrative" business. In the same year, a pregnant girl of the Hindu quarter allegedly committed suicide. A Muslim boy was accused of having started a sexual affair with her. At the condolence meeting, members of both communities offered attendance to pay their respect, an act of solidarity that also was to preempt escalation. Then, however, the Bajrang Dal skillfully intervened and organized a second condolence meeting from which Muslims were apparently excluded and turned away when they tried to attend. Pamphlets were distributed that accused the Muslim community of raping Hindu girls as a stratagem to convert them to Islam. It eventually turned out that the girl had become pregnant by her own cousin and not by a Muslim neighborhood boy, and she was killed by her own family. In 2000, after a deadly terrorist attack on Hindu pilgrims at Amarnath in Jammu and Kashmir, the entire area of Naroda Patiya was tense and broke out in violence (QET: 9–13).

Fast-forward to 2002. Initially there was an odd discrepancy between the official designation of inner-city areas as "highly sensitive" and the sheer enormity of the attacks in areas such as Chamanpura in which Naroda Patiya and Gulbarg Society are located. The uneven death toll was widely ignored in print media analyses in the English and Gujarati vernacular press, which reported events as "communalism," "communal flare-ups," and "communal clashes"—as if between equal groups of miscreants—giving a distorted picture of the events while they were unfolding. While the Godhra incident was deemed extraordinary, the reaction to it was officially described as routine communal violence. There is much evidence, however, that the uneven death toll did not go unnoticed. In an exception to the general thrust of news reportage, Anil Pathak remarked on March 3, 2002, four days into the violence:

> Thickly populated areas like Kalupur, Dariapur, Jamalpur and Raipur and Khadia remained relatively trouble free this time accounting for only six out of [the] staggering 320 deaths that have taken place over the last four days. . . . While the communally volatile walled city areas have sizable population[s] of both communities sharing space, there is also mutual respect for each other[']s strengths, than in areas where

one or the other community is hopelessly outnumbered and targeting them was easy for the mobs. . . . Perhaps for the first time in the history of communal flare-ups in Ahmedabad, it is not the walled city areas which are on the news for all the wrong reasons.[2]

Pathak convincingly explained why traditional trouble spots within the walled city saw comparatively few deaths in the initial days. He did not, however, draw the obvious conclusion out of this fact. What the city had been witnessing was precisely not "communal violence" or "riots"—groups clashing all over the city in fierce street combat—but a pogrom orchestrated in front of his eyes. It is important to keep this discrepancy between what was labeled a "sensitive area" and collective mass murder in mind when I now turn to one of several massacre sites in the city.

GULBARG SOCIETY

One of the areas of systematic attack was the residential area called Gulbarg Society in the northeastern area of Chamanpura, south of Civil Hospital. Gulbarg Society is a compound enclosed by a stone wall with metal gates, part of a small middle- to lower-middle-class colony situated on the Naroda railway line but encircled by the neighborhoods of Patrawali Chali and Dhupsing Ni Chali, both listed as "slum areas" in the Ahmedabad Setu City map. The residential complex contained nineteen blocks, eight buildings, and fifty-five tenements. On the evening of February 28, it resembled a battlefield. The attacks on its residents began at 10:30 a.m., following the imposition of the *bandh* by the Vishva Hindu Parishad (VHP).[3] Already at 7:30 a.m., crowds had gathered around the entire Chamanpura region between Asarva Talav and Civil Hospital. A sizable police force arrived only at around 4:30 p.m., by which time most of the action was over. For a full six hours, the colony was left to defend itself.

Residents reported seeing six or seven people in the early morning forcing shops to close and attacking people in the neighborhoods surrounding the colony. Concerned parents summoned home their children who were taking early tuition classes in the colony. Hearing of the *bandh*, panic-ridden Muslim residents from neighboring *chawls* (a typical building type with living quarters) sought refuge in Gulbarg, appealing for help to Ahsan Jafri, a former trade unionist who was a Congress Party Member of Parliament (MP)—and a Muslim.

Despite knowing that Jafri had campaigned against Narendra Modi in the Rajkot by-elections just five days before, Muslim residents in that area felt it safer to be close to the *sa'ab* (Sir), a *mota manas* (big man), who had connections. In a speech in Rajkot earlier in the year, Jafri had openly encouraged residents not to vote for Modi because Modi was an RSS man (that is, because he supported Hindutva, violence, and anti-Muslim rhetoric). Despite heightened tensions between Hindus and Muslims in recent years, Jafri and his family resisted the trend of well-to-do Muslims to escape to all-Muslim areas or to one of the middle-class neighborhoods in west Ahmedabad. They remained in Gulbarg, in what some considered a "dangerous area" since the Muslim compound was surrounded by poor Hindu residential areas.

The attack was also not the first on this isolated Muslim compound, which borders working-class areas, abandoned mills, and lower-class Hindu homes. Gulbarg had also burned during the 1969 riots and during several of the communal conflagrations in the interim decades. In the past, trouble in Gulbarg had spread all over Chamanpura into the neighboring Asarva district. This time, however, the attacks "zeroed in on this society" (CCT: vol. 1, 32).

The published affidavits of survivors, eyewitness accounts, and numerous analytic reports give the impression that the hours-long siege of the colony was carefully considered and planned. When early-morning crowds gathered in the open streets, there were few attacks on Muslims. The isolated individuals who were being intimidated fled to the colony. There were hardly any of the typical stray stabbing incidents that had characterized violence in the previous years. On the contrary, it appeared that initial intimidations were merely supposed to convince Muslim residents living in the area not to wander outside of the colony.

After receiving a telephone call from Ahsan Jafri, the Ahmedabad police commissioner visited the colony together with two Congress Party officials at 10:30 a.m. The police commissioner gave Jafri personal assurances in front of several witnesses that reinforcements would be sent and that he would be fully protected. Human Rights Watch quotes a forty-five-year-old witness, "They [the Muslim residents] wanted to leave by the railroad behind Jafri's house, but the police commissioner said, 'No, don't you trust me? You must stay here'" (HRW-1: 20). The Concerned Citizen's Tribunal also cites several eyewitnesses who saw the police commissioner arriving and talking to Jafri, "He said to Jafri, 'We are making all arrangements for you and sending additional police force—you don't worry.' Jafri sa'ab told [the police commissioner], 'If you cannot make arrangements for us and if you don't have enough men, then arrange for us to go away from here—just let us know'" (CCT: vol. 1, 29).

Those not acquainted with the communal realities of Ahmedabad might easily conclude that the residents of Gulbarg simply miscalculated the seriousness of the situation. The residents, however, were in no way naive about the dangers at hand. All those who have lived in Ahmedabad knew quite well that this was going to be a dangerous day. They knew that, as in past communal trouble, the day would end with several Muslim and Hindu deaths. Ahsan Jafri trusted his past experience as well as the unambiguous assurances of the police commissioner.

For over three decades, Ahsan Jafri had idealistically invested in the subsistence of this Muslim residential colony. He expected the usual incidents of spontaneous and partly instigated violence, and he was perfectly aware that if an organization like the Bajrang Dal or the VHP were to launch a frontal attack on Gulbarg, the colony would be defenseless without police help.

Just a few minutes after the police commissioner left, the Zahir Bakery and an auto-rickshaw directly outside the complex were set on fire. Within minutes, a large mob had gathered. An eyewitness and survivor told Human Rights Watch,

> At 10:30 am the stone throwing started. First there were 200 people then 500 from all over, then more. . . . We threw stones in self-defense. They had swords, pipes, soda-lemon bottles, sharp weapons, petrol, kerosene, and gas cylinders. They began shouting, "*Maro, kato*" [Kill them, cut them] and "*Mian ko maro*" [Kill the Muslims]. I hid on the third floor. (HRW-1: 18)

The initial First Information Report (FIR) filed by K. G. Erda, a senior inspector of the Meghaninagar police station, estimated the initial crowd at Gulbarg Society to be as large as 20,000 to 25,000. Other estimates ranged between 5,000 and 15,000. The crowd continued gathering force, coming from all directions, and only around 1:30 p.m. became a "huge crowd" armed with *talwars* (swords), *lakdis* (wooden sticks), pipes, and kerosene, according to the initial police report. The police shot tear gas to disperse the crowd, but that only incited the crowd to throw stones back at the policemen. "The mobs had put obstruction on the roads and were looting the shops. We let off tear gas and warnings, we even lathi-charged but the crowd was 'possessed' and shouting 'Jay Shri Ram'" (GG: 28).

The Concerned Citizen's Tribunal reported that Gulbarg Society itself was stoned within five minutes after the police commissioner had left, followed by the throwing of acid bulbs, bottles, burning cloth balls, petrol bombs, and stones into the complex from the back. Eventually objects were thrown from all sides, resulting in a continuous melee, injuring countless residents and setting fire to all houses in the colony. The mob also started to hurl lit cycle tires taken from the Muslim Ankur Cycles shop opposite the colony.

At the entrance to the colony was a house with a terrace and a full view over the entire compound. It belonged to a Hindu, Dayaram Mochi, and his family, who fled the scene in the morning.[4] Originally a small house, two stories had been added in recent years. Its terrace became a platform for deadly attacks on the Gulbarg residents. It is unclear precisely how the crowd seized the premises to have perfect access to the rest of the Muslim colony. The Concerned Citizen's Tribunal met with Dayaram Mochi and his wife, who reported that the crowd gathered around 9:00 a.m. and looted their house, but they were allowed, as Hindus, to leave safely. They gathered their grandchildren and fled to a nearby school. They claimed to have lived for many years on good terms with their Muslim neighbors. Two of the three sons of the family are policemen and were on duty that day in Shahpur and Dariapur.

There are some twists, however, in the story. The Mochis testified that initially they saw only four or five policemen and that police vans arrived with reinforcements much later, and when they arrived, the policemen took chairs from their home to sit and watch the rampage. The family also claimed not to have recognized any of the assailants, although Muslim survivors recognized neighbors who were involved in the attacks. There is little doubt that the Mochi family feared serious consequences if they identified neighbors and other perpetrators. The Tribunal reports, contrary to his testimony, that during the initial stone throwing, Mr. Mochi actually encouraged the mob to enter the compound and shouted that there were very few Muslims inside, indicating that storming the society should be easy (CCT: vol. 1, 31).

Whatever the actual role of the Mochis, big boulders and many stones were thrown from the terrace of their house. According to the assessment of the Tribunal, this caused the greatest damage because as attacks continued from the terrace, it became impossible for the remaining Muslim men to effectively protect the gates and compound walls. Without the terrace, the residents of the compound might have been shielded longer (ibid.). The attacks continued until 1:00 to 1:15 p.m. In at least one affidavit, an eyewitness claimed that a policeman fired a gun at the Muslim residents from the terrace itself. Meanwhile, the colony ran out of water, so that the fires within the buildings could not be put out. Someone had apparently emptied the water tanks of Jafri's house and garden.

At 1:00 p.m., Yusuf, one of the residents of the colony, was caught, severely injured by swords and blades, and set aflame—in full view of the horrified residents. The crowd then broke down the gate at the rear of the compound around 2:30 to 2:45 p.m. By that time, nearly eighty persons had found refuge in Jafri's house, hoping from there to withstand the attack for the longest time and waiting desperately for the police or firemen to arrive.

Those Muslims who remained in the compound courtyard to fight off the attackers eventually tried to flee to other houses, many already on fire, while being pursued by the incoming crowd. Many women and children hid on the second floor of the burning apartments and watched their relatives downstairs being killed. From below, the crowd first launched kerosene-soaked cloth balls and then burning tires against the windows of occupied apartments. Women inside frantically threw the burning tires back, singeing their hands. They hurled carpets and other objects out of the windows to prevent the encroaching fire from engulfing them. The mob caught one female Muslim resident, but a Hindu neighbor spontaneously and courageously intervened, declaring her to be a Hindu servant held against her wishes; the woman was saved. Once outside of the inferno, the woman tried to return to save her children, but the Hindu man who had intervened on her behalf begged her not to go back as that would cause the mob to kill both of them.[5]

Commenting on this stage of the massacre, the initial police report alleged "private firing" by Muslims. Chief Minister Modi picked up on this in a statement on March 1, 2002, referring to Gujarati newspaper reports of incidents of private firing at Gulbarg Society in previous years. At Gulbarg, he argued, things went out of control only after the politician Ahsan Jafri had fired his pistol into the crowd. The mysterious references to "previous incidents" of "private firing" at Gulbarg Society appealed to the general suspicion that there was a weapons cache somewhere in Gulbarg's residential colony, invoking the specter of armed Muslim terrorists.

The Gujarati newspapers had indeed referred to the 1992 riots after the demolition of the Babri Masjid, during which Ahsan Jafri had fired into the air with a private revolver to disperse an attacking crowd. But had Jafri used his revolver this time also? Witnesses interviewed by the Concerned Citizen's Tribunal denied this firmly. Moreover, Jafri actually called and talked to the chief minister personally on the phone—a fact Modi conveniently omitted. According to a witness close to Jafri, the politician lost hope after he received a "callous response" from Modi (ibid.: 32).

By the time the back gate was broken down, Jafri had made numerous phone calls (as many as two hundred), including the one to the chief minister, another to Gujarat's home minister, Gordon Zadaphiya, and still other urgent calls to the police commissioner. Jafri even arranged for a fax to be sent to Sonia Gandhi, the leader of the Congress Party in the capital, New Delhi, for help. For hours the crowd had targeted Jafri's home specifically and shouted for him to come out. Between 2:00 and 2:30 p.m., his phone line was suddenly disconnected. At 2:45 p.m., all hope had vanished for the besieged residents. In a last desperate attempt to save the remaining survivors, Jafri surrendered himself bravely to the attackers.

One of the survivors, incidentally a female member of the Parsi community, witnessed the last moments of MP Ahsan Jafri before he was put to death and gave a detailed account of his murder to the Concerned Citizen's Tribunal. Jafri, speaking in Gujarati, first pleaded with the mob for forgiveness: "He said that all the residents of Gulbarg would leave without any belongings, only their lives." Members in the crowd responded, "You burn our parents, our sisters, so we will not spare you." The Parsi woman herself shouted,"I am a Parsi—we are neither Hindus nor Muslims," to which they replied, "We know no Parsis or anything else." As the Concerned Citizen's Tribunal had it, the crowd was in a murderous mood (ibid.: 29).

Jafri allowed himself to be dragged out of his apartment. He piously folded his hands as he was beaten. "He was stripped, paraded naked, and asked to say, 'Vande Mataram!' [Hail the Mother(land)] and 'Jay Shri Ram!' [Hail to Ram]. He refused. His fingers were chopped off and he was paraded around in the locality, badly injured. Next his hands and feet were severed. He was then dragged, a fork-like instrument clutching his neck, down the road, before being thrown into the fire" (ibid.: 27). The triumphant crowd took their time, drawing out the perverse mutilation. Many others were caught and killed, including members of Jafri's family. A man called Anwar was slashed and burned in one of the four prepared funeral pyres with wooden logs brought from the nearby Sansar Bakery. Another victim, Hafi Mohammed Munawar Sheikh, was "cut into three pieces" and burned (GG: 27). The many others missing were likely killed.

After Jafri's body was burned, the crowd set fire to his home. The Parsi witness remembers, "The mobs were shouting 'Jay Sri Ram!' and 'Kill! Slaughter! This is what they did to us in Godhra. We will do the same to them here!'" (CCT: vol. 1, 28). Other witnesses stated that gas cylinders ordinarily used for heating and cooking were brought together from all the abandoned homes as ammunition for the attacks. Chemicals were thrown on the floor. The people trapped inside begged to be let out, but the crowd showed no mercy. Several women were in fact allowed to leave or pulled out under the pretext that they would be saved, but one eyewitness who testified before the Concerned Citizen's Tribunal saw those women being raped and killed (ibid.: 30).

One twenty-three-year-old eyewitness who suffered a serious head injury told Human Rights Watch:

> First they took everyone's jewelry. Then they raped the women, then they cut them up and then they burnt them. They should get as strict a punishment as possible. . . . I was hit with a pipe. We ran outside when the gas cylinder exploded and then later the police came and we left. (HRW-1: 19–20)

This woman also witnessed the murder of her husband's brother and wife:

They pulled them out and cut them up. When we came out then we saw that he was cut in the stomach, the chest, and the head. They came with *trishuls* [tridents]. My sister-in-law was burnt. First they took her jewelry. Then took her into the kitchen and exploded the gas cylinder. They wanted to get rid of all the evidence. They had been married for fifteen months and she was five months pregnant. (Ibid.: 19)

Another witness, incidentally a Hindu neighbor, reported,

They pulled the babies out with the men, then poured petrol over them, and burnt them. Police stood back. (GG: 27)

Between 3:30 and 4:30 p.m., ten to twelve women were gang-raped, mutilated with sharp weapons (*guptis*), and then thrown into the fire (ibid.).[6] Petrol in plastic bags was thrown on the surviving victims, so they would eventually catch fire more easily. By this time, only one room of Jafri's home was not on fire, and that was where the rioters now directed the attack. Anyone who came out of Jafri's home was killed, either with swords or by pouring kerosene over them and torching them (CCT: vol. 1, 28). In any case, most of the trapped victims had already lost consciousness and collapsed from asphyxiation. Chemicals had been spread into the only remaining room that was not on fire, and then, after their seals had been removed, gas cylinders were thrown in. With fireballs providing the spark, the cylinders exploded like bombs. The blast was so powerful that it exposed the structural steel rods behind the peeling plaster.

At around 4:45 p.m., police reinforcements arrived, and most of the attackers fled. A survivor who had not been in Jafri's house urged the assistant commissioner of police to help the people trapped inside, but the officer hesitated. Nonetheless, twenty-one residents of Gulbarg colony survived and subsequently gave depositions. They were stoned as the police escorted them out of the compound. According to the Concerned Citizens Tribunal and Communalism Combat, seventy people were killed in this six-hour-long mayhem. Human Rights Watch claims sixty-five were killed. The Gujarat government initially published the number fifty-nine, an exact equivalent to the number of Godhra victims. Of the dead, forty-nine were residents of the compound, ten to twelve came from adjacent neighborhoods as they had sought refuge in Jafri's home during previous bouts of violence. The final official death toll was sixty-seven, while other sources speak of higher or lower numbers (IIJ: 123).[7]

These reports describe in great detail the way in which the bodies of the victims were treated during and after the act of killing. Women's bodies were given detailed attention. Not simply tortured, raped, and burned, their body openings were also penetrated with sharp weapons and their genitals mutilated. This suggests an obsession with female body openings, and in cases of pregnant women, a desire to destroy the fetus.[8]

A twenty-year-old female survivor testified:

I state that finally at around 6:30 [*sic*] in the evening, I went out of the hiding place. I saw dead bodies of women lying on the road. None of the bodies were covered. They were all burnt and shrunken. There were a few bodies of women, where '*loha dandas*' [iron rods] were shoved up their vagina. Looking at the sight I fell dizzy. In spite of that I could see a few Hindus standing aside and laughing at us. They were saying '*aare yeh miya kaha se bachke nikal gaye?*' . . . [oh my, how did these Muslims get saved, from where did they come out?].[9]

A twenty-six-year-old female survivor testified:

I found the body [and] saw the torn clothes of my sister-in-law and traced her dead wounded body near my house in the garden. Her throat was cut open with a sword. I state that she was also raped because I found her private parts severely injured and mutilated.[10]

A thirty-year-old survivor testified:

I state that I witnessed Kharum Bano . . . being gang raped by around 15–20 unidentified men who were part of the mob. First her clothes were stripped using swords and she was completely rendered naked. Even as she pleaded for mercy, she was raped, after which swords were thrust into her stomach and she was thrown into the fire which was set ablaze close by, to die.[11]

The Concerned Citizen's Tribunal reported:

The extent of the macabre delight that perpetrators took in the crimes committed was evident in what some residents saw on the evening of February 28. When some witnesses returned to the area later that evening, they saw neighborhood goons "playing cricket" with the skulls of the dead. (CCT: vol. 1, 31)

VISIT TO GULBARG

Eleven days after the inferno, in March 2002, I convinced my friend Ranjit to visit Gulbarg Society with me. I was wary of venturing into the area alone, unsure of what to expect and insecure about how I would be received. No investigative report had yet been filed, but newspapers had published short accounts, and massive rumors were circulating about their content and veracity. I was unsure of what to do. Gulbarg Society carried the air of horror and death, while the city was still a site of violence in progress.

Ranjit had three sisters living in Ahmedabad, all of whom he visited regularly in their respective in-laws' homes. Only one of Ranjit's sisters lived in a "sensitive area" with a large Muslim population, Kalupur, within the old city. The other two lived in the far eastern areas of the city where Gulbarg Society and Naroda Patiya are situated. I made it a habit to accompany Ranjit on his visits and witnessed the unique Indian form of care between siblings. Whenever we spent time in this specific area of the city, he insisted on checking on his sisters' wellbeing, especially during stints of collective violence. Being in their proximity without visiting them was insufferable to Ranjit.

We were both nervous when we left. Many people we knew would never have ventured into this area so soon after the massacre. Chamanpura was characterized by the symmetrical lines of its matching houses, all small quadrate family dwellings. The dwellings resembled containers airlifted onto the street. The houses were mostly humble, designed for the working or unemployed poor, yet ubiquitously brightly painted with many symbols and signs marking them unmistakably as Hindu. These religious markings were the only thing that rendered them distinguishable from one another.

What would be typical in a German suburb seemed particularly rigid here in Ahmedabad. The usual density and confusion of urban space had given way to a multiplication of identical lower-class family houses, all placed exactly adjacent to one other, all cement and concrete. The houses looked too tiny and meek for their shrieking colors announcing their Hindu existence. None had more than one story and, from the outside, most seemed to consist of but a single square room. This bizarre style of one-room quadrate houses in extensive sprawling settlements was architecturally devised by a group of mill owners from the beginning of the twentieth century, when the existing clay and thatched hutments no longer were sufficient for housing the growing numbers of workers (Breman 2004: 31–32).

What was absent in the houses' height, however, was balanced by a proliferation of rectangular cement street temples lining the streets, each one 1.5 meters high. All were made of bathroom-tile temples and, significantly, did not impede the normal flow of traffic. In middle-class areas of Ahmedabad, street temples are often placed right in the way of traffic. They adorn minuscule traffic islands or road dividers, bulging out into the street, as if to position the gods and their poor purveyors (the self-fashioned priests and saints) in the way of a neglecting public in an endless river of vehicles. The temples often slow down the self-absorbed commuter machinery to remind the drivers of the timeless gods and, by the same feat, help small religious entrepreneurs to make a living.

Here, however, the temples were placed neatly on what could have been a sidewalk out of traffic's way, as if by plan. One temple looked identical to the next as if produced in an assembly line, and I wondered if they had been erected the exact same day. Usually temples are constructed where a divine being is said to have appeared, outside of the logic of urban planning and foresight. I wondered if all these gods and goddesses appeared at the exact same minute, on the exact same road, in the exact same spatial interval from one another: Hanumanji, then Amba Mata fifty meters farther down the road, then Chamunda Mata another fifty meters farther down, then Ramdev fifty meters farther again, and so on. I felt too nervous to take pictures.

At the first crossing in Asarva, we asked for directions from a group of four men standing in the shade of one of the rare trees. They stood with a woman at their side, quarreling over something. One man had a large cut on his head, right over the eyebrow. Even under the bandage the wound looked quite deep, and I caught myself wanting to disinfect it. Ranjit and I could smell alcohol, but the group behaved in a civil manner. The men explained the way to reach the one and only "Muslim society" of the area but then told us that it was "dangerous to go inside." I wondered for an instant what they meant exactly by dangerous since the massacre had ended. There was no Muslim left in Gulbarg. All survivors were living in relief camps. Did he mean that there were ghosts of the murdered victims haunting the compound?

Ranjit surprised me, however. Interrupting my thoughts he visibly stiffened up, took off his motorcycle helmet, and said in an indignant tone, "I am a Hindu; this is a foreigner." One of the men could not help but smile and said somewhat apologetically, "That's not how I meant it. . . ." I wanted to know what precisely was dangerous, but Ranjit's mood had gone sour and he wanted to leave without any further exchange of words.

"They were Vagri people," Ranjit said as we drove away. They actually pointed us into the right direction, but Ranjit was nervous and got lost, blaming it on the drunken men. We had to ask again. There were many people on the street. On one corner an entire group of colorful Sadhus were gathered for reasons I could not fathom. What were they doing here? I wondered. I found it strange to see so many saints visiting such an area, but there was no time to inquire. People seemed engaged in their daily work, but some residents seemed to eye us intently. We reached a crossing where a *pan* shop was located at which a group of men had gathered. The entire group, including all the rickshaw drivers, pointed us in direction of Gulbarg without even waiting for us to stop our vehicle and ask a question. Obviously, we were not the first ones visiting the site, and we seemed to stand out like a red flag in a white desert as not coming from this area.

Gulbarg appeared suddenly on the road, as if out of nowhere, on our right. It was visibly a wealthier apartment complex, surrounded by brick walls. In the front, several shops pointed toward the street. In the back behind the wall, there were several huge Ahmedabad Municipal Corporation (AMC) Slum Quarters and an AMC Labor Quarters where a railway track leads to Himmatnagar. Opposite the front, only relatively poor people seemed to be living. We asked the permanent police guards at the gate if we could enter the enclave. They declined and directed us to get permission from the officer in charge. We could not find the officer in charge, however. Later we realized that he was hidden from sight in one of the neighboring shops watching the Zimbabwe-India cricket match. Not one of the neighbors told us.

We entered the compound without permission through another door. Inside, we met a journalist from Delhi, a clean-shaven man with a handsome face and a soft voice. He was from *The Tribune* writing a piece on the massacre at Gulbarg. He was the first person we saw who seemed as disturbed as we were. He had employed a city guide named Shankar, from the AMC. Ranjit and I joined them and we walked around the devastated colony. Plants were burned, walls blackened, and doors broken. The empty colony was eerily quiet as no sound entered it from the streets. The surrounding residential areas were immersed in watching cricket.

We saw many remnants of burned-out vehicles; parts of scooters and motorcycles were strewn across the compound (see figure 4). Suitcases lay in the sand, with their rims burned. Some were opened, and clothes spilled out of them like the insides from gutted human beings. The clothes were dusty and had lost all color, scorched by the incredible heat of the fires.

Shankar, the guide, gave an account of the massacre in three sentences, more or less: A huge crowd came and overtook the outnumbered police, who in turn fled in panic. Then the crowd attacked the colony and stormed in after the MP Afsan Jafri (he said Afsan instead of Ahsan) foolishly had fired a "private gun," killing members of the crowd. Then the wall in the back was broken through, and members of the crowd entered from the front and the back simultaneously, killing everybody in their way. Shankar made it sound as if what had happened in the colony was a tragic sequence of acts: the police should not have panicked and left, Jafri should not have panicked and fired, the crowd should not have panicked and taken revenge for the shooting. To give his account authority, he pointed to the remainders of Jafri's house on the corner where we were standing. It was terrible, he added.

FIGURE 4: Gulbarg Society, inner courtyards, March 11, 2002

There was a large pile of schoolbooks, and Ranjit, being a college teacher, picked one up. The schoolbook contained a child's handwriting and the pages were neatly divided in color crayon. One page was written in Gujarati, the adjacent one in English. The child's name was Shail. She was in third grade. She had painted two Netaji pictures in the back and front of her notebook, with the carefully written and boldly underlined subtitles "This is Gandhiji" and "This is Nehruji." We looked at the painted pictures and Shankar, at last, finally stopped talking. All four of us remained silent from then on. We exited the compound and found ourselves back on the main road. The police officer in charge finally showed up. He did not mind that we had entered Gulbarg without his permission. He excused himself, saying, "My India is playing Zimbabwe." He reached toward me to shake my hand, smiling, while still gazing at the TV in an adjacent shop. He had absolutely no interest in us.

All the neighbors at Gulbarg firmly declined to speak to us. The trip was a complete failure. We were told by an approaching bystander in the street that no one had anything to tell us. I was astonished, because elsewhere in the city at the time, people were more than willing to narrate observations and even admit to participation in violence—at times in hyperbolic detail. A woman selling groceries waved us away from afar as we approached. Even Ranjit, who spoke the best fluent Gujarati in our small entourage, was unsuccessful at convincing people to talk to us. Another man told us sternly to leave now. We left, feeling uncomfortable. We saw people gather on the street corners in little groups to watch us departing. Perhaps we just imagined the heightened attention. Maybe we were too hesitant and cautious, or maybe this neighborhood had just been visited already once too often. Perhaps residents had been tutored, or even threatened, not to speak with anyone. I do not know.

Touch in an Untouchable Space

After visiting Gulbarg Society, Ranjit and I were shaken. We drove to the residence of one of his three sisters, immediately north of the society in an area of Meghaninagar where few Muslims live. His sister lived in a "ghetto," Ranjit explained, populated by the Vagri and the Chamar communities. Many Vagri are vegetable sellers and a low caste while the Chamar, traditionally tanners and leather workers, are a formerly un-touchable caste, now called a "scheduled caste." Many residents in the city will consider the Vagri an untouchable caste as well. Today, there is a pronounced hierarchy between the two communities, in which the Chamar claims unambiguous superiority over the Vagri, partly because they have been part of an urban working class for a long time.

Many lower-caste and formerly untouchable communities, as well as Muslims, had been recruited as factory workers in the mills from urban and then surrounding rural areas in the nineteenth century. Labor in the factories was divided by caste membership where untouchable communities—Dheds, Chamars, and Vankars—were put to work in spin-ning shops while weaving was dominated by Kanbis and Muslims be-cause they were obligated to suck yarn onto the shuttle with their mouths when weft bobbins needed to be replaced. The division of labor in the mill on the basis of caste was replicated in the housing arrangements provided by mill owners in the residential structures surrounding the fac-tories (Breman 2004: 15–18, esp. 17).

Ranjit's sister suffered frequently from mysterious symptoms that he referred to as "cancer." On top of that, someone recently stole all the cash from her house. Ranjit was worried about her. She, too, was very upset, he explained, and had asked him to pay a soothing visit. The ghetto we drove into is one of the areas that many attackers of Naroda Patiya came from. Ranjit advised me sternly not to say anything stupid while in the *nez* (a small village-like neighborhood). I should leave all talking about violence up to him.

When we entered, I saw people with wounds lingering idly. Young men had cuts on their lower limbs or on their arms and heads. People stared much at Ranjit's fancy motorbike. Wounds from communal clashes remain visible for a long time. Often these actors stay for weeks in their neighborhoods in order not to be seen with their marks, in case the police became too attentive and chose to grab an unlucky one to ask for bribes. I had seen wounded young men regularly in specific areas of Ahmedabad, but there was an abundance of them here. We were literally surrounded by injured young men after several days of battle.

The urban *nez* was so dense that as Ranjit directed me through the labyrinth, I touched what felt like a hundred people. We passed tiny alleyways and even plazas with temples that together formed what seemed like a miniature labyrinth city replicating the larger surrounding one. The difference from ordinary urban space was that many dwellings were mere hutments (called *jhupdu*), while a few larger structures resembled the symmetrical cement houses around Chamanpura. The accompanying cement temples were more sophisticated architecturally than the hutments, as if the gods had to be housed better than their human purveyors in the neighborhood. Ranjit told me that, as around Gulbarg, many of these temples had been financed by local Hindu organizations as a sort of spiritual developmental aid.

Walking with Ranjit through this small, crowded urban neighborhood, I had a memorable corporeal experience of a strange sort. My initial trepidation about walking amongst men who were attackers metamorphosed into a dizzy daze. In the overcrowded small lanes, I realized that the density of space compelled a very special bodily hexis, with whose rhythm I was fundamentally unfamiliar. Every physical movement—walking, sitting, talking, standing, drinking, smoking, or driving a vehicle—was already a sort of physical dodging of the next adjacent person, one passing by, or a body overtaking from behind. Everything everyone did in these lanes was already a making room for someone else. Hence the body was forced to move in a sequence of evasions. People made room for the other without having to take cognizance what they did. I was familiar with this experience from walking on very busy streets in Bombay or Manhattan, but here it seemed intensified manyfold.

When we passed a man standing in a group of people, he intuited us and swerved gently to the front to make room without either looking or changing the tone of his voice. I wondered if he was even conscious of us. He was concentrating on something else but his body swung back automatically. Physical flexibility was habitual because the frequency of passing another person was so high. Such routine physical movements were part of the condition of possibility to inhabit such a dense location in the first place. There was no alternating sequence between occupying space and making room for cows, people, and vehicles. Rather, inhabiting the space was a material occupation and simultaneously its opposite, an evading and evacuation from space. Without interruption, the physical body constantly had to get out of the way of others by simultaneously perceiving and bending, flexing and thinning, expanding and retracting, anticipating and estimating.

Lacking such synchronicity, the muscles of my body knew not how to move. When I tried to roll my shoulder out of the way of another shoulder, I had to make sure that my elbow did not bump into the person behind me while keeping away from the torso in front of me and remaining wary about crashing my head into the low wooden beams of huts which stuck out sharply. All this simultaneous motor control was necessary, and the bodies of the residents seem resilient against these obstacles. Residents were thin, wiry, relatively small, and their bodies flexed. Their movements were smooth and no one seemed unnerved. People seemingly sleepwalked while dodging cows, dogs, kids, humans, bikes, goats, garbage, and excrement.

Naturally, I felt like a fat sack dragging myself through a geography of bodies and buildings that seemed to evade others but into whom I crashed, pushed, and tumbled spastically without control. I had never learned how to walk, how to stand, or how to pass through such a teeming environment. It was the first time in my life that I moved through a space that I felt unable to properly master. And yet, what might have led to a fistfight or angry words in Germany was taken in good spirit here. People dwelling in this ghetto were generous and even amused at times about my obvious clumsiness.

Although the *nez* had a makeshift feel to it, its residents arranged themselves to stay and live there for good. Goats, children, even cows, clogged the narrow pathways, which were not big enough for a single overlarge man. There were many old and young men, but also women. The women had no problem looking me straight in the eye, even though some chose to look away. Many lacked the usual timidity and ubiquitous piety of the typical chaste Hindu upper-caste or Muslim women, who avert their eyes or remain veiled. There were also an endless number of children whose individuality I lost any sense of, a typical numbing effect of India's masses on me. I felt nothing for all these children. It shocked me to recognize this about myself.

All houses were painted with symbols and signs, colorfully inscribed as if they were tattoos. The tattoos on bodies resembled the painted houses. It was as if one had rubbed off on the other in the general concentration of all objects, which are forced to touch on another. There was something incredibly appealing to the vibrancy of the place, which I have difficulty articulating.

Ranjit parked his large bike on the side of a minuscule alleyway, making it thus impossible for an oncoming cow to pass. The blocked cow looked blankly at the bike and simply stood still. Ranjit's sister was not in, but a male cousin was present. He, like the sister, had a throat problem. He showed me the terrible enlargement on his throat. The visible growth had prevented him from marriage and he was now being "sidelined," Ranjit told me in English so that the cousin could not understand it. Ranjit also showed me the papers from the doctor, which the cousin was unable to read, as they were in English. The cousin wanted me to translate the diagnosis one more time, uncertain as to whether prior translations had been correct. He was trying to grasp what he was suffering from. He did not understand what was happening to him.

The doctor, a Jain, had discovered the unnatural growth on the cousin's throat several years ago and advised him to stop drinking alcohol, smoking, chewing tobacco (*gutka*), and eating nonvegetarian food. I told Ranjit that he should rather go to a proper hospital. But Ranjit responded that other doctors would not be able to help him. They would simply affirm that he had a cancerous growth. I wondered what made such a young man have an external "cancer" at such a young age. I mentioned nutritional deficiency, or perhaps the pollution by chemical waste of the textile mill's industry around this area. Ranjit nodded silently. They had already thought of all that. But the cousin had other suspicions that he did not want to share. Ranjit hinted at claims to sorcery, which he did not want to elaborate.

We then discussed the theft. A few nights ago, the one-room house of Ranjit's sister had been broken into. A single cement room with one door and one window, it allowed for very little light. In her small place, much room had been made for a house temple in honor of her *kuldevi* (her lineage goddess). It is a typical "ready-made temple" that one can buy in a store to attach to the wall. There is also a shelf on which she stored some suitcases, and it was from these that the money was taken. Only knowledgeable people could have known exactly where the money was hidden. Why did she keep cash at her house? Why not deposit it at a bank? She cannot read or write and has never been inside a bank. She had always left interactions with financial institutions to men like her brother. Hence control over income translated into keeping it in cash in the house, rendering her vulnerable to theft in turn. We discussed the possibility of neighbors being the thief.

Finally, Ranjit's aggrieved cousin told us about the "riots." He was eager to tell us his story. He had seen things, which finally made him feel a little more important in this city of neglected and forgotten denizens like him. He saw many killings, and he witnessed how limbs were cut off, he said. He made the typical butcher-type gesture with his hands that is also used when silently indicating nonvegetarian foodstuff. He explained, addressing Ranjit, how he saw one Muslim woman completely pierced through with a sword. He stood up, and showed us where the sword had entered and where it had come out of her body. He sat back down and smiled, proud and happy of the attention we gave him. Because he was just an observer, he did not know who the people were that did this. But there were many people and many killings, he concluded. An odd silence followed.

Since his sister was not at home, Ranjit called for his sister's neighbor to prepare tea and bring water. We disturbed her afternoon nap, but Ranjit insisted on waiting until she served us the customary brew. Neighbors take over family obligations for one another in this way. Taking tea from the neighbor's hand fulfilled the obligation of a brother towards his sister. Many children surrounded the neighbor woman while we spoke. Too many for such a poor family, I caught myself thinking. Ranjit sat silently on the bed, sternly pondering over something and slurping tea with a loud noise from a saucer. There was no more opportunity to ask questions. When we left, the cow was still standing in front of the motorbike. After Ranjit moved his vehicle, she considered the fortunate turn of events with a flap of her ears and then continued with a slow pace.

Although walking in a neighborhood from which many young men involved in the violent events a few days earlier undeniably had hailed from, I did not come away from Meghaninagar with the impression that I had walked among killers. The place Ranjit had taken me was a world onto its own, not unlike the city's dense Muslim ghettos, which followed their own laws and had their own forms of life. I realized that I knew nothing about these people or about the squalor in which they were forced to live, and that if I really ever wanted to understand their participation in violence, I would have to return for a much longer stay.

VISIT TO NARODA PATIYA

On April 5, Ranjit and I visited the ruins of Naroda Patiya, a residential area divided into two spatial moieties—one Hindu and one Muslim. One section was completely blackened, with doors broken and windows missing, while the other was not. I wondered how long before the grey of the street dust would cover the black of the charred buildings. Unlike Gulbarg Society, Naroda Patiya was a very poor residential stretch. The area was not visibly demarcated by walls or fences. Everywhere, in this already depressingly bleak area of Ahmedabad, black holes stared at us.

Ranjit and I met at the apartment of Mr. Chauhan, one of Ranjit's colleagues, and were served water and afternoon tea. The Chauhans' son, Lalobhai, was willing to lead us around the location of one of the worst massacres in Ahmedabad. The Naroda Patiya massacre had taken place less than five weeks earlier, on February 28, 2002. At the time, it was said that over 125 people were killed there within a few hours.[12]

Lalobhai's parents invited us for dinner. They had just moved there three months ago. The father came from the same rural district as Narendra Modi, a fact that he communicated proudly. The family had thought Naroda a "good area." I was surprised to hear that. They had been told that there had never been any altercations between Muslims and Hindus in this area, which they still thought was true. In fact, Mr. Chauhan said, "All the attackers came from outside." Yet, as indicated earlier, the neighborhoods of Naroda Patiya had burned before.

Between afternoon tea and evening dinner, we left with Lalo for a tour of the entire area. Unlike his father, Lalo was unsure if this was still a "good area." He indicated this with a weak, doubtful smile. He had been there, after all, and witnessed the attack on the Muslim neighborhood. He himself had thrown some stones, he admitted. In the first three weeks of violence, many Ahmedabad residents confessed to me such participation, but seldom did they acknowledge this with such shyness in a lowered voice. For many people, throwing stones was like saying, "I was there." At the time of violent action, participation was a proof of loyalty and of behaving properly in the moment when *hindu dharma* (Hindu religion) needed protection from the devils of Godhra, when Hindu religion was supposedly under attack. Lalo felt uncomfortable about his own trifling participation, and more so about what he had been forced to witness.

Directly in front of the apartment complex where the Chauhans rented their flat, there used to be a series of small shops. We saw some construction workers busy rebuilding them. Piles of bricks flanked half-destroyed and charred walls. Corrugated iron covers were being refitted for use as ceilings. The shops used to belong to Muslims and now were taken over by Hindu families. The new owners, sitting on several beds (*kaatlo*) in front greeted us as we were passing by. Leaving the courtyard, we entered the road, but Lalo suddenly paused. He pointed to an empty space in the dust at the compound wall we just had exited. Not seeing anything, we looked at him, waiting.

He told us that a Muslim woman with torn clothes had sat on that very spot on the day of the massacre. He pointed to the other side of the road where the neighborhoods of Naroda Patiya began. She had fled the killing from there and simply sat down here. The woman was dressed all in black, completely veiled. Her dress was torn in places. She did not utter a single word. Day and night, in the full heat of the sun, she sat here, right in front of his apartment house, for four full days. She rested in silence, Lalo remembered, framed by her torn clothes, her back to the low brick fence, fixed in the dirty sand. She barely made a sound.

Whenever Lalo went to the hospital, where he worked as a medical assistant he passed her sitting there. Whenever he came back home, he passed her again sitting on the same spot. People complained about the woman and tried to chase her away, but she did not react to anyone anymore. Lalo eventually heard the police abuse her with foul language—words and expressions Lalo did not want to utter in our presence. She stayed nonetheless. After two days, Lalo could no longer bear it and brought her some water to drink. But neighbors got angry with him, he recounted, and he had to bring her water and biscuits at night, around 12:30. Finally, someone took her away to a Muslim refugee camp. He never learned her name. He never asked her, either. Nor did he ever think of taking her into his home for protection. That would have been impossible at the time, he said. He had not even seen her face, he told me. Today, Lalo cannot pass the space where she sat without thinking of her. She used to be his unknown neighbor, then became a living ghost on the side of a busy road, and then disappeared into some relief camp.

Lalobhai was an earnest young man. He showed us around with fearlessness and sincerity. His matter-of-factness bespoke someone who had become conscious of having witnessed something unusual. It seemed odd that he was so open about what happened. But such candor was not uncommon in the first weeks after the Godhra incident. I had the impression that Lalo wished to revisit his own neighborhood to try and understand the mayhem that occurred just weeks earlier.

We reached Naroda Road, and I saw the burned-out Noorani Masjid, a mosque, adjacent to what Ranjit held were a series of meat shops, which were now gutted and in ruin (see figure 5). We looked at the remnants of tandoori ovens where chicken had been cooked and sold. The entire area was blackened and abandoned. Muslim residences had lined both sides of the road. On the other side, where trucks sped by, spreading an unbearable sandy dust, a police post had been positioned. As we spoke, policemen sat in front of the municipal bus depot. They watched us curiously.

On our side of the road, a man guided a camera crew through the site. He claimed to be from the police and had a revolver at his side but wore no uniform. We wanted to get a clear picture of the destroyed mosque, and he chased us away, as if we were little kids playing soccer on private property. We spotted a family, either Vagri or Rabari, sitting on bedlike structures in front of an unspoiled shop. They covered their faces as the cameraman tried to take a picture: the man used his hand, the women pulled down part of their saris. Obviously, their shop was the only one

FIGURE 5: Noorani Masjid Noroda Patiya, April 5, 2002

that had not been attacked. I felt sorry for them. Lalo told us that when the crowd came, these people had been safe, because they were considered Hindu.

The three characters viewed us as well as the camera crew with palpable suspicion. Eventually one woman addressed us. "There is no one there anymore," she lamented, while ignoring our initial question about what they had seen. "There is no one there anymore," she repeated in a melodic voice. She said all the attackers came from outside, they were not locals. While she talked, loud trucks and buses passed by, swallowing up her thin voice and spraying us all with that fine dust. Lalo asked if they would not be in trouble once the Muslims returned. "No," said the man firmly, somewhat angrily, "We all had enough of this trouble." The other woman, carrying a blank face, nodded as she eyed Ranjit and me, indicating that she, for one, was not completely convinced by her husband's assertion.

The man indicated that he no longer wanted to talk to us. We left. Lalo was certain that Muslims would surely target the family in the future, because theirs was the only unscathed establishment in the entire neigh-

FIGURE 6: *Jay Shri Ram!* Incorporation through destruction

borhood. Their own former neighbors will resent them, he contended. We passed a house where someone had written "Jai Shri Ram" on the wall and mounted the picture of a goddess Ambaji Mata next to it (see figure 6).

I used a moment of silence to ask Lalobhai what he had actually seen during the attack on Naroda Patiya. As if he had been waiting for this question, he immediately responded, "The police did absolutely nothing." Some policemen actually cheered and shouted *"Jai Sitaram,"* he added. Turning to Ranjit, a swift giggle rolled out of him, as if he still could not believe this. Spectators who did not throw stones or otherwise participate were called to order by the nearby VHP leaders and forced to take part, he adamantly asserted. "You were supposed to do something, like throw a stone or carry kerosene for the others." The leaders commanded and if someone refused, members of the VHP went to the nearby police and told them: "Get him. He is obstructing." Those who hesitated were arrested and accused of rioting, while those who rioted were left alone to do their bit.

Lalo pointed to the side from whence a large mob had gathered, and explained how the crowd attacked the Muslim shacks and shops. He pointed to an alley that entered into the Muslim neighborhood between now-charred remainders of the former shops. At first, the attackers could not venture inside because the Muslims were waiting behind that first corner ready to strike and protect their neighborhood with weapons. He remembered his astonishment that a few Muslims could keep so many attackers in check for so long.

That day, at Naroda Patiya, he also saw more than one local vendor sell tea and hand out water to the mob. Snacks were provided, and they were handing out plastic water pouches for free. The "refreshment areas"—he pointed them out to us—were staffed with VHP people, men wearing white *kurtas* (Indian chemises) with cleanly folded saffron scarves over their shoulders speaking incessantly on cell phones. They also gave the orders. He saw policemen arrange for tea to be brought to their corner over there. He pointed at the spot. The VHP decided how to advance, how to attack, how to provoke reaction. All "refreshments" were free—paid by the VHP, and he gestured again to where the refreshment stalls were located.

There was a second picture that Lalo wanted to share. He saw the killing of a young Muslim woman that he could not forget. She must have suddenly lost her mind inside the Muslim *nez*, because she tried to drive away on a scooter. She seemed to think somehow that no one would attack her, so she drove out from the compound onto the road right into the murderous crowd. She was stopped and, without ado, dowsed with kerosene and set on fire. "Why did she try to leave?" Lalo asked himself while addressing me. "It [the compound] was being attacked!"

We wanted to enter deeper into the neighborhood behind the road, but the police, while not unfriendly, told us firmly, "Not today." They encouraged us to return tomorrow, the day after tomorrow, or best some day after that. When I insisted on a reason why we should not enter the compound, they told us that officials were counting houses and doing investigative work right now. Not really convinced, Ranjit and Lalo decided to make a large detour to enter the inner areas of the Naroda Patiya compound from the other side.

We passed an area with more sophisticated wide roads and large, two-story houses, with fences and servants and nameplates on the mailboxes. I did not know that such dwellings existed here in Naroda. This area had pleasant temples of tasteful religious architecture. On our way, we passed the now-infamous large field where an even greater mob had gathered and many Muslims were killed. It was an open dusty area usually used for cricket and other sports. As we walked, we asked the people present about the events. Some acted as if they did not know what we wanted. Others told us freely what they had seen. Two young boys joined us and showed us the way to enter Naroda Patiya from the back, passing what was obviously a Hindu neighborhood immediately adjacent to the destroyed Muslim one.

The destruction was demarcated with surgical precision. Charred ruins were everywhere. Here it was Hindu; there it was Muslim. In one lane all the houses were unscathed; in the next all houses were burned. Ranjit observed that this selective burning did not accord with the nature of fire. Fire does not know Hindu or Muslim. It just travels and catches hold on anything flammable. These fires, however, had been well planned and tightly controlled. They targeted only Muslim homes, which were left as blackened ruins.

In the alleyways of the Muslim residential compound, destroyed objects covered the sandy ground: bicycles, cables, vehicles, tires, tables, and broken glass lay around like skeletons. Hundreds of little hutments whose guts were spilled out lay in front of them. A group of older men suddenly appeared, wordlessly shooed away the young boys, then replaced them in accompanying us in silence through the rest of the Muslim area.

It was getting dark and we prepared to leave. Lalo got a glass splinter in his foot. One of the men said that all the Muslim residents were in camps now, but not the Hindus, who were with their "relations" (*sambandh*). However, we perceived some lights farther inside the Muslim part of the neighborhood. Ranjit stopped and felt uncomfortable seeing signs of life deep in the charred Muslim section. Who were these people? Why did they risk coming back? We returned to the roadside of Naroda Patiya and, by hiding behind heavy night traffic, tried to pass without being noticed by the lounging policemen who had told us earlier not to enter. Since the road lacked any streetlights, this was not too hard to accomplish. I wondered why the five men had accompanied us and who they were. The Hindu neighborhood watch, explained Lalo.

I asked Lalo how it was possible that residents of Naroda Patiya would make their immediate neighbors responsible for the incident in Godhra. Lalo responded that early in the violence, two Hindu representatives visited the Muslim *nez* in order to keep the peace, but the Muslims mercilessly hacked them to death. First, there was a small Hindu man, he said, and the Muslims hacked him into pieces. Then a big, strong man went inside. He was also hacked to death. Lalo demonstrated how his arms were severed. Only then did a Hindu mob gather and start to attack, he continued. These murders inaugurated the real riot, he explained. I asked him the names of these Hindu representatives, but he did not know them.

This narrative is typical for many neighborhoods where atrocities were committed in the city. At some point during the pogrom, the incident in Godhra was no longer sufficient to provide the rationale for the targeted violence. Nor did stories of the abduction of women in the media suffice. There was always the supplemental story of some courageous Hindu who entered unsuspectingly into the Muslim area alone to make a peace effort in the name of his community *before* violence broke out. That individual never returned, and no one ever knew his or her family name or exact identity. Versions of such stories were so numerous that they barely made it into fact-finding or news reports. The murders detailed in these fabrications were taken to be the local spark for the reaction unleashed against the neighborhood Muslims.

In this way, violence was fueled by localizing and splintering into smaller instances through side narratives and rumors that multiplied wildly. If violence began with an incident that happened elsewhere, it metamorphosed into myriad smaller incidents directly implicating local neighborhoods. The logic underlying this movement is not simply accumulative but follows the fault lines of a progressive spatial internalization. The more one inquires about reasons for violent reaction, the more productions become geographically confined while their factualness is obscured. In other words, violence is always added on to. As we shall see in the next chapter, this movement does not stop at spatial boundaries of the city but moves further inward toward the intimate surfaces of the body.

On Detail and Denial

In my conversations with residents of Ahmedabad about the events at Gulbarg Society and Naroda Patiya, middle-class Ahmedabadis either simply denied the massacres or they explained everything by the reciprocal logic of anger (*krodh*), riot (*tofan*), and reaction (*pratikriya*). Most middle-class residents of the city speak pejoratively about the quality of life in the mill areas of east Ahmedabad, and they invoked these notions when accounting for the violence there. They routinely refer to a lack of economic discipline and ethic cultivation as explanations for social neglect and destitution (Breman 2004: 34–35). But several members of lower social strata whom I knew admitted openly to having "seen" things connected to the massacres in and around the city, or they claimed to "know" something about them, usually as spectators. This willingness to portray and depict horrific events lasted for roughly three weeks, after which it became increasingly difficult to get anyone to talk about these experiences.

Initial accounts most often took the form of descriptions of what happened, what was seen or done. I rarely used a recording device, and I took no notes while people talked. I also did not later try to verify their specific statements and observations, which would surpass my capabilities.

It was never quite clear to me if the "knowing" (*mane khabar chhe*) and the "seeing" (*me joyu*) of the people I talked to actually meant they had been present and seen with their own eyes. People also frequently used ambiguous expressions, such as *je thayu te joyu* (what has happened, that I have seen), in their depictions. Lalo was one of the few exceptions to this general fact.

In contrast to this ambiguity in the relation of the speaker to what was seen, there was often clarity of details that I had never asked for, narrated in an air of unself-conscious fascination. This mode of talking led me to conclude that most of the details were from secondhand accounts and not personally witnessed. Also, people might have been ambiguous in their accounts because of an understandable fear of the consequences if they were to reveal their presence at a killing or massacre. In the initial days of violence, on the other hand, fear of prosecution seemed largely absent.

Despite the different locations of witnesses, they seemed confident when describing what happened to the bodies of the victims. For instance, some referred to the number of pieces into which a specific victim was cut, or whether a sword was stuck into a woman from the front or in the side, or whether the sword actually exited on the other side, or whether the head was severed before or after burning the torso, or whether some limb was severed and, if so, which limb. Others described cutting (*kat karvu*), burning (*salgavavu, balvu*), and stabbing (*stebing, ghayl karvu, cheri marvi*), piercing (*bhokvu*, penetrating), or severing (*kapvu*, disjoining). Fact-finding commissions reported similar detail, compiled and generated by local activists who had had some direct contact with the violent actors or their victims. As with the interlocutors, the material produced to give evidence to the violence seems fundamentally contaminated by the always hyperbolic and excessive forms of describing violence. These forms exist on both levels, on the level of concrete acts that we can be sure had occurred as well as on the level of representation and individual imagination.

Given the circulation of photographic images, sacrificial terminology, and rumors as described in the previous chapters, for those reporting on the violence after the fact what they had actually seen or known is difficult to distinguish from what was reported in newspapers like *Sandesh* or recounted at a tea stall. People's recollections were interpolated by the events in a way not accounted for by terms such as "agency" and "participation." In initial accounts during the violence, regardless of the source, what was seen or imagined, or precisely both together, still had power over the speaker. Spoken words did not yet create distance between word and deed.

In sum, there is a unifying quality underlying all of these representations, be they of actual violent acts, mere rumors and imaginations of acts, or explanations after the fact. That quality is something singular yet collective, with various aspects inextricably interwoven. It is as if, when pondering the horrific nature of violent acts, instead of parsing fact from fabrication, people add hallucination to fact. In this way, violence is mustering ever more of the same material. What exactly is being articulated here?

CHAPTER 4

The Lack of Muslim Vulnerability

HOW CAN A FAMILIAR NEIGHBOR, with whom one frequently interacts and even shares laughs, arouse extreme forms of disgust, fear, or anger? This chapter examines how, in the time of the pogrom, the neighbor was turned into a stereotype. It explores how the distance between stereotype and the experience of the neighbor suddenly collapsed as cliché coalesced with experience. Chapters 1 and 2 presented the imaginary grid that emerged in media representations and in the circulation of rumors during pogrom violence; chapter 3 presented more documentation of the pogrom. This chapter depicts how residents of Ahmedabad articulated oversimplified notions of the "other," some of which were drawn directly from the imaginary grid, and in doing so became accomplices in the violence.

The pogrom demanded not one but several types and degrees of complicity, dependent on functions and locations within complex hierarchies of gender, caste, class, and religion. The most pervasive form was also its most perplexing—intimate participation in the imagery invoked by the sinister appeal of familiar stereotypes. This material did not hallucinate novel attributes but harnessed ideas that circulated earlier and more widely. Once this material becomes condensed in the figure of the Muslim and inhabited by residents in the context of the pogrom, it brings forth forms of complicity.

Complicity of this type was quite differently motivated than the participation of both active perpetrators of the pogrom violence and those responsible for its political orchestration. It is more subtle yet nonetheless important for facilitating an atmosphere in which other actors were able to engage in largely unfettered violence, and in which their exceptional behavior resulted in support for extralegal impunity after the events.

Stereotypes always carry a kernel of truth, as their power lies primarily in the psychological material they can evoke. In the pogrom, they worked as residues of individual subjective experiences that became articulated collectively. Ethnographers are peculiarly situated in relation to such evocations, since they witness them in the very moment of their interlocutor's sense making. When this residue takes on a stable form by being projected onto the Muslim, that figure becomes a phantasmagoria: an embodiment of the most pronounced form of perceived threat, and a danger that appears confined to this figure, controllable despite its blurred and shifting nature.

In the account that follows, the phantasmagoria of the Muslim is drawn from certain culinary and dietary habits, most succinctly stereotyped in the meat eater or butcher. I track this stereotype as it appears in the explanations of three separate members of three very different communities: Jain, Rajput, and Dalit. None of these individuals were sycophants of Hindutva ideology or members of the BJP. While they share membership in the city's middle class, they differentiate themselves, and are frequently distinguished from one another, in their relation to diet and other practices.

Whereas Jains are identified with very strict vegetarian practices, Rajputs are in general identified with beef prohibition (though not necessarily with vegetarianism). By contrast, Dalits risk signifying every possible transgression—in this case, beef as well as all meat consumption. All three individuals expose a need to identify something excessive in Muslims that can serve to legitimate the infliction of violence upon them. After delineating these individual types, I then turn to describe the way in which Muslims inhabit such stereotypical forms. Finally, I present the remarkable "autobiography of a goat," a story that attempts to position the reader inside the mind of, and hence create empathy for, the animal that is frequently slaughtered and eaten in Gujarat.

SOMETHING IN OUR HEART

Shortly after the pogrom I met Sejal, one of my former language teachers, and Payal, her former student, for lunch at a vegetarian Panjabi restaurant called Mehfil. Located near Sejal's home, Mehfil offered an acceptable assortment of dishes that she was able to eat. After we had finished eating, Sejal told me, "They finally learned what it is to get hurt, what it feels to get tensed. To have fear, they have finally learned vulnerability." Sejal's words took me aback. Payal fell silent. It was the first time I saw them since the violence began. At first, Sejal had hesitated to address the unfolding events. Putting one hand on her stomach, she started complaining grouchily about the food to deflect my own attempts to talk about the violence that was engulfing the city for nearly two weeks. Sejal made sure that there was neither garlic nor onion in the dish she ordered. Both are spices she finds revolting, and above all they signify to her the preparation of nonvegetarian food.

The waiter, whose dark blue uniform made him look like a French *flic* (colloquial for policeman), swiftly approached the table and patiently repeated all the ingredients of the dishes in front of us. He was habituated to this sort of elite culinary suspicion. Payal, less sensitive in dietary matters, didn't mind the risk of swallowing a piece of onion, but she repeated three times, after I brought the topic up, that she did not want to talk about what was happening. She told me she did not really think about any of "this"—leaving unsaid what exactly she was referring to.

Thirteen days earlier, both Sejal and Payal had urgently called me on the phone of my apartment. They warned me that I might be mistaken for a Muslim and should therefore not leave the house because of the "riots." Like other acquaintances of mine in the city, they advised me not to utter my name in public as long as the situation was "like this." All over Ahmedabad, people were being stopped on the road and killed just because they were identified as belonging to the minority Muslim community.

If I had to introduce myself somewhere on a road in the city, Sejal had suggested, I should shun my first and last name, "Go by the name of Peter." My roommate Bharat suggested "Michael," and an academic friend "John." I frowned at the New Testament character of the proposed names, especially since Christians, too, had faced attacks by violent Hindu activists in the state just a few years earlier. I reverted to another strategy. More by coincidence than planning, I started pronouncing my name with my native German accent, which to Gujarati ears curiously sounded like an Indian name. Pahvis (for the Persian Parviz) sounded like a mispronounced Bhavesh, an unambiguously Hindu name. Thus I avoided the danger of becoming a local Parvez, which could be construed as Muslim.

Our favorite meeting place used to be Abhilasha, a fancy vegetarian restaurant close to the university with several whirring air conditioners on the first floor. But that restaurant burned down in the first week of violence. All restaurants owned by Muslims had been surgically excised, leaving behind charcoaled ruins in a line of unspoiled shops uncannily beckoning to someone passing by. In the better areas of the city, Muslim restaurants were without exception strictly vegetarian, with names such as Tulsi, the basil plant sacred to Hindus. Most proprietors of these establishments came from the merchant Muslim Memon community, who were not recognizable in any way as Muslim. By contrast, nonvegetarian restaurants were run by non-Gujaratis and carried names such as Upper Crust Café, Neelam's Lutaf, or Tomatoes. Run mainly by Panjabis and Marwaris, their employees were often Nepalis. It was rare to find Gujarati employees in nonvegetarian restaurants in the west city.

Around Gujarat University, at L. D. College of Engineering and a little further down the road, an entire series of former restaurants had blackened interiors. Students gathered at several roadside teashops, sitting on tin drums, and were surprised that no one ever knew these places had actually been Muslim. Better-off students had been regular guests in them. Abhilasha was located a little farther up the road opposite the Panjarapole, an animal shelter, in which ahimsa (nonviolence) and *jivdaya* (compassion for all life), was put into the concrete practice of animal care—especially care for old cattle. The owners of Abhilasha did not wear Muslim caps or typifying beards. On the face of it, it would have been difficult to know that it was a Muslim establishment. Payal, too, had no clue that we had been regularly eating in a "Muslim" restaurant.

I asked Sejal to explain herself, but to no avail. After a long pause, she said that people like her did feel some compassion (*daya*) for Muslim victims.[1] But she wanted to be "transparent" to me. "Somewhere in our heart, there is a spot, a corner. That spot says 'yes.' That was good." She paused, before concluding, "They finally learned what it is to get hurt, what it feels to get tensed. To have fear." Sejal turned the noun "tension," which might describe a state of being, into a state of being acted upon— "to get tensed." She was unapologetically telling me that Muslims have finally learned vulnerability. With diffidence, I told her that I appreciated her honesty.

Usually when I met with Sejal and Payal, we discussed men and the trials of marriage. Both had, since my student days, become my friends. Payal recently got married but always explained it as "purely for financial reasons." Sejal, too, was planning to get married again after a history of divorce, failed legal proceedings, and years of successful circumvention of the marriage question as a promising academic. Recently, after malicious rumors spread about her emotional proximity to her PhD supervisor, she planned to marry again to a Brahmin widower with a daughter. As she explained her choice at the time, "I am marrying a motherless daughter."

As we talked about the violence that had erupted in the city, Payal seemed discomforted about her former teacher's candor, but Sejal continued unperturbed: "We have always been the victims. Always we have taken their aggressions. Muslims always start." This would be the first time, she added, that Hindus had fought back.

Sejal worked as a teacher in a Muslim girl's college in an all-Muslim area of the old city and thus had many years of close experience with Muslims. As a Jain, she was one of only two non-Muslim faculty members in her school. In the past, she had expressed pride to me about this minority position at her workplace and she had never indicated that she felt discriminated against. In many ways, Sejal understood herself as following in the footsteps of her academic adviser, a prolific Brahmin writer, who was a member of the RSS in his youth. But then he turned Gandhian and made the conscious decision to teach at this Muslim school.

I remembered, a few years back, when Sejal had confided in me her emotional attachment to some of the young Muslim girls in her college. She identified her suffering as a woman, along with her traumatic marital experiences, as that which she thought many Muslim girls went through. In our more intimate discussions she had even seemed to me at times like a woman on her way to discovering formerly foreclosed erotic possibilities, as she described her complete indifference to marital life, and especially sex with men.

When she talked of her experiences with sexuality in her failed marriage, a shadowy picture emerged of daily nocturnal abuses and what she understood to be bizarre demands by her former husband, for example, to include another woman in their sexual activity. Sejal did not elaborate on these issues, always displaying a certain degree of revulsion. Usually she digressed quickly into more general questions about married life. To make matters worse for her, during her divorce proceedings in 1997, her lawyer, too, demanded sexual favors in exchange for good legal work. Sejal therefore dropped the lawyer and subsequently never received any marital compensation from her husband, a dire situation for most divorced women. Fortunately her family was relatively wealthy and her academic supervisors appreciated her academic skills.

Although Sejal never had intimate contact with a Muslim man and was never personally approached or propositioned by one, today she thought Muslims were naturally "tough." She expressed fear of them and, after a long digression, concluded, "They got it once." I had to work to contain my composure to her suddenly explicit understanding if not sympathy for the violence being directed against Muslims around us. Over the years, we had spent significant time together discussing the Jain conception of nonviolence. I was unsure what to make of the fact that Sejal suddenly sounded like other interlocutors I had talked to. I asked her to explain this Muslim nature. She replied, "They do not see what is right, what is wrong. They see the blood. If they can kill animals without a thought, how can they have problems killing humans?"

ROUGH AND TOUGH

Back in 1999, three years earlier, Sejal spoke very little English, and our language study was nearly all in Gujarati. Then she had a penchant for using rhyming English word combinations such as "rough" and "tough." She seemed to think that "tough" was the answer to "rough." She held on to this linguistic peculiarity even when she became more fluent in English.

When Payal spoke about the difficulties in her marriage, for example, which she often did in tears, Sejal told her to get "tough," using the English word in a Gujarati sentence. I believe it was the letter "t" in tough that Sejal particularly liked, as she always overemphasized the retroflex pronunciation of "t" which made it sound like an original Gujarati word.

By "rough," she meant coarse and prone to revert to bad practices. I often heard "rough" asserted as characteristic of communities considered backward and uneducated, though not exclusively those. The terms with which one typifies entire communities reappear frequently as characteristics of individual members of one's own group—preferably one's own husband. If Payal's husband displayed signs of being "rough," Sejal suggested becoming "tough." My naive advice that in so many versions suggested getting rid of the guy always made them both laugh and giggle. While they were amused by my simple-minded recommendation, for them I also displayed ignorance of the realities of married life for a woman in Ahmedabad. What Sejal meant to say was that in the absence of a possibility to divorce, the only solution was to mobilize an inner strength to withstand the humiliation: to become tough.

Sejal had always insisted on her privileged position of insight into Muslim women's troubles in marriage. But the few times when I visited her college, I got the impression that at least some of her female Muslim students acted overly reserved in her presence. She displayed a self-confident posture with them that not all of her students were comfortable with. When students answered my questions in class and inadvertently used an English or Urdu expression, Sejal reprimanded them strictly. Although the students submitted quickly to her authority, I could not help but perceive a slight mocking in the young faces at Sejal's conceited insistence on speaking only Gujarati and elaborating frequently on things Gujarati in a Muslim girl's college. Perhaps this was caused by the fact that at least some of the female students related to me automatically as a Muslim, that is, a non-Gujarati.

Sejal's overly strict insistence on Gujarati was odd, I believe, not simply because she was a Jain working in a Muslim college but rather because she acted as if engaged in a disciplining and civilizing process that contradicted the logic and self-understanding of the school, which was to help Muslim women achieve an education on their own terms. Sejal acted as if the invisible barriers that she herself signified and affirmed as member of the Gujarati elite were altogether absent, and as if the distance between her and the students was simply a matter of becoming more or less properly "Gujarati."

Sejal attributed roughness to members of particular groups, traditionally lower-and intermediary-caste groups, but it was not a fixed condition. If prompted, she would, like many of her teacher colleagues, say that

FIGURE 7: Surgical strikes

all people are redeemable through care, discipline, and education—the qualities that she felt responsible for providing as a teacher to her Muslim students. What bothered the Muslim students, on the other hand, was that they did not necessarily conceive of becoming more "Gujarati" as an improvement, because this word unambiguously signified to them "Hindu." Or, to say the same thing, what in Gujarat was historically Muslim had become erased in dominant Hindu middle-class discourse. If it appeared, it was couched in unmistakably negative and insulting terms. Sejal acted as if she were fundamentally unaware of these subtleties.

MUSLIM, NOT GUJARATI

During our discussion at Mehfil restaurant, Payal related an anecdote of a female Muslim roommate she had in the college hostel. The roommate was a foreign student from Egypt and had been her close friend until the day they had a disagreement. The friendship ended in a serious quarrel. Payal explained that this friend had an angry demeanor and, although there was no physical altercation, she became very scared of her. Payal, a fragile woman with a thin frame, felt intimidated by her roommate because there was "this thing in her eyes"—she used the Gujarati expression *majli akh* (uncanny eye), often used to describe especially light colored eyes, green or blue, that seem to glow. Later Payal told me that the Egyptian student also had a dark complexion.

"They are very honest," Sejal interrupted with a certain surprise in her voice, as if to say something good about Muslims. They are "a hardworking people," and "sober," like the subordinate peon she had in school. But, "They are not like us, they do this butchering business." Payal continued that the problems between Muslims and Hindus have been going on since Partition. "They speak not our mother tongue. Our mother tongue is Gujarati, not Urdu," Sejal added, regaining back the initiative. "They will ask me, '*Tame Gujarati?*' [Are you Gujarati?] as if they were not from here. This all has been going on since Partition," she concurred with Payal.

Sejal's claim that Muslims generally negate being Gujarati is, on the face of it, absolutely correct. If one were to walk through any Muslim neighborhood of Ahmedabad and ask, "Are you Gujarati?" most will certainly respond, "No, I am a Muslim." And yet, Sejal's interpretation is nonetheless astonishing in this context. Payal is a Maharashtrian Brahmin and her mother tongue is Marathi although she was born and raised in Gujarat. If someone were to ask Payal, if she was a Gujarati, she too would decline and explain that she is Marathi, as I have witnessed her do many times. Payal spoke Marathi and English at home, not Gujarati, as well as in her new in-laws' home (although she was fluent in Gujarati—as are the majority of Muslims). The familial customs and festivals she followed, too, were self-consciously Marathi, not Gujarati.

Furthermore, Payal's husband, Hritik, was from a different Marathi Brahmin subcaste than her natal family. Gujaratis as well as other Marathi Brahmins tended to look down upon this subcaste. They were said to "take it" (*e loko le chhe*). "It," here, meant meat, usually chicken and fish. In middle-class and upper-caste Gujarat, eating meat strongly connotes moral degradation in a way similar to consuming alcohol. Hritik's family had invited me several times for delicious fish and chicken dishes in the Hindu middle-class neighborhood where they lived. They complained about their Gujarati neighbors' rigidity and the clandestine discriminations they had to endure for being what they called "cosmopolitan," a synonym for having nonvegetarian food habits.[2] Some neighbors thought they must be Christian due to the smell of cooked meat, which her in-laws took as an offense. Being a relaxed vegetarian, Payal did not mind cooking chicken for her in-laws, although the smell of fish nauseated her. In this discussion, Payal nonetheless felt no need to disagree with her teacher.

It was not the first time I had heard complaints about how Muslims had become excluded from Gujarati identity. The first time, a prominent professor of literature described to me how as a young man in the 1960s, he had attempted to join a cultural student organization at M. S. Baroda University. He hailed from Saurashtra, a region in the state of Gujarat with a distinct identity whose people call themselves Kathiawadis. The reason he wanted to join the organization was that most of their members were Kathiawadis, too. His peers, however, turned him away claiming that he was a Muslim and not a Gujarati. He insisted that he was in fact a Gujarati Muslim and, on top of it, from Saurashtra, as they were—but to no avail.

In other words, while he was a Muslim Kathiawadi at home, at M. S. Baroda University he became a generic Muslim, not allowed to inhabit the identity of a Gujarati. While his Hindu peers had made the transformation from Kathiawadi to Gujarati, he was barred from such a categorical shift. It was as if the price the members of the organization had to pay to be considered properly Gujarati was the expunction of the category "Muslim." What Sejal referred to here is not the unwillingness of Muslims to become internal to Gujarat, but the product of shifts in the categorization of identities that began with the political consolidation of the state and its various regions. This shift facilitated practices of exclusion by those groups who successfully have come to occupy the terms associated with "Gujarati."

Payal often emphasized a distinction between "those Gujaratis" and "us Marathis," the same way Sejal often drew the line between "those Hindus" and "us Jains." Being a Brahmin, however, created no ambiguity as to whether Payal was a Hindu, and being a Jain did not cast doubt as to whether Sejal was a Gujarati. The two forms of externality to Gujarat, the Muslim and the Marathi, were asymmetrical and not substitutable. While both Muslims and Marathis keep themselves apart, the separation that Muslims assert is unstable and more difficult to merge with Gujarati on a higher, more encompassing level. This is not because Muslims are more "other" than Marathis but rather the opposite. The category "Muslim" comes to stand for something that is kept in psychological suspension: it implies something that cannot be affirmed.

The asymmetry between Marathis and Muslims began with the regional integration and reconfiguration of Gujarat after Indian Independence and with the administrative and territorial consolidation of the state in 1960. Marathis were frequently held in contempt as foreigners in earlier times (Yagnik and Sheth 2005: 57–58). Furthermore, while regions such as Saurashtra and Kachchh remained largely peripheral to Gujarati identity in the nineteenth and beginning of the twentieth centuries, these provinces now became internal to a reformulated Gujarati-ness, engendering new anxieties about boundaries and borders (Ibrahim 2009: 32). The sense of strange familiarity that brings about fear holds especially true for the region of Sindh in Pakistan immediately north of Kachchh with which it shares so much in history and yet from which it is separated by a national border. The national border with Pakistan is a barrier that generates psycho-geographical effects. Whatever its actual porosity or asserted impenetrability, it is psychologically more momentous than any desert could ever be.[3]

The way Sejal constructed a collective "Hindu we" was not at all unusual for middle-class Gujaratis of diverse background or religious tradition. As a Jain, she is bound to the ethical norms of one of the stricter vegetarian communities, closely identified with nonviolence. Therefore, she sometimes distanced herself quite sharply from those Hindus whom she considered "rough"—for example, from the two roommates with whom I shared my apartment, members of a community that belongs to the "other backward classes" (OBCs), or from members of the Sindhi minority.

But Sejal's "we" related nonetheless to an inclusive social universe of friends, colleagues, and academic advisers, mostly from Brahmin, Vaniya, and Patel background sharing a middle-class habitus. They spoke *shuddh* Gujarati (proper Gujarati language) and in varying degrees ate *shuddh* Gujarati food (pure vegetarian food). They were able to command a controlled speech, indicative of refinement through "education," they were opposed to animal sacrifice, and their food habits revolved around cleanliness and a concern for nonviolence. For Sejal, Payal, the self-assertive Marathi, too, belonged to this category. And as Sejal planned to marry a Brahmin, a Hindu, she herself was preparing for her final and unambiguous entry into the category "Hindu." What Sejal's spontaneous exhortation about Muslims at the moment of their victimization suggests is a relay between her female vulnerability vis-à-vis men's sexual demands in general and the suspicion of excessive sexuality on the part of Muslims. What warranted protection from this demand was the unmarked cultural style of middle-class Gujarati Hindus.

FASTING AGAINST SACRIFICE

On February 23, 2002, three weeks before we met at Mehfil and four days before the Godhra incident that inaugurated the Gujarat pogrom, Sejal held to a strict fast (*upvas*). Although she was sick and feeling weak, she joined her parents and neighbors in a Jain locality of the west city where she lived. When I called her on the phone that morning, she told me I should not come to visit her. She was feeling weak and would fast the entire day. The reason for the fast was Bakri-Id—a Muslim festival at which goats were being slaughtered. Jains all over Gujarat were unhappy about this, she explained. Some Jains would eat "no white, as goats are white [sic]."[4] Some would not even touch water for an entire day.

Perfectly aware of her dietary regimen, I was nonetheless astonished at her rationale for fasting on that particular day. I wondered what effects this insistence on fasting might have on her relationship with Muslim students. She was fasting at the very time her students were getting ready to wear their new clothes, embracing one another by saying "*Id-Mubarak*" ("Happy festival of Id"), and indulging in culinary delicacies for one of the most joyous and colorful festivals of Indian Islam. At the time I could not think of a tactful way to ask Sejal about that. Instead, I asked her if the collective fast she participated in was due to the yearlong 2,600th birthday celebration of Lord Mahavir, the Jain champion of nonviolence, which the Indian Prime Minister Atal Bihari Vajpayee had inaugurated in April the year before.

Sejal scoffed at my question. Instead she insisted that the fast was a traditional Jaina practice. She had already fasted against Muslim animal slaughter when she was a child, and, sensing the direction of my question, she added, it had nothing whatsoever to do with the politics of the BJP. It was true that she had always been highly skeptical of Hindu communal ideologies and aggressive politicking. But, she exclaimed, "They have no right to kill only for a festival." The goat is killed in the house privately, and the meat is given to friends and neighbors. Every year, many members of the Jain community would be very upset about this practice, she added.

Sejal knew perfectly well that nonvegetarian restaurants in west Ahmedabad were filled with members of the middle class, Hindus as well as members of her own community. She also had more than an inkling of practices of animal sacrifice among specific Hindu communities in the state. But even if she was underestimating the level of subtle dietary obfuscation in the city among middle-class Gujaratis, for her these deceptions would in any case be mere aberrations. To be modern and cosmopolitan included engagement in decadent and morally precarious practices based on contemporary fashions or a misconceived ritual tradition. The fact that a Jain ate meat changed the truth expressed in Jainism as little as the fact that a Dalit, who considered himself a Hindu while consuming beef, changed the truth expressed in cow worship.

Sejal equated Muslim practices of ceremonial animal sacrifice with the practices of rural communities, who sacrifice buffalos or goats to the Mother Goddess—often still performed today but in relative secrecy. Sejal considered such worship practices backward and superstitious (*andhshraddhalu*), a sort of false worship. These rituals were unnecessary, based upon false premises, not acceptable in any way whatsoever.

For Sejal, every ceremonial blood sacrifice of this sort was a murderous slaughter. Although she expressed tolerance for Islam as a religion, she rejected its claim to special cultural rights to take the lives of animals.

When Sejal referred to Muslims as "honest," she meant that they would neither hide nor be ashamed about their worship practices or dietary habits—unlike members of other communities. Assertive of their cultural traditions, they would not easily calibrate their behavior to fit the proper norm. Muslims were "honest" in Sejal's understanding, because they did openly what others concealed. This sobriety however did not in any way redeem them for what they did. They were honest, yes, but they were still unnecessarily taking life.

I asked Sejal if she was aware of the religious justification of the festival, part of Middle Eastern traditions of Abrahamic sacrifice, in which Muslims commemorate Ibrahim's sacrifice of Ishmail (Abraham and Isaac in the Old Testament). She told me it was about a pious man, whom God asked to give him his most precious and valuable belonging. "His son, his only son, he wanted to give as that was his most precious gift. Thus he cut his son's throat, but then it was a goat."

Sejal acknowledged the deeper religious meaning of this festival, but she dismissed all symbolism in contemporary times: "Nowadays, Muslims do this only for taste." To kill an animal just for the sake of taste was unacceptable. She used the English term "taste" here informed by the Gujarati term *svad*, which means "taste, relish," as well as "pleasure." For Sejal, *svad mate* (for taste) means "for pleasure." Today everything was about pleasure, about *santosh* (satisfaction). Muslims were killing for the pleasures of taste. For Sejal, they lacked vulnerability, an instinct for injury.

Because Muslims indulged in pleasures, Sejal's community abstained from all pleasure on Bakri-Id and kept a strict fast. Her abstention was directed explicitly against Muslim slaughter. One group's sacrificial ritual of substitution, displacement, and expenditure became the rational for another group's collective practice of inverse internalized sacrifice, that is, renunciation. In this way, what she conceived of as Muslim transgression was inscribed onto her body. Their pleasures became her injuries.

According to traditional Jaina thought, what grows less in the body is valued positively. There is no fault in dying, only in engaging in injury. Fasting means conscious life and overcoming death by embracing severance from an injurious world of violence. Sejal, however, was no renouncer. She had no intention of attempting to die in a fast unto death, the highest ideal in classical Jaina thought. Hers was not a renunciation that severed the ties to the world but rather an inner-worldly care for all forms of life. Recently she had grown thinner and more lifeless, in reaction to, and in a sense compensating for, the violent expenditure of life in

Muslim animal sacrifice during Bakri-Id. Sejal in this way internalized the Muslim ritual slaughter. It was she who was sacrificed by them. Sejal took the place of a goat. Or, to say the same thing, somewhere in the goat there was a cow, the mother that Sejal always wanted to be and the reason she was planning to marry a motherless daughter.

Hindu Coward, Muslim Bully

Shortly after walking through the spectral remainders of the Muslim quarters at Naroda Patiya (see chapter 3), Mr. Chauhan, Lalo's father, suggested that as a foreign researcher, I should ask myself why Muslims are such constant bullies. Ranjit and I were sitting on the couch in his living room, waiting for our dinner and still pondering the depressive stroll through the abandoned quarters. Mr. Chauhan authorized the characterization by paraphrasing Mahatma Gandhi, who had said, "The typical Muslim is a bully and the typical Hindu is a coward." How can one be a friend to a bullying person? Mr. Chauhan asked.

As a matter of routine, I inquired what precisely made Muslims so bullying. Mr. Chauhan did not hesitate to point to the diverse forms of killing in sacrificial slaughter. Every young Muslim boy of five years of age is taught by his father to slaughter a chicken halal-style, he explained. To slaughter an animal *halal*—according to Islamic injunction—is considered particularly cruel in Gujarat, as the knife has to cut the throat while the heart still pumps out the blood (considered impure by Muslims). Hindus, by contrast, when and if they would slaughter, do so only *jhatko*, which is by one single stroke, not by cutting slowly.

"The boy will take a knife and cut the hen's throat mercilessly," Mr. Chauhan continued. The fact that young Muslim boys learn to slaughter a hen was the reason, he said, that "Muslims are always ready to kill—they kill even their blood relations. Hindus are always the sufferers." Ranjit nodded. I argued that members of Rajput communities like him also indulged in meat consumption. But Mr. Chauhan insisted on something exceptional about Muslim carnivorous practices besides the distinction between *halal* and *jhatko* butchering.

"They even eat the female goat, and the young animal. They are always ready for nonveg." He listed the animals that Muslims are ready to eat, "Goat, buffalo, dove, duck, cow, peacock. They eat the meat of any creation, which has their backs to the sky [*sic*]. The Hindu [by contrast] has *maryada* [boundary, limitation, modesty]." Ranjit again agreed. Like Sejal or Payal, Mr. Chauhan would not understand himself to be genuinely "anti-Muslim." Whereas Sejal is a Jain working in a Muslim college, Mr. Chauhan claimed to have a Muslim "best friend."

As an example of what many Gujaratis think of as the utter perversity of the Muslim act of slaughter, they point out that the Muslim butcher will utter the name of God in the very moment of killing. Many will add that they find incomprehensible to invoke compassion in the moment of killing. Indeed, the Islamic prescription of halal demands that the *hajji* (pilgrim returning from the Haj) who slaughters should recite, "*b-ismallah al-rahman al rahim*" (in the name of Allah, the compassionate, the merciful). Sometimes the ritual *takbir*, "Allahu Akbar," is also used. According to my observations, Muslims usually utter the *takbir* three times when killing the sacrificial animal.

In Gujarati idiom, a butcher is a *kasai* or a *khatki*. Some dictionaries also define the term *kasai* as "a heartless person," "a brutal murderer," and a "cutthroat" (cf. ASD, GED, TMGED). In its verbal form, it compels the adjective *nirdaya* (without compassion or pity), that is, cruel and merciless (cf. GCD). The Islamic ritual slaughter invokes compassion while the Gujarati term for butcher lexically signifies the opposite.

Consequently, the most frequently invoked idiom in conversations about Muslims was the figure of the Muslim butcher. Ranjit, who himself was neither vegetarian nor particularly anti-Muslim in his stance, asserted the typical attribute of the Gujarati Muslim butcher, "They kill rather mercilessly." Over the years I have had many discussions with Ranjit about his own precarious status as the only middle-class Dalit in the college where he taught, about the way his colleagues secretly suspected him of many vices and showed minute interest in what, where, and with whom he ate.

Ranjit could not risk entering the main temple in his home village, which was run by the local Patel community. Although legally enfranchised, such an act, he explained to me, would be perceived as a clear provocation spelling consequences for his relatives still living in the village. His best friend, Gautam—also a middle-class Dalit—recently converted to Buddhism in protest of the Hindu caste system. Ranjit was one of the most educated men in his home village and never struck me as particularly opposed to Muslim meat eating. In the 1980s, during severe anti-Dalit violence, he had personally experienced what it meant being member of a social category that is collectively held to be abject.

What Ranjit voiced here was less his own opinion, I believe, but more something like a suspicion, almost a superstition, in the form of a typical Gujarati stereotype, a discourse that existed before and apart from him and that came to inhabit him in the context of this discussion with Mr. Chauhan. In the moment when he had reached the status of a middle-class Hindu, he had become a potential target for Muslims. Something took hold of him, and he thought, "They kill rather mercilessly." When Mr. Chauhan claimed that Muslims even kill their own kin, he referred not merely to Ibrahim and Ishmail in Islamic sacrifice but also to former Muslim kings known to have killed family rivals to the throne.

Many people talked to me in much the same spirit, invoking diet and sexuality to characterize Muslims. The indifference to the smell and sight of blood, the eating of all kinds of meats (such as intestines) and the meat of young animals as well as the consumption of the female—be it does, cows, young Hindu women, or close kin—formed something like a continuum of fantasized objects that were referenced repeatedly to characterize an excessive expenditure by Muslims which is ever encroaching upon Hindus. The imaginary that informed and legitimated the violence of the pogrom relied on this totemic character of communal identification. The difference from Muslims was most pronouncedly expressed in the idiom of one's relationship to animals and diet, forms of slaughter and killing. This relation is expressive not so much of an estrangement between communities as of a deep intimacy, where the "other" comes to stand for those parts of the self that are to be vehemently denied.

HIDDEN COW

Stereotypes are not only projective devices used by majorities against minorities. Individuals from minority communities also inhabit these stereotypes with an astonishing regularity. In this relation of projection to internalization, stereotypical behaviors can be understood as the result of intersubjective symbolic processes essential to the definition of society. If stereotyped projections name a perceived danger and give it form, they can give some comfort to the subject also. For those subjected to stereotypes, the response can range from rejection to introjection. Introjection is not merely an act of submission but an attempt to turn social abjection into power. In this section, I take up such introjections as attempts by minority subjects to divest themselves of negative stigma through jokes and double entendres.

Jokes are often the privileged site of employment of stereotypical material. From 2001 to 2003, I tried to collect jokes to understand something about contemporary Hindu-Muslim relationships. Jokes by Hindus about Muslims were extremely rare, whereas jokes by Muslims about Hindus were common. My Hindu interlocutors did tell me jokes about other communities, especially Sikhs and Sindhis, but they resisted making fun of Muslims in the same way.

While speaking with a group of mixed-aged Muslim men, whom I met in September 2001, I was told several jokes that more indirectly made use of such ambiguities. The following conversations took place during the emotionally charged atmosphere of 9/11 in the United States. While a few individuals of the group were well situated, running local businesses and safely lodged in their marriages, most were despondent about their lives, had not yet taken off, with little income or employment or marriage perspectives. The group met regularly at a telephone shop on the street for tea and conversation.

One day I brought an American magazine, too expensive for most to acquire, which showed pictures of the catastrophe in New York. Some Muslims showed compassion. A young Sudanese cleric residing in Gujarat for his studies embraced me in sorrow and empathy. But within a month, the register changed fast as the vast mountainous regions of Afghanistan became the unlikely target of US military aggression. At the time, many Hindus, too, disagreed with what most interpreted as American imperial intent in what they considered their natal South Asian hemisphere.

After a certain initial empathy, this particular group of Muslims became extremely contemptuous and derisive. Arif, an unemployed and unmarried man in his late twenties, always insisted on wearing the longest possible Pathani *kurta* (Indian chemises for males). His thin body, nearly skeletal compared to some of his already skinny comrades, seemed even more elongated in these *kurtas*. After the carpet bombing of Tora Bora in December 2001, he started calling the garments "Afghani." In urban Gujarat, they designated him as unambiguously Muslim. He wore a less-than-full goatee and dyed all his hair red, both signs of Muslim today. Arif's thinness compared unfavorably to the appearance of his more self-assured cousin, Mohammed, a handsome and clean-shaven man in his early thirties with black curly hair.

Waiting for a grand change in his life, Arif spent much time on the Internet in designated cafés. One day he brought a printout depiction of George Bush being anally penetrated by Osama bin Laden, which created a minor stir amongst the group. His uncle Jehangir chastised him for circulating such evocative material and especially for showing it to me, a foreigner living in "Amireka."

The next time I joined the group, Arif greeted me with a joke, "Penta is gone, Pentagon!" and he waited for my laughter. Then he said, "Do you know Abubaqr?" Arif explained to me, that the Arab name Abubaqr literally meant "father of cow." He elaborated that the son of a cow is a "cowboy," that is, a quintessential American. It was cowboys, the sons of the cows, who were now attacking the Taliban in Afghanistan. The mother of cows, in turn, was the "*gaumata*," that is, India and its Hindu people. He asked me triumphantly, "Who then is the big man? Who is the boss?" All looked at me in anticipation.

They laughed at the joke before I could fully understand it. The word "Abubaqr" said it all, because in Arabic *abu* means father and *baqr* means cow. According to patriarchal logic, the father of the cow is situated above both, the son and the mother (the American cowboy and the Hindu *gaumata*). Thus, by default, Abubaqr is the hierarchical apex, the father of cowboys as well as of cows. Superiority over Hindus and Americans is here expressed through reference to two implicit forms of incorporation, beef ingestion and sexual consumption. Muslims are ingesting the flesh of cows, instead of venerating the animal, and they relate as husbands to *gaumata*. Such was the doubtful linguistic triumph that the Arab name Abubaqr presented for Arif.[5]

Arif's joke is a good example of how a word play making use of three different languages (English, Hindi, and Arabic) allowed an entourage of Muslim men to reverse, for a moment, what they felt was a growing atmosphere of abjection. To allude to slippages and ambiguities of expressions through double entendres is a favorite pastime of Gujaratis. Although a joke, it was much more than that. It expressed a sort of linguistic practice of defiance and a secret truth that they felt only few were able to see: a sea change was coming for Muslims in South Asia and the world at large.

Yet there is another angle to the Arab *baqr* and how they used it. The name for the Muslim festival of Bakri-Id derives from the Arabic word *Eid* (feast day) and the local word for a female goat, *bakri*. However, the sound of the word *bakri* (*bakru* and *bakro* for neuter and masculine respectively) resembles closely the Arab term for cow, *baqr*. Although few Muslims in Gujarat understand Arabic, this similarity has not gone unnoticed. Hindu nationalist organizations will point it out, as will Muslims who want to define themselves as particularly orthodox. A real Muslim is to slaughter a forbidden cow for the festival.

Foreign students from the Middle East who study in Gujarat often point out that Indian Muslims rarely have the linguistic competence in Arabic that many claim. The Muslim prayers (*namaz*) are learned in transcribed form by rote, in Gujarati, Hindi, or Urdu script. The Qu'ran, too, is read in Gujarati, Urdu, and English and merely recited in Arabic. The way Arabic is used by local Muslims resembles the way Sanskrit verse is used by many Hindus. Much of the attractiveness of ritualized speech comes from the pervasive inability to actually understand ancient and scholarly language.

Even if aware of the onomatopoetic link between *baqr* and *bakri* many Muslims would not want to allude imprudently to this resemblance of sound. It is fundamentally uncanny as it summons a constant implicit allegation. Muslims are frequently accused of cow slaughter, often falsely, and without doubt, even more habitually than Dalits. The practice is not only strictly prohibited in the state; the prohibition is also rigorously enforced. Nonetheless it is not impossible to obtain cow meat from butchers in Muslim areas, especially at night, not least because beef is the cheapest of all meats. This fact conveniently marries economic frailty with pious defiance.

That the very term used for a Muslim festival inclusive of ceremonial animal sacrifice of bulls and goats references that killing of which Muslims are always accused, which is cow slaughter, provides the key to understanding the structure of the entire slaughter discourse in Gujarat. It points to what is centrally omitted in it: the cow as the most forbidden object of sacrifice in Gujarat. Being only suspended this omission generates effects, as a form of secret signification, the kind that makes for community—and a barrage of jokes as well as double entendres.

That Arif would reference Muslim domination over cows in a world where the "Pentagon is gone," bin Laden sodomizes an American president, and cows are slaughtered for Bakri-Id reveals how the global triangulation of identity between Hindu, Christian, and Muslim is internal to India. The Christian is infantilized as a boy and the Hindu feminized as the mother. But who is the father? Where is India's paternal authority for Muslims? The ostensible father is Abubaqr, an Arab and a Muslim, the master of cows as well as cowboys.

Note that a cow's husband could also be the bull. The bull is venerated in India but is also sacrificed and ingested during Muslim as well as certain Adivasi festivals. One of the Gujarati terms for bull—*balad*—is used figuratively for someone who is doltish or stupid. There was also the possibility that Arif could have thought of Mahatma Gandhi, the father of the nation, as the symbolic parent. But in popular Gujarati discourse, Gandhi is too Hindu, too docile, too vegetarian, too emaciated, and feminine a figure for this role. In truth, Gandhi vehemently opposed cow slaughter and attempted to transform the issue into the opportunity for Muslims to show their self-chosen kindness towards Hindu religious sensibilities. Being a Gujarati, Arif is undoubtedly aware of this fact, yet it has little weight in the present climate.

Jehangir, Arif's uncle, immigrated to Karachi after the 1969 violence in Ahmedabad. One day Jehangir confided in me that he had been profoundly unsettled by his extraordinary experiences in the city that year, in which he had lost most of his non-Muslim friends. In Pakistan, however, he was badly treated, even physically assaulted, and he found no opportunity to start a good business. He soon returned to Gujarat, impoverished and disappointed, and had to begin anew.

Arif ignores his uncle's experience and, projects all that is good onto the neighboring country. In Pakistan, a country that he takes as the authority in all things Islamic, residents eat a much larger amount of meat than in India, Arif claimed. Whereas well-to-do Gujarati Muslims ate meat maximally thrice a week, Pakistanis would eat meat daily—*kheema* (hashed mutton or beef) for breakfast, butter chicken for lunch, and tandoori for dinner—he believed. They also would start every meal with a choice of fruits—something that elite Gujaratis did not appreciate. The chaste Hindu upper-caste diet is limited to vegetables, *gol* (sweet molasses, jaggery), and ghee, which are eaten together with *rotli* (bread). Pakistanis also knew better how and what to prepare when it comes to proper meat dishes, Arif explained. Finally, they are allowed to eat beef, even from the female cow, which is according to Arif, the healthiest and best of all meats.

A few months after we met, Arif began to engage in a new set of personal strategies to overcome his skeletal build. For one, he started to learn Arabic at the local branch of the Islamic Research Foundation, as suggested by his uncle. The nonprofit organization, whose president is Bombay's popular Dr. Zakir Naik, teaches Indian Muslims one of multiple "real" versions of Islam. The organization is also active in defending Muslim culinary practices against Hindu claims of impurity and moral impropriety. In one of its myriad publications, a video with the curious title *Is Non-Vegetarian Food Permitted or Prohibited for a Human Being?* Naik debates the former president of the Indian Vegetarian Congress, Mr. Rashmibhai Zaveri. The debate took place in 1999 on the premises of the foundation in Mumbai.

Naik appears meticulously dressed in all his video lectures and speaks in an highly self-assured tone. In this debate too, he is well prepared and obviously steals the show. The recording is immensely popular among those urban Muslims in Gujarat who suddenly came to realize that they were discriminated against for a long time when confronted with what they perceive as an arduous dietary stigma. Naik's self-confidence is performed through a scrupulous English articulation and show of scientific knowledge. What some might identify as arrogance fascinates a growing Muslim audience. Arif discussed the video recording as if it were a form of acquittal, relieving him of something. But of what? As a Muslim he was never a proper vegetarian anyway. Arif took profound joy in Naik's triumphant exhortations, blissfully unaware of how peculiar the performed preaching and counterpreaching about the benefits or dangers of animal-flesh foods sounded to an outsider like me.

In the recording, Naik argues as a doctor, a scientist, a community leader, and a Muslim. In his overly confident demeanor, triumphal at times, he represents all that local Muslims seemed to aspire for: the rationality of science, the knowledge of the scripture, the magnanimity of a balanced and sincere mind, and the scholarly sophistication of a pious

Muslim as well as the courage to name and oppose the clandestine discriminations expressed in quotidian Indian life. Through the foundation's materials, the discriminatory rejection of Muslim dietary habits by elite Gujaratis, far from becoming insignificant, has reached a new level of reflection within Muslim communities. Watching the video supported the perception that something was wrong, that somehow Muslims were increasingly treated as if they were the new untouchables, as if they had something to be ashamed off, a blot that needed to be cleansed.[6]

Arif, for one, only recently started eating animal intestines, and he was proud of this dietary accomplishment. While he had eaten chicken and mutton for longer than he could remember, the insides of animals had always disgusted him. It took him many years to get over his revulsion for such delicacies as liver, brain, and kidneys. Intestines were fried in oil, butter, or ghee, heavily spiced, and served during Muslim festivals. In his own sense of self, Arif has become more adult, more Muslim, and thus more masculine. Part of the ascent to Muslim adulthood was ridding the self of what he considered to be Gujarati—that clandestine effeminate Gandhi within himself.

Mohammed once invited me to a domestic dinner. As is the custom in most Gujarati homes, we ate with our hands—no utensils are provided. After dinner, Mohammed kept me from utilizing soap when I wanted to clean my hands. By not washing the hands with soap, he explained, we preserve the smell of cooked meat on them. I smelled his hands, then mine, and did indeed smell curry and asafetida (*hing*). Mohammed had turned what amounted to a problem for others into a daily act of perfuming himself. When Muslims who eat meat interact regularly with strict vegetarian Hindus, they often fear smelling of meat. For Mohammed, this smell defined him as a "real" Muslim, who no longer cared what upper-caste Hindus or Jains might think of him.

For both Arif and Mohammed, eating meat was much more than a dietary choice or a health issue, as much as they tried to make it seem that way. It was an assertion of an adult masculine Muslim identity, which derived its impulse and strength from an antagonistic relation to elite Hindu and Jain practices, perceptions, and stigmatizations. Vegetarianism was not an acceptable choice to them, despite the fact that Islam does not in any way prescribe meat eating, as Dr. Naik frequently points out. More indirectly, both identifications while opposed to one another on the surface actually converge in their implicit address of the West: Islam by mustering science and especially medicine to make its overly rational, nonvegetarian case; Hindu and Jain religious tradition by mustering medicine as to the negative health effects of meat eating as well as the attractive ideal of nonviolence and compassion extended to all forms of life.

In their conscious embrace of identification with meat eating, Arif and Mohammed stood in opposition to the handful of Muslim Gandhians in Gujarat, who are self-consciously vegetarian, or to certain rural Sufi saints and ascetics who prefer to eat vegetarian. For Arif and Mohammed, meat signified "Muslim" in the exact way it did to Sejal. The elite Hindu's repugnance for meat became their opportunity for defiance against everything "Hindu." Along these lines, meat signified power for some exactly because it constituted abjection to others. It goes without saying that such a defensive and aggressive posture placed Arif and Mohammad in a difficult relationship to the notion of a *shuddh* Gujarati.

Stereotype and Humor

The themes of ritual sacrifice, butchering, and meat eating continually recurred in the Gujarati discourse about Muslims. They formed an important part of the imaginary grid of the pogrom and allowed for the mobilization of strong collective resentment. Hindu-identified individuals seemed more eager to be explicit in their discussions with me about their quotidian associations and idiomatic expressions concerning meat. Vegetarian arguments emerged when all other arguments for the legitimacy of violence seemed no longer reasonable and the speaker needed to hold on to a distinction in relation to Muslims. They form a psychological defense and a linguistic regression into a familiar domain of dietary and ritual reflection—but now taken at face value. That such a defensive posture was deemed necessary, despite its absurdity, shows the serious nature of communal conflict in Gujarat, where violence is experienced as erupting without any way to stop or make sense of it.

While vegetarian arguments were constructed and sustained in order to insist on religious difference between Hindus and Muslims, if one looks closely at them—their implicit logic, structure, source, assertion, and counterassertion—they are predicated with certainty upon one another. Instead of a clear-cut opposition, they form something more like symbolic continuity. The concern for meat as a substance, its smell and effect, bespeaks a fundamental similarity lacking all difference between the two aggregate communities. Furthermore, what was claimed about Muslims versus Hindus could easily be said about Dalits versus Brahmins, Rajputs versus Vaniya, or men versus women.

In this context, when the distance between one's purported ideals and one's actual behavior was lost, Hindus came to believe most stubbornly in their own nonviolence despite all signs to the contrary. This inversion of perpetrator and victim not only misrecognized the Muslim neighbor's vulnerability but encouraged Muslims to turn abjection into false sense of power, that is, to assume and inhabit the very qualities that rendered them strong in the eyes of their frightened Hindu contemporaries.

In the context of the pogrom, irony—the ambiguity and distance it might establish between stereotypes and their assertion (as for example in the not uncommon claim of dietary hypocrisy of the vegetarian classes)—was lost. Suddenly stereotypes and clichés, which at other times might have been laughed at, were taken dead seriously, and words came to mean brutally what their content expressed. Reality is not funny when it is threatening. Irony and laughter were no longer available to create distance between one's prejudices and one's experience.

The Autobiography of a Goat

In Ahmedabad's old city, in the lanes around Manek Chowk not far from Pustak Bazaar, I came across Gopinath Aggarwal's *Vegetarian or Non-Vegetarian: Choose Yourself*—a little booklet in its fifth edition. What the seller described as an important work of nutritional science was really just a leaflet of forty-three pages. Its unassuming appearance did not prevent it from becoming popular. In seventeen short chapters, Aggarwal's collection draws together descriptions of physical attributes of non-meat-eating animals and of carnivores, nutritional and financial analyses of diets, lists of the diseases and health risks, religious bans on flesh foods (including Islamic Sufi teachings), and, finally, the moral and spiritual degradations caused by meat eating. The section most pertinent to my argument in this chapter is by an anonymous author who inhabits a goat in the first-person singular. It starts with reminiscences before actual birth and ends in a restaurant, long after the narrator, a slaughtered goat, is dead (Aggarwal 1991: 33–35).

The "Auto-biography" of a Goat

Like all other animals, after traversing through many rebirths, when I entered into my mother goat's womb, and suffered the ignonimity [*sic*] of being encaged there for five months and took birth, I found this world a nice and pleasant place to live in. Man and his little children treated me with affection, held me in their laps and gave me tender green leaves to eat. Drinking my goat-mother's milk, I began to grow quickly. Her master used to pet me and take me to his farm, where I used to feed myself on green leaves. He was not annoyed even when I evacuated my body waste in his field. When I asked my mother the reason for this, I was told that our waste turns into manure for his plants, giving him great yields. That is why he was never angry with me.

Time continued to pass gradually and I went on living contentedly with my companions. After about an [sic] year and a half, a stranger came to my master. They talked for some time and then my master brought together about 40–50 of my companions and we were made to stand in a group. Then a big van arrived there and we were forcibly thrust into it. I wanted to go to my mother, but could not. When I moved toward her, an ugly-looking man hit me with a stick. Helplessly, we squeezed, ourselves in the van. My head began to reel due to over-crowding. My companions were also in bad shape. Fear was writ large on every body's face and the jerks caused by the moving vehicle was scratching out [sic] skins. The day went by and night fell and another day and night passed but the van was constantly on the move. Twice the van-owners threw us some food but it barely sufficed to fill half our bellies. Next day, the van stopped in a big city. A tall, bearded man approached the van, he gave the van-owner something and we were all turned over to him. Our new master drove us with sticks to a house. He made all of us stand in the sun. Restlessness caused by sunshine, hunger and thirst, and to top it the fear of the stick were driving us towards our death.

After a long wait we were pushed into the house. A man sitting there was examining my companions with some tube attached to his ears. When our turn came our owner gave him some thing, and he sent us inside without checking.[7] I could not understand this but a senior companion of mine told me that he was a doctor and it meant our death was approaching us. Already half-dead with hunger, thirst and tiredness, I lost all my appetite on hearing this and could not swallow whatever little was given to us. Even water hurt instead of soothing my throat. Then the door of an adjoining room was opened and what I saw made me tremble with terror. My legs refused to carry my weight and darkness appeared before my eyes. Cries and wails of my companions coming out of that room made me weep. I tried to cry but the voice could not come out of my mouth and throat. I tried to run out but a man caught hold of both my hind legs and threw me into that room where a horrible person looking like a giant was slitting the throat of one of my companions with a massive knife. Suddenly, a thought flashed in my mind. Is this the same man who claims to be the descendant of sages and saints and who always sings songs of pity and nonviolence? No, this cannot be the same man because even wild animals, who are solely dependent on flesh diet, never indulge in such mass killing as he was doing. While such thoughts were passing through my mind, a man caught hold of my ears and pushed me toward that horrible man. The pain now turned my fear into rage, I tried to pull myself away, but in vain. My frustration resulted in boiling of my blood, froth started oozing from my mouth and involuntarily I passed urine and solid waste. But no on took pity on my helpless condition. Rather two other person[s] caught hold of me. One caught me by the legs and the other one started cutting my throat with a dagger. Fountain of blood spurted from my neck and my entire body was filled with pain. Now there was no alternative, but to pray for instant death. I only wished they would kill me with one blow and not prolong my agony. But no, I was destined to suffer more because the knife went only half way through my neck. Death was still far away and every moment of this torture dragged on like a year. Cursing my fate and remembering God, I continued praying and waiting for death.

Darkness gradually began to descend before my eyes and I started losing consciousness. Perhaps breathing had also stopped. It seemed as if I am dead and messengers of death were carrying me to the sky. But wait what is that? My body still lay in that slaughter-house and now two persons were pulling my hide away from the flesh and fat below my hide. They threw my hide on one side and flesh on the other. After some time a person purchased my flesh and took it to the kitchen of a hotel. There a person sliced my whole flesh into small pieces. Probably, all these tortures were too little for this God like man, because it is his hereditary habit to rub salt on the wounds and this was still due. Why they should leave it for me? So after changing my meat to pulp he not only added salt and chillies [sic] but fried me on fire too and thus gave ample evidence of this barbarity. I was wondering what next, when I saw another person arranging my meat in a plate and taking it out of the kitchen into a big decorated room where a young couple was sitting. As soon as the plate was laid before the couple, the male among them started eating my meat with a flourish of delight. But the female sitting opposite him appeared to dislike eating my meat and it seemed that she was just giving company to her husband.

By now, I had reached the court of "Dharamraj" and was standing in the queue of many souls. The loud voice of "Chitragupta," who was narrated [sic] the account of good and bad deeds of everybody, attracted my attention. On my turn, Chitraguptaji revealed that in my previous birth I had feasted on the flesh of a goat. As a consequence of that, I had to born [sic] as goat and offer my meat to others. He also revealed that the persons, I had seen in the hotel eating my flesh were my own loving children of my previous birth, whom I had loved so much that for their sake I had staked everything in life. "Now that they are eating your meat in their present birth, they will have to suffer similar punishments for this in their next birth." Hearing this my soul trembled. How could I like my progeny to suffer the same tortures as had been inflicted on me? I, therefore, requested Dharamraj ji to forgive all of them because I[,] too, had forgiven them and wanted no revenge of any kind. Dharamraj ji took pity on me and graciously ordered that, since as a goat I had eaten only leaves and creepers, and had done no one any harm, and had forgiven everyone, I should be reborn next as a man. My soul was thus sent to earth to take the human life.

Entering into my next re-incarnation, I vowed that now I would behave with the utmost rectitude and be a votary of truth and nonviolence. Far from killing any bird or animal or eating its flesh, I would desist from causing the least pain to any living being, nor do anyone any harm. I would always offer protection to every living being. With these thoughts, I entered the womb of my new mother.

ANIMATE MEAT

In this account of a goat's experiences, the violence of animal slaughter is expanded far beyond the mere act of killing in the slaughterhouse. The text is not only about animal death but also about the animated life in the flesh of an undead goat. The violence of killing flows as "torture" into the activity of both the preparation and consumption of meat. Violence contaminates all persons and activities associated with the animated flesh of the goat-victim. Even the mere witnessing of meat consumption in a restaurant by a wife ends in the horrific revelation of an incestuous cannibal feast of two siblings devouring their own father. How did it come to this?

The goat, after leaving the womb, describes its happy life with a farmer and then the death by the hand of a "bearded man"—the Muslim butcher. The goat is killed in a cruel manner, not with one stroke ("I only wished they would kill me with one blow and not prolong my agony"), a reference to the distinction between Hindu ritual slaughter (*jhatko*) and Muslim ritual slaughter (*halal*). As I mentioned earlier, the Muslim way of slaughter is considered crueler in Gujarat as the animal has to be cut and bled, in order to evacuate the blood, which is considered impure.

After a moment of surprise, the goat's spirit finds itself back in the slaughterhouse after its own physical demise. The author says: "It seemed as if I am dead and messengers of death were carrying me to the sky. But wait—what is that?" Although the goat is now dead it can nonetheless "see" and can "feel" what happens next. In other words, after the goat is killed, its consciousness becomes bifurcated: one part experiences entering the heavenly realm of Dharamraj (the judge of actions), the other witnesses what happens to the remains of its former physical body on earth.

An orgy of violence follows the killing. The goat experiences "changing my meat to pulp," the burning sensation caused by salt and chilies ("hereditary habit to rub salt on the wounds"), the heat of the cooking fire ("fried me on fire too"), and finally the experience of being served and eaten ("arranging my meat in a plate") in the "decorated room" of a restaurant.[8] The separation of material body and spiritual body is blurred. It is as if the spirit, the goat's soul, remains present in its own flesh while being butchered, cooked, spiced, and lastly eaten. The consciousness of the goat is characterized by simultaneity or timelessness. The physical body of the dead goat is animated and still feels pain and thus becomes "tortured." Then the account suddenly stops. But one wonders, why here? Why not continue the voyage of flesh through the digestive organs of the meat eater to its evacuation? Perhaps because the text has already completed its work. It stops after having established a relation between butchering, preparation, and ingestion, a relationship that allows assignation of blame to the butcher, the cook, and the meat eater. This unification of roles—procurement, preparation and consumption—is reminiscent of formulations in the Manu *smirti*, the Hindu law codex (Alsdorf 1962: 577) and elsewhere in the Hindu canon (Bryant 2006: 194–203). But ancient scripture offers a confusing play of contradictory layers of prohibition and permission. While meat consumption is discouraged in one moment it is permissible in another (Alsdorf 1962: 572–578; Doniger and Smith 1991: xv–lxxviii).

The above text wants the cooks and consumers of meat to understand their complicity and guilt in killing by conveying to the reader that life lingers in meat after animal death. When the nonvegetarian eaters look at meat, they are supposed to see a conscious goat, not a mere substance to eat. The eater is supposed to inhabit the goat's flesh, which sees a human being eating it. The eater is supposed to see himself (a goat), seeing someone else eating goat's flesh, a remainder of the narrating "I." The meat eater is supposed to put himself into the meat that he is eating. This perspective powerfully depicts a vegetarian ethos through the evocation of disgust and total identification with the animal victim exemplifying in an astonishingly transparent form what Kolnai (2007 [1929]: 48–55) described as "life's excess" (*Lebensplus*) in the exciting experience of disgust.

This portrait radicalizes ahimsa, which at the time of its emergence as an ethical doctrine explicitly allowed for nonvegetarian consumption so long as the eater of meat was not the killer of the animal, and so long as the animal was not killed explicitly for the eater. There was no disgust at work in this early doctrine. Meat was still permissible, sometimes even preferred, as food (Alsdorf 1962; Schmidt 1968; Smith 1990; Jha 2002: 73), while the contamination of killing was countered either through ritual means or by a ritual division of labor. It was possible to eat meat and still escape the terrible consequences of the animal victim's revenge by not falling under the shadow of its reciprocal violence or the impurity of killing. The complementarity between monk and layperson, or of traditional occupational groups (castes), with their diverse hereditary functions and food habits, secured a workable separation that guarded against the threat of contamination with the violence unleashed by killing. Certain necessary activities were relegated to those in the ritual hierarchy who could complete the work with less danger (Pocock 1973: 81–93).

In the above text, however, complementarity finally collapses and makes room for a complete identification with the animal victim, finally focusing on the remaining flesh itself. The identification is so strong that the victim's spirit is hesitating to ever leave the flesh of the dead animal. The spirit is completely transfixed on the meat-ness of meat. But of course it is the human author's own consciousness in writing that really is the spirit in the dead animal's flesh. That consciousness yields to a reverie in which it somehow cannot let go of this meat. An entire series of persons (the butcher, the laborer, the cook, and the restaurant couple) are portrayed only in their relation to the slaughter of the animal victim and the preparation and consumption of its meat, which is animated and still holds life by retaining consciousness. As if the moral outrage over killing was not enough, the text needs to paint a precise picture detailing the materiality of the killed substance in butchering and eating.

As the finality of death cannot be imagined, the author invests in the animated life after death and creates a figure of the living dead. The author's imagination is spectral. It follows the logic of a Hollywood horror movie, where flesh or body parts become animated and all boundaries have been shifted and are reversed. It becomes questionable whether such an imagination in the register of disgust is the product of compassion, empathy, and care for an animal victim. Compassion for the vulnerability of the living animal, objectified as food and killed by the butcher, is strangely truncated through an obsession with the remaining quivering substance of the kill: animate meat.

The violence of the slaughter contaminates all protagonists of the story. The "bearded" butcher is the killer, the "ugly-looking man" is a daily wage earner,[9] the cook preparing the animal victim for consumption tortures the flesh with his burning spices, the wife of the couple allows her husband to consume the victim's flesh, and the husband eats it. As if that were not enough, however, accountability is also introduced through the transgenerational logic of karmic reaction. The slaughtered goat is not only punished as an individual for the transgression of indulging goat meat in his previous birth, but this punishment includes children eating the flesh of previous generations. The couple in the restaurant morphs into siblings in a previous birth, the son and daughter of the victim's previous birth as a human father. Children eat their own father.

Interestingly, the woman in the restaurant (in this birth a wife to a man, and a sister to her brother in a previous birth) is never actually accused of ingesting meat. Yet at the end of the account she is guilty of participating in the cannibal feast nonetheless. The cannibalism of children eating their own father in the form of a goat, as a punishment for his consumption of goat meat in a previous life, leads them inevitably to rebirth as animal victims themselves in future incarnations. Moreover, any animal that humans can eat potentially could be one's own relative. Not only cannibalism but kinship is invoked here. To the horror of cannibalism is added the horror of imagining being eaten by one's own children or eating one's own father—highly incestuous adumbrations. Meat eating strikes at the center of the social unit: family, incest, and genealogy. In this way the ancient notion of retribution, which was considered a common fate—that what men partake of in this world will eat them in the yonder world unless specific ritual precautions are performed—is substantially radicalized (Alsdorf 1962: 570; Schmidt 1968: 644).

Disgust

Of all the human aversions, the affect of disgust is certainly one of the most powerful. Although less useful compared with anger when trying to focus aggression onto objects, and less contagious than fear, disgust most effectively links mental image to somatic symptom and bodily experience. While hatred easily leads to harming or destroying a particular object, and fear arrests the subject in flight, disgust initially seems less existentially momentous. More a continuous irritation, the experience is accompanied by a strangely magnetic impulse causing the subject to concentrate and focus on, even obsess about, that which is repulsive (Kolnai 2007: 13–20). The intentional structure of disgust directs all attention to specific properties of an object of perception culminating in a form of exploration, which "almost savors its object at the same time that it is revolted by it" (Smith and Korsmeyer 2004: 9).

Most often the disgusting has to do with the collapse of corporeal boundaries and too much proximity through category confusion: food, waste, bodily refuse, and all sorts of organic matter (Douglas 2002 [1966]: 36–50). Proximity, however, does not necessarily precede and cause disgust but rather *accompanies* it. In other words, the aversion recurrently effectuates an experience of invasion by a foreign substance when no objective reason for the propinquity can be found. Indirectly, there is some form of life intuited in the disgusting material: seedy and sordid substances are always somehow animated. Completely inorganic and lifeless materials do not usually arouse strong repugnance. Thus the repellent force of disgust is more frequently about the uncanny life that lingers in death and the rotting corpse is accordingly the nauseating object par excellence.[10]

Disgust is most effectively carried by senses such as smell and taste, touch and sight, while, significantly, not by hearing.[11] Its main domains are food and sexuality, offering possibilities for the oscillation between desire and revulsion, ingestion and evacuation, incorporation and expiation. Physically, disgust causes nausea, sickness, gagging, and even vomiting, as if the poisonous substances were already internal when perceived from a distance or merely imagined, while moral disgust compels contempt, loathing, and abhorrence.[12]

Disgust is fundamentally ambivalent and betrays an attraction caused by the exciting substance. Like fear, it disrupts the existence of a self through a foreign presence, but it does not need to make the object real; it can fantasize its presence as something foreign within (Kolnai 2007: 22). In psychoanalytic language, the affect of disgust is an expression of desire, a strong defense against a particular and forgotten wish that has been rendered unconscious. The relation of and to disgust is an ambiguous one because that which is repressed is still present and effective, more so by the fact that it now wreaks havoc from the position of the unconscious (Freud 1974 [1929/1930]: 229–230). Disgust can thus fuel itself through its own inverse, the unconscious longing for the object, which remains inaccessible, and thus uncontrollable, to the subject, suffering from bouts of disgust.[13]

In the autobiography of a goat, renunciation of the undeniable violence of animal butchery, and the complicity in this violence through the act of eating flesh, is opposed through a series of imaginative pleasures: tortures of the body and mind, invoked as revenge on the cruel or the ignorant but in reality entertaining the hyperbolic vegetarian who lives in bad faith, hallucinating his own nonviolence while simultaneously enjoying the excessive imagery of violence. Vegetarian disgust does indeed spare an animal from becoming a mere object of consumption. But in its cultivated obsession, it feeds on the most cruel and most violent of imaginations. In the attempt to fix a particular substance and its ambivalent appeal to a stable representation that remains morally unambiguous, its own intention becomes subverted through the intervention of a disgusted affection and its morbid hallucinations.

CHAPTER 5

Vibrant Vegetarian Gujarat

IN 2003, NARENDRA MODI, weakened by international criticism of his leadership during the Gujarat pogrom in the previous year, commemorated the 135th anniversary of Mohandas K. Gandhi with a speech in Porbandar, the birth town of the Mahatma. The chief minister reassured Gujaratis of their nonviolent credentials, despite the pogrom, by meditating on "Bapu's principles"—Gandhi's unique blend of social reform, village economy, removal of untouchability, and the Khadi movement. He also devoted considerable time to the "hidden strengths" of Gujarat, that is, to the treatment of animals and vegetarianism:

> Gujarat's main strength lies in its vegetarianism. Most Gujaratis are strict vegetarians. The concept of "*Chappan Bhog*" or 56 different dishes is native only to the Indian context, and more especially to the Gujarat culture.[¹] The beauty of the Gujarat palate lies in its variegatedness [*sic*]. Vegetarianism is the first step for a healthy society. When Gandhiji went abroad at a young age, he took a vow that in any event he would not indulge in the consumption of animal flesh. According to the ancient Vedic texts of India, it is mentioned that there is "fire" or "Agni" in the stomach (*kund*). It is this fire or heat that digests the foods and provides nourishment, and strength to the body as a whole. According to our Sanskrit scriptures, if a vegetable, or fruit, or food grain, is put in fire, then that fire and its container is called a "*Yagya kund*" [vessel or pit for sacrificial fire], but if dead flesh is put in fire, then that fire becomes the fire of a "*shamshaan bhoomi*" [still earth, ground of death, burial ground] or the fire of the funeral pyre. The fire of "*Yagya*" [sacrifice] gives life, energy, strength, and piety, while the fire of the "*Shamshaan*" [crematory fire] consumes and converts dirt to dirt and ashes to ashes.

The distinction Modi drew between *yagya* and *shamshaan*, sacrifice offering life and consumption signifying death, is analogous to that between eating vegetarian and nonvegetarian food, as well as to that between Hindu and Muslim. Those who consume vegetables make a sacrifice by renouncing meat and thus attain life. Those who eat flesh, however, convert themselves into a funeral pyre. They become the death that they have ingested. Thus eating death, as Modi expounded, "converts dirt to dirt and ashes to ashes." In the elaborate cannibal symbolism of Indian mortuary rites, the digestive fire allows for a process of expiation, distilling the good from the bad by consuming the latter and preserving the former. Through fire, sins are consumed while pure essence is preserved (Parry 1985). In Modi's version, the good is distinguished from the bad by reference to substances of ingestion, which determine the outcome of the ritual metabolism.

He continued:

> As per Bapu's principles, vegetarianism is unavoidable for the purity of thoughts and action. It is a kind of purity of means. You reap what you sow. The grains, vegetables, fruits etc. provided by nature are sufficient to maintain life and to gain necessary physical strength. Its moderate use provides best nutrition to our body without any impurities. Our geographic position is not in such a way that we have to maintain our life by killing other animals. From all viewpoints, vegetarianism is the perfect food. Vegetarianism is also a solution to protection of animal life. We have to listen to and understand the pain of speechless animals being taken to the slaughterhouse. Bapu said that it is a very dangerous situation when a dead animal is more precious then [*sic*] a living one. . . .[2]

During the Navratri celebrations in honor of the Mother Goddess that year, Modi again glossed the theme of vegetarianism at the traditional festival. This time he combined the theme with the promise to offer Gujarat *abhaya* (fearlessness), after the disconcerting experiences the year before. In this way Modi started a new "Vibrant Gujarat" campaign to attract international investors to Gujarat in order to counter the large economic losses accrued due to the violence. And yet, to offer *abhaya*—fearlessness—carries a deeper symbolic significance. In the context of world renunciation, *abhaya* is synonymous with ahimsa (Schmidt 1968: 636). The apprentice Brahmin, too, who in the first stage of life takes the vow of nonviolence, offers the world *abhaya*, promising fearlessness to all animate beings (Schmidt 1968: 649, 651). During his spiritual apprenticeship as *brahmachari*, the neophyte is not supposed to eat flesh, kill a living being, or engage in any behavior that is considered contaminated by violence similar to the *sanyasi* (world renouncer). The original reason for this prohibition was that the celibate neophyte was not yet deemed able to ritually counter the reciprocal effects of rebounding violence—*pratikriya*.

During and immediately after the pogrom, the collective violence was explained to be a result of Pakistan-sponsored localized terrorism and of the violent nature of Muslims, which in turn led to the "spontaneous violent reaction" by the Hindu people. Now, however, Modi, with great confidence, promised nonviolence and calm, business as usual. What had been constructed as impulsive and uncontrollable was now rendered tamed and controllable. And it was Modi who implicitly held the key: the power to will or abjure violence.

Although Modi was widely understood to have supported, if not orchestrated, the anti-Muslim pogrom in 2002, he spoke in the voice and birth town of the Mahatma, the father of the nation. Many contemporary Indian politicians share this desired locution and the chief minister of Gujarat invoked the Mahatma not for the first time. Gandhi's name was used repeatedly as a flexible relay between regional subnational pride (*Gujarat ni asmita*) and as a figure of international renown with national scope (Baxi 2002: 3521–3522). Even more significant than the invocation of national unity through Gandhi, however, were the references to diet, sacrifice, and death: three conceptually linked phenomena that were relentlessly articulated in diverse forms during the pogrom. Modi invoked vegetarianism at a moment when Gujaratis were unsure of themselves, when national and international condemnation of the violence of the previous year peaked (Modi was later denied an entry visa to the United States for his involvement in the pogrom), and when political opponents began to taunt the chief minister.

Modi had won reelection in December 2002, and yet doubt was spreading among Gujaratis whether this man whom some called Nakamo—an acronym for N. K. Modi, while the adjective *nakamu* means "useless person" in Gujarati—was not a moral catastrophe for the state. Ultimately, the chief minister survived the storm well, and as I make clear in the postscript, even increasing his popularity by allegedly bringing greater economic development to Gujarat. His invocations of ahimsa through recourse to vegetarianism and *abhaya* cemented his dominant political following. I will return to his speech in Porbandar at the end of this chapter.

BOVINE NATIONALISM

Many traditional institutions in Ahmedabad, and central Gujarat in general, are identified with practices of ahimsa, including animal shelters,[3] popular gurus, Mahatma Gandhi's Sabarmati Ashram, the Institute of Indology (which is mainly an institute for the study of Jainism), social reform organizations, the Ahimsa Research Center at Gujarat Vidhyapit, and numerous vegetarian circles and societies. While most of these organizations pursue ahimsa as nonviolence, there is also a strong discursive affinity between the insistence on ahimsa and militant agitation against any form of animal sacrifice, in particular cow and bull slaughter by Hindu nationalist organizations. In Ahmedabad at least since the early 1990s, privately run cow protection organizations such as the Ahimsa Devi Trust, for example, have systematically combined issues of animal slaughter with extremist anti-Muslim rhetoric explicitly in the name of nonviolence.[4]

This affinity between ahimsa and religious militancy found one of its most acute expressions in recent local politics. In March 2000, the Gujarat Assembly unanimously passed an amendment to a bill, the Gujarat Prevention of Anti-Social Activities Act (PASA, passed in 1985), declaring cow slaughter as well as gambling illegal and punishable. In 2001, the prime minister of India, Atal Bihari Vajpayee, inaugurated a yearlong celebration of the birthday of Mahavira, the Janma Kalyanak of Lord Mahavira. During the inaugural proceedings for the 2600th anniversary of the saint, a Jain Tirthankara, the doctrine of ahimsa was hailed as "India's spiritual and cultural heritage."[5]

From the moment he assumed political office in 2001, replacing Keshubhai Patel, Modi engaged in a micropolitics of ahimsa, which he deployed whenever it seemed convenient. One of his first promises as acting chief minister was to clamp down on illegal slaughterhouses, which in Ahmedabad were incidentally all owned by Muslims. In this, he continued the groundwork laid by the former home minister of Gujarat, Haren Pandya, who had for several years together with local animal-rights activists and cow-protection organizations—including offshoots of the VHP and the Bajrang Dal—pressed for stricter cow-protection legislation.[6]

In the weeks leading up to the Godhra incident, beginning February 2002, Modi announced an "effective drive" against illegal slaughterhouses in cities all over the state, apparently in response to the demands of "Jeev daya organisations." Newspapers alleged illegal cow slaughter by Muslims butchers.[7] A week before Bakri-Id 2002, a Jain organization in Juna Vadaj threatened an agitation (*andolan*) against a mutton shop, which was little more than a small roadside shack. Reportedly, the small mutton shop had opened in a neighborhood where there had never before been any meat sold and thus became an excuse for an offensive.[8] On February 24, in Tankaria village near Bharuch, a young Muslim man was shot dead by the police during a raid in a village in which cows were allegedly slaughtered during the Muslim Bakri-Id festival.[9] Moreover, within weeks of the gruesome pogrom, the Modi government cynically proposed to develop "Ahimsa tourism" and to open a modern "Ahimsa University."[10]

Figure 8: Mr. Shahkahari

Mr. Shahkahari

Coinciding with the start of the pogrom, but delayed several weeks due to the violence, the McDonald's corporation opened a new franchise in a prominent middle-class district of Ahmedabad opposite the former Shiv Cinema on Ashram Road. This McDonald's outlet—allegedly the first of its kind in the world—accomplished what many local nonvegetarian restaurants were never able to offer: two menus, vegetarian and nonvegetarian, on the same premises, without one automatically contaminating the other. Its slightly Indianized American fare addressed openly a vegetarian middle class without offending their sensibilities, despite selling meat dishes.

It collapsed the usual sharp demarcation in Ahmedabad's restaurant business between "pure vegetarian" (*shuddh shakahari*) and nonvegetarian. The advertisement board announcing the new outlet addressed the city residents with "Special treat for Mr. Shahkahari" (figure 8). The mascot, Mr. Shahkahari (literally "Mr. Vegetarian"), was depicted as a slightly overweight, good-natured man with a thin civilized moustache, wearing eyeglasses indicating education. The term *shahkahari* includes a pun, suggested by the green color of the word shah. *Shah* is one of the most common surnames amongst Vaniyas in the city, identified with the strict vegetarianism of Hindu Vaishnavas and Jains. Together with the Patels, many of whom are members of the Swaminarayan *sampradaya*, this segment of society would be most likely to agitate against a local mutton shop in that city area. The advertisement suggested that the fast-food giant offered only vegetarian fare. And, indeed, many residents in the city spontaneously called the new establishment a "vegetarian McDonald's," although factually this was not the case.

Restaurants in Ahmedabad frequently switch fares, converting from vegetarian to nonvegetarian or vice versa, in response to the changing diets of their customers. The food a restaurant offers stands in a significant relationship to its geographic location within the urban spatial matrix segmented by community, caste, and class composition. The establishments are thus sensitive to sociological changes in their surroundings. The more territorial locations of restaurants are in tension with the religious profiles of customers—say, an upper-caste Hindu Vaishnava at a Muslim *tandoori* chicken stall in Jamalpur—the more this tension allows for joyful release. The transgression will often be performed boisterously.

McDonald's, on the contrary, true to its universalizing capitalist spirit, addresses as many socially diverse customers as possible while simultaneously making sure that such precarious indistinction does not alienate its financially most promising customers hailing from the Gujarati middle class which belong mostly to upper castes. There is little lively performance of transgression here, as there is no tension between religious sensibility and marked urban territory. No husband can hide from his wife at McDonald's, since it is a family institution where everyone is supposed to consume jointly. There is arguably only the tension of the wallet as meals at the establishment are considered expensive. As long as you can pay, all customers are treated the same.

There was already a precedent for this McDonald's nearby. In 2001, an all-vegetarian Pizza Hut had opened on CG Road in Ahmedabad, and it soon became a successful venue. A year later and around the same time as McDonald's, a Domino's Pizza opened. The respective marketing strategies of these various fast food restaurants illustrate the challenges that meat posed in Gujarat at the time. If Pizza Hut renounced all meat and diverted attention into the question of mushrooms and onions on their pizzas (both toppings are eaten by many Vaishnavas but not by Jains),[11] Domino's Pizza solved the intractable problem between desire and the transgression of meat with the relative secrecy of private home delivery. McDonald's appeal to the vegetarian elite in the name of its products was an ingenuous solution outmaneuvering Muslim or Sikh restaurants as well as Nepalese street vendors.

The usual reason given for restaurants to convert to a vegetarian fare is that strict vegetarian Gujaratis will not eat vegetarian food in a restaurant that also serves and prepares nonvegetarian food on its premises. Regal Restaurant, for example, a small establishment just a few meters away, had turned vegetarian years earlier to attract a larger clientele in this part of the city. A majority of the strict vegetarians in Ahmedabad will eat no food from a kitchen where the cook has touched and handled putrefied flesh. Plates, utensils, and all cooking vessels, too, are potentially contaminated. A restaurant owner that calls his establishment "vegetarian" but dares to offer meat could face consequences as serious as those facing the mutton seller who is caught selling beef. After the new McDonald's opened, Regal subsequently closed due to competition from the fast-food giant.

In some of Ahmedabad's older cafés and restaurants, one can find a message on hand-painted boards written in Gujarati: "*Nat jatino bhedbhav rakhvo nahi.*" Translated it means "On these premises separation will not be kept." The assertion that separation based on social differentiations will not be kept made the idea of the modern urban restaurant possible in the first place. These messages address the customer and caution that the dishes served are not prepared or distributed differentially by caste or community. An untouchable might drink from the same cup as a Vaniya, sit in the same corner, perhaps at the same table. These boards are fast disappearing, perhaps marking their increasing obsoleteness.

Restaurants are spaces for all castes, communities, and classes to mix in a public place, and mixing is very common, though it is also the major reason why some Gujaratis choose categorically never to eat out or only in carefully chosen venues. The ubiquitous separation between vegetarian and nonvegetarian, the intimacy of cubicles, the partitioned family room, and the engineered darkness in many posh nonvegetarian restaurants express the search for a solution to the problem of how to maintain boundaries when society is slowly divesting them of salience. Some restaurants in socially and ethnically more homogeneous areas cater to this limited upper-caste, middle-class clientele through elaborate daily *puja* performances, such as Rasvatika in Naranpura. Here, sacred sounds echo piously through the neighborhood in the late afternoon for one hour before the restaurant opens, making the gastronomic experience akin to a chaste communal temple feast.

In general, consumers of meat have no qualms about eating in a purely vegetarian establishment. Thus, in certain parts of the city, it is economically wise to offer a vegetarian menu to attract a larger pool of customers. Hence, ironically, in the western part of the city, all Muslim restaurants are strictly vegetarian. How, then, did the American fast-food giant escape this predicament?

Figure 9: Dark consumption in a nonvegetarian restaurant

The new McDonald's outlet is not a vegetarian restaurant in the sense that Regal Restaurant was. It is not a typical high-end meat-eating establishment with darkened glass and private cubicles, either, however. It offers its food in open light, with a visibility like that of purely vegetarian restaurants such as Rasvatika, or the unapologetically nonvegetarian ones like Motil Mahal near the train station in Kalupur, a predominantly Muslim area. Nor does McDonald's offer a food buffet where nonvegetarian dishes are placed on the left and vegetarian dishes on the right like many luxury hotels of the city do.

Instead, in the new McDonald's outlet, color-coding is the key: products and utensils are separated by color. Burgers are neatly wrapped in green paper for "100% vegetarian" and in a pale orange for nonvegetarian. "Meat" is a euphemism for the bland substance of the McChicken sandwich, which has the same consistency and color as the vegetable mix in the McVeggie or McAloo Tikki burger. The restaurant serves 100% eggless mayonnaise, 100% eggless cheddar cheese, and 100% eggless milkshakes. Employees use separate equipment and machines to prepare vegetarian and nonvegetarian items, which is advertised on every menu card. The assembly lines of the restaurant, as well as the menu, are clearly separated into green and orange sections, and all cooks who prepare vegetarian items wear green aprons and are theoretically forbidden to cross into the orange section.

Strict vegetarians, then, can visit the outlet openly, without unease. In contrast to many posh nonvegetarian restaurants in Ahmedabad, the McDonald's outlet heralds complete transparency, avoiding even the darkened glass and intimacy of private cubicles, which is most necessary for the consumption of illicit alcohol that often accompanies carnivorous escapades by vegetarians. Eating at the fast-food outlet heralds a kind of consumption that is not associated with excess, secrecy, or transgression but with modern bourgeois consumption. The only remnant of excess is the routine habit of stealing paper towels from the washroom—the only place that allows for some privacy. Consequently there are never any paper towels available.

The "Special Treat for Mr. Shahkahari" advertised on the billboard at the time of opening described an experience where being vegetarian no longer means feeling excluded from consuming "cosmopolitanism" through the inscription of distinction by orange and green colors. Following the American ethos that anything goes, one can be a vegetarian, but it does not matter. Nothing exemplifies the communicative aspect of meat eating better than this wrenching away of the meat-ness of meat, through the color green, or for that matter, a the pale orange that poses as "red." The clever marketing strategy of the fast-food giant enables the middle class of Gujarat to enter a nonvegetarian restaurant without being contaminated by the meat eaten there. In fact, part of the enticement for customers is to enter a nonvegetarian restaurant *as vegetarians*, the way Gujaratis experience public consumption in Mumbai, New Jersey, or London.

From the use of disposable packages to the paranoid visibility of the kitchen, the restaurant aligns itself well to local sensibilities, signifying the contemporary contradictions of Gujarati vegetarianism. This contradiction comprises the tension between a rich cultural heritage concerning the exchange of food pregnant with sacrificial themes, including the more recent one-sided preference for renunciation, and a new imperative delivered in a loud and clear voice: Consume! The restaurant enables a demonstration of the moral superiority of vegetarianism while pretending to overcome the concrete limitations it sets on desires in modern life. Ingesting America cannot be the same thing as eating death.

This then, illustrates the advent of a new form of vegetarianism: an abstention that no longer simply defines ascetic and particularistic community practices but represents an individual choice to consume as a vegetarian communicated to others. The modern vegetarian no longer has to conceal or abstain, to find compromises by choosing between descent (parental authority), affinity (marital), ritual status (caste), and community. The modern consumer instead assumes an "identity of vegetarianism" in full view of others. In this new context, hiding in full view from one's own secret desires, the traditional compromise that allowed for the curious interplay between taboo and transgression now becomes increasingly read as hypocrisy. But if meat as a substance poses less of a problem once it becomes packaged and assembled as a processed food substance rather than through slaughtering, butchering, and cooking, what happens to the signification of meat?

The Hyperbolic Vegetarian

The ethnographic examples in the preceding chapter illustrate the communicative aspect of meat and the idiomatic forms that stigmatization assumed. In all three cases—Sejal, Mr. Chauhan, and Ranjit—the qualities that are rejected and denied coalesce in the image of a phantasmagoric figure. From this figure speaks back the danger of excess, but to some degree this danger becomes stabilized and confined in its representation, which marks one of the few points where there is stability in the discourse of distinction between Hindus and Muslims.

The effects of identification with the phantasmagoric figure of the Muslim are not always stable, however. At one time, Sejal condemned Muslims for their supposed subdued aggressiveness, but at other times she related with great tenderness to her Muslim female students. Her focus on aggressive male sexual behavior, she argued, crisscrossed all ethnic and religious boundaries. Alternatively, Mr. Chauhan claimed to have a Muslim best friend. Both he and Ranjit were greatly amused by sayings and jokes that rebuke and make fun of upper-caste claims to vegetarian purity and nonviolence (of which there exist many in Gujarat). It was in the moment of high tension, during the pogrom and its aftermath, that all three interlocutors defensively insisted on the exaggerated stereotypes as if they needed to assure themselves of something they did not completely believe in.

In the following section I hope to shed light on a less equivocal and more severe form of identification, what I am calling hyperbolic vegetarianism. Through a case study of an upwardly mobile member of what is generally conceived of as a "lower" social category, a proponent of Hindutva, I explicate how articulation and confinement into representations that stigmatize do not lay to rest an existential threat. The case focuses on a specific new form of cultivated digestive disinvestment: identification *with* and *of* disgust. Here, meat is experienced as the veritable risk it can pose to the subject's own sense of coherence with a fragile self.

RAW CHICKEN COLLAPSE

It was an inauspicious moment for a vision of *mas* (flesh) when, on February 8, 2002, Bharat, one of my Hindu roommates in the city of Ahmedabad, described to me the first time in his life that he saw raw meat. As described earlier, Chief Minister Modi had begun his campaign to close down illegal slaughterhouses, and newspapers alleged illegal cow slaughter by Muslim butchers (see above). On February 24, in the village of Tankaria near Bharuch, the police killed a young Muslim man during a raid. During the Muslim Bakri-Id festival, cows had allegedly been slaughtered. Things would get much worse. The stage for sacrifice was set.

Bharat's encounter with raw meat had happened in 1998 in Ahmedabad. Though raised in the countryside, he explained, he had never before seen uncooked meat. Hence his shock one day when he went to Lal Darwaja, in the old city center, and by accident walked right into the chicken market at Patwa Sheri, a small lane with Muslim-run fish and meat shops: "I got sick; disgust overwhelmed me. I saw a raw chicken. I had no idea what I was getting into. I walked right into the area. Suddenly I saw something hanging from a hook, just next to me. I looked up and I saw it hanging. 'This is a chicken,' I thought. 'This is a chicken.' Then I began to gag."

Bharat's face turned serious as he narrated; he portrayed his reaction graphically, gagging several times to demonstrate. The light aluminum armchair on which he sat creaked loudly under his movements. "I sat down after the gagging. I had to catch my breath. Then I vomited, and someone brought me a glass of water. I sat there for five minutes. Then I returned the same way I had come, and I have never gone back into this area of the city again. For three days, I could not eat. I always saw the chicken on my plate." Bharat exited the lane the very same way the food exited his body: that is, he went backward (*bekwad*), much as his vomiting (*ulti*) was meant to reverse ingestion, to turn something inside out.

Almost three weeks after Bharat told me of this harrowing first encounter with meat, on the morning of February 27, 2002, we heard the news of the Godhra incident. Bharat understood the fire on the train in Godhra as having been provoked and instigated by Pakistan in collaboration with local Muslims who, in his view, had acted as proxy agents of the enemy state. He described the scenes on the streets of Ahmedabad that followed as a legitimate punishment of the Muslim community as a whole, something that had to be done. The ongoing pogrom violence, he said, was "purification" (in English). Several months later, he illegally purchased what is locally called a "country-made revolver."[12]

"Edukashun" in the City

I first met Bharat in 1999, when his guru and academic adviser at Gujarat University recommended that he share a room with a foreigner from America who was going to do research and language study in Gujarat. He was a thin, meticulously groomed man, with a closely trimmed moustache and oiled hair smoothed to one side. Bharat was in his mid-twenties at our initial encounter, and he wore his best, gold-embroidered *kurta* and brand-new sandals. He spoke no English, nor did he address me in Gujarati, but he ceremoniously handed me a red rose, a token of our future friendship and gesture of welcome to India. The shy farmer with the red flower is a memory that has stuck with me.

At that time, I had already completed an intensive field study between 1995 and 1996 in rural Gujarat. I was, however, unfamiliar with urban Gujarat. Bharat and I began to experience Ahmedabad together. In the following years, whenever I lived in Hindu neighborhoods, I invited Bharat to live with me for free. He always thankfully accepted the offer, as the student hostels were in lamentable shape and became especially hazardous after a devastating earthquake in 2001.

Bharat came from a family of farmers (*khedut*), but he left the farm business behind to live in Ahmedabad. He never told me so, but I suspect that this decision was reached shortly after the sudden death of his father, which elevated him prematurely to the male head of his extended family household. At around the time his father died, in 1991, Bharat joined the RSS in his home village—"*mara imej mate*," as he explains, "for my image."

For the RSS, he at first only served food at marriage functions and did kitchen work, activities he calls "social work." But today he has become the most successful export from his home village to the big city. Farming needs water, and after years of drought in Gujarat, water has become scarce. Degrees are readily available, however, and therefore they are more accessible for someone like Bharat than is water for farming. To send the oldest son off to become a teacher while the younger one stays home to tend the fields is the family's first step in obtaining an urban foothold in government service.

Bharat's kin tried to emulate what they had seen many Patel farmers do in generations before them. The Patels of Gujarat, the Patidars were once classified as Shudra, the fourth Varna associated with lower status (Pocock 1972b: 29), a fact alluded to today only with nervous circumlocutions. The two main caste branches of Patel now belong to the most economically successful as well as politically powerful groups in all of Gujarat. Many are members of the middle classes and have relatives in the United States, especially in New Jersey.[13] When talking to members of the Patel community in Ahmedabad, one will often hear "Edison," "Elizabeth," or "Metuchen," place names that have a spectral ring to Bharat but are definite destinations of relatives for members of the Patel community.

Our life together, always in strictly vegetarian Hindu middle-class housing societies, and often joined by friends and caste brethren from the countryside, soon became routine. Bharat treated me as his *mota bhai* (older brother); he usually prepared food and took care of the household while I paid the bills. Given my prior field experience in rural Gujarat, I insisted on occupying a separate room where I could work at any time of day or night—drawing my boundary. Bharat soon complained that whenever I was traveling he felt lonely in the large apartment building, especially at night, when the empty and quiet darkness of a large middle-class flat caused him to have nightmares. Bharat consequently invited Pratab, a fellow caste member and friend from a neighboring village, to live with us, and I consented. Bharat had soon delegated all housework to Pratab. Although the youngest of our group, Pratab was no bachelor. His wife and children remained in his home village with his parents while he pursued a degree in Hindi at Gujarat Vidhyapit, a university founded by Mahatma Gandhi. Pratab, who planned to write a thesis on Gandhi, treated both Bharat and me as his gurus and older brothers. We three, then, lived together for about seven months.

At Gujarat University, where I was still studying Gujarati, the knowledge that Bharat and Pratab were cooking daily for me, the Westerner, soon led to a series of inquiries among my teachers, as well as suggestions for alternatives. When I once complained about a stomachache, for example, they quickly questioned Bharat's cooking with medical, if not alchemical, precision. At another time, I grumbled in passing about the excessive oil in the food that I had eaten (which caused me considerable weight gain). I was advised with sudden sternness to seek out another cook.

One teacher explained that the overuse of oil (*tel*) in food was a sure sign of the *guna* of *tamas* (attribute of darkness): that is, of typical *tamasi* food. Food that is considered *tamasi* in Gujarat carries negative associations, as it is linked with poor intellectual abilities (mental slowness and inertia), lustful thoughts (sexual rapaciousness), and proneness to violence (bloodlust) in those that consume it—signs of weak control of the passions. I initially found these reactions very puzzling, but I came to understand that while Bharat and Pratab kept strict vegetarian diets, their academic superiors nonetheless continuously ascribed to them typical lower-caste practices, such as the consumption of nonvegetarian food, which for them has unambiguously negative connotations.

For example, one day my Gujarati language class was rescheduled to the early afternoon. My teacher commented on the smell of onions on my breath—an intimate remark that took me by surprise. Indeed, I had eaten lunch in the university cantina together with Bharat, as I normally did, shortly before the class. The cheap lunch was purely vegetarian and included two dishes: *khichadi* (rice and lentils) and the usual salad of raw onions mixed with lime juice. For my teacher the smell of raw onions (or garlic, for that matter) was not only disgusting but also, and more importantly, indicative of nonvegetarian food habits. While she sought to ease my embarrassment, she was less generous about someone like Bharat, whom she considered *asanskari* (uncivilized). The incident reminded me of my first German girlfriend, whose parents complained that their daughter smelled like garlic after she had spent time at my home.

What surprised me were three things. First, the sincere sense of revulsion that my teacher displayed; second, the generosity she showed me, the foreign student, after my continuous lapses; and third, the unambiguous rejection she expressed for Bharat. It was as if her generosity toward me had been subtracted from him. The German version of olfactory rejection stressed not so much a purported lack of civilization, but rather a pronounced cultural alterity.[14] Muslim women, in turn, will often opine with a mocking smirk that Hindu men must be passing gas all the time when engaged in sexual intercourse, because they ate too many vegetables not easily digestible.

According to Bharat, his initial motivation to come to the city and enter a university was a desire to teach and aid the educational progress of his community, the Jadav, whom he considers largely "illiterate" (*abhan*). For Bharat "*edukashun*" is the attribute that distinguishes Jadav from those groups whom he calls "*unchusthan*" and describes as "higher-level *upar*," such as the successful Patels, Vaniyas (Hindu Vaishnava and Jain merchant groups), and Brahmins. I once asked Bharat why out of all possible disciplines he had chosen to study the subject of Gujarati, given that it is the least likely degree to translate easily into a prospective job. He replied, somewhat indignantly, "But I am Gujarati."

He used the same intonation when saying "I am Hindu"—as if these two identities were intertwined, if not altogether the same, and could be taken away from him. To Bharat it made sense to study what one is, that is, Gujarati. This claim, however, meant much more than simply membership in the state of Gujarat as a linguistic and political entity. Today, being a Gujarati also unambiguously denotes being a Hindu. As indicated in chapter 4, members of the numerous Muslim communities of the city would not call themselves Gujarati, as this term is exclusive of the term Muslim, even though many Gujarati Muslim communities identify strongly with the state, speak fluent Gujarati as a first language at home, and are distinguishable in many ways from Muslims in other parts of India.

Bharat's academic advisers explained to me that language study for someone like Bharat is an appropriate discipline because with language comes cultivation, which he lacked (*sanskar* = "politeness, respect"; and *sanskruti* = "civilization," like the German *Kultiviertheit*). Bharat's main academic adviser, his guru, told me bluntly, "Bharat is not smart, but loyal." In other words, Bharat is still in the process of becoming a proper "Gujarati."

Bharat aspired to be a successful man from a locally respected family. And indeed he seemed to command considerable status in his rural home. When I visited his family and kin in his natal village, his younger brother Mahesh proudly showed me sacks full of stored grain millet worth tens of thousands of rupees. We visited Bharat's school friend who had taken the vow of celibacy and decided to become a world renouncer. He lived as a celibate at a local Hanuman temple and officiated as a temple priest. Bharat talked to his old friend as if they were two entrepreneurs meeting after many years of separation; one was successful in the business of religion, the other in the business of academia.

We rode on a fancy blue tractor to inspect the fields and to do worship for Bahuchar Mata—the family *kuldevi* (lineage goddess)—at the small temple in the middle of a sizable piece of land. At night, the usually very taciturn Mahesh offered me the *hukkah* pipe and cigarettes to smoke but made me promise not to tell his brother. All the neighbors laughed and giggled, as Bharat had acquired, in his new life in the city, the annoying habit of calling everyone to order for their bad habits.

When Bharat was in the city, however, he evoked a different sense of origin. Despite his landownership, savings from stored agricultural produce, and high status among his village peers, Bharat referred to himself as "poor" (*gharib*) and his kin at home as "backward." The Jadavs are *nadoda rajput*, a *pachhat varg* (a backward class), classified among the other backward classes (OBC; see Parikh 1998: 75). Since the implementation of the Mandal Commission recommendation in 1990, 27 percent of government-related jobs are reserved for other backward classes such as his.[15] In the city, Bharat's insecurity about the status to which he can aspire led him to calibrate his behavior strategically and with caution.

When speaking of the social status of his community, the Jadavs, Bharat employed no Gujarati term; he instead used the English word with a local twist: "bekwad." The Gujarati language contains many adjectives associated with groups considered backward: for example, *halka loko* (inferior people; *halku* means "low, thin, light"), which is usually contrasted with *ujliyat loko* (literally, "the radiant people"), denoting members of either traditionally higher castes or symbolically prestigious communities. For Bharat, the term *halku* conjured up something dirty and disgusting, from which he always wanted to distance himself. Bharat stressed that the Jadavs are *bekwad*, not *halka* (that is, backward but not inferior); they are perhaps *abhan* but not *nich* (that is, illiterate but not low). While he never called his own community low or inferior, but only *bekwad*, he was less careful when describing other groups.

Although both Bharat and Pratab came from the same community, they had different personalities. While Pratab had a friendly nature, an almost effervescent jolliness all around and about him, which allowed him to befriend easily the daughter- and mother-in-law of the neighboring Patel apartment (for example, cutting vegetables for lunch together with them), Bharat was a more solemn figure, with a stiff demeanor, and was overly self-conscious. Although he did have a sense of humor, others did not often laugh with him.

Once when we visited by foot the drive-in cinema in the north of the city, he almost provoked a fistfight with a terrified young man who accidentally touched his arm with a cloth while cleaning the tables of an eatery. At another time, when a street tea seller overcharged me, Bharat threatened him with violence by his entire natal community. To be fair, these were exceptions to his usual behavior. But they reflect his tendency to take his own masculinity seriously, perhaps because he then was still unmarried, while Pratab, who already had two children, felt more confident in that respect.

Both, however, shared a rejection of Muslims, and saw in Hindutva the logical extension of proper democratization—the fact that the majority should have its way in the face of a recalcitrant minority, the Muslims. In the competitive atmosphere of Ahmedabad, Hindutva seemed to prop up who they wanted to be: Hindus. But while Pratab often voiced the circulating stereotypes and rumors about Muslims, he was nonetheless uninterested in political matters and somewhat immune to a more pervasive anti-Muslim rhetoric. Bharat, however, took things much more to heart, possessing an earnestness that led him to be more active during the 2002 pogrom.

In the many years we knew each other, Bharat never found it important to tell me that he was a member of the RSS, although he knew perfectly well my interest in the organization's ideology and national-ritual practices. This, it turns out, is an experience I share with many Gujaratis, especially with Muslims. Many local Muslims told me that more than anything else that had happened in the eventful history of communal alienation in the state, the discovery that a Hindu friend, neighbor, or colleague was working for the RSS led to strong feelings of betrayal. For many, such betrayal began years before the violent events of 2002, or even before similar events in 1992–93. One Muslim acquaintance traced its origins back to the aftermath of the 1969 communal violence in the city, when he realized that one of his best friends was encouraging his son to engage in RSS activities.

Yet I have met no Muslim who ever actually confronted his friend or neighbor with these feelings, which in any case are only rarely expressed directly. Whenever I suggested to Muslims that they break their silence and address suspicions and concerns about RSS membership openly, I was accused of being naive. Insistence, they said, could lead only to the eruption of a dangerous cycle of disputes among neighbors, acquaintances, and "friends"; they were satisfied with an uneasy but peaceful calm.

Shortly after the pogrom had begun, Bharat told me how his involvement with the RSS had started. I had expressed shock about the absence of the rule of law on the streets of Ahmedabad and the organization's obvious involvement in the violent mob scenes that I personally witnessed. Consequently, our discussions became more directly political and confrontational. Busy with his studies, he had not visited a local branch of the RSS for some time, but after the pogrom he became involved again and proudly showed me his khaki uniform. At around the same time, Bharat's academic advisers told me that they, too, had formerly been members of the RSS but no longer agreed with all of the organization's goals.

Assimilating Lack

Like many of his peers, Bharat does not speak English well, and his lack of marked improvement while living with me led others to attribute his slow progress to the stigma associated with his social background. Yet, I found Bharat very astute in his selection of English words. Some listeners perceive his selective use of English simply as betraying his low educational status; despite his studies, his use of foreign words and concepts reveals a fundamental unfamiliarity with a wider English-speaking world. In this regard, he is quite unlike many bilingual professionals; at the same time, he is also unlike the large number of residents in the city who, despite weak active English skills, will nonetheless fall into what a linguistics professor in Varodara has referred to as "Gujarezi."

Gujarezi is used mainly in Ahmedabad and Varodara in varied forms that depend on the English vocabulary and general linguistic competency of the speaker. For the most part this linguistic practice is incomprehensible to a non-Gujarati speaker, as English words are imported into Gujarati syntax and pronounced in accordance with Gujarati phonetic rules. By contrast, in Bharat's use of English words, there is a more decided semantic shift at work, with an even stronger indigenization of concepts and words whose similarity to English can obscure differences of meaning.

Bharat has never attended a school where English is taught or taken an English-language course at the university, nor did he ever enjoy a movie in English. He takes in English words through the Gujarezi that he hears practiced on the street. His selective appropriation of new words—a practice he shares with his peers, like Pratab—is a formidable technique for incorporating the modern world of the city, as he essentially assimilates its power in order to overcome his relative lack. Although these words will not appear in standard Gujarati dictionaries, their experimental and creative use evolves into collective understandings.

For example, Bharat refers to techniques of dress and style in the city as productive of "*personaliti*"; to communal conflagrations, marital conflict, or sexual frustration as "*tenshun*"; to the wished-for outcome of job interviews, class presentations, marital negotiations with affines, or first scenes in Bollywood movies as the power of "*entri*"; and to all sorts of transgressive behaviors involving wasteful expenditure as "*enjoi*."

As already mentioned in chapter 2, the term *enjoi* was widely used by young men like Bharat on the streets during the pogrom to refer to rape, looting, and the destruction of Muslim bodies and property. Initially taken from the very successful Coke commercial "Enjoy, Enjoy!" that entered India some time in the 1990s, *enjoi* is incorporated into typical Gujarezi constructions, such as in *enjoi leva mate* (in order to enjoy). *Enjoi* reaches into the semantics of the Gujarati verb *bhogavavu* (to enjoy, to suffer) and the noun *bhog* (pleasures, the victim of a sacrifice) and expresses the idea of excessive and wasteful consumption. The deployment of this term suggests how economic liberalization and the circulation of new goods in an atmosphere of accelerated consumption is experienced and assimilated by a younger generation. Its semantic differences from the English word point to ways in which the term reaches deep into the collective unconsciousness of Gujaratis.

The words *personaliti* and *entri* are employed in different but not completely unrelated ways. Bharat often insisted borrowing a leather belt of mine, bought in an expensive traveler's store in Berlin many years earlier, that he fancied. The belt had an elongated hidden pouch on its inner side where I used to keep my *Notgroschen*—emergency cash kept ready in case of sudden illness or accident. Many of my Gujarati friends were fascinated with the secret device and fantasized about what else could be hidden in it. Whenever Bharat had to give a presentation in class, he asked to borrow this belt.

Bharat enjoyed his class presentations, in which he declaimed wise sayings and recited poems with spiritual value. With great concentration, he practiced at home in front of a minuscule mirror for hours, memorizing the smallest details of gesture, rhythm, and tone. When he practiced, he acted as if he stood in front of an attentive audience wearing a clean, freshly pressed white shirt, a black leather belt, a watch with a golden wrist band (he did not like mine, which was a silver Sonata watch), and spit-polished shoes. Naturally, I was Bharat's audience.

Entri is the power of catching someone else's gaze. It can be wielded with the help of a fancy belt, a wristwatch, an expensive pen in one's shirt pocket (a symbol of literacy), or an impressive motorbike. This desire to stand out and be gazed at is the inverse of the traditional threat of being looked at desirously, the fear of *najar* (the effect of the evil eye): both belong to the same class of phenomena. The gaze is powerful, whether desired here or feared there—be it in *entri* or *najar*—and loses none of its potency. Bharat is not afraid of jealous looks. In fact, he often desires to be the recipient of a gaze that might betray the jealousy of others.

When I asked Bharat to offer me another example of the phenomenon of *entri*, he mentioned Bollywood movies in which the actors' frequent entries to and departures from the screen are highly stylized. Within the same movie, the main hero or heroine may make many different entrances, each time in new clothes and with a different musical overture. Audiences frequently welcome these scenes with a sigh of pleasure, a call, or some other sound of recognition. The assortment of outfits and other accoutrements that the actors display are studied and, if possible, copied. The staging of the entry of hero or heroine has a particular aesthetic importance.

The cinematographic practice is also reminiscent of the sequencing of Vaishnava worship in Gujarat, in which love and care for the deity take the form of an elaborate *puja* (worship ritual). The anthropomorphic image is undressed, bathed, and then dressed and adorned again with clothes and jewelry. And the practice by which Bollywood superstars such as Amitabh Bachhan, Shah Rukh Khan, and Ashwarya Rai are divinized in their own right through temples and shrines is regarded with amused detachment by Bollywood fans.

Bharat's *personaliti* and *entri* concerned first appearances in encounters, which manifest the essence of a person (*vyaktitva*) expressed through a mark, sign, or symbol of recognition (*olakh*). The fetishistic power of the object that promises to produce such *entri* was supposed to cancel out the initial impression made by his name and appearance, permanent qualities linked to caste and class. Bharat tried to get rid of *bekwad*-ness and did not want to be confused with *halka*. He tried to take control of the identification he was in danger of being subjected to. The point is that the techniques to produce *personaliti* and *entri* can be learned, managed, and manipulated. They are supplemental devices that seem to make possible control over what Bharat was in constant danger of signifying in the city.

When Bharat stood in front of the tiny mirror that he had been able to save from the student hostel (where items change owners so frequently),

his skin dark against his freshly pressed and starched white shirt, he reminded me of my father, an Iranian who immigrated to Germany, as I
knew him in my childhood years. Standing in front of his own reflection,
Bharat performed *entri* to himself, imagining the way he might appear
to others, trying to perfect that magic of charisma that might allow him
entrance into the world of the city. Whereas my father had picked up
the obsessive practice of wearing dark ties, white starched shirts, and
fancy suit jackets from watching black-and-white Hollywood movies in
Teheran in the 1950s, Bharat took on the style of urban Indian university
students, replacing his usual *kurta* with pants and shirt.

And like my father, when Bharat became aware that I was watching
him at his most beautiful self, he could turn the fantasy into irony, joking about his smartness and sophistication to make me laugh. He often
teased me about neglecting style in clothing (reminding me of my father's
disapproval)—a bad habit I picked up in the bizarre timeless and classless
space of cold war Berlin in the 1980s, where the West German government subsidized housing, education, and public life to compete against
the alleged attraction of state-sponsored socialism in the east. Only in
the mirror, with the belt around his thin waist, did Bharat find a self that
made sense to his aspirations and that enabled him to be generous. I really liked him in these moments.

Boundary and "Weakness"

In our daily conversations, Bharat often referred to his *maryada* (boundary, limitation, modesty) as his "weakness" (in English). This weakness—a space within him, which he maintained as unreflected—found no
expression in his village but must instead have developed, or taken concrete form, after he arrived in the city. His professor and guru at Gujarat
University had initially identified this "weakness" as a strong disdain for
Muslims, which was why he explicitly told Bharat to live with me, a foreigner sporting a Muslim name. Over the years, Bharat himself repeated,
"Muslims are my weakness."

In making this claim, Bharat meant that he could lose his balance,
his temper, in relation to Muslims. He could "lose it," so to speak, in
relation to "them" (that is, lose grip over the boundary that separates
him from them—*maryada*). Violence between Hindus and Muslims in
Gujarat emerges when this boundary, which separates them by rules of
modesty and limitation, is lost. Such violence is intimate, because it becomes possible when the boundary evaporates. Violence is an effect of
too much closeness, not too much distance. In cases of mixed marriages,
for example, the transgression of marital boundaries is often considered

a violent act in itself, thereby legitimating communal posturing (and the logic of "reaction"—*pratikriya* or *pratighat*).

The shocking positive attitude of many Gujaratis—Muslims and Hindus alike—toward violence cannot be comprehended if one fails to recognize the authority generally possessed by such boundaries. Community and caste boundaries are, from this perspective, a sort of frozen violence—petrified into structures that keep communities apart in some respects while allowing for innocent interaction in specific contexts.

But though Bharat followed his professor's advice to live with me, and thus struggled with his weakness, he did not overcome it. On the one hand, his views conformed to the dominant discourse in central Gujarat, which stigmatizes Muslims as abject. On the other hand, he identified me—his vice-ridden, higher-status, light-skinned, German-born, American-educated roommate—as a Muslim, and he initially had trouble making sense of me. In fact, despite all the vices I engaged in, some of which, like meat consumption, are stereotypically linked to Muslims, he came to treat me genuinely as a friend.

Like many other Gujaratis, Bharat views religion (*dharma*) as a matter not simply of belief (*manyata*) but also of group membership, which implies much more than just philosophical or spiritual orientation. *Dharma* is connected to forms of social organization as well as to what one does, whom one marries, what one eats, and whom one interacts with on what basis. Consequently, marriage and conversion are understood to be synonymous. My insistence not to signify anything in the register of religion, despite my Iranian-born father, always seemed phony to Bharat and others. He understood the marriage between an Iranian man and a German woman as one between a Muslim and a Christian, which made me irrefutably Muslim. In this regard, Bharat's perceptions of me did not differ from those of local Muslims.

In retrospect, I must admit that he was correct, in a way, because I not only sported what he considered a Muslim name and knew no dietary boundary in relation to meat, but I also constantly crossed into the local Muslim world without hesitation, visiting Muslim neighborhoods, religious sites, and houses. Although I initially asked him to accompany me, he never did (unlike other Hindu friends who did). Muslims in Ahmedabad, in turn, seemed eager to incorporate me as one of their own from overseas. Thus I became, in a very special way, Bharat's "Muslim acquaintance"—the one Muslim he could deal with despite his prejudices about those belonging to that category.

While touring Bharat's home village with him, I became aware that he had already introduced me everywhere as a Muslim. He did this again in my presence, even after I had corrected him several times. Given the extreme anti-Muslim atmosphere in the state, I was not too pleased with this loss of control over my signification. Bharat, now a local success, had obviously taken steps to overcome his "weakness," as his guru had advised him to do. He was just showing off his "Muslim friend." Back in the city, he introduced me to people as "Amerikan," a practice that I had grudgingly assented to, as the category "Jarman" (German) seemed not to make much sense to him.

That I could alternately signify what is most desired or most despised, "Amerikan" or "Muslim," speaks ardently to the intertwined logic of stigma and phantasma at work in these identifications. Yet there might be another factor at work. The Muslim population of Bharat's home village consisted of two houses of the Fakirani Jat, a poor Muslim community in the region whose members work as ritual specialists at Muslim shrines. Muslims today often ridicule this community for being too "Hindu," and it occupies an unequivocal low social status. The only other Muslim presence in the area was spectral by contrast: the descendants of the former royal family of a nearby regional town, who now live in America. While Bharat claimed that his own community was exploited and persecuted by these former Muslim rulers, his maternal grandfather told me that relations between the Jadavs and the ruling Muslim family were fine.

Although I was living mostly a vegetarian life with Pratab and Bharat, I did eat street food and visit nonvegetarian restaurants and Muslim homes. For Bharat, nothing signified "Muslim" more strongly than "meat," and his insistence on calling me a Muslim (despite the fact that as a German I do not hesitate to eat pork) is consistent with his refusal to ever consider such dietary ventures "cosmopolitan," a common euphemism employed to excuse the consumption of nonvegetarian food in urban Gujarat. My own association with meat is mostly with a festive German *Sonntagsbraten* (Sunday roast) or *Weihnachtsganz* (the roasted goose served at Christmas), which, deposited in the middle of a large table, is a symbol of extended collective commensality with friends and family—inclusive of wine, cigarettes, and vibrant late-night talk. For him, instead, meat connoted the absence of all that is funny.

Bharat, who thought of himself as a *pakka hindu* (a staunch Hindu), was annoyed by my inability to feel shame or hide my occasional indulgences. A middle-class Dalit whom Bharat knew dissimulated his own meat-eating behavior in Bharat's presence. Although we had eaten meat together many times, this friend frequently, in my presence, claimed to third parties that he was a pure vegetarian. For him, this behavior constituted not hypocrisy but a "smooth style" of social behavior: the absence of the desire to hurt religious sensitivities. I, by contrast, initially did not understand how to manage my "vices"; nor could I later bring myself to adhere absolutely to a strict vegetarian regime or misinform about what I had ingested. In many ways my stubborn insistence on remaining utterly transparent in such matters was rude, and it certainly did not give "Jarman" a good name.

To befriend and even live with a meat eater like myself, Bharat risked disapproval for his association with a "lower category." Yet I, frequently identified as Muslim, also commanded an enviable status when I interacted with academics, religious authorities, activists from nongovernmental organizations, neighbors, shop owners, and businessmen. There was a generosity and forgiveness displayed towards that which Bharat considered my aberrations—meat eating, wine drinking, smoking—that puzzled him. Bharat was reminded of what he lacked precisely because he so strongly aspired to it himself. It was highly unlikely that he would ever receive such a reprieve in these matters.

Bharat's near reverence for some of the status that I commanded automatically led him to overlook the real reason for his own weakness: he was a farmer in the city, a member of the OBC (other backward classes), in a society that harbors many silent prejudices against rural villagers known for their "roughness" (asanskari, dhamaliyu). The attractiveness of categories such as "Gujarati" and "Hindu" lies in their promise to efface and overcome these firm stigmas.

For Bharat, nationalist organizations like the RSS or the Vishva Hindu Parishad (World Hindu Council, or VHP) were not simply protectors of the Hindu nation, but they also were knowledgeable about "culture" (sanskrutini jane chhe).[16] He explained to me that if there existed any form of maryada (limitation, boundary, modesty), then the memory of it should be kept (je maryada che ene janvi rakhvu); and if there existed any custom, then that too should be protected (ritrivajo sachvi rakhva). Thus "culture," for him, essentially consisted of rahenikarni (the manner of living; the way of doing things) and khanipini (the manner of eating and drinking; what is eaten and drunk).

Bharat's conceptions of commensality and traditional boundaries of caste coalesced with the discourse of the Hindu nation, in which the definition of "culture" was reduced to certain core symbols that are conveniently deployed in electoral campaigns—the politics of yagya and yatra (sacrifice and pilgrimage). In political discourse, this has led to a proliferation, even preference, for blatant Hindu kitsch—a fetishistic version of tradition, easily appropriated and used (Rajagopal 1999: 135). Second-generation nationalisms often come in the form of an "awakening" to an imagined aboriginal essence that, even if historically associated with elites, is suddenly accessible horizontally to everyone (Anderson 1991: 195). Along these lines, the defensive and authoritarian use of identity and culture can be understood as a reaction formation against the experience of the self splintering, pulled in too many different directions by new temptations. Bharat's defense, his maryada, helped him fortify his sense of self against the effects of capitalist consumer fragmentation, a self constantly attacked, and often defeated, by so many seductions, so many occasions to experience lack.

In the stern rage of the *pakka hindu,* there lies a promise of something as yet unadulterated by the ugly compromises and corruptions of city life, where boundary maintenance can conflict with access to what one secretly desires. An aggressive response to a perceived injury can, from this perspective, become a sign of authenticity, and complicity in violence can then be explained apologetically in terms of uncontrollable emotions or affects. In short, Hindutva organizations not only protect Hindu neighborhoods from Muslims but also, and perhaps more importantly, protect Hindus from themselves, from the possibilities of their own desires. They fortify what Bharat referred to as his *maryada* regarding Muslims, an impulse to maintain an emotional distance that was his "weakness." Bharat knew he did not like Muslims, because they were identified socially as a threat, but his feelings concerning Muslims were more anguish about those aspects of himself that he shared with them. These were the same feelings he shared with members of lower-caste or tribal groups that differentiated them, according to local logic, from proper Hindus. His academic advisers identified those same qualities in him: lack of restraint and self-control, unsophistication, inertness, illiteracy, and uncleanliness of mind and body.

These negative stigmas were not, however, affixed to me, the meat-eating "American Muslim" who received an automatic recognition that Bharat did not. Bharat was not invited into houses for dinner, or approached flirtatiously by upper-caste Hindu women of the middle class, as I was. None of these women would ever criticize him because he ate too much garlic or his breath smelled of onions. Bharat complained about this, realizing that it signified a lack of *entri.*

I am unsure, even after the passage of time, how our friendship was able to sustain itself through these events. For me, the experience of the pogrom changed things dramatically. Bharat's self-conscious and calm affirmation of the pogrom violence angered me greatly at the time and even made me mistrust him for a while. Following the advice of concerned friends, I moved away from Hindu middle-class Naranpura in West Ahmedabad, where we had been living, to Shah Alam, a Muslim area in the eastern part of the city.

Although we met each other frequently, it took Bharat almost a year to come visit me in my "Muslim flat," as he called it, a middle-class apartment building not unlike the ones we had lived in together. By then, with the help of an RSS uncle, he had married, obtained a job of lecturer at a college, and was expecting his first child. In 2005, Bharat bought a fancy middle-class apartment with a large loan secured from the son of his former academic adviser, who owned considerable real estate in the city.[17]

While I condemn Bharat for his complicity in the pogrom, I also believe that he went out of his way to protect me on the first day, when the violence in the city was unchecked. In the early morning hours, Bharat and I quarreled about venturing into the city. He did not want to accompany me, arguing that he was afraid that his brother's motorbike would be seized and burned, but he also did not want me to go alone. I compromised by joining him on a visit to a Hanuman temple, where I received a *tilak*—a mark signifying "Hindu"—on my forehead. I felt confident wandering in the city alone, as I had some experience with urban violence in the city. I expected to be able to interview policemen and participants in a relatively controlled environment. I did not, however, entirely understand the magnitude of the events I was to witness. During the day, I left the Hindu mark untouched, and I cannot help believing that it somehow protected me from harm.

The Nausea of Mobility

Vices come in clusters in Gujarat, and they are believed to reveal something about the essence of the person who engages in them. One vice always implies another, eventually leading to a series of addictions (*vyasano, tevo*). If someone takes drinks (*daru le chhe*), it is likely that he will also take *gutka* (form of chewing tobacco) or smoke a cigarette if offered. The most extreme vices in this series are the consumption of meat and the engagement in illicit sex. But vices do more than accumulate and collect around certain individuals lacking resistance to them. By extension, they also affect entire categories of people naturally prone to them. It was thus important for Bharat to be explicit about his adamant resistance to vices, because his surname, Jadav, revealed a caste that was potentially associated with stigmas. Jadavs, who consider themselves Rajput, are closely associated with alcohol, tobacco smoking, and, to a lesser degree, consumption of meat.[18]

Hence Bharat refused tea even when offered by his academic superiors and other authorities of social importance. His superiors often showed a certain stiff astonishment at his refusal, to which Bharat added that he also fasted three times a week, eating only *anaj* (wheat), ghee, and *gol* (sweet molasses). Far from being disingenuous in such meetings, Bharat communicated a complete series of unspoken values beneath and between the few words that he uttered shyly. In addition to abstention from tea and pious fasting (*upvas*), he also implicitly communicated that he was *shuddh shakahari* (pure vegetarian); did not smoke cigarettes, *bidis*, or the *hukkah* (as did his uncle or brother); and was unlikely to take "drinks" (always used in plural) or chew *gutka* (a stimulant with tobacco and betel nut) or *pan* (betel leaf).

When he first explained his caste to me, Bharat insisted vehemently that all Jadavs were and always had been strict vegetarians, with a few impious exceptions. But on visiting his home village in 2001, I found that while most members of his community professed vegetarianism, older members openly admitted to nonvegetarian practices in earlier times as well as to distant contemporary relatives who would still indulge in meat. This history of dietary practices is shadowy and complicated by the community's sudden upward mobility.

Even back in 1999, when we shared a house during my initial language training, Bharat was particularly offended when Tejendra, a neighbor with a Rajasthani Rajput background, invited me to a chicken dinner at his place. Tejendra claimed that a real Rajput (literally "son of kings") ate meat, implying that Gujarati Rajputs were not authentic because they were vegetarians. Behind Tejendra's claim was an Indian stereotype of the Gujarati male—Rajput, Vaniya, and Muslim alike—which insinuated that they are particularly effeminate, lacking in courage and strength. Bharat's relation to vegetarianism and meat eating was, in one sense, an attempt to distance himself from this stereotype, to assume Gujarati-ness while remaining strong and firm.

Here, then, we must return to the incident with which I began: Bharat's bout of severe nausea at Patwa Sheri, which caused him to collapse in the aisles of a Muslim meat market. This was not the only time I heard of sudden afflictions in the face of meat. Restaurant owners of nonvegetarian restaurants in Ahmedabad have much to tell about such strange behaviors—so-called hesitations and sudden averse reactions—especially among affluent Gujaratis, Jains, or members of the Swaminarayan branch of Hinduism. One owner, himself a vegetarian Hindu from South India, explained to me that something like a "vegetarian majority" had emerged in the city.

The severest form of these "hesitations" was what frequently is called *alagi* locally, a condition in which the object (the allergen) puts the entire subject at risk. Abstaining from meat was one of those behaviors about which Bharat seemed to have no doubt; he never seemed to stray (in distinction to his actions regarding liquor or sex before marriage). His affect of disgust appeared brutally simple, yet it remained highly ambivalent. Something in Bharat could not let go of meat, and he obviously expended much more energy than did others to fend off its intimate appeal to him. Pratab—Bharat's former roommate—laughed at Bharat's affliction with *alagi*. Although also politically conservative, and a vegetarian himself, Pratab had no problem with the sight or smell of meat and even encouraged me to eat it. "It suits you" (*tamne fave chhe*), he said. He simply did not want to ingest the stuff himself; he remained in control in his relation to it.

Investigating the phenomenological nature of the abject, the nauseating power and the revulsions of the body when it seeks to turn itself inside out, Julia Kristeva (1982: 1) maintains that "the abject is not an object." That is, the abject is not something that can be named, imagined, and thus tamed. It does not allow for the "I" to remain autonomous or detached. She adds, "The abject has only one quality of the object—that of being opposed to I." What is Bharat attempting to relieve himself of as he retraced his way back through the lanes of Patwa Sheri in order to reverse his encounter with a raw chicken? What is opposed to the "I" here? Since he never actually ingested any meat, he seemed to be trying to relieve himself of a sight that through his eyes penetrated deeply into his body. It is the very presence of meat that caused him to collapse in front of it, in the meat's sight. And, finally, why did he recall the chicken as being no longer on the hook but suddenly on his plate, as if he were poised to eat it?

PARALYSIS AND SPLIT BODY

Despite the historical influences of vegetarian Vaishnava traditions, Jainism, the salience of Mahatma Gandhi in Gujarat, and its current index of the abject, meat eating is not simply associated with disgust. It also carries great potency, and can signify power. Traditionally meat eating was not simply identified with impurity and vice, but with power and chivalry, symbols of royalty and Kshatriya status. For many Gujaratis, the substance of meat even today carries an almost medicinal value, as it is said to counter weakness, emasculation, ineffectualness, and impotence (Alter 1992: 42–43; 2000: 135–136; Tambs-Lyche 1997: 230–233; Osella and Osella 2008). In other words, if meat eating was on the one hand identified with vice and with groups considered backward or even abject, it could alternatively also be associated with erotic attraction and an alluring potency, modern decadence, and cosmopolitan freedom, an association gaining ground especially among the young.

The dual valence of meat is acutely present in how members of lower-caste groups explain, legitimize, and rationalize their own practices of meat consumption or abstention. During the numbing months of violence in 2002, I was told by Hindu residents in the most tense areas of Ahmedabad that Bajrang Dal leaders offered chicken and whiskey, as well as cash, to members of Adivasi and scheduled caste groups as incitements and rewards for attacks on Muslim neighborhoods. Along these lines, meat is equated with the need for strength as well as sex, and its consumption has the quality of an excessive release, like that connected with sexual climaxing. I have seen many men from middle-class Hindu and Jain communities consume meat at night, out of the view of their wives, in the predominantly Muslim-owned meat stands and restaurants of the old city. But their meat eating, unlike that of most Muslims, is coupled with the consumption of illicit liquor, despite the fact that Gujarat is a state in which alcohol is officially prohibited.

Muslim restaurant owners and meat-stand proprietors, many of whom are religiously conservative, were not generally pleased about serving inebriated customers. What this middle-class consumption shared with the bribing of Adivasi with chicken and whiskey to incite them to attack Muslims was the desire for transgression. Meat seemed to enable the Hindu consumer to cross a certain boundary and confront the image of the ever-powerful masculine Muslim either as a coconspirator in festive consumption or as a rival. The release of violence was akin to a relinquishing of the self to *enjoi*, an excessive expenditure and a form of letting go.[19] In this sense, it is somewhat obfuscating to insist that meat eating pertains to nonvegetarians and abstention to vegetarians. The insistence on such a separation remains on the surface of things in Gujarat. Instead, meat is the relay of a form of communication that structures intimacy in which one practice derives its significance for the subject only in light of the other.

Two insights are important here. First, ingesting meat (or seeing blood) can result in, or is indicative of, power—heat—that, once summoned, has to be tamed or expended. Meat consumption not only defines the wretched but also the noble, the royal, the king. It is a form of heat, which provides power similar to the ritual heat of ascetic practices (*tapasya*). Second, as Harold Tambs-Lyche (1992) has demonstrated in contradistinction to the Dumontian dichotomy of Brahmin and Kshatriya, caste complementarity in Saurashtra can be traced historically to the relation of the merchant to the king, the Vaniya to the Rajput, and to their respective regimes of value. These values culminate in what Tambs-Lyche (1997) calls a "Vaniya model of culture," which stresses vegetarianism (with an emphasis on ahimsa), asceticism, and a business ethic, whereas the "Darbar model of culture" stresses chivalry, honor, and animal blood sacrifices in the context of *shakti* worship, the ritual forms and conceptions surrounding the Mother Goddess complex.

In Bharat's affliction of *alagi*, this complementarity has finally collapsed, leaving him with nothing but pure disgust and in a relation to the "other" as a challenge to him. Needless to say, not all vegetarians in India, or in Gujarat, suffer *alagi* and fall sick when exposed to the sight of raw flesh. But for Bharat there was something still alive in the meat that took cognizance of him, and this sensitivity marked him as a very special Jadav. His aversion was more radical than a mere "hesitation."

Today members of those social categories traditionally associated with arms-bearing activities, such as the Rajput and Adivasi, or those associated with impure practices, such as Vagri and diverse Dalit groups, are called upon to emulate the "forward classes" (*savarna*). The later consist mainly of Hindu Vaishnavas, Jains, and Patels, who all share a strong mercantile and vegetarian ethos. Similar developments seem to have occurred in neighboring Rajasthan, where Babb (2004: 225) goes even further and attests a "transmutation of trader social identity into a political ideology." New constituencies are mobilized through a politicization of nonviolence that resonates deeply with local traditions as well as Hindu nationalism (ibid.: 227–228). As groups considered Rajput abstain from those practices they used to be identified with, and which in the traditional ritual order granted them access to a certain kind of power, the symbolic space they have vacated came to be signified by Muslims—who, in turn, now inhabit a form of power simultaneously desired and rejected.[20]

Caught within a confluence of these historical influences, Bharat was arrested by contradictory impulses: the desire to ingest meat (in his account, it suddenly appeared on his plate) and the visceral disgust at flesh, the substance of a being that was killed unnaturally for consumption. Ingesting meat risked the undoing of all that he has been so laboriously externalizing (vomiting): his backwardness (*bekwad*), inferiority (*halku*), and lowness (*nich*); his "hesitations" toward an enticing world, cultivated through fasting (*upvas*) and abstaining from vices (*tevo*); and finally his claim to represent the "essence of the Hindu" (*hindutva*).

At the same time, however, he claimed proudly to be a Rajput—a man fit to rule—and thus the holder of the exact power signified by meat. Bharat's desire for that power was so great that any open argument about his status as a true Kshatriya (a Rajput, warrior) was a hostile challenge.[21] Meat signified that part of himself that he wanted to spit out. It is when the raw meat looked back at him that something in him realized what he is: the other side of power—that is, powerlessness, inferiority, and disgust. This "malady of *alagi*" is a manifestation of being caught in a maelstrom of impulses no longer neatly separate in a symbolic division of complementary values and roles.

If desire implies the wish to devour, then disgust takes the form of its opposite, revulsion and the impulse to vomit. As the symmetrical reverse of the desire to devour, now introjected and become corporeal, it has no language. It is pure affect. Yet how can something that has never been swallowed be vomited out? As we see in Bharat's case, the object to be evacuated was mental, not inside the body. That which is to be vomited was that which had been rendered unconscious: the desire to devour. Something in Bharat wanted to devour meat and thus assimilate its power. In the end, and quite ironically, this affliction of *alagi* enabled Bharat to reinvent himself as a new subject in the context of Hindutva—a *pakka hindu*, a man with an identity, a man of action.

When Chief Minister Modi, in the Porbandar speech quoted at the beginning of this chapter, explained vegetarianism by alluding to Vedic sacrifice and when he insisted that those who ingested death become the death they were eating, whereas those who ingested vegetables attained life, he was doing much more than just engaging in empty Vedic phraseology. To be sure, Modi is neither philologically trained in Sanskrit nor a competent Indologist. Acutely attuned, however, as this chief minister always is, to his audiences and to the enormous prestige that anything "Vedic" and vegetarian has in Gujarat, Modi is making sure that people like Bharat keep on vomiting, even if they have not ingested anything in the first place.

By contrast, persuaded by his Muslim friend Sheikh Mehtab, Gandhi himself famously ingested meat when he was young to appropriate the physical virility of the British. He even confessed relishing its taste for a while (M. K. Gandhi 1927: 18–20). Gandhi subsequently abandoned the practice and turned to *brahmacharya* (celibacy) in order to gather the strength needed to overcome political domination and, later, ethnic violence. Although he was certainly a very strict vegetarian and felt guilty for his transgressions, Gandhi never expressed disgust for those who ate meat, nor did he warn of contagion from those whose profession or traditional occupation brought them into contact with it. In this way Gandhi's relationship to meat, and by extension his relationship to Muslims, always remained sovereign—not an act of bad faith.

There are many passages in Gandhi's voluminous writings that attest to his acute understanding of the relation of stigma to diet, notwithstanding his own strict dietary regiment. For example, discussing the nature of Sanatana Hinduism at the height of Hindu-Muslim conflict, he writes in *Young India*:

> Unfortunately today Hinduism seems to consist merely in eating and not eating. Once I horrified a pious Hindu by taking toast at a Musalman's house.[22] I saw that he was pained to see me pouring milk into a cup handed by a Musalman friend. . . . Hinduism is in danger of losing its substance if it resolves itself into a matter of elaborate rules as to what and with whom to eat. . . . [A] man eating meat and with everybody, but living in the fear of God is nearer his freedom than a man religiously abstaining from meat and many other things but blaspheming God in every one of his acts. (M. K. Gandhi 1987 [1921]: 32–33)

Whereas Narendra Modi, a celibate who is rumored to have a secret wife (or a girlfriend), inscribed ahimsa and vegetarianism into Hindu nationalism in order to mobilize disgust against Muslims, Gandhi's renunciation of meat was complete: the substance no longer exercised any power over him. Gandhi's strict abstemiousness, despite appearing obsessive to some contemporary observers, did not translate into the overt denigration of character of members of lower castes, tribal groups, or Muslims. Though he needed to mobilize the masses for national independence, and though he did indeed connect this political activism to a regimen of bodily discipline, he at the same time maintained emotional sobriety vis-à-vis the inevitable cultural and individual differences that defined India then, as they do today.

The hyperbolic vegetarian, by contrast, vomits his own forbidden desires and feels disgusted by those who come to stand for what he himself signifies. Bharat's disgust was fueled by this fundamental proximity to Muslims owing to symbolic equivalences established between him and them by those from whom he desired *entri,* which means to say recognition. In this way, disgust makes argument or persuasion unnecessary. It becomes a weapon to establish a new relation to the Muslim, one informed by Hindu rage, at once corporeal and instinctual, almost innocent. In short, Bharat's weakness of disgust, his malady of *alagi,* becomes a formidable power that Hindutva can harness. In turning this affliction into a sign of true "Hindu-ness" (*hindutva*), the expression of an uncompromising *pakka hindu* (staunch Hindu), the subject is made to externalize those elements of himself that are, for the moment, associated with the phantasmagoric figure of the Muslim.

• • •

Shortly before I left the field in 2003, Bharat called me on the phone and asked me to invite him to the "vegetarian McDonald's," which had opened the year prior. We had not seen or spoken to one another for a while since I had moved to a tense mixed area and was living in a Muslim apartment building, which he refused to visit. I was to come from the Muslim area where I now lived, and he from the suburban Hindu area where he had since moved with his newlywed bride. We were to meet in the middle, at the American compromise restaurant. I told him that meat was eaten there, but to my surprise he insisted on visiting it anyway. Bharat felt obliged to enjoy consumption at the popular venue and knew the perfect person to join in. He also knew that I was not going to let him pay for the expensive fare.

After we arrived, he remained unimpressed throughout. He ate an un-accustomed vegetarian burger and I ate a chicken burger right front of his eyes, which came cleanly wrapped in green paper and pale orange paper, respectively. Bharat was, perhaps unsurprisingly, more interested in the clientele than in the food. In the meat of the burger I ate there, some-where was the fleshy remainders of a live animal, a chicken in fact. But the flesh had been transformed into a sanitized substance, meat devoid of any visual or olfactory residue that could risk signifying the two simulta-neous aspects of pollution: death and the teaming fertility of rotting life. The meat strangely lacked the very meat-ness of meat.

We agreed that we did not like the taste of our respective burgers and decided to visit pious Rasvatika for their magnificent *thalis*, vegetar-ian and wholesome, turning our backs on the garish Ronald for a more solemn smile of Ganesh. This was the first and only time I ever ate non-vegetarian food in Bharat's presence. There was no *alagi* attack, and the presence of processed meat did not affect him. While Mahatma Gandhi traversed his desire for meat to reach a position of sovereignty in which renunciation did not constitute a loss of enjoyment, Bharat's jouissance is ultimately caught up with Muslim meat eating. Other meat does not interest him in the least.

CHAPTER 6

Ahimsa, Gandhi, and the Angry Hindu

The Thumbnail Version of Nonviolence

On May 1, 2002, the government of Gujarat published an advertisement in English in *The Times of India* commemorating the forty-third year of the existence of the state, founded in 1960. It appealed for a "present of peace and harmony to the state of Gujarat." The advertisement included an astonishing mistake, the omission of the prefix "non" in the word nonviolence—a printed Freudian slip.

A picture of Mahatma Gandhi stands at the head of the spiritual lineage, followed by pictures of three prominent Gujaratis: Sadar Vallabhai Patel and Ravishankar Maharaj, who fought for independence with Gandhi, and the current chief minister of Gujarat, Narendra Modi.[1] With the possible exception of Modi, the other leaders certainly considered themselves Gandhians. Each picture is accompanied by a sentence in English. Only Modi looks directly into the eyes of the reader, perhaps emphasizing his role of arbiter of the national genealogy represented by the other leaders.

The chief minister is depicted as saying: "Trust is the mother of peace. Rumours always shake the foundations of trust. Trust is the assurance of peace. Peace is our collective responsibility." Ravishankar Maharaj is depicted as saying: "Let us not put to shame the deeds of Gandhiji. Destruction of national and others' assets will only make us poorer." Sadar Vallabhai Patel is depicted as saying: "You may be weak physically, but develop a lion's heart; Guard your self-respect at the cost of life. Keep away the disintegrating forces with your intellect." Mahatma Gandhi, the father of the nation, unexpectedly contradicts the others: "Violence is not a shield to hide cowardice. It is the greatest asset of the brave."

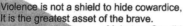

Gujarat has stepped into its 43rd year of journey
Let us give a present of Peace and Harmony

Violence is not a shield to hide cowardice,
It is the greatest asset of the brave.
          - Mahatma Gandhi

You may be weak physically, but develop a lion's heart;
Guard your self-respect at the cost of life. Keep away
the disintegrating forces with your intellect.
                    - Sardar Vallabhbhai Patel

Let us not put to shame the deeds of Gandhiji.
Destruction of national and others' assets will
only make us poorer.
                    - Shri Ravishankar Maharaj

Let us build peace and harmony

Trust is the mother of peace. Rumours
always shake the foundation of trust.
Trust is the assurance of peace.
Peace is our collective responsibility.
                    - Narendra Modi
                    Chief Minister, Gujarat

Our Gujarat Distinct Gujarat

FIGURE 10: Violence Gandhi

The omission of the three letters of the prefix "non" before the word "violence" negates Gandhi's well-known consistent affirmation of the practice and philosophy of nonviolence. It is very likely a printing mistake, though it might have been a joke on Gandhi's stern insistence on *a-himsa*, nonviolence. It certainly would not have been the first humor at the mahatma's expense. People on the streets of Ahmedabad tell many jokes, and some with considerable charm, about the father of the nation. But it is difficult to understand the depiction as a joke, given the immediate context of the pogrom. In effect, the advertisement had the mahatma ventriloquizing the local discourse of violence by proponents of Hindutva. The next day, the newspaper printed the correct citation, and the Mahatma is made to say, "Non-violence . . . is the greatest asset of the brave."

I asked a reporter at *The Times* about the omission. He understood my discomfort and called it a particularly unfortunate "bad coincidence."

**Gujarat has stepped into its 43rd year of journey
Let us give a present of Peace and Harmony**

Non-violence is not a shield to hide cowardice,
it is the greatest asset of the brave.
- Mahatma Gandhi

You may be weak physically, but develop a lion's heart;
Guard your self-respect at the cost of life. Keep away
the disintegrating forces with your intellect.
- Sardar Vallabhbhai Patel

Let us not put to shame the deeds of Gandhiji.
Destruction of national and others' assets will
only make us poorer.
- Shri Ravishankar Maharaj

Let us build peace and harmony

Trust is the mother of peace. Rumours
always shake the foundation of trust.
Trust is the assurance of peace.
Peace is our collective responsibility.
- Narendra Modi
Chief Minister, Gujarat

Our Gujarat   Distinct Gujarat

FIGURE 11: Non-violence Gandhi

This coincidence transpired at the time the city had barely begun to recover from weeks of violence in which reference to *himsa* and *ahimsa*
were rampant. He assured me that an apology had been printed somewhere in the paper's back pages, not wanting to draw too much attention
to it. I never found the apology, however, though I perhaps did not look
hard enough.

As we know from E. E. Evans-Pritchard's classic study of witchcraft, an
untimely coincidence is usually no coincidence at all. Witchcraft is more
likely. This chapter hopes to shed some light on the omission of "non,"
on the significance and consequences of a missed negation. The mistake
of *The Times* is symptomatic of how ahimsa, the doctrine of nonviolence,
and attitudes toward the enigmatic figure of Mahatma Gandhi, its most
famous proponent, can so easily obtain its opposite charge and become
implicated in the production of the violence it claims to renounce.

THE TRUTH OF COWARDICE

No other concept or notion is hailed in the West with such unadulterated admiration as the Indian doctrine of nonviolence—ahimsa. Its ancient origins, its modern association with Mahatma Gandhi, its assimilability to the Christian notion of "love thy neighbor" or Islamic notions of compassion, and its universal appeal to the practice of resistance against state power all over the world have made the ancient concept one of India's greatest gifts to the world.[2]

Contemporary ahimsa is a concept that everyone can affirm. At the same time, unlike popular modern ideas such as justice, law, democracy, or equality, whose origins are multiple, ahimsa seems unquestionably a product of the East. On the surface, it does not appear tainted by Christian or Enlightenment thought. In Gujarat, it is understood to be an indigenous term with a long tradition in the state. Although the local effects of the intense Western affection for ahimsa are seldom openly acknowledged, that affection has become internal to Gujarat.

Not surprisingly, for the nationalist Rashtriya Swayamsevak Sangh, founded in 1925, the political deployment of ahimsa by Gandhi has been a problem since the day the popular leader began employing it in his anticolonial struggle. While many followers of Hindutva today appropriate the rhetoric of Gandhi's nonviolence, they generally find his style of political activism utterly embarrassing. This embarrassment is much older than the contemporary attractiveness of Hindutva and runs deep in Gujarat (cf. G. Shah 1975: 47).[3]

The Sanskrit term *ahimsa* means the "absence of the desire to kill" (Biardeau 1989 [1981]: 31), or the "non-desire-to-carry-out-any-attack" (Oguibénine 2003 [1994]: 65). It is a privative compound word composed of the negative prefix *a-*, followed by the radical *hims*, a form of the desiderative mode of *han*, meaning "to assault, to kill" (ibid.). According to the Indologist Louis Renou, privative compound words in Sanskrit are infinitely more nuanced than their positive reversals, and can conjure up a wide variety of meanings. The positive counterparts are semantically scarcer than the negative forms. Terms such as *abhaya*, *amrta*, *advaita*, *avidya*, *adroha*, for example, allow for a dispersion and scattering of meaning with connotations of their own.[4]

In the case of states such as *abhaya* (fearlessness, security), *amrta* (nondeath, immortality) or *ahimsa* (noninjury, harmlessness, nonviolence), not only does the positive term stand for one single reality, but that reality is also to be denied in its negative form. In consequence, the positive root *hims* connotes a type of evil inherent in the desire to kill that is negated, creating a morally positive term, *ahimsa*, which is the negation of the former (Oguibénine 2003 [1994]: 67). Thus good is always evil negated, and if "the term ahimsa itself is affirmative and positive, it continues to bear traces of that which is negated: the desire to kill is offset by the affirmation of another desire, that of not killing" (ibid.). These two aspirations are clearly designated in the compound form of the terms in question. "[I]t represents the frequent and typical to and fro swing of ancient India, which places opposites, the positive and the negative, on the same plane" (ibid.).

While an older translation of *ahimsa* is "innocence" (M. K. Gandhi 1996: 41; Rolland 1923: 29), and the term has sometimes been misunderstood as passivity, more recent renderings have included a lack of courage, a sign of timidity, or cowardice. Gandhi had already confronted such interpretations and countered that "A man cannot . . . practice ahimsa and be a coward at the same time" (M. K. Gandhi 1996: 40). Discussing the concept a few years later, Gandhi related an exchange with his son Harilal. After Gandhi told him of an experience of physical assault by a Pathan in South Africa, his son asked him what his duty would have been had he been there at the time of the attack. Gandhi responded:

> It would be a sign of cowardice if you ran away or did nothing to protect me. If you could not protect me by taking the anger upon yourself, you should undoubtedly do so by attacking the other man. It is any day better to use brute force than to betray cowardice. (1996 [1920]: 70–71)

After relating this anecdote, Gandhi continued:

> I hold this view even now. It is better that India should arm itself and take the risk than that it should refuse to take up arms out of fear. . . . It will be evidence of India's soul-force only if it refuses to fight when it has the strength to do so. (Ibid.: 71)

The "soul-force" of which Gandhi spoke was the strength he located in ahimsa, the ability to renounce and forgo retaliation. For Gandhi, forgoing brute force meant not weakness or cowardice but the strength indispensable for attaining *swaraj* (freedom and self rule). *Swaraj* included overcoming colonial rule as well as one's desire for revenge. Gandhi acknowledged that a soldier might show fearlessness in the face of battle when confronting the enemy. What distinguished the soldier from the Satyagrahi (the one who strives for truth), however, was the latter's stern adherence to truth. Because man is not able to know the absolute truth, he is not competent to mete out punishment. What distinguished *himsa* from ahimsa then is not cowardice versus bravery, but truth, which for Gandhi had the status of a God (ibid.: 55, 50–51, 45).

During the dark spring of 2002, the head of the RSS, K. Sudarshan, a guarded man who generally refused to speak to the public media, explained in a rare interview:

> Ahimsa is a negation of himsa, violence. If you have the capacity to do himsa and still do not take recourse to it, then it becomes ahimsa. A coward cannot follow ahimsa—Mahatma Gandhi used to say this—because he does not have the capacity to practice himsa. I've got the capacity to slap someone if he abuses me, but I can walk away, thinking he is ignorant. If I do not have the capacity to retaliate—then ahimsa has no meaning. So we must first have the capacity, the strength. After having the strength, then if we do not retaliate, that is ahimsa. Ahimsa is not to be followed by weak persons.[5]

Sudarshan is saying that only if you are absolutely sure that you possess the capacity to inflict harm can you choose nonviolence. If you are not violent, how do you know that you actually possess to ability to be violent? Your lofty ideal of nonviolence may simply be a denial of the fact that you lack courage. The internalization of nonviolence and your emotional equanimity may simply hide your utter ineffectualness. Do you actually have a choice to opt for violence or nonviolence, respectively?

In the logic of Sudarshan, violence is equated with the affirmation of power. The powerless lack not only the strength to retaliate but also the ability to opt for nonviolence. The powerful, in turn, the one who is capable of retaliation, can choose to opt for nonviolence. Hence, the weak should not try to be nonviolent, as it will never be a sign of strength but only of cowardice. In contradistinction, Gandhi had suggested that nonviolence need not be of the strong but must always be of the truthful (M. K. Gandhi 1996: 42).

Sudarshan's clever elaboration succeeds in agreeing with Gandhi's wording while simultaneously communicating the opposite of what the Mahatma meant to say. If Gandhi rejected revolutionary violence against a British minority presence by colonial subjects, Sudarshan inverts this claim by insisting on the violent possibilities of a majority population against a minority today. Such inversions are effective in manipulating young men from lower social backgrounds who feel challenged and frequently humiliated by the defeats they experience in daily life. Instead of encouraging nonviolent means to resist one's proclivities for violence, as Gandhi would, Sudarshan tries to co-opt anger and the propensities for violence for the ends of the RSS.[6]

Gandhi's position is similar to that of Hannah Arendt, who understood violence to be the expression of *Ohnmacht*, a lack of power, and not the opposite (Arendt 1970: 35–56).[7] Violence speaks when authority is lost. The act of empowerment and license that violence allows for comes at the price of negation, that is, destruction, and the realization of truth. Gandhi's position differs from Sudarshan's precisely in that Sudarshan thinks that destruction is not defeat but might very well be absolute necessity in order to achieve one's goals. The Hindu when confronted with his own ineffectualness should appropriate the ability to mete out violence and not attempt repossession of the self through abstention, that is, through self-discipline and acquisition of what Gandhi considered the higher power of nonviolence.

In consequence, Sudarshan suggests that nonviolence can only be achieved when violence has first been meted out. This is because the timid and nonviolent Hindu has to prove capable of defending himself against the ever bold and naturally violent Muslim. The continuity established with Gandhi's wording willfully misconstrues the current state of India, no longer a colonial regime under the grip of a ruling minority class but a modern democracy. Most Muslims are part of a poor and disaffected social stratum and suffer many forms of discrimination. While the Hindu has to learn to overcome his nonviolent nature (in order to achieve "real" nonviolence), the Muslim has to be taught a lesson so that he can overcome his own violent nature and inculcate his own vulnerability, that is, his respective "lesson."

During the Gujarat pogrom, many residents in Ahmedabad—including Dalits and Adivasis—represented the violence unleashed as a successful experiment in overcoming Hindu timidity and attaining the strength to be bold and retaliate. They claimed, contrary to fact, that this was the first time the Muslims had been at the receiving end of collective violence. After the pogrom, prominent members of the Sangh Parivar were ecstatic about their success at social engineering, and those among them that held no public office (and thus did not risk public rebuke), made their excitement widely known.

GANDHI UNSCATHED

Pratab, a young Hindu man of twenty-three whom I initally met in Ahmedabad in early 2001, studied daily the writings of Gandhi, copying and collating sayings and paraphrasing the author's work. He did this even during the pogrom violence itself. He was completing a degree in Hindi literature at Gujarat Vidhyapit University. His thesis was on the impact of Gandhi's thinking on a collection of Hindi literary texts, a topic suggested by his Hindi teacher.

More specifically, Pratab wanted to understand the origin of Gandhi's "strength" (*prabhav* = luster, majesty). This entailed an investigation of the mahatma's thought, biography, and lifestyle and how all these aspects of

Gandhi appeared in the work of specific writers. He had already read about thirteen books by Gandhi, concentrating especially on those sections in which Gandhi gave vows (*vrato*). He also read all the sections on ahimsa, the welfare of cows, cleanliness, and celibacy to understand the mahatma.

In a long discussion that began as an interview, Pratab told me in a language that seemed not his own that Gandhiji was about perfect life, the essence of completeness, and the pureness of his ideal model, which enters into thought and sight. Pratab referred to Gandhi as *sampurn*, which denotes complete, whole, and carries a sense of perfection.

Pratab is married, but he left his wife and two children behind at his parents' house in his home village to complete his studies in the city. In 1999, he enrolled to learn Hindi at Gujarat University, but now he worked in the library and with the professors of Gujarat Vidhyapit, a university founded in 1920 by the mahatma.

Seemingly disoriented and insecure in the big city, Pratab was fortunate to have been assigned a student hostel room, although he did not particularly like the location of the accommodations. Vejalpur is a Hindu area adjacent to the large Muslim area of Juhapura at the southwestern outskirts of Ahmedabad. City residents already referred to Juhapura as the quintessential "mini-Pakistan" long before the 2002 pogrom. The ghetto was the spatial expression of inner-city migration due to rounds of violence in prior decades. The area invoked the specter of a Muslim suburban zone, material evidence for the deepening division between Hindus and Muslims. Pratab was relieved when Bharat invited him to come and live with us.

While Pratab was proud not to suffer from the "malady of *alagi*" like Bharat, he was pleased that the hostel warden prohibited the cooking of meat. Still, he recounted that in the hostel he was made to cook "chicken" secretly by many of his Rajput caste brethren. He also stressed that many students were engaging in "eve-teasing" and "brawls," activities of which he could not brag.[8] Whereas Bharat was thin but muscular and strong, Pratab was a true featherweight, although he always emphasized that he was a "farmar" (in English) indicating strength and physical endurance.

What is the RSS? I asked Pratab. He explained, "The RSS is a collective of pure Hindus, believers of dharma and of one Hindu nation." And he added that in 2001, after the Gujarat earthquake, it was the RSS who were first to arrive at the scene of rescue helping the victims in affected locations such as Anjar, Bachau, and Bhuj.

Moreover, Pratab explained that only as a member of the RSS was he able to obtain a college room in a student hostel in Ahmedabad. His 2,000 rupees college scholarship, too, was due to RSS intervention. He confided that he had joined the organization when he turned twenty, but he did not want me to share this information with others. Unlike Bharat, he never went to an RSS branch in his home village, but in Ahmedabad he visited the RSS branch close to the hostel where he lived.

Sensing my suspicion of RSS involvement in student access to fellowships, Pratab explained that these practices had nothing to do with discrimination or corruption. Instead to be associated with the organization meant that one was expected not to lie or to use the scholarship money for other purposes. The organization simply makes you a little more respectable, he elaborated, and that would open all kind of doors. RSS association compensated for the lack of social capital and prestige of newcomers like him. I took away that the RSS had successfully usurped the role of moral authority where it seemed lacking by supplementing social and cultural capital.

Pratab could choose to visit any of the many RSS branches, called *shakha*. The one he attended taught him to teach his children selective readings of the Hindu epics, the Mahabharat and the Ramayan, to recite national prayers, in addition to Yoga postures, physical games and exercises for national protection. He also learned about Swami Vivekananda's famous lecture on Hindu religion from the Congress of Religions in Chicago in 1893. Vivekananda is considered one of the founders of neo-Hinduism, and, as Pratab pointed out proudly, he was a nineteenth-century saint who praised the Gita in front of the entire world.

Pratab liked his time in the organization because "If you are an RSS man you get help immediately when you need it. You are not alone." The *shakha* created a network of support in an alien urban environment and fostered a "feeling of unity" by ignoring caste and class boundaries. RSS members arranged transportation for him to go back and forth to his home village, and they supported him when he had to deal with all academic bureaucratic matters. Now, however, Pratab no longer had time to attend meetings, as he had to finish his thesis and prepare for exams. He was aware, he explained, that if he did not offer something in return, the RSS would not keep up relations (*sambandh*). Attending a *shakha* implied a certain risk, like the obligation to agitate or fight in the streets. That is why Pratab no longer attended their camps. "I do not want to fight," he admitted. "I am afraid of that."

I asked if they discussed Islam in the *shakhas* he attended. He reacted with indignation: "Muslims are not talked about. The word 'Muslim' is not even uttered." The RSS was not a political organization at all, he insisted; there was no direct talk about Jawaharlal Nehru and secularism, or Jyotindra Phule. On the other hand, its members did discuss Babasaheb Ambedkar, Sadar Vallabhai Patel, and Mahatma Gandhi, he explained.

But then, although they did not address Muslims topically, they did explicitly say, "If you walk on the road and you see it's a Muslim, beat him, that's it." You should also hurt them economically, paraphrasing what he took away from *shakha* sessions. I was surprised by the simplicity and directness of Pratab's understanding of what he had been told. When I pushed him for clarification, he simply explained that for the RSS, Muslims should not exist (*"musalman loko hova j na joie"*) in the sense that they are a sort of unnecessary nuisance. They are not often directly talked about, but it is clear what one's relationship to them should be.

According to Pratab's RSS instruction, although Muslims were not mentioned by name, they nonetheless appeared in passing as that which should be negated. According to this understanding, Islam as a religion was not the issue because Muslim conceptions of a formless god caused no conflict for a Hindu. A Hindu could choose the name of his or her god because Hinduism was a tolerant and inclusive religion. Thus the conflict is not one of theology or belief, but one of assimilation and discipline. Muslim demands for recognition were particularistic and should be ignored.

Pratab had already had one experience of disciplining Muslims. He recounted how several years ago, a girl of his *samaj* (community, caste), whom he knew personally, had been caught having an affair with a Muslim boy close to his village. The relationship was terminated violently. Pratab told me, "We went and broke his arm." I could not really imagine jovial Pratab physically assaulting another person, but he recounted the details: a group of youngsters entered the Muslim boy's village, gathered locals around, and beat the boy up badly, resulting in a fracture of the boy's arm.

Pratab appeared to me caught in an unresolved impasse: his identification with Gandhi's notion of nonviolence conflicted with his membership in the RSS, which provided benefits and responses to some of his daily needs. I asked him what Gandhi would do if confronted with the recent violence in Ahmedabad. He found this a formidable question and lauded me for it.

Gandhi would fast, he said, he would neither eat nor drink. He would pray to God. He would not go and harass Muslims, he would make Hindus understand, and while fasting he would pray to God for support to deal with this misfortune. Gandhi's "weapon" to cast out the British from the country was only one single thing: fasting. If anyone slaps your cheek, give him willingly the other one, Pratab continued. And Gandhiji, he emphasized, was really practicing this. If Muslims are attacking Hindus, we should not retaliate, because any revenge is merely another challenge; to attack will bring the entire country to war.

Like many Gujaratis, Pratab understood Gandhi's thoughts to be primarily based on notions of Hindu spirituality and, ultimately "Hindu dharma." But Pratab's affirmation of Gandhi was not characteristic of all Gujaratis I met. In several settings, other interlocutors reacted to my references to Gandhi, and my research on ahimsa, with a certain degree of antipathy. For example, one man contended that Gandhi knew very little Sanskrit and misrepresented the scriptures, that the mahatma was more a political practitioner than a philosopher; another criticized him for his involvement with Christians and Muslims; a third faulted Gandhi for completely misunderstanding the ancient doctrine of ahimsa; a fourth one for his many personal inconsistencies.

These critical representations may have been reactions to my presence, and uttered to me because people identified me with the West. They expressed a palpable resentment that the West has invested heavily in lending recognition to the figure of the mahatma, but not in Hinduism or Jainism at large, which many considered to be philosophically more momentous. For many city residents, what marked Gandhi as special were not his concrete ideas but his obstinacy in following them through even after personal setbacks and failures. As one person told me, Gandhi was simply the opposite of a hypocrite—someone obstinate, that's all. Gandhi was stubborn and acted out his lofty ideals without compromise. Some felt that Gandhi's particularly principled stand rendered his followers incapable of reacting adequately to any form of aggression. Gandhi's celestial strength rendered them weak by association as well as by comparison.

Pratab, in turn, made no distinction between a practical and a philosophical Gandhi. He, too, understood Gandhi's strength to be partly his obdurateness, his stubborn insistence on truth. This very same strength characterized those Hindus that are called *rudhichust* (orthodox), a word with which he also characterized agitators for Hindutva. Pratab contended that Gujarati people, Hindus as well as Muslims, believed that Mahatma Gandhi was a very good person, who served his people his entire life. Employing a language that is usually applied to RSS activists, Pratab said that Gandhi's followers were his *swayamsevako* (volunteers), by which he meant Gandhian Satyagrahis. These followers did their service (*seva*) fully.

The Symbolic Source of Violence

But then, without my prompting, Pratab insisted that Gandhi made one mistake (*bhul*). That mistake was to grant Muslims a separate nation. He created a separate Pakistan. Pratab repeated the phrase often used by Gujaratis when referring to Partition, "*Emne alag api*" (They were given separate, or They were given something separate). That is why Nathuram Godse murdered Gandhi, and, Pratab continued, that is why Hindus and Muslims were fighting each other today in every village in every corner of the country. Gandhi's *valan* (mental inclination) was such that he thought a separate nation of Pakistan was the solution to their demands. But it was not, because many Muslims remained in India.

For Pratab, that Muslims stayed back in India did not demonstrate loyalty to their ancestral home but constituted the continuing headache. If all Muslims had gone to Pakistan, Pratab explained, this question would not have arisen. Now they had both, a homeland for themselves in Pakistan while mingling also within India. As many Gujaratis told me, Gandhi was a great man, but his "soft spot" for Muslims was a flaw in his immaculate character, exemplified by his childhood relation with his Muslim friend Sheikh Mehtab.

When I argued that it would be unfair to blame Gandhi for Partition, I realized that Pratab did not know that Mahatma Gandhi was not India's first prime minister but Jawaharlal Nehru. When I corrected him, he said, "Yes, right—the condition became bad because of that Jawaharlal Nehru." Pratab clarified that Gandhi was confused at the time and, reversing the usual logic of the Edwina-Nehru affair, he alleged that Nehru sold out to Pakistan because of an affair with some woman (he meant Lord Mountbatten's wife).[9]

In analyzing the secret of Gandhian luster (*prabhav*), Pratab opined that the British knew very well that they could not harm Gandhi, as that would have seriously jeopardized their rule in India. Gandhi was too well protected. The term *chhaya* means "shadow or shield": the mahatma was shielded by his own people. Pratab said, "People left their households in order to join the agitations. . . . Gandhiji is the best." Such a leader had never appeared in the past, did not exist today, and would not emerge in the future either.

What did Pratab express in this conversation? After painting an ideal Gandhi, an "idol-Gandhi" decorated with a little ahimsa, *satya* (truth), and a final brush of *sampurn* (perfection), Pratab quickly moved to blame the very same Gandhi for Partition. Partition, of course, was for Pratab the source of all misery, the cause for all violence in the state and elsewhere in India. It was when the mother country was cut into pieces, and the promise of unity became the reality of division, and all innocence was lost.

Pratab's ambivalent feelings towards the father of the nation were shared by many others in central Gujarat. The mahatma was first erected as *sampurn*, and then there was but this one little mistake, said Pratab. The little mistake turned out not to be minor at all but the source of all trouble, into which all resentment and bitterness was poured. Gandhi's *bhul* (mistake) led to the dissection of the country in the moment of independent state formation. The gesture with which the figure of Gandhi was erected as *sampurn* was the same gesture with which he was also held to be responsible for the single most devastating national catastrophe. In this way, Gujarat's Gandhi stood in the shadow of Partition, and in relation to that traumatic event, his assassination was often assimilated to a national sacrifice.

Note that when I criticized Pratab for unfairly blaming Gandhi for Partition, he did not insist on his prior point but evaded by conjuring up someone else, Jawaharlal Nehru. The figure of Nehru caused no cautious reserve in Pratab. He did not mention the prime minister's small mistakes. Rather, Nehru is blamed entirely by alluding to his moral character: a sexual scandal. In other words, Nehru is dismissed without inhibition. Not so with Gandhi, who was whole and complete. His was but a *bhul*.

In Gujarati, you do not make a mistake actively, but you are associated with it passively. A mistake is a form of visitation: *mane bhul thai gayu*, which translates literally into "a mistake came over me" or "to me a mistake happened." In conventional English translations, the passive is usually rendered active. When Pratab averred that Gandhi made a mistake, he implied that the mistake happened to him like an unfortunate accident, "*emne bhul thai gayu chhe*" (a mistake happened to him). There is implicit in this construction a sense that Gandhi did not by intention harm the country.

One reason that Gandhi cannot be outright rejected is the recognition he receives as the world's most famous Hindu. The power of Gandhi, the mana of the phenomena one might call "global Gandhi," is the recognition that the condensed figure of the mahatma commands internationally. "Global Gandhi" can be used as an emissary of all things "Hindu." And because the West has become internal to India through the recognition extended to Gandhi and his use of ahimsa, those who follow Hindutva desire control over the very power that radiates from Gandhi into the West. In this way, Gandhi has become internal to Hindutva.

POLITICAL IDOLATRY

Pratab's relation to Gandhi reveals a form of national idolatry, which allows distancing from Gandhi in the same moment as proximity through veneration is claimed. It is in this sort of veneration that the fundamentally ambivalent and unresolved emotions sustain themselves. Worship consists in the act of placing the national figure on an pedestal, in order to not have to confront the urgent Gandhian imperative. An idol, representing an ideal, allows for control over one's relationship to the piercing demand that it communicates. One can act out ambivalent emotions much better because pious adoration never automatically demands replication.

In fact, the idol is in many ways exposed and dependent upon the wor-shipper, who controls the mode of access to it. One can feed, bathe, clean, or neglect the deity, omitting or adding prefixes and words to his sayings, like in the thumbnail version of ahimsa. In order to resist incorporation, the sacred is controlled, kept at bay, arrested into an object of reverence.

The ambivalence towards *sampurn* Gandhi is closely related to the magnetic attractiveness of Hindutva, the new incarnation of the Hindu as legitimate anger. Since the 1990s, the majority of Gujaratis have elected the BJP (Bharatiya Janata Party) to power, and Narendra Modi has ruled in the state since 2002 with an absolute majority. In the sig-nificant election in December 2002, in which the electorate could have severely penalized the Chief Minister and his party, the opposing Con-gress party led by Shankersingh Vaghela, challenged Modi's Hindutva rhetoric (sometimes referred to as "Moditva") with what he called "soft Hindutva." After the Gujarat pogrom, a violence fomented not in the name of the symbolic father Gandhi but in the name of the Hindu, the Gujarati voter could choose between Hindutva and soft Hindutva. They chose Hindutva.

There is always something in Hindutva that proponents experience as truth, be it in the body as disgust, in sentiment as anger, or intellectually as clarity and honesty. Pratab visited an RSS *shakha* for several years and inhabited the Sangh Parivar's discourse rather well during the pogrom. Nonetheless, he still held on to Gandhi's version of ahimsa, something that he cherished. He did not display the disgust of a hyperbolic vegetar-ian (*alagi*), nor did Muslims seem an obstacle to his personal ambitions, as was the case with Bharat. He voiced his suspicion towards all Muslim men but then confessed having had sex at least with one, and he exalted in his friendships with a series of Muslim women.

Such ambivalence towards Gandhi expressed itself in more than one way. For example, on the one hand, Gandhi showed his incredible strength by using austere practices to exert pressure on the British to leave India by following traditional techniques of accumulating ascetic power. For Pratab, Gandhi attempted to appropriate the techniques of traditional ascetics by his renunciation of sex. On the other hand, Pratab thought that the British would not have dared to harm Gandhi anyhow because the entire Indian people stood behind him as a safeguard.

In the alchemical metabolism of renunciation, the traditional renouncer abstains from sexual activity to preserve his semen, which rises up through the spine, accumulates inside his head, and forms a refined substance, thus producing ascetic power (*tapas*, ritual heat). Through the technique of semen retention, the traditional renouncer is independent from the social world and can harvest his own magical efficacy (O'Flaherty 1973: 261–267; Kakar 1990a: 118–121; Alter 1997: 275–298).

For Pratab, however, Gandhi's power was not self-generated and independent from the world. Rather, his *shakti* was the power of the Indian people, the Indian nation, Mother India. Although traditional forms of asceticism are clearly invoked in the context of Gandhi's politico-religious activism, Pratab's Gandhi derived his power really from his union with the people. In these elaborations, the mahatma resembled more the traditional Saurashtrian king, whose prowess and potency to rule is ultimately dependent on the goodwill of the Mother Goddess exemplified in *shakti* worship. The king could never sustain this marvelous power on his own but needed to procure blood for the Mother Goddess in order to rule, something Gandhi was very unwilling to consent to. Once Gandhi's decision stood in opposition to the people, by agreeing to break the country through Partition, he was no longer protected by the people. A *bhul* came over him, a mistake. The mahatma was no longer shielded (*chhaya*).

Hence, what initially looks like the production of power becomes, at second glance, a form of castration and emasculation of the symbolic father.[10] Pratab has heard about Gandhi's claim—rather typical for an older generation of Gujaratis—that through the loss of semen, eyesight and health in general are put into jeopardy. He, however, did not believe in Gandhi's suggestion of self-chosen celibacy and abstention. Dryly but confidently, Pratab told me that the only real outcome if he turned sexually celibate would be that his wife would run away and find another man. This would spell ruin. It would be like the Indian people deserting their father, who chose to inhabit a woman in the moment when he should have been a man by resisting Partition.

It is important to note that Gandhi never claimed the power that Pratab asserted he suddenly lost. Although he took leadership of the Independence movement in 1919, Gandhi never held political office (Pratab thought he was the first Prime Minister), nor did he ever insist being called *sampurn* or assume the esteem of a traditional king. On the contrary, Gandhi cherished the qualities of motherhood—especially at the end of his life, after the death of his wife Kasturba.[11] To insist on Gandhi's loss of power is to insist that he ever held or wanted this power in the first place. For Gandhi, through perfect nonviolence, or innocence, man does not reach divinity but instead realizes within him the possibility to "become truly man" (M. K. Gandhi 1996: 41).[12]

In fact, Gandhi opposed Partition tooth and nail and finally relented only under pressure of close associates, resigned and devastated, trying to quell the violence unleashed. Partition broke the mahatma's heart, and he fell into a depression, communicating his wish to die or be killed (Nandy 1998a [1980]: 88). There is a certain unintended and yet decisive cruelty in making Gandhi responsible retroactively for what he so ardently opposed. Partition became the mahatma's biggest failure, and yet there is no tenderness, no repose, in making the symbolic father fully accountable for it retroactively although he held no political office or claim to possess occult powers.

For Pratab, Gandhi was one with the people until the moment when there was *bhagla vakhate*—the time of breaking. At the moment he allowed Muslims their separate country, Pakistan, he was made to be the symbolic father of the newborn nation, albeit a failed one, who stood accused of breaking Mother, the prior imaginary fullness. Gandhi became the father in order to stand accused. He stood accused because the unity of Mother—the people—had to remain intact. Hence, blaming Gandhi for Partition stood in the service of allowing the imaginary unity of the people to remain unscathed.

Gandhi eventually relented to Partition, I conjecture, only because he hoped to quell violence between Hindus and Muslims. He understood what Pratab does not want to acknowledge even today. It was the people themselves in whose name unity was invoked, and whose unity Gandhi himself had represented against the British, who betrayed this idea. It was the people and the many leaders they followed that were responsible for the enactment of violence and the mutilation of their own newly found freedom. Perhaps the people had too many mothers at the time, too many ways to feel whole to an imagined prior unity.

Pratab likens Gandhi's political strategies, such as his fasts-unto-death, to pistols or rifles. For Pratab, the idea of fasting being used merely as a "weapon" against the British, means that pistols and rifles, instruments of violence, are transformations of the Gandhian fast, an act of nonviolence. The link between renunciation and magical potentiality as described above has been a prevalent notion in Gujarat and elsewhere in India. Traditionally, all forms of penance produced magical power, and a long line of personages used self-mortification, self-sacrifice, and austerity for ritual as well as political purposes. Power seemed always to emerge in the context of withholding consumption (asceticism) or its inverse, the act of expenditure, as in blood sacrifice.

Thus the deficiency that Gandhi cured with the remedy *upvas* (fasting), a violence internalized, might as well be cured with the remedy "rifle," a violence externalized. And indeed, Gandhi was killed by a pistol in the very moment that, according to Pratab, he no longer represented the people but weakness and division. Both the fast and the rifle are transformations of each other in the same way as are *himsa* and *ahimsa*, sacrifice and self-sacrifice. They are both technologies to accumulate and channel power, a power whose source is really in the people. A single shot with a pistol by Nathuram Godse, a man of the people, and a man who in Gujarat is openly identified with the RSS, could do what the British never dared to do. The act of assassinating Gandhi itself becomes the retroactive triumph of the people over the British, who according to Pratab, did not dare kill the mahatma. Godse, after killing Gandhi, explained:

> Gandhiji failed in his duty as the father of the Nation. He has proved to be the Father of Pakistan. It was for this reason alone that I as a dutiful son of Mother India thought it my duty to put an end to the life of the so-called Father of the Nation who had played a very prominent part in bringing about vivisection of the country—our Motherland. (Nandy 1998a [1980]: 83)

Many Gujaratis today read Gandhi's murder not as resulting in a descent into violence following a prelapsarian narrative, but they blame his death on his consent to Partition. The prelapsarian narrative of the fall from a former state of wellbeing has been displaced by a sacrificial one in which his assassination can be read retroactively as the opposite of murder, which is sacrifice, for the sake of a unity betrayed. Gandhi was killed only after the unity of mother had been violated. The mahatma was thus consumed by the people, who were angry at his *bhul*. The people are she who always longs for blood. This amounts to what Nandy (1998a [1980]: 70–98) has insightfully analyzed as the "joint communiqué of political assassination," in which the idolatrous relation to the historical Gandhi is a function of identification with the murderer.

That is why, during field research, whenever Nathuram Godse was mentioned, even if not lauded, I rarely heard him be openly condemned, except by those who stood in unambiguous ideological opposition to the Sangh Parivar. After Gandhi's death, the very reason for his weakness, that which used to be his power—truth and nonviolence—became enshrined as a surrogate of the father: the ideal of ahimsa, which is now held to be *sampurn* (perfect, complete). The attribution of perfection and completeness to a man who strove his whole life to communicate his own personal failures thus seems like a form of subdued aggression. Such subdued aggression occurs with astonishing regularity whenever Gandhi is subject of discussion.

The Indian psychoanalyst Sudhir Kakar (1978: 103–139) has pointed out that in India, the son turns away from the father libidinally, but never through breaking with the father openly. The lack of open conflict between father and son is symptomatic in a society that, on the one hand, emphasizes patriliny while simultaneously making the father dependent on his son for salvation. Gandhi is blamed but preserved, mourned but held responsible at the same time, like the many mute statues erected in his honor. The statues are erected so that one can turn away from them whenever one pleases. When Ahmedabadi residents drive in rush-hour traffic, they will risk an accident to greet the many Mother Goddesses along the road in little adjacent street temples at full speed. But no one will gesture to greet a dusty Gandhi statue. Nonetheless, Gandhi remains *sampurn*.

In sum, the enigmatic relationship to this figure, Gandhi, in Gujarat consists in never rejecting the mahatma, his ideals, or his fame outright. Idol Gandhi is caught in a prison of nationalist worship. The ritual lip service reveals a relationship to the symbolic father as a broken one. To describe him as *sampurn* in one moment and identify him with a "small" mistake in the next, a mistake that ends up swallowing all other aspects of Gandhi, reveals that the preceding elevation really served the opposite purpose. Pratab's idolization of Gandhi had the function of punishing the father and turning towards the mother. If Gandhi were rejected openly and consciously, the strange identification with ahimsa and Hindu vulnerability in the context of anti-Muslim violence would have to become unhinged.

Whenever the Sangh Parivar manipulates the collective memory of Gandhi, omitting or adding the "non-" to nonviolence, it is able to give voice to a collectively shared ambivalence, which reverberates with people like Pratab. It intuits with people who think or feel in similar ways but will carefully abstain from openly saying so since the mahatma has become part of what Taussig (1997: 137) called "soulstuff." In erecting Gandhi as *sampurn*, the mahatma's ethical demand, which was fundamentally a human one, can be dismissed.

ANGRY HINDU ANONYMOUS

The text that follows is part of an edited volume, including statements by journalists, writers, Chief Minister Modi himself, and others, about the Godhra incident and "reactive" pogrom. The paperback cover of the book depicts the burning coach of Sabarmati express in Godhra. The text translated here is the second article of the volume, a sort of introduction, and significantly, like the "auto-biography of a goat," it remains anonymous, whereas all the other chapters name individual authors of the texts. The author is simply named as *ek krodh hindu*— one angry Hindu. The word "one" signifies the many that authorize the singular. I reproduce the full introduction, translated from the original Gujarati.[13] The short text describes the metamorphosis of vulnerability and division into anger and unity and is an example of the magical voice that the Sangh Parivar successfully employed to construe the meaning of the pogrom violence.

•   •   •

Why Did Anger Come? One Angry Hindu

A famous pseudo-secularist wrote a letter in a weekly. Reading it, some angry Hindu roared. Immediately upon looking at this article, his eyes turned red with anger.

Yes, undoubtedly, I am angry. My anger is appropriate. If I were not angry I would not be a human being.

For a long time I have been suffering insults quietly and until now I just have merely kept on suffering. The enemies have kidnapped my fellow brethren and rendered my numbers small. The result: My country worth worshipping was broken. My traditional right was snatched away. Afghanistan, West-, South-, horizontal land, Sindh, Baluchistan, half of Punjab, half of Bengal, and a third of Kashmir were stolen. I suffered countless violations, insults, and I was hunted in mass-killings. I was chased out of this country.

And nonetheless it is said that I should not become angry! I should not remain unbent! I should not angrily shout: This is enough!

My gods and temples were rendered unholy. They were destroyed. The attackers crushed the statues of my gods under their feet. My gods are crying out in shrieks of horror. They are looking at me for their reestablishment. If I express my suffering to them, the secularists make it seem as if I break communal harmony. They begin abusing me. You pour salt into my wounds but still expect that I should keep my mouth shut?

The main reason for my anger is your betrayal and deceit. You come to me when you need my vote. But you are promoting those who are attacking me. If I save myself from their effort [*akraman*, also invasion], then you call me communal [*sampradayik*, sectarian].

When they are shouting "we are in danger"—(even if this claim is not true)—you give them support in the name of minority. In Godhra a violent Muslim mob well equipped with weapons attacked us. The reaction [*pratikriya*, counteraction, retribution, retaliation] to this was natural. Around this, how much noise was made! But in Kashmir how many temples have been destroyed? When my brothers and sisters were driven out, there was not even a single word of protest coming from your mouth. And still you blame me for being angry?

When some Muslim or Christian heads of state come to my country and then visit a mosque or church for prayer, their followers line up in front of them as if for a lecture. That news you print in big big continuous letters in the [newspaper] columns. If not that much, then you silently praise their feeling of patriotism. But if our president or minister performs worship in some temple, you start shouting. This shows the doubt about their own "secular tradition" [*dharm-nirpeksh parampara*]. If the Ramayan is screened on TV, this, too, you are not able to tolerate. In this you see "Hindu extremism."

The logic of your arguments reveals your own double standard. The number of worldviews from followers of diverse sects is less than mine. You gave them the name "minority" and you have started advocating their rights. In Kashmir and West-East states Hindus also are in the minority. They were chased out of the region and were treated like second-class citizens. Yet still, I have never heard you advocate in favor of us [Hindus].

You failed to see the ugly face of communalism when in Kerala, the Muslim League and the "Kerala Congress"—which means the "Christian Congress"—sheltered Congress and communists who substituted their rule. When I voiced a little protest, all of you, one after another, immediately began to identify the mark [sign] of communalism in the clear picture of Kerala. If any point or issue about Hindus is raised the minority becomes upset about the issue. For you, to offer a coconut or to light a lamp is also forbidden behavior. For you, secularism means that, even though a Hindu home, there is nothing Hindu in it. And so it should be in the way of life of a nation [*rashtra jivannu swarup*, the form of national life]. In short, I am not remaining me. I should forget my identity [*asmita*, pride], that is what you are desiring.

However, you should also understand that I will never fulfill this wish in your mind. In my heart, Maharshi Arvind's voice is echoing full of emotion: "On the foundation of Sanatana Dharma India will rise again." The words of Gandhi are deeply resounding in my life: "If no Hindu lives in India, in that India, I do not wish to live." I also have not forgotten Annie Besant's words: "If Hindu dharm is ruined, then India will not remain India." Swami Vivekananda's voice keeps resounding in my heart: "Hindu dharm is India and India is Hindu dharm."

Sometimes, I feel pity for your mental corruption [*mansik vikruti*, mental perversion]. In my country there are ninety percent Hindus. You fail to grasp even such a straightforward fact clearly? For my country's Independence I shed my blood. That also you do not understand and you wish to keep me separate from the very people who openly enjoy those rights. These are those people who in private talk together with foreigners have broken my motherland into pieces. You don't want me to teach my culture and traditional spirituality to my children with love. I should not sing praise to my ancient great men . . . and those people who are annoyed about [care for] each and every holy matter. They, in turn, can teach in their school whatever pleases them. Can you not see the horrible unevenness [*bedbhavo*, differences, distinctions]? That which we are offering at the feet of our god—money earned in sweat—that money my rulers have begun to waste. The question of the so-called minority taking money must be addressed because they are nourished through my wealth. Through my helpful contribution, they go on the Haj pilgrimage. I should tolerate all this insult, injustice, and exploitation quietly? And still you dare to ask me not to become angry? Even insects are reacting, don't you know that? Am I inferior even to an insect?

You make fun of me by saying I am an "angry Hindu" [*krodh hindu*]. In my mind that is not a joke. It is a compliment [*prashansa-stuti*, a praise of admiration]. For a long time I was unconscious [*bebhan avasthama*, not alert]. I was not alert at the time when my motherland was broken into pieces. But the continuous blows on me have awoken me. Now I have started to hear, understand, and think (about) the ongoing oppression that has befallen me. This is the result of my former mistakes. Now, I will no longer remain fearful, I will not remain quiet. Now I will speak. I will become active and energetic, I will fear no challenge. I will confront them.

That you call me "angry Hindu" [*krodhit hindu*] fills me with delight. Until today, I was the angry landowner, farmer, malik [village head], laborer; and then I was the angry Kannadi, Marathi, Bengali; and then I was the angry Jat, Harijan, Brahman, Rajput; and then I was the angry Lingayat, Arya Samaji, Jain. But now you have given me a new name—"wrathful angry Hindu." In this, all can be included. Everybody is included in this. That name suggests that after so many centuries my existence [*astitva*, being] has become complete [*samagra*] and a perfectly united form [*sampurn ekam na rupe*], a Hindu form.[14] Now, I can think as one unit. I am able to have an experience [*anubhavi shaku chhu*]. I am able to do work. Is that a small gain?

I was in decline for many centuries. The main reason for this was that I was un-united and divided. I had forgotten my real and natural Hindu identity [*asmita*, pride]. Knowingly or unknowingly you admire [envy] me for my experience and, now, for resolving my mistake. Keep in mind that you yourself have accepted that my anger is not just the anger of some small flock of people. It is the anger of 90 crore people. . . . The anger of 90 crore people.[15]

Now I understand. How ignorant I was about the hard reality of the world until now. I always thought that as I gave respect to the opinions of other sects, they also will give respect to my gods and temples. I understood that I make no attack on another country, but they also do not make any attack on my country in turn. It was my expectation that if you are good, then the world is good.[16] I lay trust in the fact that in war those *niti-maryadao* [rules of moral conduct] I am observing would also be observed in the same way by my enemies. I was giving the enemy's women respect and kept the limit [*maryada*, boundary, separation]. I believed that the enemy, too, would act like that in turn. I accepted equal rights for all sectarian opinions and beliefs. Okay, their confidence and mode of worship should be according to their wishes. I believed that others would also show that kind of inclination towards me.

But alas, I have been cheated again and again. I have been betrayed. I have been stabbed in the back. Those that I had allowed to built their worship place [*puja sthan*] in my land [*bhumi*] started to render my worship places unholy and began to demolish them in return. In return for giving them freedom [*svatantrata*, independence] to continue their method of worship, they started to destroy my religion. The answer to my morality [*nautikta*] came through their immorality [*anautikta*]. I considered all as equal. They dealt with me even worse than with an animal. As compensation for my kindness I met with wickedness.

Now I also have knowledge of the dealings of the world. Now I have also decided to put into practice those rules tit for tat. There is no doubt that in the manner of spiritual ideals, my morality is in me.[17] It is my most excellent cultural treasure. I'll never leave it. Never ever. If I allow them to go, I would not remain a true Hindu. I would not remain the descendant of my great saints. But I have become vigilant now. I will no longer allow others to take improper advantage of my goodwill. To do good dealings with evil men is a vice [*avgun*, bad quality]. It becomes a bad habit.

The truth is, I am more angry with myself than with any other. I am angry about myself. For a long time I have allowed my *jaat* [tribe, race] to be deceived in different forms in the past. After Independence my *jaat* was cheated, was deceived, through the hands of pseudo-secularists.[18] How many lessons I have learned now! I will pay attention to the preaching and warnings of my saviors, protectors, great men. Shankaracharya said: "Generosity expressed towards good men is very good. Expressing generosity to evil men is not good." Shri Ramkrishna Paramahans narrated the tale [*bodh-katha*, moral lesson] of a snake. According to the story, a snake had assumed a complete virtuous conduct through the preaching of a *sadhu* [an ascetic]. The snake was rendered half dead by the throwing of stones on the part of travelers. Seeing the snake's miserable condition, the great soul said: "I told you not to bite, but not to stop hissing.[19] The snake understood its mistake and started to hiss again. Its life was saved."

Swami Vivekananda advised his own disciples in this way: "If anyone insults your mother, you experience that through the insult your blood is boiling. Okay like that, today, if any Christian missionary abuses Hindu religion, gives bad names, and then converts your religious brethren, then also your blood should boil and rise."

When making a boat trip, Swami Vivekananda threatened to throw two Christian preachers into the ocean by holding them by their feet. These Christian missionaries had kept on insulting Hindu religion. Both Christian preachers started shivering out of fear. When they stopped hurting Hindu religion and apologized, then Swami Vivekananda let them go. Shri Krishna and Chhatrapati Shivaji's method was exactly like this. In order to observe the most excellent moral behavior, they have always used their power of discrimination [*vivek-buddhi*]. It is because of these glorious men that the Hindus have remained Hindu. This fact I have now understood.

I have now experienced the importance of my anger. Because of this, fear has slowly arisen in the heart of my enemies-by-birth [*janm jat trasvadio*, terrorists-since-birth or longtime-enemies]. Out of these terrorists, a few have started to leave the camp of secularism. They have begun to realize the full extent of my anger. Not only that, but they have now begun to respect my anger. You are but one [single] knowing being and such was your vanity. As if pure reason was yours alone, only recently have a few high judges, admirers, journalists, historians, writers, professors, etc., begun to defend my position. The fortress of "intellectuality" from which you safely rained down melee and missile weapons upon me, that fortress is going to be collapsing in a short time. Beware! Now your mental hypocrisy will strike you back like a boomerang.

Before I finish my talk, I insist you understand the hidden meaning of the famous journalist's warning: "It takes time for the Hindu to awake, but once awoken, even the Himalaya is shivering. And the Himalaya is the residence of the most angry Hindu—Shiv." (Makawana 2002: 11–17)

THE BROKEN LANGUAGE OF AUTHORITY

Professor Parmar, a middle-class Catholic of Dalit background with whom I translated the text, wanted to quit halfway through, as he felt denigrated by its attacks on Christians. The style and tenor of the writing angered him. My interpretation below relies greatly on his extensive linguistic expertise. As he speculated, on the basis of the language employed, the text appears to have been written by a first-generation literate, probably a member of a lower or intermediary caste, with minimal knowledge of *shuddh* Gujarati, English, or Sanskrit. The text does not appear to be written by a University-educated author because the mix of quotidian Gujarati expressions with Sanskrit terms in an ill-informed manner for local sensibilities. English is painstakingly avoided, as the Gujarezi expressions (English and Gujarati mixed) common in speech of the urban middle to lower-middle classes are almost completely absent.

There is a marked intent not to use Gujarati at specific moments, but a strong Sanskrit presence. The text is inundated with somewhat confusing Sanskrit terms, like *prashansa-stuti, aradya bhumi,* or *nivas sthan.* The substitution of everyday words associated with "Muslim" because they derive from Farsi or Urdu with Sanskrit terms associated with "Hindu" is carried out to the detriment of elegance and readability. The author uses, for example, words like *shatruo* instead of the much more common *dushman* (enemy, opponent), which is derived from Urdu. These Sanskrit terms float into a simple Gujarati in an incompetent way. There are also mistakes in the text, in grammar, punctuation, as well as vocabulary itself (including in the use of Gujarati words).

The creation of a new purified language that no longer indexes humiliation and shame, or rather conceals it under gold and glitter, is characteristic of the style of "Vedic revival" in Gujarat, a tendency to identify everything new in science and technology as a "Vedic return." One might understand this momentous substitution of usable words with nonusable ones as expressions of Hindu kitsch, inaugurating the emergence of a language of pure adornment and decoration.

The use of Sanskrit terms in the text, indicating the speaker's relation to something Vedic, does not mean, however, that the writer attempts to claim the status of a learned Jain, Brahmin, or a someone of social stature. The anonymous voice of the angry Hindu that speaks does not try to inhabit Sanskrit knowledge and the status associated with it. Through his use of Sanskrit, the author does not establish authority over the terms. In other words, the author knows his subordinate place and delegates authority to the *mahapurusho,* the great men of the Hindu tradition. He uses Sanskrit terms only in order to indicate his own relation to them, not competency over them.

It is, therefore, not the authority of the author, but of "Indian Sanskrit tradition" that is established through the use of Sanskrit terms. By extension, the usage establishes authority over all things "Hindu." The author uses Sanskrit to express a relation to that cultural sphere he claims he is part of, in fact, a child of. In the logic of the book of which this article is a part, his lack of authority and education paradoxically authorizes him to say the things he does. If the anonymous author does not need to claim mastery over Sanskrit or religious knowledge in order to establish his own authority, in what, then consists this authority?

His authority resides in his bluntness, his directness, and, above all, his anger. The author knows that any Brahman or middle-class educated Gujarati might recognize that the speaker is not a member of an educated class, to whom the unevenness in the materiality of language of the text would be obvious. But what is much more important is the author's deference to and respect for the *mahapurusho* of the Hindu tradition. The spirit of the text tries to transcend castes and communities in the Hindu fold and reach an identification that is not dependent on claims of parity of lower-status groups with the educated language of higher castes. Rather, the identification is based on devotion following the logic of *bhakti* (devotional-forms worship). The unsophisticated use of language does not hamper that attempt but, on the contrary, facilitates it.

HEALING ANGER

What then does this text do? Above all, it overcomes the inability of "Hinduism" to create a satisfactory experience of unity. This unity is finally accomplished only in the experience of anger. The anonymous writer makes this rather explicit: *aje hu samagr ane sampurn ekamna rupe, Hindu rupe, astitvama avyo chhu* (today my existence [*astitva*, being] has become complete in a perfectly united form, a Hindu form). In *sampurn ekamna rupe, Hindu rupe*, we see the emergence of an incarnation of the Hindu in anger. The author draws attention to the angry wrathful Hindu, the name given to this new Hindu by his enemies. It is not the knowledge of Sanskrit but anger that makes perfect and whole (*sampurn*). It is the magic of becoming one, one form (*rupe*, also incarnation), in anger.

The many historical injuries enlisted come from a variety of sources and across times. They are all condensed into one so that the feeling of injury and anger can arise and sustain itself. Whereas disgust is an affect that expresses a collapse of boundaries and an instability in relation to the object, anger unifies and makes the object appear in full clarity. If nonviolence is conceived in the register of law and the Father, anger is prior to law and erupts from the imaginary, a sentiment in the register of an encompassing mother's indulgence. Unlike the paralyzing affect of disgust, which fixates on the rejected object, anger mobilizes for action. It is a good catalyst for violent activity, seeking a target and its negation or annihilation (Kolnai 2007 [1929]: 107–108).

The anonymous author addresses the anonymous "pseudo-secularists." A "pseudo-secularist" is what a Hindu nationalist calls a secularist. Application and meaning of terms such as "secularist" and "pseudo-secularist" are complex and reveal symbolic struggles over perception of the nature of the present invoking diverse *Weltanschauungen*. "Secularist" in India does not necessarily describe a position that rejects religion but frequently one that supports a multitude and equality of religions against religious nationalism and fundamentalism. Hindu nationalists, too, do not reject secularist principles per se (defined as a multitude of religions), but only their so-called Western forms, which are understood to cause a splintering of Hindu unity.

Both secularists and Hindu nationalists (who call the former "pseudo-secularists") differ on the nature of religious harmony and authority. While secularists have a tendency to view as legitimate self-assertion of lower categories of Hindu society, as well as of Muslims and Christians, Hindu nationalists are suspicious of these developments and call instead for a unified identity under the sign of the "Hindu," understood not as a particular religion but a cultural ethos, a "Hindu way of life" (*hindu jivshaili*). This way of life is usually referred to as "Hindu-ness" and is not to be confused with "Hinduism." In central Gujarat, however, such distinctions have become fundamentally unstable.

The pseudo-secularist addressed in the text is, however, unambiguously the Western-educated, English-speaking elite, who are assumed to be dismissive of the genuine religiosity of the masses. The text describes the moment of anger as a spontaneous coming to consciousness. We have encountered this elsewhere already, where Hindu awakening is described by terms like *jagruti* and where becoming "Hindu" is a coming to oneself, becoming the *tatva* (essence) of Hindu, *hindutva*. But the text not only describes "anger" but transforms it into "voice."

There is a double entendre in the last two sentences of the text suggesting the line of interpretation I have followed here. In the quotation of the "famous journalists" when describing the people's anger, the author says, "It takes time for the Hindu to awake, but once awoken, even the Himalaya is shivering. And the Himalaya is the residence of the most angry Hindu—Shiv." One might also translate the last sentence as "And the Himalaya is the residence of the Hindu's most angry god, Shiv." The text ends by conjuring up the anger of the Hindu god Shiva, the angriest of all Hindus. But there is a slippage. Why would Shiva shiver? In the face of who or what does the god have to be afraid? Is Shiva trembling because of the intensity of his own anger, or shivering in the face of Hindu anger? The power of Shiva, as some Gujaratis would say, is *shakti*, the female source of all power. Shiva's anger is always *Her* power. Even the Himalaya, his abode, is trembling once *She* is awoken. Shiva trembles in the sight of "Hindu anger," of which he himself is the most perfect expression. But his power is not his own. It is given to him by *shakti*, female power. It is She who is the prior one. In the context of Hindutva, She, of course, is the people, the primal force, before any distinction, before which even the Gods must be trembling. The auto-destructive force of nationalism lies in the successful summoning of this mythical force of the people that in its legitimacy is capable of crushing everything, even its own religious traditions in whose name it claims to act. Welcome to Hindu *rashtra*!

• • •

This chapter began with an error in a newspaper clipping, something that happened and came over *The Times of India* at a most inopportune moment. The error attributed violence to Gandhi, while it placed him in a lineage, a pantheon of important national leaders, all of whom are said to oppose violence. The last in the lineage is Narendra Modi. All of the leaders except Modi are portrayed as looking away from the reader, as if not part of this world anymore. Modi, however, who is of this world today and who stands accused to have surpported the use of violence, looks into the eyes of the reader directly, in a gesture towards the future.

The thumbnail version of ahimsa is the seemingly arbitrary addition or subtraction of "non-" to "violence," the inclusion of the *himsa* of ahimsa as part of a political movement and its cultural resources. This is what has become of the ethical principle of nonviolence in the context of Hindutva. Violence and nonviolence have become that over which one establishes mastery and thus over the appeal and power that a figure like Gandhi carries. Whether one adds "*a-*" to "*himsa*" or "non-" to "violence" does not really matter. What matters is being situated in such a way as to be able to play with both as one pleases. In that way, the one is merely the symmetrical reversal ("mistake") of the other. Here ahimsa functions in a way similar to Freud's (1931: 399–404) elaboration on *Verneinung*, a negation in which the negated part (*himsa*, violence) acts as affirmation of a more momentous desire. The play of ahimsa and *himsa* is determined by those who have the means to invoke the concept in one of its two possible forms, respectively, whenever it is suitable. In a Hindu nationalist context, ahimsa stands in the service of *himsa*, the one a sign of strength, the other a sign of cowardice. To the degree that this inscription is successful, nothing can stand against ahimsa any longer—not even its symmetrical opposite, which it already expresses, vitiating the concept of its dialectical force.

As a cultural phenomenon expressing consciousness about injury, contemporary ahimsa is reminiscent of what the young Hegel once identified as dead positivity (*Positivität*), a concept developed in his early critique of Christianity in the immediate aftermath of the French Revolution. Positivity is given when the moral autonomy of a historical subject is cancelled and disappears behind religious or doctrinal assertions, resulting in a petrified morality that is simply administered (Lukács 1973: 56–75, 134–159). In the dialectic movement of the historical process, products of intellectual labor become implicated in ways that are often obverse to their initial intention. We should no longer expect much of a concept that can no longer oppose its own reversal.

In sum, the omission of "non-" with which this chapter began was neither a mistake nor an arbitrary coincidence. It was a sudden eruption of truth, a public secret in a text authorized by the Gujarat government. "Violence is the greatest asset of the brave." Hindus are only whole and perfect if they can rule over the entire spectrum, affirming on the one hand their inclination toward nonviolence while simultaneously proving to themselves that they can also be violent. The slip expressed what too many Gujaratis would have wanted the father of the nation to have said when he really meant the opposite.

The anonymous author of the autobiography in chapter 4 inhabited a goat in the moment of death and its unfolding in order to allow for disgust and moral outrage to emerge. The anonymous author in the text above inhabits the *krodh* Hindu as a historical subject moving through empty homogeneous time, piling one injury upon another and growing a resentment that provides wholeness in anger. While revulsion is an experience of vulnerability causing collapse and instability in the subject, anger allows for a firmness of sentiment and the hallucination of coherence and unity.

CHAPTER 7

Split City Body

DIVISION

A series of contradictions mark the urban experience of Ahmedabad. The city is Gujarat's largest and one of India's major commercial centers. It has an official and fast-growing population of over five million residents. In normal times, it is felt to be safer than most metropolitan Indian cities. Residents are proud to point out that instances of rape, murder, and robbery are much more frequent in Bombay, Bangalore, or Delhi. Yet there is something conservative and staid about its cultural scene, meaning that despite the general perception of safety, many of its younger residents frequently aspire to move to other large urban centers in India or even to international destinations like London or New York. Often I was asked, "Why did you come here?" as if the places from which I came must, in any case, be better.

Ahmedabad is also a city with a continuous history, and unlike Calcutta, for example, it is not steering headlong into "unmitigated decline" (Kaviraj 1997: 86). Although it has witnessed calamitous events like floods, earthquakes, and communal riots, it is also, for many of the residents, a city of calm and prosperity. In quieter times, the city busies itself with infrastructural improvements in an atmosphere of endless growth. Its entrepreneurial class has proved capable, to a large extent, of insulating the local economy from the devastating ups and downs of international capital markets. While the city is strongly divided along class, caste, and communal lines, at the same time, it remains integrated through community borders, cyclical occurrences of violence, spatial urban imaginaries, and an economic division of labor.

Divisions of the city fall into sharp relief during times of violence or in its aftermath, when one difference is able to bridge all others and becomes more prominent. The Hindu-Muslim divide is the default mode of all divisions. In periods of violence, the city behaves like a gigantic organism, closing the many interfaces between areas and communities, as if it were a giant cell reacting against chemical intrusion: bridges become structures of confinement; police posts define borders, which in turn become spaces for provocation and violent performance; sacred structures become sites of conversion, identity assertion, and injury. Then any traversing of urban space is fraught with immense psychological stress and incalculable risk. This chapter describes experiences of separation and how they become expressed with reference to the city's hardware: its bridges, police posts, roadside temples, and the use of interstitial space for urban expiation rituals.[1]

THE CITY'S BRIDGES

What is a bridge? At first blush, this question seems simple enough.

Bridges are ingenious structures that allow passage over and above an obstacle: a gorge, a river, a highway, or train tracks. It seems commonsense that bridges unite separated spaces. In the notoriously congested Indian inner cities of Bombay and Surat, for example, many overpasses function as bridges to facilitate the flow of traffic over and above busy intersections. Local residents call these flyovers, as if to suggest a meaningless intermediary space that must quickly be overcome by a continuously rolling traffic.

The Sabarmati River is traversed by seven modern bridges—large, elongated tongues of steel and cement. The bridges over the river connect the eastern part of the city with its western counterpart, the new city, and there are plans for additional ones. For the first-time visitor, Ahmedabad's bridges can seem bereft of purpose—merely uniting two sides of a large, sandy ditch or ravine—because the riverbed is dry for most of the year (figure 12). Yet the waters of the Sabarmati are deceptive, and the city's history is satiated with occurrences of great floods with devastating consequences (Edalji 1986 [1894]: 297). Historically, the river has never been a navigable waterway (Gillion 1968: 14–15, 99, 130–131).

There are other bridges that pass over land or railway tracks, such as the Chimanbhai and Kalupur Bridges, or that pass beneath obstacles, such as the Shahibag Bridge: underpasses that residents call "underbridges." During riots and collective violence, underbridges are particularly dangerous, as they allow attackers to throw stones onto frantically jumbled traffic.

The historical city of Ahmedabad, founded by king Ahmed Shah in 1411, knew no bridge over the river, nor did it expand onto the western shore. By contrast, today, the city has grown far beyond the old city wall into the east, as well as into the west, creating two halves of a city divided

FIGURE 12: Under Ahmedabad's bridges

by a river as in many other places, too. Ostensibly, Ahmedabad's bridges over the Sabarmati unite two opposing shores to expedite travel between them, and thus increase what is called "trafficability" (Gazetteer of India 1984: 479).

The anticolonial rebellion in 1857 caused suspension of most public works programs, but British officials renewed efforts after its suppression, and emergent nationalist elites then began to appropriate the scientific and technological projects of imperialist rule (Prakash 1999: 6–7, 159–161). In Ahmedabad, this transformation led to a restructuring of the city's morphology: a revaluation of city space, in which an older cosmological scheme integrating ruler and ruled in the old inner city was replaced with a new spatial order, with immediate benefits for the new urban elite (Raychaudhuri 1997: 16–24, 124–129; 2001: 680).[2] By the 1920s, during the height of anticolonial struggle, town-planning schemes led to a "new system of signification" (Raychaudhuri 2001: 710), attributing higher values to city areas on the west shore. Thus was created a new ceremonial center of the city around Gujarat Vidhyapit, a university founded by Mahatma Gandhi, replacing the old one around the Bhadra citadel (ibid.: 712).

This twentieth-century shift of the city's symbolic center from an old city, marked by a Muslim ruler's past, to the west was made possible by these bridges over the Sabarmati. The heavy travel over them replays daily the historical shift all over again. The movement that the traffic performs seems like a gigantic, everyday flight into the west: from the crowded, intimate space in the inner city, full of dense lanes and *pols* (minuscule alleys and cul-de-sacs), to the *puras* (suburbs) on the western shore, with its residential areas, wider streets, and highways.

The oldest bridge over the Sabarmati, Ellis Bridge, named after a British colonial officer, was built in 1870 and rebuilt in 1875 after a devastating flood destroyed the original.[3] Construction on the western shore of the Sabarmati, however, only began in the early twentieth century. The famous Sabarmati Ashram, founded by Mahatma Gandhi in 1917, and the older Satyagraha Ashram, founded in the village of Kochrab in 1915, today both lie securely within the west city. They used to lie outside the city proper. As tourist attractions, they bear witness to the immense expansion that followed independence on the west side, which today is unambiguously considered the better half of the city. Referring to the mahatma's ashrams, an acquaintance put it to me, "Where Gandhi is, there is peace."

Most other bridges over the Sabarmati are named after modern Indian leaders, all of whom were proponents of national unity. From the far south of the city, after Vasna Barrage, one encounters Sardar Bridge (built in 1939); further up in the very city center, Ellis and Nehru Bridges (the latter built in 1962); then Gandhi Bridge (built in 1940) to the north, followed by Subhash and Indira Bridges in the far north, both built after independence. Much as these bridges divide the two halves of the city (as I explain below), Gujaratis are divided and ambivalent about the legacy of their national leaders.[4]

More recently, the city bridges have been widened frequently to facilitate commuter traffic. In 2000, Gandhi Bridge was widened and Ellis Bridge became Vivekanand Bridge. In the context of the contemporary Vedic revival, it was renamed after one of the heroes of the nineteenth-century Hindu reform movements. The old bridge was not reconstructed but added onto. At the west end of the bridge, a large statue of Swami Vivekananda now stands opposite the Ahmedabad town hall, next to the Ellisbridge police station. The new structure is built around the older in such a manner that what was once its main causeway is now an odd, abandoned, and unused middle strip, flanked by two large new roads wide enough for white Tata Sumo jeeps, several trucks and buses—old Ellis has literally become engulfed by Vivekananda.

In the way that locals reference these immense cement constructions, however, they reveal a different imaginary, one in which bridges have little to do with unifying space: two halves of a city, two shores of a river, east and west. City residents habitually perform a typical hand movement gesturing to the opposing river shore. Not incidentally, middle-class residents in west Ahmedabad will often claim that Muslims live "on the other side of the river." They live "inside" (*ander*) meaning within the old city, which is on the eastern side of the river. Sometimes, people will use the hybrid expression "inside area *ma*," or the more proper "*juna shaher ma*" (in the old city). Residents in the west city have a tendency to insist that violence is happening "there," and the new McDonald's is opening "here." Muslims and Dalits are living "there," and we are living "here." Killings are "there," and Gandhi's ashram of nonviolence is "here."

These references in idiom, speech, and gesture are overdetermined. They intend to execute a desired result more than describe an actual empirical fact. Indeed, it is easy to mobilize counterfactuals. Not only do members of all communities live on both sides of the river, as well as inside and outside the historical old city; liquor, meat, communal violence, prostitution, and crime are available all over Ahmedabad. Not only is Maninagar a better-off Hindu area in the eastern city. But there are also overcrowded ghettos without access to water in the western suburbs, and the Muslim ghetto of Juhapura lies in the southwest of the city.

Such communicative acts, contrary to fact, are exorcisms of sorts, which perform a categorical expiation in the act of speaking, during which the object to be designated is relegated to the other side. As speech acts or gestures, they are approximations and describe an experience grounded in the historical development of industrial labor, town-planning schemes, and urban growth as well as inner-city migration of elites to the new city after every major outbreak of communal violence (Breman 2004; Nandy et al. 1995: 111).

Nor are these references one-sided or unidirectional. In the old city, or alternatively in the larger eastern stretches of the city, residents will as naturally refer to the western side when indicating the existence of full facilities: broader roads, desirable jobs, greenery, commodities, and well-paying customers. Here, the logic is not one of expiation, but of anticipatory projection, a dreamlike wish fulfillment. Everything imaginable that is unavailable or unaffordable "here"' beckons from "there." If young men desire premarital sexual adventures, which are impossible "here," it is likely to be possible "there," as the western city has many colleges filled with well-to-do and "modern" girls.

In most neighborhoods of the west, low-paid workers—such as watchmen, washmen, milkmen, vegetable sellers, cleaners, tobacco sellers, and tea brewers—cater to a middle and upper-middle class in their petit bourgeois lives. Many consider themselves fortunate to be able to do so in this part of the city. They journey daily over the bridges by bus or bicycle, while some have even found affordable housing in the west. The contact between classes of diverse income levels in apartment buildings and housing societies is frequent and allows them to see, touch, and smell the good life.

When I considered places to stay during my field research visits, I was confronted with these dichotomies and an array of rationalizations accompanying them. While I was warned about choosing to reside in the inner city, areas to the far east, outside the former city walls, were considered beyond the pale for a Westerner like me: they were simply considered unsuitable. For a century, the industrial crescent around the old city had witnessed frequent public unrest. But even in calm times, the area is considered unruly by default.

The terms with which this unruly quality is frequently understood by better-off city residents are truncated and heavily clichéd. Already in 1909, the Dhed Sabha, an organization for the uplifting of untouchables, campaigned locally against liquor and meat consumption among the working class (Breman 2004: 36–37). Today, also, many organizations do not stress labor relations or housing conditions but religious and cultural reform as goals to be achieved. In this, they stand in stark opposition to the silent work of non-governmental organizations that attempt to ameliorate conditions of the working poor and are often slandered by political actors. From the time of my very first visits to Ahmedabad, I made it a habit to conceal my destination from my middle-class acquaintances whenever I ventured into these areas.

CITY MIRRORS

This uneasiness of middle-class residents living in west Ahmedabad was based on an exaggerated perception of the unruly character of inner-city Muslim communities as self-consciously opposed to Hindu communities as well as of the far-eastern city areas, where low-caste and poor migrant laborers scramble for cheap places to live in an atmosphere of dust and poverty. This latter perception is grounded in a spatial grammar of the city characterized by "border areas" and police posts.

Indeed, in the congested bowels of the old city (for example, around the Bhadra citadel), the ubiquitous Muslim presence is felt to be too close for comfort. Not only the presence of Muslim neighbors as such but that of a Muslim past inscribed into the city's center has begun to pose a point of contention for middle-class Hindu residents. One can say that in this way the old city has remained the ceremonial center of communal posturing, stone throwing, and recurrent neighborhood clashes. Beyond the old city, in the unfinished industrial landscapes of east Ahmedabad (such as in Behrampur, Dani Limda, or Gomptipur), poverty is indexed by poor public works, alcoholism, and frequent outbreaks of community and family feuds. The neglect of public works in this part of the city has a long history and is closely related to the overall spatial configuration of the city (Breman 2004: 31–36).

INSIDE THE OLD CITY

In the historical old city, most living space is structured through *pols*, traditional residential arrangements mostly organized by caste and professional group, which result in an immediate spatial proximity of group members in adjacent alleys, entrance gates, and cul-de-sacs inclusive of secret doors and unknown passageways.[5] In every corner of the old city, the familiar spatial intimacy of different castes and communities is in danger of becoming unfamiliar today. In this way, Ahmedabad consists of three distinct urban spaces, each one connected to a specific urban imaginary as well as to concrete facts on the ground, relating uneasily to one another: the walled city, its eastern periphery, and new Ahmedabad on the western river shore (Nandy et al. 1995: 110–123; Yagnik and Sheth 2005: 229–230).

These divisions of the city's urban morphology were preconceived as town-planning schemes and were implemented during the height of nationalist struggle in the 1920s. The city's elite leadership wanted land in Ahmedabad to be "neatly arranged into working class areas, middle and upper class residential localities, commercial areas, and industrial areas" (Raychaudhuri 1997: 128). They successfully achieved the spatial segregation thus preconceived. The functional organization of urban space by economic and social status promised a new elite control over an increasingly recalcitrant working-class segment (ibid.: 89–151). Today, moreover, this rationalization of space has become internalized, part of an instinctual mapping of the city that is easily divulged by interlocutors when asked to describe their city. This mapping is not congruent with empirical facts on the ground, which are in any measure changing rapidly.

THE WESTERN MIRROR

The residential areas in west Ahmedabad seem much better planned than those in the east, with large green areas like the public parks around Gujarat University that I often frequented to recover from the hustle of urban congestion. Nonetheless, many green areas are uninviting, marred by barbed wire, and special entry gates to prevent city animals, in particular cows, from eating on the green spaces. They can at times be completely barred from use. Commercial roads like Ashram and CG Road have a more sophisticated feel to them and seem less decrepit. Poorer residents refer to CG Road, the local abbreviation for Sheth Chimanlal Girdharlal Marg, as "cheating road," due to what they perceive as its inflated prices. Many regions are marked by the complete absence of the ubiquitous call to Muslim prayer from the mosques, despite their proximity to historical Muslim shrines and mosques.

Although generally less raucous than quarters in the old city or the far east, many neighborhoods in the west have pockets where migrant communities such as Marwaris, Vagris, or Rabaris have encroached. Their festivals are noisy and defiantly fill the air at night, to the dismay of middle-class residents, especially those in secure gated communities. Unlike in the eastern and inner areas of the city, the battle of the winds is uneven, and the noises of these communities always dominate over other sounds. A few Muslim middle-class families also live in these areas, but they are not visible as a minority community.

Habitually, Muslim rickshaw drivers, in order to work in these better-off areas, abstain from wearing a beard or decorating their vehicles with paraphernalia that could be considered Muslim. Middle-class Muslim residents there usually desist from wearing a *topi* (cap) openly on the street. All Muslim-run restaurants in the west city are strictly vegetarian and carry what are increasingly understood to be "Hindu" names. The Muslim proprietors of these establishments are indistinguishable in comportment, gesture, speech, and clothing pattern from their Hindu colleagues. This tendency is not always a conscious choice due to the dangers of 2002 but preceded the pogrom, temporarily forming an emulative practice of Muslim residents who wanted to fit in. I have also met Muslim rickshaw drivers who pose as Hindus by using Hindu names for themselves and decorating their vehicles with Hindu paraphernalia, but such obfuscation can have dangerous consequences.

The nonvegetarian restaurants and meat stands in this part of the city are run not by local Muslims but exclusively by Nepalis, Panjabis, Marwaris, or other communities that originally come from outside the state. In 2002, the atmosphere in the city was so tense that one of my professors at Gujarat University, by birth a Marathi Brahmin who lived in Vastrapur, shaved off his own beard in order to not be mistaken as a Muslim by his Hindu neighbors. He did this despite the fact that he had been living in the area for several decades.

Far-west city areas, like Vastrapur and Satellite, have a distinctly different feel than the old and eastern parts of the city, with large, broad roads, high-rise apartment buildings, and cleaner air. Here, where urban space expands into the surrounding rural countryside, the city has a modern feeling and thinks of itself in the way it manages and plans its future. A sense of remoteness and aloofness to the struggles of the inner and east city predominates, coupled with a cultivated propinquity to everything American or Western.

This propinquity is self-confident and cautious, not simply a postcolonial emulation of the West. In among the high-rise apartment buildings, where one white-tiled balcony faces another, a sense prevails that there is much to come in the future. It is easy to find resident hosts who are still unaccustomed to their own middle-class amenities. They will automatically escort the visitor through each and every spacious room, culminating in a show of the bathroom with twenty-four-hour water access and incessantly flushing white toilets. Large numbers of activists and NGO personnel live in these areas, as do an increasing number of middle-class Dalits, a first-generation experience for them to live in immediate proximity to their upper-caste neighbors. The always-white-tiled bathrooms of middle-class Dalit families seem the shiniest and cleanest of all, as if an unspoken prejudice is to be cautiously preempted.

At the far-west border of the city, one finds the Sarkhej-Gandhinagar highway, with modern lifestyle amenities indexing the recent and immense economic progress in the state. Here, a veritable "New Jersey-fication" of Gujarat is under way, in many ways reminiscent of what Partha Chatterjee aptly identified as a suburbanization of the middle classes, inclusive of a proliferation of segregated and protected sections for elite consumption (Chatterjee 2004: 131–132). The middle class has not reclaimed the same old urban space but migrated away from it, and, perhaps peculiar to Ahmedabad, it does not care too much for the preservation of architectural and cultural heritage since much of it lies in the old city and is considered Muslim.

Shopping and entertainment malls have appeared next to a series of fancy restaurants and new monumental religious edifices, such as the Swaminarayan and ISKCON temples.[6] They, in turn, are flanked by sport clubs with names like Karnavati and Rajpath Club, whose lifetime membership costs up to a million rupees (US$25,000). Fun Republic— a multiplex building—has its name painted in bright yellow, red, green, and blue, while Reliance supermarkets promise an orderly adventure when purchasing consumer goods. There exists a strange homology between the

experiences of new entertainment centers and the modern religious structures advocating worldly renunciation despite all obvious contradiction.

At multiplexes such as Fun Republic, Iscon Mega-Mall, or Wide Angle,
there are airport-style security checks at the entrances, largely to prevent
any undesirables from entering. When prompted, guards will explain that
the complex has to be defended against possible attacks by Pakistani-
sponsored Islamic terrorists. The same reason is given for why taking pictures is not allowed inside—rules that are frequently flouted. Uniformed
guards manage the traffic, search backpacks, and use mounted mirrors to
examine a vehicle's undercarriage for possible hidden bombs in the mall's
large parking garage. What they usually find, instead, is illicit liquor to be
smuggled into the fancy compounds—Gujarat is officially a "dry" state.
The spacious underground garages also conceal rare discotheques, in
which mostly privileged young clienteles can dance, free from any public
oversight.

These security provisions manage to keep out an entire section of the
local population who do not look as if they could ever afford any of
the colorful activities lurking inside. While I myself was always treated
with politeness, I frequently observed how the low-paid uniformed guard
would quickly drive away an underclass denizen who wanted to take a
bedazzled peek into the colorful array of unattainable commodities. The
same middle-aged guard will mumble uncomfortably when a teenage girl,
not even half his age but a member of the sophisticated class, teases him
self-confidently about his stiff and uneasy demeanor.

The malls and multiplexes include cinemas, coffee shops, stores, bou-
tiques, and restaurants, as in such places anywhere else in the world.
One mall has a House of Horror in which mechanical as well as live
"ghosts" and "monsters" haunt the visitor for a few minutes, for the price
of one hundred rupees. Surprisingly, the supernatural beings resemble
not so much the terrifying *bhutpret* or *pishach* of Gujarati folklore but
American Halloween masks and Disney paraphernalia. The backside of
the entry ticket warns the expectant visitor of possible heart attacks and
forbids carrying weapons inside. The live ghosts want to scare the visitor
without the risk of becoming targets themselves.

Once visitors have passed the security checks, the malls allow for long,
leisurely strolls in wide, air-conditioned spaces full of translucent glass
windows and for rides up and down escalators to controlled sounds and
smells. In the districts of Satellite, Vastrapur, and parts of Memnagar,
the traffic islands and curbs are painted yellow and black and are often
strewn with flowers. Some squares have water fountains and police
booths to protect the officers from the blazing sun. The fancy supermar-
kets, which sometimes sport a Ganesh statue to greet the customer at the

entrance, have a wide range of food items that cost up to three times as much as anywhere else.

The new entertainment complexes reorganize the contradictory impulses of capitalist society by separating the spaces for production from those of enjoyment. Middle-class consumers in these malls thus find puzzling the integrated life in the bazaar of the inner city, where, by contrast, labor, life, and work flow into each other without much demarcation. Those who find neither time nor money for consumption nonetheless participate at times of violence in the palpable energy of *enjoi*, when they can abreact those heterogeneous impulses not completely appropriated by the productive cycle of labor and domestic life.

By contrast, in the new palaces of consumption, all play is relegated to entertainment and the expenditure of money. It ends at ten o'clock, when children should go to bed. Shopping and consumption adventures always include the entire family, not individual anonymous neighbors with whom one meets. This disintegration of living and playing in western sectors, with their new emphasis on particular social forms, bespeaks the conformity that the new spatial order increasingly demands. Not surprisingly, the most extreme stereotypes about the dangers of inner-city space, or of the malevolence of specific minorities, can be heard in the high-rise buildings of middle-class suburban zones. In the monotonous residential valleys, the mobile phone and the internet have established their rule, much as the extended bourgeois family has. Everything that used to be close is now far, and what used to be unattainable now seems close.

THE EASTERN MIRROR

On the eastern shore of the Sabarmati River, the old city is surrounded by Ring Road, where the historical wall used to be. The wall was demolished under considerable protest in 1925 (Raychaudhuri 1997: 79–88). Even in the absence of a visible wall, the road demarcates the inside and outside of a disappeared barrier. When spoken of in English, the historical city is often referenced as the "walled city." Within it lies the former Bhadra citadel, the site where the city's founder, King Ahmed Shah, situated his fort. The citadel lies in the immediate vicinity of the older trading sites, Karnavati and Asaval, which today are juxtaposed to Ahmed Shah's city, thus claiming historical priority from Muslims. There have been repeated agitations to rename the city of Ahmedabad as "Karnavati," and in 2002, hundreds of signboards were placed all over the city on road dividers, plazas, and street corners that greeted passersby with "Welcome to the Hindu Nation of Karnavati" (see figure 13).

FIGURE 13: Welcome to the Hindu Nation of Karnavati

The area between Patwa Sheri and Machhli Bazar, not far from the majestic Juma Masjid (Friday Mosque), includes a fish market flanking Bhatiyar Gali, the meat market in the old city center next to Tran Darwaja, a predominantly Muslim area. Both lanes are joined at a revolting garbage heap, which provides food to dogs, cats, and other roaming animals. The smell of the heap sometimes penetrates unpleasantly into the meat stands and surrounding eateries. The olfactory and visual concentration of meat and fish shops and restaurants in one small area (one *gali* and the adjacent *sheri*) creates a formidable spatial confinement and staging of the spectacle of meat. People can walk through this confined, concentrated space and see meat or can decidedly avoid it, go round it, flee it.

In this way, the spatial confinement allows an urban body to orient itself in relation to the central staging of meat, by abreacting the affect of desire or disgust through physical movement in space. A motorcyclist might speed up when driving through this area; a bicyclist might avoid the sight by lowering his eyes and uttering a small purificatory prayer. This fact also has consequences for the imagination of meat. Residents of the city who want to describe something horrendous in matters of food and butchering often refer to these two lanes, although slaughterhouses and nonvegetarian restaurants are found in many other areas as well. Spontaneous evaluations of Bhatiyar Gali and Patwa Sheri tend to attract hyperbole, both positive and negative, as if mental geographies and competing imaginaries intersected here in high metaphoric density. Some residents claim that the food is particularly good there; others express their dislike and mention the poisonous and unhealthy odors at the market.

Within the confines of the old city, Muslim sartorial styles differ considerably from elsewhere in the city. In the districts of Kalupur and Dariapur, for example, one finds a preponderance of women with burqas and bearded men with *topis* (caps) and long flowing *kurtas* (chemises for men). The heightened visibility of Muslim dress stands in stark contrast to its relative scarcity in the new city. When I bought such *kurtas* with large collars in the old city and began wearing them in my residential district in the west, I was repeatedly taken aside and politely informed that this clothing style identified me as either Panjabi or, worse, as Muslim. I was told to match my attire to the area in which I lived, so that no "misunderstanding" could ensue.

Because Muslims are present in great numbers, daytime is structured through the call to prayers of mosques (*azan*). The day is interspersed by five appellations to remember the one and only God, amidst the ubiquity of many others who make themselves heard through jingles, bells, or artificial sounds. Hindus, too, orient themselves instinctively according to these *azan* noises and even know the chronometric delay of competing mosques, which try to capture those Muslims afoot who missed a particular prayer.

At night in the densest parts of the old city, men play chess or carom, drink tea, and exchange news at street corners, in a lively, vibrant atmosphere. City residents like to exchange worldviews, rumors, and other fantasies circulated in fast succession on the street. Most interactions are between men, but women sometimes pick up food from stalls or communicate from balconies or windows. Interactions are full of energy until late evening, without any alcohol. This stands in considerable contrast to private Hindu consumption patterns in middle-class dwellings of the west city, or to underclass alcohol abuse in shantytowns and around gas stations in the far-east city. Some Hindus will venture from across the bridges to join the mainly illegal Muslim meat stands. A lone person can easily join and depart from these gathered groups without much ado. Men enjoy walking the dense city at night, and unlike what Chakrabarty (2002: 71–75) described for the bazaar area in Calcutta, anonymity in Ahmedabad does not automatically translate into strangeness or danger.

Ahmedabadis seem to have a deeper grasp for the anonymous familiarity to one another than, say, residents of my hometown. Even today in Berlin, a city that has not witnessed a pogrom since the 1930s, I would hesitate to wander alone at night in remote designated areas on a weekend for fear of encountering violent neo-Nazi street actors. In Ahmedabad, a city where not a year passes without deadly violence between Hindus and Muslims, one can encounter Hindus at Muslim stands consuming kebab at night and debating the world around them.

With a rather keen sociological understanding, residents in Ahmedabad recognize other city dwellers and can distinguish them competently from outsiders or visitors despite, or perhaps because, of the complexities of caste, community, residential area, and ethnic group. It is safe to say that many even enjoy sharing this cognitive labor of classification. At times, these reflections takes the form of social play, full of double entendres and ironical remarks. Recognizing someone as belonging to a specific group, even if that group is not particularly liked, does not hamper or hinder polite exchanges, informal discussions, and pronounced joking relationships. I have witnessed such interactions also in tense areas time and again.

What goes by the name of "Muslims" and "Hindus" interact so frequently in certain city areas that the unaccustomed observer is always astonished when this possibility suddenly collapses during violence. In many ways, Ahmedabad does not feel like a divided city filled with residents who perceive one another as vicarious strangers opposed to a domestic interiority—quite the contrary. The outside street between *pols* is a meeting place, while the same ground, as we shall see, is also the preferred site for communal posturing. Only when transgressing physically into the most private space of *pols* is suspicion at hand also in normal times. But that suspicion is not defined merely by ethnic or religious belonging.

THE CITY BEYOND

Beyond and around the old city in the east, the sky is adorned with chimneys, giving material evidence to Ahmedabad's former status as the "Manchester of India." It was here that a new labor class emerged in the nineteenth century to work in the prospering textile mills that mushroomed in a semicircular fashion around the old city. Most of those mills are closed today, but the descendants of their employees, now in a constant search for jobs, remain in the east, living in the shantytowns that dominate large parts of this area.

The poorly constructed extensive settlements known as *wadas* include many chawls (*chalis*—buildings with rooms organized in rows) and provide affordable living quarters for the large underprivileged class, internally separated by caste and religion (Nandy et al. 1995: 110–111; Breman 2004: 32–33). Initially, most workers came from the surrounding rural regions of the city and were distinct by religion, occupational status, and community but not by region or language.[7] This changed with later phases of labor migration from other parts of Gujarat and the country as a whole (Breman 2004: 148–149).

Many middle-class Ahmedabadis who live in the west have not visited the industrial areas for years and have no plans to do so. During the latter half of my field research, when I took residence close to Dani Limda in the east, only a few of my lower- to middle-class Hindu friends came to visit me. They not only feared poor Muslims but also wanted to avoid encountering the large Dalit population that lived in the east, many of whom are migrants from outside the state of Gujarat. A few Christians live among the Dalits and Muslims; most of them are from a Dalit background themselves.

In this part of the city, the dust accumulates exponentially, and one has the impression of a city half-finished as if suddenly interrupted in its development. Time acceleration became expressed spatially as capital accumulation and labor migration were quickly followed by sudden disinvestment, industrial collapse, and inner-city migration. Everything now appears degraded; past boom times did not create any visible permanent structures worth living in, and the profits made were siphoned off and invested elsewhere. The landscape appears empty and bled out.

In tense areas, the Muslim call to prayers competes audibly with the Arti noises of myriad small temples. Always technologically enhanced, the competing echoes bounce against one another in midair like battling kites at Uttarayan—the yearly kite-flying festival. The more sugary and melodious the Arti tunes, the more sober the Islamic calls to prayer seem to become. Reflected from walls and corrugated iron ceilings, the nightly soundscapes resemble recurrent drunken, discordant concerts. The disparities and spatial segregation of living space between the far-western and the far-eastern industrial areas of Ahmedabad could not be starker.

Bridges That Keep Apart

We return to our initial question: what is a bridge? Bridges link disparate terrains, facilitating flows across space. Yet in defying the ontological priority of space (*Raum*) over place (*Ort*), Martin Heidegger (1954: 139–156) has complicated this usual understanding. For Heidegger, it is only with the bridge (*Brücke*) that the human space around it actually emerges. By building a bridge, one does not simply connect formerly separate spaces; rather, one creates a place divided by a bridge.

To understand bridges as simply uniting places by manipulating objective space is to imagine a world without relation between things, objects and human beings. Bridges do not simply unify; in many ways, they do the opposite: they exacerbate existing separations and even add and create new ones. Heidegger argued that a bridge creates a place by bringing a surrounding area in relation to the bridge's function: overcoming physical or geographical distance. The problem of division that a bridge is supposed to solve comes into its own once people become related to each other through the very object that was supposed to bridge physical division. Now, the bridge becomes complicit in the division of the place that it has helped to create. The bridge is not the cause of social division but a part of it, through exacerbation by organizing new forms of access and escape that take diverse shape in expiation, anticipation, contagion, estrangement, displacement, or imaginative projection.

What Heidegger drew attention to here is that through the bridge, the question of closeness (*Nähe*) and remoteness (*Ferne*) suddenly becomes defined merely by physical distance: the space between two things (what he called *Zwischenraum*). Separation can be "bridged," in the sense of the Latin *spatium*, by the ingenuity of the engineer and the skill of the construction worker. *Spatium* can be overcome by building bridges or, by extension, constructing roads, railways, and airports. Such devices accelerate time, minimize distance, and promise solutions to physical separation. Bridging physical space, however, can have the contradictory effect of becoming a metaphor of division, a language that expresses or imagines apartness, and thus, recreates through its metaphor and utterance its very own sense of separation.

Nothing expressed this implicit perception of separation better than the attempt of the McDonald's Corporation to organize a "human chain," linking the west city with the east via the old city, which it announced and planned for March 2002. The commercial gig, which attempted to attract attention to the opening of a first fast-food outlet in the west city, was overtaken by the Gujarat pogrom at the end of February. The "human chain" over the bridges, uniting two halves of a physically and spiritually divided city, was never realized. Instead, the fast-food giant chose to open its first outlet silently a few weeks later.

The more bridges the city of Ahmedabad has built, the more unequal it has become. Instead of being a solution to the problem of separation, these structures have assumed its very form. In ordinary life as well as during extraordinary events, residents of the city use these bridges not simply to span space and to gain access to the other city half but also to escape and confine, project and displace, and even to remain hidden while in full view. Those divisions that the bridges were meant to over-come have become expressed through the division of the city through bridges. The bridges have become the language of their own failure. In this way, they are part of the experience of inequality in Ahmedabad.

Division and Invisibility

Violence in the city always includes a closing of the bridges through obstacles—whether psychologically through anticipatory fear or physi-cally through large stones, policemen, or plastic cubes at their entrances. Yet, in everyday life, residents will venture at night onto these bridges in search of cool and calm. On top of the bridge over the Sabarmati, despite the ubiquitous urban gaze, one can remain invisible, as here one is finally in between the city or, better, on its very surface. The liminal space of the bridge is the location where lovers meet at night or couples promenade side-by-side freed of the gaze of their neighbors, parents, or in-laws: Hindu or Muslim, Dalit or Jain, from east or west, all enjoying the rare breeze, away from the city body and the logic of extended family or community.

It is where Bharat could softly take my hand, imagining his planned marriage to Renjenben, and where Merunissa could meet her Pravin for shy kisses. There is an air of neutrality blowing over the sparse and empty cement space that constitutes the bridge, an interstitial space that has not yet become assimilated to the city proper. Promenading on its top strangely feels as if one is at the city's margin, even though the structures are geographically in the city's very center. When the water of the Nar-mada does not reach, the riverbed below Nehru or Gandhi bridges is used for drying clothes or playing large cricket matches during the day. At night, its unlit darkness provides a space for relaxation or forbidden love, as well as for crimes such as murder.

In 1997, the Ahmedabad Municipal Corporation (AMC) initiated the Riverfront Development Project, which has today become one of Naren-dra Modi's main political vanities, similar to the late Keshubhai Patel's Science City. In 2008, Modi celebrated the completion of the reconstruc-tion at Kankaria Lake in the east, which was supposed to improve the value of real estate in the eastern urban regions. In the Riverfront project, both river shores are being transformed into developed public space that will include gardens, walkways, promenades, golf courses, amusement parks, water sports facilities, shops, and restaurants. It can be expected that these changes will appropriate the median space of the bridges and inadvertently change the way they are used by residents.

FIGURE 14: Permanent police post

THE UBIQUITOUS POLICE POST

In the grammar of inner-city space in Ahmedabad, the existence of permanent police posts that mark border areas make visible and bring into
consciousness the Hindu-Muslim binary, often permanently inscribing it
in the city landscape. This was especially true in the period between 2001
and 2003. It is not the dyadic relation between the two aggregate communities, however, but their spatial triangulation with the police posts
that objectifies their opposition. The police are incorporated as precarious players in moral, legal, and political transgressions. This triangulation has the effect of effacing all other distinctions. Suddenly there are
only two communities, divided by a border.

City areas and localities in which communal violence is likely to
erupt receive the designation "sensitive area." Every resident carries in
his head a precise geography of risk concerning street corners and neighborhoods, the numerical relationship between minority and majority, as
well as the resulting local modalities of interaction. In times of tension,
it would be foolish to ignore the fault lines that structure the intimacy
between communities.

Intimate knowledge can be relevant for the assessment of risk in moving through these spaces, as others tend to classify one as Hindu or Muslim. Thus, there always remains the danger of becoming the medium and object of communal communication, something to be consumed: smashed, killed, and destroyed. In times of communal effervescence, the victim's property or physical body becomes the site of a sacrificial possibility whose destruction communicates complete sovereignty over the victim. As a foreigner, I was relatively safe because I was not classified as part of this intimacy and remained external to the conflict—a fact that I came to exploit unwittingly as an ethnographer.

Sensitive city spaces are of two kinds. In the so-called mixed areas, Hindus and Muslims actually share physical space, living intimately among one another, rubbing shoulders, buying in the same shops, driving through the same lanes. The second kind of sensitive space is that where a predominantly Hindu area is immediately adjacent to a predominantly Muslim area. This segregation is usually the product of former bouts of violence. One entire side of a street can spatially confront the other: a Hindu street corner across from a Muslim street corner. All residents know these border areas well.

In anticipation of communal violence, a mixed area can easily metamorphose into a border area, and members of one residential minority may choose to move temporarily to safer locations. These urban border areas replay explicitly the logic of national borders and recall the cataclysmic events of Partition. Hindus refer to Muslim areas as "mini-Pakistan"; Muslims refer to the surrounding areas as "Hindustan." The surest way to identify a border area is by the ubiquitous permanent police post.

The police post, or *tambu* in local idiom, is a large tent with water jugs and beds for the officers to rest on, positioned strategically at street corners, intersections, and plazas where communal violence is thought to be endemic. Ahmedabad has permanent police posts all over the old city. They also mark the entrance to the large suburban zone of Juhapura, considered a Muslim ghetto, and the border to Vejalpur, an adjacent Hindu majority area in southwest Ahmedabad.

Even when the posts are removed, the terrain they helped to define remains a "border area" in the public imaginary. Residents point the respective residential areas—Muslims there, Hindus here. Even though envisioned as temporary, the *tambus* are permanent. Some are even depicted on local city maps then referred to as "police chowki."[8]

Armed policemen live in these *tambus* and slowly blend in and become part of the neighborhoods they divide. In tense times, the posts are assigned extra men. In calm times, the policemen who usually sit at street corners caressing their moustaches and scratching their scrotums will frequently wander around and engage residents and shop owners in discussions. Recently, small rectangular shacks made of smooth metal have replaced many of the older tents, emphasizing even more their permanent nature.

Once in a while, a police superior unexpectedly visits and inspects the posts. Then the panicky constables hurry to smooth their hair, adjust their uniforms, and find their rifles. The superiors take the chairs and bark at their subordinates, who stand caught in the act or scurry around. During curfews, residents are not allowed to exit their houses or the side lanes of *pols*. As I wandered the streets in the first week of violence in 2002, they seemed to welcome me as an international distraction from their idle talking and silly joking. They rarely asked me for a curfew pass.

While policemen may not appear particularly competent or receive much recognition as executive representatives of the state, they nonetheless command an immediate local authority, not based on an appeal to the rule of law, but on direct access to the means of exercising arbitrary violence. They take the right to discipline by beating or humiliating, which residents escape only with good connections. People fear arrest more than harassment or the occasional beating. Women are also subject to these controls, and during curfew receive much verbal abuse, which they invariably ignore as if they do not hear it. A few times I witnessed strange disciplining measures, such as holding an arm or leg up for long periods while standing in the sun, or doing squats and push-ups—"Yoga exercise," one officer joked at me.

Policemen offered me tea every time I stopped by a post, but the officers who invited me did not pay, which spoiled the invitation. They took advantage of the local vendor, who they assumed would provide it free of charge. Often they demanded the same free service for lunches or snacks. While policemen complained to me about the low pay they received and the risks to safety they allegedly faced, I could not but perceive the incredible boredom of their jobs. For this reason they frequently inspected my backpack, and my German passport, page by page, sometimes upside down, over and over again.

Even in normal times, these posts can become grim impediment for city residents on their daily travel to work or back home. At the entrances to the Muslim suburban area of Juhapura, for example, policemen frequently stop lone late-night travelers and ask for illegal bribes. To be caught late or early in the morning by these policemen can swiftly translate into uncomfortable scenes.

It can hardly be said that Ahmedabad's police posts promise security or alleviate local fears of violence. Their failure is often attributed to alcohol consumption, but I personally have never experienced inebriated policemen. Yet police do often transgress the laws they are employed to enforce. The proximity between the police and criminality as extralegal activity is one reason why some people choose to apply for police work in the first place. The low pay is compensated for by access to the goods of the underworld—bribes, prostitutes, booze, weapons, often confiscated in raids.[9]

In 1999, for example, I witnessed a memorable scene at a border zone next to a teashop during the Kargil riots in the old city at Prem Darwaja, where the police who were present failed to compel any caution or discipline. An older male customer was waiting for his collective order of hot brew when a middle-aged man snuck behind him and simulated anal intercourse through a pumping motion of his hips, to the amusement of everyone around, including several stationed policemen. They had become a consuming audience of a tasteless performance. The older man ignored the fact and left, intimidated and dishonored. Such lewd behavior could be dangerous at other times or places. But the permissive atmosphere allowed for the enactment of violence on the one hand and mockery on the other. The immediate vicinity of police posts thus becomes the site for enactment of boldness, overconfident performances, or ridicule, especially but not exclusively by young men.

THE SIMPLIFIED COMMUNITY

In the spatial grammar of the city, the border area inclusive of a police post defines that space which carries the potential to reduce human encounter to that between communities, irrespective of demographic particularities. Sociologically, there are always many more communities involved in any give area than just the two artificial aggregates of "Hindu" and "Muslim." But conflict does not automatically arise where a man who could be classified as Muslim happens to live next to a man who could be classified as Hindu. Posh apartment complexes in Vastrapur, Satellite, or Navrangpura, as well as many mixed areas in the city that are not considered "sensitive" attest to this fact.

Equally, it is never hard to find an individual in Ahmedabad who disavows division and introduces you to his friend from the other community at the teashop or the eatery where they regularly meet. One can always find the seemingly sane person who points out the seemingly good relations with their neighbor of the other community. The person in question will usually elaborate passionately in the presence of his friend about the absurdity of inner-city communal division.

The absence of hostility or suspicion between friends, colleagues, and acquaintances across religious lines is often explained by reference to specific distinctions like, "He is a Memon" (that is, a Muslim merchant caste) and "Memons are very peaceful." Perhaps it is stressed that "He is a Shi'a, not a Muslim," or "He is an educated man," or even just "We are best friends." Alternatively, a Muslim might claim, "He is a Brahmin, and they are the learned people," "He is a BC [backward class], and they are not so staunch Hindus," or "He is a merchant, [Jain or Hindu Vaishnava] and they are a soft-hearted people."

All these examples can be inverted, however, and what is an explanation for one person's benign quality becomes another person's reason for suspicion. The members of a "BC *kom*" (backward community, scheduled caste) can then be more dangerous than Brahmins, precisely because they are beyond the Hindu pale (beyond any *sanskruti*, civilization). Or the Vohra (Muslim merchant caste) is more aggressive than the Fakir (lower-caste Muslim), because the Fakir is a simple-minded person and anyway almost a "Hindu," whereas the Vohra is a proud character. In other words, rationalizations for notable exceptions exist in abundance and are spun circumstantially here and there. The most distinguishing feature of these stereotypical depictions of collective characters is that there is nothing stable in them.

Stability, however, is provided by the perception of danger and the necessary calculation of risk. It is here where the inner-city border comes into its own and provides the space where one's fear can finally meet a concrete target: the threat at the border. Thus is constituted an amalgam of many distinctions into two single entities that constitute the "minority" and the "majority," divided by the idea that they are separate and opposed.

Consequently, the risk of violence is highest where the two communities encounter each other qua religious community, that is, where other possible distinctions have become redacted by the aggregate binary of Hindu and Muslim community, respectively. Analytically, then, there are two forms of social encounter: one is the encounter of two local residents: two fathers, two mothers, or two friends who happen to be members of different communities; the other is the encounter of two religious communities via the conduit of two individuals triangulated by the state. Most hostility results when the stress is on the latter, on religious community, which constitutes that form of experience where one encounters the rival community in one's neighbor, the corner tea vendor, the shopkeeper, or, for that matter, the local policeman.

When space prioritizes this stress on two entities, tension looms large. The police posts and the bridges are integral in this reordering and unmixing of space in relation to community sentiment. In acknowledging this psychological complexity of communal relations in Ahmedabad, one can then appreciate the successful symbolic labor of the Sangh Parivar, the family of Hindu organizations that promote Hindutva, and the less successful attempts to resist this.

The Sangh does not deny caste or ethnic distinctions within the larger Hindu community but rather seeks to bridge those differences in particularly affective moments, channeling energy to one target, to one space: the inner-city border. The instrumentalization of existing or new boundaries is the most important symbolic labor that these organizations are engaged in. The inscription of borders, internally on bodies (for example, through hyperbolic vegetarianism and disgust) and externally through city or national borders (myriad "mini-Pakistans"), is only successful if residents come to understand their intimate experiences in the terms of the Sangh's divisive discourse.

The RSS, in particular, attempts to make people sacrifice their petty mutual differences in order to concentrate on a larger difference, which can accommodate the project of Hindu nationalism: Hindu and Muslim, India and Pakistan. If successful, this symbolic labor allows for a creation of a feeling of unity while at the same time defining its lack and limit: the Muslim. An activist friend from Varodara, a Marxist who had many family relatives in the RSS, described the organization's training camps: "You see, in those camps what they do is, they create a subconscious mind." A "subconscious mind" is a mind that lays itself to rest, and hands itself over to an affective mood. Every affect, however, compels an ideational content because as affect it is fundamentally empty. The inner-city border becomes that content, the form for one's fears, the content of one's nightmares.

Once there are only two, the communities are artificially brought into a relation of equivalence, although they are fundamentally unequal given the fact that Muslims, divided internally into many subsections of caste and community like Hindus, consist de facto of many "minorities." To assume the two communities are comparable allows for the antagonism to arise. As equals they compete for everything: strength, prestige, population numbers, influence in local politics, street visibility, inner-city space, and economic power. The more the two spectral communities' claims to recognition collide, the more the perception of tension. Muslims, too, inhabiting this false logic, often behave and talk as if they were a community on par with the Hindus.

REPEATING PARTITION

The assumption of equivalence is one reason why so many residents in 2002, when asked what could be a possible solution to communal violence in the city, propose in full sincerity the further segregation and dissection of urban space. We see a return of the very logic that Pratab claimed to be Gandhi's mistake (*bhul*) in chapter 6. The solution to tension is the division of space conceived through a scenario that replicates the historical experience of Partition in exact terms. The proposal to repeat that very event, which at other times is profoundly lamented and named as the original cause for all misery, bespeaks the dangerous intellectual and emotional state of paralysis among city residents. How can Partition be made responsible for all troubles while inner-city segregation is at the same considered the solution to neighborhood conflict?

Thus the logic of Partition returns, although it is disavowed. According to this logic, Partition eliminated the need for Muslim recognition in India—by territorial displacement, India no longer had to deal internally with the demands of Muslims. The conflict of recognition became an external one of two countries fighting a prolonged battle, inclusive of wars, against one another. In Pakistan, the Muslims became a border beyond which they have access to a certain kind of recognition.

The same is imagined for inner-city partition in Ahmedabad. To create separate spaces means (a) to envisage the other community as one single entity, (b) to contain that community territorially, and (c) to displace conflict with that community onto the border, a marked space symbolized by police posts, religious structures, and other contested sites. It is lamented that Muslims were given a separate state (*emne alag api*), while at the same time, everything presently moves in the direction of doing precisely that.

It becomes clearer now, when the *Sandesh* newspaper (chapter 2) claimed there were terrorists inside the border (*sarhad ni ander*), why it was fundamentally unclear which border was meant. Was it the national border to Pakistan, the borders of the state of Gujarat, the regional borders of Saurashtra, Kachchh, or south Gujarat? Or was it the border of inner-city areas, marked by police posts? In this way, external threat moves inward to become intimate, the stuff of everyday life, where urban space becomes interspersed with the border areas of many mini-Pakistans and Hindustans. If the psychology of communal relations is based on an intimacy of shared space, it is nonetheless not caused through the manipulation of social or physical distance. It is expressed in space but is not of it.

Autoimmune Target

The culminating effect of this severe development can be grasped by the automatic transformation of personal and family conflicts into communal conflict, which makes for the contamination of violence in particular city areas, especially in the aftermath of repeated bouts of violence. These smaller clashes can be sparked by trivial incidents, such as traffic accidents, rows over prices at a shop, eve-teasing, rude behavior, or nonpayment at a food stall.

A few months after the pogrom, I moved from a Hindu district into the Muslim area of Shah Alam. After encountering many problems finding a place to live in the east city, I contented myself with a "border area." Sandwiched between the districts of Maninagar, Behrampura, Shah Alam, and Dani Limda, there is a cloverleaf situated not far from a large relief camp, which was still housing displaced Muslim refugees of the pogrom. My apartment building, a middle-class high-rise, was a mixed one—not between Hindus and Muslims but between Sunnis and Shi'as—and surrounded by lower-class Hindu service castes and Adivasi groups.

While I was living in the house, I grew close to Munavar, the house guard, a rural Pathan by caste. One day in February 2003, he came to me, exasperated and worried, and told me the following story. In the neighboring lanes of Dani Limda, a poor and low-class settlement of unemployed former factory workers, which included members of both respective communities, Munavar witnessed a quarrel between two Hindus that soon turned ugly. The incident happened at a recently electrified new temple next to a tea shop in a decrepit area with unpaved roads and dusty huts that is regularly flooded during monsoons.

A Rabari girl (Hindu) had been "touched" or "bothered" by a young Hindu man. She told her father, who got a stick and began beating the transgressor. This resulted in a row between neighbors and family members. But then, within half an hour, after more people had gathered, stones were thrown towards the local border (i.e. "the Muslims"). The barrage was answered within minutes by the other side, inaugurating what amounts to a mutual ritual of stone throwing for about an hour.

This was not a quarrel between Muslims and Hindus, Munavar assured me emphatically. He warned that the entire area was tense, and I should be cautious when leaving the building. Only with the arrival of uninvolved residents did the incident turn truly serious, which for Munavar always signified altercations between Hindus and Muslims. Police eventually arrived at the site and calmed the situation down. When tension are perceived to grow out of hand, first there is an incident, then stone throwing, after which the entire area becomes tense. "Tenshun" (tension) is a familiar state in Ahmedabad and is always most acute at a border, one of the city's many nerve endings. Men threw stones at the shape of a Muslim, because, as in Bharat's elaborations of *maryada*, the Muslim had become the border.

This time, as far as I know, the rather routine incident led to no serious injuries. Yet although it was not a communal issue at the outset, it exemplified the microscopic transformation of street aggressiveness into a volatile situation between communities. That it occurred without the direct involvement or manipulation of the Sangh Parivar is testimony to the Sangh's success in regularizing, elaborating, and ritualizing reactions to minor incidents. I witnessed another round of stone throwing at the same locality in 2005.

The stones, sometimes the size of a small fist, inadvertently land in a densely crowded space, echoed by the loud bang when it hits corrugated iron ceilings of poor dwellings—a sound now so familiar to me that I can distinguish it from any other, even in thick traffic noise. It is particularly popular to hit a religious structure or a dignitary of the other community. The target is never talked about as a neutral bystander but always conceived as either a Muslim or a Hindu. The person hit is assumed to be a representative of the other community, because only thus can any injury be retroactively legitimized.

Border conflicts leave urban scars, reminders of former bouts of violence. Once the police post inserts itself spatially into this scar, it becomes a sure site for future violence. Where the state has thus inserted itself physically into the neighborhood, it not only configures a tense space but also constructs a specific localized memory. The separation that the border signifies becomes naturalized and inscribed permanently into urban space, resulting in a peculiar local paradox: nobody really feels safe living near a police post; however, most feel even less safe without them. Interaction in view of the police is an interaction at a border, be it a national, physical, or an inner-city border.

Mushroom Temples

If bridges link an urban expanse that remains psychologically divided, and police posts configure a split intimate space that is physically shared, then street temples and shrines cluster within the matrix of these existing fault lines. These miniature city constructions seem to have a will of their own. They chaotically expand into the middle of roads and on street corners. They either grow larger and impede traffic or recede back to the margins at the side of the street.

Urban micropolitics determines this movement in space. Small-scale religious entrepreneurs compete with city officials and the police, who are charged with controlling building or regulating traffic in the city, and with residents as well as extremist organizations. Although these street temples and shrines increasingly flag city corners as belonging to one religious community alone, their spread and growth are not reducible to political or communal machinations. Much of their existence has to do with the indifferent flows of money and traffic through the city.

There are many religious sites in Ahmadabad. While large historical temples and shrines and prestigious modern edifices are depicted on city maps and tourist guides, the more dynamic minor structures are not. Counter to intuition, the slighter and more insignificant a temple or shrine, the more it connects the residential contiguity to its spatial signification. The reason for this is simple and has to do with the social background of the clientele that makes use of the structure. If a temple grows large and becomes well known, it will attract a different set of visitors from all over the city than if it remains small and relatively insignificant.

In extreme cases, such as the fancy Akshardham temple on the Ahmedabad-Gandhinagar highway, or the series of wealthy ISKCON temples, visitors often include middle-class Muslims and Christians who want to see spectacles of the divine during Sunday picnics. Likewise, the Usmanpura Dargah, a fifteenth-century tomb of Sayyid Usman (built around 1460), nowadays located in a middle-class Hindu neighborhood, attracts many Hindu visitors in search of a cure for spirit possession, broken heart, or disease.

By becoming tied to diverse categories of visitors, the more developed edifices escape the immediateness of their surroundings, overcoming boundaries of class, caste, or religious composition within a respective neighborhood. In other words, physical growth encourages transcending of the sociological makeup of surrounding space, and although physical size makes a structure more visibly present, its visitors tend to be much more transient and less tied to the structure's concrete location and its political geography.

Successful sacred places become the site of city pilgrimage and official recognition, patronage, and finally, city police protection. An attack on one of these structures will lead to investigations, arrests, and trouble with the authorities. This in no way excludes their destruction during times of violent unanimity, however, like pogroms. In contradistinction, minor improvised structures are more dependent on their immediate surroundings, supportive neighbors, or the demographic dominance of a particular community. When the air is filled with communal posturing, they inadvertently become or are turned into community markers.

Small structures, on the other hand, can often make it big. Bulging constructions on major traffic arteries frequently fill out what was earlier an empty traffic island. Several of these can be found on Ashram Road. In one, an adolescent street temple grew into a place for street worship for middle- to lower-middle-class commuters on the way back home. The success of the structure is predicated on its creative ability to attract the fleeting residents into short-lived economic and spiritual transactions.

FIGURE 15: Adolescent street temple

Most miniature street temples or shrines have doors that can be closed, and even if not, their walls create an enclosed space, protected from the outside, framing and symbolically demarcating the inside. Usually, but not always, the walls and doors, as well as the cement platforms on which they are frequently erected, are later additions, after the structures become economically viable or some patron offers a religious gift to improve it. The platforms often create an open space that is kept clean and serves as a seat for neighbors on the street. The edifice is elevated above the dust of the road.

On occasion, the structure's entrance is positioned at an angle to the street in such a way that passing drivers are compelled to look into the temple when its tiny gates are open, lights are lit, and deities are present. Conversely, some are turned away from the traffic to allow visitors to stay safely off the road when performing *darshan*, the visual exchange with the divine. As they grow, temples in particular have a tendency to gravitate sideways towards the center of the road (figure 15). In some cases, they find a balance on slim road dividers or traffic islands. All such growth invites congestion and even leads to accidents at times. Although commuters often express annoyance, the general atmosphere is one of great tolerance. This tendency to imperceptibly encroach onto the road tentatively reverses the rationale of enclosed space. The protected inside of the temple is brought into direct contact with the rolling vitality outside, placing it directly in the way of passing movement.

The impulse to expand, encroach, and insert the edifices into the busiest of urban flows is constantly perceivable. The hierarchical distinctions of social distance in city space, expressed most pointedly through guards, gates, and bridges, are supplemented through these structures, which introduce a more encompassing verticality of the sacred: in relation to invisible forces all city residents are really equal—gods, goddesses, ghosts, demons, or, for that matter, the distribution of destiny and bad luck. And where are these uncontrollable forces more palpable than in the unstoppable commuter traffic?

Traffic, by connecting all unequal places, leaving no one present unaffected or isolated, is a collective phenomenon that, like money, defines the experience of modernity. While it always implies the danger of misfortune in accidents, road travel becomes blocked during violence, constituting one important element of the extraordinary atmosphere during violent conflicts. Then devices that minimize distance, vehicles like cars, scooters, and motorbikes, are destroyed. If the transience of space is interrupted when the city engages in violence, it is not hampered in peaceful times but tapped strategically by improvised religious structures.

The smaller concrete temples, round or rectangular, are usually decorated inside and out with white or colored bathroom tiles depicting even more colorful deities. The Muslim version is a small shrine, a *dargah*, with the grave of a saint or two and painted green. Sometimes small street structures mark a particularly busy corner, or a large tree where cows gather, producing a localized charm that residents enjoy and often attribute to the supernatural powers of the divinity or saint. The aesthetic value of such sacred assemblages is appreciated across religious lines, as both Hindus and Muslims hold similar ideas.

Since the BJP took power in central Gujarat in the 1990s, miniature temples have progressively sprung up everywhere, not only in urban Ahmedabad. Recently, in the eastern expanses of the city, a series of identical Hindu structures, always rectangular, have been placed strategically in border areas in fast succession to one another (compare chapter 3). Many of the replicates were patronized by the VHP. They are frequently built with walls and doors, grills and platforms, all at once, displaying a more aggressive colored presence, and they seldom impede traffic by horizontal shift or displacement. They are easily recognizable because they resemble one another in size, height, material, and the overall monotonous appearance.

Although erected by local neighbors of specific castes and communities, they signal a generalized Hindu presence in urban space. During the 2002 violence, these structures on Gita Mandir Road became gathering places for armed killers, who stopped Muslim ambulances or individual vehicles on the east-west city axis. Another strategy is to erect such structures immediately in front of peace activist or NGO buildings that are considered opposed to the chauvinist goals of Hindu organizations, such as the one in front of Prashant, a Jesuit center for human rights, justice, and peace in west Ahmedabad. It is dangerous to oppose such planned and willful construction as it can invite unpleasant accusations of anti-Hindu bias and conspiracy theories.

For me, most miniature structures in the city offered wonderful opportunities to sit, drink tea, and ask locals about their gods and beliefs in an informal atmosphere. My questions about the age of the temple and the actual context of its erection were, however, generally considered intrusive. Most street temples were erected illegally. Once a temple is erected, it is very difficult to demolish, since followers insist that no human agency was involved in its emergence. The deity or saint in question had "chosen" the place of appearance and had magically surfaced in some form, usually an idol or image growing out of the ground beneath the asphalt. In fact, bubbles and lumps in the asphalt, that to me appear due to overheating and heavy vehicular traffic, are often interpreted as signs of sacred intervention. This source of authority joins them in kinship to larger and more successful structures of the city. The gods can appear to the poor as well as to the better-off.

The social lives of such bathroom-tile temples track the intersection of religious interest with small-scale economic entrepreneurship in contested urban space. If space allows, the small temples invariably grow into big ones within a few years. And the larger they become, the older they are claimed to be. When the grueling traffic flows by, riders on two-wheelers greet the deities with a nod or a brief placing of a hand on the heart, risking accident but amazingly optimistic that nothing will harm them at that very moment.

Often a *pan*, a tea shop, or both quickly arise next to small temples. Ultimately, most religious entrepreneurs seek to become *sadhus* (world renouncers). Then they and their followers tell elaborate stories and draw pictures of their spiritual predecessors and of the ancient origin of the temple, even when residents of the locality know very well that five years earlier, in the place where the temple now stands, there was only a concrete traffic island on which traffic police smoked their *bidis*, spit their *pan*, and wielded their *lathis*.

One *sadhu* now runs a former street temple the size of a small truck off a busy commercial road. He told me that the biggest reward for him after all these years is to see people greeting the goddess when they drove by. A congenial older man, he felt proud to participate in the road traffic at a lifeline of the city. He has become part of what used to ignore him as they rolled by—the people with work, with families, on their way to the west and back. He speaks to them and he feels acknowledged. As he explained, he is with them but not of them, a true renouncer.

This particular man had managed to scrape a living by inhibiting traffic, slowing down time, providing an increasingly hurried clientele a way to worship on their way to work. Around his structure, a minuscule and bare bazaar area has grown, inclusive of a street barbershop, a Muslim garage, a tea shop, and a fruit-juice vendor. Through the attraction and propitiation of the goddess Chamunda Mata, he provided work for relatively poor city dwellers, all members of the city's informal economic sector.

The final sign of upward integration of street temples into urban public life occurs the moment when neighbors and residents from far-off places come to visit during religious temple festivals. Then the temple becomes their central place of worship. Electricity lines or prestigious telephone lines are suddenly provided (the latter in fast decline due to the ubiquitous spread of mobile phones). Neighbors offer electricity, allowing for a connection from their houses to the temple. The electrification of a temple becomes a religious gift and a sure sign of patronage and status. Those who openly disagree with this practice do sometimes accuse the small temple entrepreneur of electricity theft.

Once the temple is large enough, it is often protected by a ceiling and encircled by a large red grille to keep out thieves, monkeys, dogs, and stray cows. During "riots," the grille also protects from vandals, Muslims, and "petrol bombs" (street jargon for Molotov cocktails). If a stone lands on a temple during collective violence, newspapers report, "Hindu temple stoned."

At some spots, small Islamic structures attempt to rival the mushrooming Hindu temples. But given the demographic dominance of Hindus, and the financial patronage of the VHP, the territorial competition in Ahmedabad is obviously one-sided. In the end, there are always many more Hindu deities than there can ever be Muslim holy men for whom it would be suitable to build shrines. There is also a pronounced and openly acknowledged bias in the city municipal authority itself against small Muslim structures. Additionally, Muslims lack a powerful and feared organization such as the VHP to seriously challenge and pressure the city administration on religious matters.

The distribution of Muslim shrines compared with Hindu temples reflects the general configuration of city space. Muslim community pres-

FIGURE 16: Hulladia Hanuman

ence is concentrated in delimited zones, while Hindu markers spread and mushroom. In many regions of Gujarat, a Muslim shrine defines a marked sacred space that signifies a sphere symbolically separate from society—external to caste, identity, and community division. In Ahmedabad, however, Muslim shrines increasingly signify the same thing that mosques do: Islam and a local Islamic population, which stands apart from other communal divisions.

In areas formerly inhabited by Muslims, local Jain and Hindu proprietors often still tend to older shrines, if they have not been converted into temples. The reverse can equally be true but seems more atypical and is increasingly rare. I have discovered former temples used for storage space in what are today Muslim neighborhoods but never one that has been transformed into a Muslim place of worship. While these urban transformations were caused by inner-city migration, especially from the old city that left abandoned Muslims and Hindu religious structures, respectively, they also indicate a shift in worship styles.

Muslim shrines are now primary targets during times of violence. In the 2002 pogrom, many smaller urban shrines simply disappeared. Some

FIGURE 17: Destroyed Isanpur Dargah (16th century)

were destroyed; others were converted into Hindu temples. Some of the converted structures were referred to as "Hulladia Hanuman" (angry, riotous Hanuman).[10] The marked tendency to destroy and convert Muslim shrines has much to do with eliminating sites where religious boundaries were transcended. Traditional Muslim shrines have tended to be places that welcome people from all social or religious backgrounds. While competition between communities and individuals for the spiritual patronage of religious preceptors was common, conversion was not.

As spoils of urban warfare, converted structures loudly announce Hindu-ness. The religious iconography, especially the idols dwelling inside, lack aesthetically the creative individualism of other smaller improvised Hindu religious sites. The retainers at these temples interdict photography within the sanctum in opposition to most other street temples, where a photo is usually strongly encouraged. Ironically, the prohibition is thus most acute where there is no need for a photo anyway.

As depicted in figure 16, Hanuman is announced from the outside kneeling in pose, using identical reproduced images. Inside, there is not the usual collection of diverse forms and designs of the divinity. While small Muslim shrines provide an easy target during violence, even large historical edifices were attacked and partly destroyed in the pogrom, with the help of the city administration (figure 17).

These developments correlate with larger social shifts. In a curious way, the ideologies of Muslim reform movements and Hindu nationalist ideas concur. Whereas for the former, traditional worship practices at Muslim shrines are a symbol for a false or anachronistic Islam, too "Hindu" to be acceptable today, for the latter, the very fact that Hindus visit Muslim sites for worship and supernatural help render them formerly "Hindu" in the first place.

Perhaps most significantly, a fundamental asymmetry structures the relation between religious locations in space to alleged emergence in time. While every Muslim sacred spot is today quickly suspected to hover over an older destroyed or abandoned Hindu or Jain site, the reverse never appears to be of concern. Although recently, as well as in former decades, a series of Muslim shrines have been violently "reconverted" to Hindu sites or destroyed, Muslims can never claim temporal priority for any of their sacred sites.[11] Reacting to this asymmetry, Muslims will sometimes claim self-importantly that this was so because their shrines are actually historical and not mythical. While Pir Sayyid Usman was a historical figure, for example, Hanuman is just a figment of the imagination. In regard to smaller and more insignificant Muslim urban structures, however, this certainly cannot be affirmed since small-scale Muslim religious entrepreneurs, too, are constructing new miniature structures whenever they can.

Remainders of Urban Magic

Temples, shrines, and police posts visibly delineate inner-city space. As central markers and sites of worship placed on the side, in the middle, and between things, they separate what is locked together in an embrace through being held apart by doors, platforms, gates, and projected dangers. But it is not only deities and policemen that dwell in the open city. There are also structures such as birdfeeders (*chabutaro*), often hailed as symbols of nonviolence; animals such as cows, goats, pigs, and dogs; and humans such as beggars, saints, and migrant workers. And finally, there are elemental beings such as ghosts, who inhabit in-between spaces along the city's arteries.

There is something transient about these nonplaces, where one can be invisible without disappearing. This transience is heightened when traffic rolls by and the street is full of busy movement. The space between divergent roadways, the center of a road crossing or intersection, and the midpoint of four-ways or six-ways (*char*- and *che-rasta* in local idiom),

FIGURE 18: Magical remainders on traffic island

in which all directions meet, where everything begins and everything ends, are also the preferred sites for remainders of urban magic. These in-between spaces are inhabited not only by benign beings but also by an evil that must be avoided at all cost. In fact, a popular practice often referred to as "superstitious" (in English) and disavowed but never disappearing haunts the street crossing. The evidence consists of magical waste left behind, the stuff of *bhutpret* (ghosts), often flattened by the rolling traffic (figure 18).

If an evil spirit is identified and held responsible for some misfortune or disease, residents of the city perform an exorcism in a small ritual called *utar*. The remainders of this ritual become a potent magical waste that still must be gotten rid of, somehow. In the case of such ritual remains, the usual means of garbage disposal will not do. In the residential areas in which I lived, all middle- to lower-middle-class housing societies, normal garbage was either picked up at the door by garbage workers or thrown off balconies onto the street itself, where the poorest of the poor and animals (in Hindu areas, often pigs) scavenged it. What remains is usually burned, lending a peculiar tangy smell to many residential neighborhoods throughout the city.[12] But it is more difficult to get rid of magical remains, as it may contain possible evil that does not lend itself easily to elimination without some form of concerted action. The remains after

FIGURE 19: Magical remainders on Relief Road

puja worship are called *prasad*, the food remainders of the gods, and are a form of blessing. Magical remainders of small exorcism rituals, by contrast, are a dangerous pollution, the symmetrical opposite of *prasad*. It is not ingested but avoided at all cost.

The small exorcism ritual, sometimes merely performed pro forma, consists of placing several objects like red thread, red powder, limes and a coconut into a metal plate. The plate is then waved or circled around the afflicted person seven times in order to confuse and constrict the evil element within. That element, usually a *pret*, a sort of ghost, becomes entangled in the thread and enclosed in the objects on the plate.

Josephbhai, a converted Catholic from scheduled caste background who lives in Navrangpura, speaks with the authority of a priest. He qualifies coconuts or other remainders left on the streets as "cast down evil spirits" that were taken from a family member or from the dark corners of a house. The term *utar*, a masculine term, means, "I cast down, descending, the evil spirited material," as Josephbhai related it. The evil substance is then caught in substances, which become the carriers of the evil essence: magical remainders. "No one will even touch it," Josephbhai warned. The ghost becomes caught in the coconut. In a way, the coconut is possessed now. "One goes away from it, one does not touch it."

At the end of the ritual, it is absolutely incumbent to leave the objects demonstrably behind. The physical movement away represents the symbolic departure from the ghost's location. The charged substances must be placed at locations such as road crossings or traffic junctions, where everyone is moving away, where divergent directions lead away from a single center.[13] According to Josephbhai, at certain junctures of the year, the practice is particularly prevalent, for example, during Diwali, the Indian festival of lights.

Salim, a Muslim in his late thirties, and Matuben, member of a scheduled caste in her mid-forties, discussed with me the practice of *utar*. Both had performed the ritual several times. In the morning, one has to circulate the chilies, limes, and an earthen vessel (*matlo*), over the head of the person afflicted by disease or misfortune. The effective substances that cause harm through disease or from the evil eye (*najar*) are thus captured in the objects and the ware, but not the ghost itself. Unlike in Josephbhai's elaboration, Matuben and Salim insisted that the ghost was still haunting the road. Only the effects of the evil spirit are confined into the earthen vessel or the coconut, which is thus called *utaro*, which they described as evil leftovers. As in Josephbhai's stipulation, the pollutants of the purification ritual have to be left behind demonstrably, acting out a definite departure from them, by placing them where others pass by: in-between roadways, in the middle of squares or intersections.

The former president of the city's Muslim butcher community also explained to me his views on these common practices of urban magic. He made a distinction between visiting specific religious sites and these roadside rituals. During the college examination period, for example, business and health problems are particularly prevalent in the city, he observed. Therefore, some residents of the city visited places of worship, while others sought help by performing the ritual of *utar*. "They give some donation, sometimes only stone of green and red, and then they wish for something: If God gives me success, I promise to come [to worship] every day until my death," he explained. "I will give my presence every Thursday there [in the shrine or temple] until my death and by the will of God, if he gives me success, then I will have to fulfill [that promise]."

Invisible forces that lurk about can cause much unexpected harm and must be taken into account. "It is some element we can't see, like horror, like *shaitan* (demon), invisible powers. If they [the forces] are harassing me, someone will suggest to me to take one coconut, circle it seven times around [my] body, and then keep it in a four corner [a cloverleaf road junction]." This is done in order "to escape from that element who [which] is punishing me." Butchers perform the same practice with the remainders of animal slaughter. An animal liver is circled seven times around an afflicted person's head and then kept at the junction. "The

FIGURE 20: Magical remainders in the way of others

vultures will eat it." Thus the evil is carried away. I asked if one could touch the remainder. He responded, "It is indeed, dangerous. If you enter or touch these spaces where this is kept, you will become patient of that *tatvo*" (that is, the victim of that element, that elemental force).[14]

Other residents told me that live chickens were formerly slaughtered at intersections, and their blood was spilled about in an expiatory exchange of death. I was unable to witness such a practice, and it no longer seems to be performed to any significant degree. Today all chickens have been replaced by coconuts, but blood is still signified by the red color of the thread and powder used. As with so many things, exorcism, too, has largely become a vegetarian affair today with the exception of the butcher's reference to liver.

These small rituals are practiced by all groups of Ahmedabad's diverse society. Although one might expect that members of the middle class will perform them less frequently, these practices are prevalent across caste, religious, and even class divisions. There is no group or community that can convincingly claim not to be harmed by misfortune or to be immune to the attraction of such convenient ritual solutions. The practice needs no expert specialist and can be performed by anybody at any time. Accordingly, such magical waste can be found in all parts of the city. It does not accumulate necessarily only among specific social status groups but instead in neighborhoods where street dividers and traffic islands abound, the in-between spaces of the city, where all directions begin or end. If such raised circles and pavement structures are absent, the magical remainders at times are also placed simply in the middle or the side of a road, always halfway off the road while never completely out of the way (figure 20).

In a society concerned with distinction in worship and religious practice, the universality of this practice is unusual. The reason is that these acts are not exactly based on a particular positive belief system but rather constitute the underbelly of all existing religious belief. It is difficult to substantiate and describe in detail the procedures at hand and their rationalizations. They have a decidedly negative core, which all interlocutors expressed in one way or the other.

People will speak about these practices in different ways. Many a city resident speaking English will use the word "doubt" when a native English speaker might have used the word "belief" to describe this sort of urban ritual behavior. For example, the speaker might say, confusingly, "Yes, he is doubting" (in English), when he means to indicate that someone believes in, say, a ghost or an attack by an evil spirit or element and engages in the practice of *utar*. The statement "he is doubting" here does not mean that the person in questions doubts whether there are ghosts but rather that he is in doubt of the assertion that there are no such beings as ghosts. In other words, he is entertaining a doubt (*vahemavu*—to entertain a doubt, to be suspicious).

That, however, does not mean that he positively affirms his belief in ghosts either. The speaker is not affirming the existence independently, as if a ghost were a car, a house, or an elephant. The person in question is not thought to be delusional: rather, he is doubting the fact that the ghost is not there just because he cannot see it. In relation to such forces that can cause much imminent harm, caution is in order. Since ghosts cannot be seen usually anyway, there are other indicators that can perhaps lend evidence of their presence, such as repeated and inexplicable misfortunes. That evidence is the stuff of everyday personal lives and varies from case to case.

In other words, even when people claim that they do not believe in it, this merely means to say that their belief is not *of* it. To believe *in* something means to draw closer, constituting access and proximity, and at times creating an obligation. To perceive is to be perceived, as is the case in the mutuality of *darshan*. Stating "*hu manto j nathi*" (I do not believe in this or that) can therefore nonetheless imply a suspicion, or a doubt, indicated by the Gujarati term *vahem* (suspicion and superstition). That is why members of higher castes will often refer to deities associated with, and propitiated by, lower castes, for example, those demanding blood offerings, as "superstitions." But when prompted, they will not claim that these propitiated entities do not exist as such but rather that their particular form (including the forbidden objects they demand as offering) reveals the low nature of those believing in them.

In Ahmedabad, most religiously identified individuals are acutely aware of the fact that the divine is a *Vorstellung* (a representation), and its imaginative form reveals an aspect of the one engaged in the particular act of cognition. Many competitive caste, religious, and sectarian divisions are motivated by claims to a privileged access to the divine or to a better method to comprehend the supernatural. Thus, to say one does not believe in ghosts often merely indicates that one does not consider oneself associated with such a dark belief. Such a stance does not to suggest that invisible and malevolent forces are absolute humbug. Belief and doubt are contingent upon one another in what constitutes *Aberglaube* (a faith in the register of a "however," a *super-stitio*). The Gujarati dictionary understands the term *vahem*, originally derived from Arabic, to denote both a "deep thought" and a "whim," while it also has come to mean "suspicion, doubt, fancy, misapprehension, freak, imagination, conception"(!) and finally "superstition" (cf. TMGED).[15]

In short, Ahmedabad's inner-city superstition is not simply a belief that one can assume, openly affirm, and believe in, or choose to dismiss. It is not a positive assertion of a presence but rather a negative reversal of the given, a possibility that logically can never disappear. One can always be suspicious of the given and fear its reversal. To be superstitious is to be credulous that things are connected in ways that are not obvious. Accordingly, someone behaving superstitiously is someone who is fundamentally in doubt, apprehensive of the normal order of things. It would make sense if this stance would accumulate more among desperate sections of society, but it seems that there are considerable qualms among members of middle classes too.

The other words often locally used in the sense of superstition are of Sanskrit origin: *andhshraddha* (false worship, superstition) and *andhshraddhalu* (blind faith) (GED). They are the opposite of *shraddha*, the proper ceremony, or ritual. They are the proper ritual in reverse, not the absence of any ritual at all. Superstition can never cease because it is the logical underside of belief, a belief in the register of an endless "however."

All magical remains of misfortune and disease are placed without exception on unoccupied traffic circles, at crossroads, on road dividers, or in the middle of a square; between at least two roads or in the middle of four directions; and with a coconut or some red powder symbolizing blood and a lime. These substances carry the evil pollutant extracted from someone. Sometimes there is an unbroken coconut, sometimes a broken earthen vessel. And sometimes the substances are concealed in a black, red, or green bag.

Why is it so important to place the magical remains at a crossroads? These interstitial spaces, it is said, confuse the evil spirits and ghosts, and they cannot find their way back to their bearer. In fact, Ranjitbhai explained to me, to do it properly, one has to bring the evil remains to the road crossing by walking backwards (although I have never seen anyone actually doing so). Walking backwards confuses the evil spirits about where one came from (recall that Bharat, too, retraced his steps after fainting at the sight of meat, claiming to walk backwards; see chapter 5). Others claim that after one has positioned the remainders on the crossroads, one has to walk backwards away from it—again to confuse the spirits.[16]

The beginning or end of pathways and the center of crossroads are locations characterized by their relations to a distinctive spatial directionality. At the interface of different directions, the spirit, and the affliction it causes, can better jump onto other people passing by. In its most sinister version, placing the remains of exorcized misfortune on road dividers and traffic islands serves the function of redistribution and displacement of the evil one has been able to get rid off onto others. As in comparable conceptions elsewhere, here, another person's affliction helps with one's own, especially if that person swallows it whole.

I had one such encounter with concentrated evil of the urban kind. Driving my scooter down the busy Gita Mandir Road in the hot afternoon sun in east-west traffic, I came across a red cloth bag in the middle of the road. It had obviously fallen down from a traffic divider and rolled onto the street. In a moment of absentmindedness, and because the dense traffic allowed little room for evasion, I tried to drive over the bag, realizing too late that something was inside of it. My front wheel slid sideways and came under the tires of a bus to the left of me.

By chance, and because I had been driving slowly, I was able to drop myself before my legs went under the large slowly moving bus. I landed on the pavement while the bus's rear tires, almost in slow motion, crushed my vehicle's front wheel. The bus paused for a moment with a dramatic sound of its brakes, as the driver made sure he had crushed my scooter and not me. The passengers in the bus stared at me in frozen postures from their open windows while swaying gently in unison with the vehicle. Then the bus, which had almost become my undoing, moved on.

Recovering from light wounds at the side of the road, I was offered water by a friendly garage owner, who introduced himself as Ramesh, a man in his twenties whose repair shop was conveniently located close to the place of accident. He was able to replace my squashed front tire quickly and thus restore my precious vehicle within a few hours. While recovering from the shock of the accident, I complained about the custom of placing coconuts in bags that roll in front of moving wheels. Ramesh listened silently. He agreed and nodded while competently repairing the squashed wheel. It was not the first accident he had witnessed at this specific traffic divider right in front of his garage. He finally spoke, with great authority.

Ramesh did not think my accident was a coincidence. He did not actually witness the incident, as the bus had blocked his vision, but he avowed that he would never dare go and clean up the road divider of magical waste (*utar*). No sane person would. The remainders rot, large vehicles crush them, and animals swallow them, he explained. To try and come close to them would be looking for trouble. I had tried to ignore that which had left the road divider (the space where there is no clear directionality) and which had placed itself directly in front me. Thus it assumed my direction, that is, the evil assumed me.

I objected to this explanation of intent, but Ramesh remained unimpressed by my objections. I had dared to touch the magical remains of an exorcism. They had been placed on the road divider a few days earlier and had rolled off onto the road. Someone had decidedly placed them there, between where four roads meet, precisely in order to step away from them, to get rid of them. The only way to avoid the evil would have been to slow down and steer clear of the remains, drive away from it. The concentrated evil contained in the coconut had immediately assumed a new victim and almost killed me, he was sure. From the moment when my front wheel had touched the coconut I had been incredibly lucky. I knew he was right at least about the last part, about my good luck. Unnerved about a custom that places objects in one's way and then defines the dangerous outcome as willful misfortune, I paid for the repair and drove off.[17]

INTIMATE SEPARATION

There is something analogous between the leaving behind of magical waste on the street and the practice of inner-city stone throwing in border areas. *Utar*, an evil harvested from a person, is placed in the middle, on the side, or between roads where others pass by. A stone, in turn, is thrown because there is tension, a perceived danger, in the concrete direction of the border.

The police post in the neighborhood marks the danger of a very intimate and familiar kind found in one's immediate neighborhood and its residents, whose physical proximity becomes the instance of imagining their social distance (in religious practice, in allegiance, in loyalty). Their very closeness becomes the impending danger through the police post. The community of the other becomes one's boundary, the border and target at which to throw a stone. The target is the object of focus, while one bridges for the time being all internal division and displaces all that is unwanted in one's own community onto the other. In chapter 6, Pratab complained that Muslims were given something separate (*emne alag api*), a land of their own. For Bharat, Muslims are his *maryada*, his own boundary (chapter 5). Sejal fasted, renouncing ingestion, in order to protect herself from Muslim dietary transgression (chapter 4). For all three, to encounter the Muslim is to encounter one's own very intimate corporeal boundary.

Both *utar* and communal tension displace violence from the self onto some interstitial space, allowing for a strange sort of anonymity of intent and agency—the abstract other community, or the transient road traveler, one among many in a city of thousands of vehicles. In the logic of inner-city division, the other community becomes a representation of what is secret in one's own. The Muslim community mirrors what is a secret in the Hindu community, the malevolent intent to harm, sexual fantasies, disgusting practices.

The practice of *utar*, by contrast, hands the magical waste over to chance, to the anonymity of a city and its rolling traffic. Once it is placed correctly on the road divider, the waste can't look back at you. In both cases, what was once internal has the chance to be made external, but whereas in *utar* the evil is carried away, in the communal mirror it always looks back at you through the border. It looks back at you and you recognize it, because you see the malevolent intent in the other, but you misread its origin, which lies in yourself.

While the superstitious practices of *utar* transcend all communities, since the targets of evil are individual victims of chance, inner-city tensions imply the opposite. Communal tension feeds on the idea of collective communities acting as an organism. Thus it seems that communal tension is a form of reversed intensification of the superstition of *utar*, where the displaced violence no longer chooses a random target, which carries the evil away and out of sight, from whence it can't return. Rather, in the context of communal tension, the evil, the malevolent intent, finds a fixed target: the other community, Hindu or Muslim, respectively. The other community never goes away, however. It looks back at you, now filled with your own intent, which you understand as *its* intent. The neighbor becomes a possible enemy even more monstrous the more he is familiar to you.

This, of course, reveals the structure of the *Unheimliche*, where what is familiar returns externally as something that is perceived as strange and thus frightening, eliciting a strong reaction. The uncanny is in truth that which is secretly one's own. The intensity of inner-city tension far surpasses in significance the practice of *utar*. The origin of the fear, and its spatial expression in inner-city division, lies in the malevolence of those who are scared.

CHAPTER 8

Heterogeneity and the Nation

DIFFERENCE AND INCLUSIONARY EXCLUSION

Romain Rolland, a French author and contemporary of Mahatma Gandhi, recounted an anecdote of Gandhi's school years: since the obstinate young Mohandas often brushed against untouchables, his mother recommended he then touch a Muslim in order to cleanse himself from the contamination accrued (1923: 78). David Pocock mentioned the same practical solution to pollution when witnessing similar scenes in rural Gujarat during his fieldwork some eighty years later (1972a: 5–7). Comparing this solution, the touching of a Muslim, to a game of tag, Pocock explained that the contradictory nature of the Muslim in caste society provided the possibility of reinstating the jeopardized separation between Hindu and untouchable.

Among the many attempts to explain the Gujarat pogrom, Ornit Shani (2007) and Jan Breman (2004) have most directly linked the issues of Hindu unity to Muslim expiation. Shani traced the emergence of what she calls "ethnoHinduism" in Gujarat to the violent antagonisms over reservation politics in 1980s, which laid bare the internal antagonisms of Indian society. Since Independence, this society had to integrate those sections that traditionally were not part of the Hindu moral and ritual order, such as Adivasi and untouchables. The assertion of a unified Hindu identity began gaining ground in response to the changing relation of caste to the state, "a shift from the politics of redistribution to the politics of recognition" (Shani 2007: 155).

Breman, in turn, while not considering political Hinduism an altogether new phenomenon, identifies as a major factor the "informalization" of labor after the demise of the mill industry in Ahmedabad beginning in the late 1970s (2004: 134–135, 287). The competitive climate of social Darwinism led many urban workers to regress into "primordial loyalties" along the lines of caste and religion instead of fostering the class-based intercommunal solidarity that preceded this shift (ibid.: 221–231, 285–291).[1]

Both accounts convincingly link the antagonism between upper and lower castes, as well as upper and lower classes, to the increasing lethality of Hindu-Muslim violence in urban Gujarat. However insightful for a general understanding of violence in Gujarat, they nonetheless elide certain specific aspects of pogrom violence. Breman's (2004: 230–231) frame of analysis, that the attractiveness of Hindutva in the late 1980s is caused by a regression into primordial loyalties, misses the utopian impetus of nationalist unity, its rhetorical departure from distinctions of inherited caste and subgroup belonging. Shani, while delineating the switch from caste to Hindu-Muslim conflict in the 1985 violence, cannot account for prior Hindu-Muslim violence, nor does she theorize about the role of national identification.[2]

Other authors point out that processes of excluding Muslims were apparent long before the 1980s, and even before the inception of Hindutva ideology in the 1920s (Bhatt 2001: 7–76; Sarkar 1983: 233–242). However one might choose to weigh such competing interpretations, it remains undeniable that while Dalits have incrementally become internal to Indian politics after Independence, the Muslim presence in India has become increasingly hazy (Mendelsohn and Vicziany 1998: 21). Hindu organizations in central Gujarat mobilize this ambiguity through a resolute symbolic labor and a hyperbolic rhetoric of suspicion. It is important to acknowledge that what these organizations purport openly is what many Gujaratis feel but might desist from expressing.

The relationship between a paranoid extremist ideology and its silent reception by a wider audience is one of the most complex issues haunting the political climate of contemporary Gujarat. My own experience of the pogrom has convinced me to explore more fully this relationship between overt ideology and an unspoken and complicit delegation of authority to violent actors. At the center of this question lies the fascination with power in the context of democratic political form and the unwillingness to submit to the limitations of legal norms or state institutions. The possibility of foiling institutionalized legal and political norms in the name of the Hindu people can overwrite emotional and moral hesitations that help keep destructive tendencies at bay.

This delegation of authority, which, in the Gujarat pogrom, seemed to entitle Hindus to deride and punish Muslims, is not merely found on one side of the equation. Muslims, too, can delegate authority to obscure actors, and they can clandestinely approve their punitive activities. In Gujarat, however, any form of material support for violent Islamic organizations is suspected of illegality and involves great personal risk. In the act of such delegation, Muslims individually confirm what they know they already stand accused of collectively. Delegation by Hindus during the pogrom, by contrast, resulted in a discovery of new possibilities through accessing extralegal forms of power that authorized violent expression not through law or illegality proper but on the basis of what legitimates the legal structure of the polity in the first place: the power of the majority. There is no parallel power to which Muslims can appeal.

For all the change in India since Independence, Gujarati Muslims remain simultaneously ideologically excluded and empirically internal, which in part explains the pogrom's dangerous eliminatory tendency. Muslims are an intimate element of the group, but unlike the stranger in Simmel (1992 [1908]: 764–771), they are not new arrivals on the scene. Mainly from the twelfth century on, outsiders brought different versions of Islam to the Indian subcontinent, which local groups that were already present appropriated in various ways. Hence most Muslim communities are considered converts and betray cultural and religious styles that resemble the immediate surroundings within which these unfolding encounters took place.

This resemblance is not one of uniformity or homogeneity. The internal differentiation between Muslim communities on the basis of cultural forms and religious styles compares with that in the rest of Gujarati society (Misra 1985: 69–125). Even the relation of Muslim communities to one another reflects local idioms and realities. Hence, there exists a deep reciprocal imbrication between all the empirical elements of cultural phenomena traversing the categorical labels "Hindu" and "Muslim."

Muslims in Gujarat form no political or cultural unity, and there is no single voice that can speak in their name. By contrast, in the symbolic labor of the Sangh Parivar, Islam is made to signify Pakistan, and every Muslim is walking evidence for the imagined historical humiliation of female abduction, dissection of the country, religious conversion, and colonial invasion. Like Simmel's stranger, however, Muslims will not be leaving anytime soon. Hence the solution of the pogrom: what cannot be reconverted or expulsed and resists leaving can be killed, ritually undone by violence. The way Muslims were killed neither expresses underlying cultural incommensurables, nor were they motivated by religious antagonisms. Rather, the motivation to eliminate expresses an instability in which Muslim neighbors who fail to be all that different nonetheless can no longer be recognized. The internal heterogeneity of communities labeled "Muslim" escapes the dominant understanding of Indian national cultural integration. In Gujarat, Muslims are already internal. In this way, Muslims have become strange in their familiarity.

Along these lines, the effervescent experience of "Hindu awakening" is a veritable dissolution and rebirth into a social collective held together by negativity (Simmel 1992 [1908]: 533–538). It awakens destructive impulses, a nihilist guarantee of group cohesion, that enable an abreaction in an orchestrated environment, one often termed "riots," which, while carrying many incalculable risks, appears nonetheless micromanaged and controlled. The national referent "Hindu" in juxtaposition to caste and community distinction might shed some light on Pocock's puzzle concerning the game of tag cited above: How does one rid oneself of pollutants, and what happens to the Muslim as the location of the untouchable is caught in a process of ongoing re-signification?

Traditionally, Muslims were, for all practical purposes, outsiders to the Hindu moral order, yet they were thought of as insiders, whereas the insiders, the untouchables, were thought of as outsiders. In rural Gujarat, these two locations were always ambiguous, yet still assumed form within local hierarchies. Muslims were never implicated in the same way in the machinations of ritual status as were untouchables. Above all, untouchables were a necessary element of the system, included only by formal exclusion, by signifying the negative pole, the impurity enabling the signification of purity by the caste Hindus. Muslims, by contrast, were outsiders, yet the many individual Muslim communities were treated as various insiders. Muslims were not necessary for caste to exist but stood in a relation of complementarity to it.

What happens to the Muslim, to what Pocock (1972a: 5) calls this "conduit for restoration of normality," when the Hindu and untouchable are instead, as effected today by the ideology of Hindutva, joined together to form a homogenous national unity? Rejection of Muslims in Gujarat is contemporaneous with the rise of the lower sections of society onto the political stage and their symbolic integration into the category "Hindu." The former relations of internal externality (untouchable) and external internality (Muslim) thus unravel. The category "Muslim" loses its ability to inhere in a complementary position; Muslims become aggregate objects of expiation.

This changed signification has come about not only with the transformation of the traditional ritual and moral order but through the work of Hindu nationalist discourse, which has displaced the idioms of ritual and caste on a larger scale. Partha Chatterjee (2004: 17) has stressed how imperceptibly the idea of a homogeneous India slid into the idea of the homogeneity of the Hindus. Terms like "Hindu" and "Muslim" are now national as well as transnational identifying categories, with the latter especially problematic in that the Muslim today risks becoming potential traitor and terrorist with reference to Pakistan. This shift from caste complementarity to transnational identification transforms the vertical, integrative relation between communities into a horizontal Schmittian friend-foe binary.

Sangh Parivar discourse most effectively makes use of the way the state organizes abstraction and intimacy in classifying populations, with its origin in colonial administrative practices. But while many citizens in India successfully distinguish between empirical realities on the ground and imperatives of the state, in central Gujarat, Sangh Parivar organizations have been particularly effective in discursively controlling the logic of aggregate opposition. The result is an optical shift that reaches down to the affective dimensions of social life, engendering visceral experiences that while relatively unstable are at times overwhelming, as we have seen. At the base of these experiences is an unresolved intimacy in the relation between Hindus and Muslims. Through a sudden realization of a ubiquitous presence, what should be no surprise—the heterogeneity of a Muslim—suddenly has the power to overwhelm, at least momentarily.

ABDUCTION AND RECOVERY

The imagination of abducted women in the pogrom is not a new trope in modern Indian history, but builds on several memories, including, of course, the large-scale abductions that occurred during Partition. Veena Das (2007: 18–37) has importantly argued that the figure of the abducted woman during Partition belongs to the foundational moments of the two enemy states, India and Pakistan, and that these abductions set the stage for a particular relation between the social-sexual contract and the state. By creating the legal category of the abducted woman, she argues, the post-Independence Indian state sanctified a conservative and masculinist definition of proper kinship norms of purity and honor. The "origin of the state," she concludes, lies in the "rightful reinstating of proper kinship . . . and recovering of women from the other side" (ibid.: 21).

This social contract comes apart, however, as Hindus and Muslims keep returning to this initial battle over the control of sexually and reproductively active women in recurring states of exception: for example, the veiled Muslim women in chapter 1 and the missing girls discussed in chapter 2. For Das, abductions were followed by the "correct matrimonial dialogue of men," that is, an exchange of women which cemented the subjugation of women under fathers and husbands (ibid.).

Relating Das's insights to the Gujarat pogrom might lead us to reconsider the valence of several of her central categories while not departing from her insight. More specifically, Das collapses the category nation into that of state, claiming that both are masculinist. On one level, it is true that the other group's women represent a lack, as something either unattainable or, the more intermarriage becomes a real possibility, attainable.

One's own women, in turn, are always in danger of being objects of the other group's desire, creating a vulnerability about what is one's own.

On another level, however, the nation incorporates its citizens in a maternal register—as Bharat Mata, ideally free of social divisions and corrupt politics, a nation as womb, pure and prior to all conflict and distinction. And as the imagery during the pogrom suggests, the Hindu nation is not about law or politics, not masculinist, but conceived in the register of a people without divisions, and, as such, theoretically in tension with the state. The pogrom revealed plainly this tension and how it is integral to Hindutva ideology, which flouts law but appeals to an official "Hindu way of life" (*hindu jivshaili*) that is supposed to recover not only women but all those sections of society (including men) that are not considered integrated. This recovery, then, also entails expiation of those elements not considered assimilable.

Charu Gupta (2002 [2001]: 222–258) has shown that the origin of national imaginaries of abduction reach further back than Partition, at least to the 1920s, when such material was already circulated widely. Partition imaginaries were then an instantiation of a prior fantasy: the moment when the Hindu nation became initially manifest as a collectively imagined project against the colonial state and its divisive administrative practices in the second half of the nineteenth century. It is conspicuous that this development was contemporaneous with the imagination of an *Indian* nation as opposed to a *Hindu* nation. The former included Muslims as a more or less *separate religious community*, whereas the latter rejected such a form of inclusion. While this ideological distinction is formally true on the surface, in nationalist practices it becomes much more blurred. Something in the nature of national consciousness itself is conducive to both possibilities, although they have historically been in opposition to each other.

In Gujarat, Hindu nationalist consciousness insists vitriolically on aggregates. It is the insistence on this register, which creates a relay to local Muslim communities, whose women now become sites of "Hindu loss." The experience of Muslim women as Hindu loss would be quite inconceivable without their prior aggregation, because that would collapse the entire edifice of marriage and social organization, which is regulated and controlled in comparable ways across caste and religious community.

EXPIATION AND THE LOGIC OF SACRIFICE

In its minimal definition, sacrifice is the creation of a loss to constitute the social, and as Georg Simmel (1989 [1900]: 55–92) and Georges Bataille (1992 [1949]: 45–77; 1991 [1967]: 43–61) have alternatively argued, sacrifice thus belongs to a general theory of economy and exchange. It is an act of regenerative expenditure involving both destruction and abnegation as well as production and symbolic appropriation. In sacrificial killing, destruction is a function of incorporation because when the victim is destroyed, it is taken out of circulation. In this way, the victim's being-for-others, its thing-ness, is eclipsed and the victim (the destroyed thing) becomes solely one's own.

The mechanism of establishing absolute sovereignty over someone else through violent incorporation works on two levels. First, for Hindu nationalist demagogues, Gujarati Muslims are not really Muslims but only converted Hindus. This encompassing logic of the Hindu is grounded on a refusal of recognition, in this case, of the very difference that Muslims are trying to assume. The heterogeneity that Muslims are made to represent, the excess they are identified with, is to be expiated and the Muslim rendered civilized, read "Hindu."

This inclusiveness of Hindutva ideology is indebted to what the German Indologist Paul Hacker (1957) has termed "neo-Hinduism," a product of the experience of colonial humiliation in the nineteenth century. With prescience, Hacker distinguished the aggressive posture of *Inklusivismus* rather sharply from *Toleranz*, terms that many Western scholars equated (1983: 14–23).[3] The traditional Hindu ritual and moral order, by comparison, was characterized by an absence of a need to define externality and internality through aggregate categories of national registers in quite this way.

Second, the violent actions during the Gujarat pogrom, dramatized through word and image, forced home what belongs to "India" in the first place. When the Muslim is killed, he or she becomes a Hindu again, though only as corpse, a dead body image. When Muslims are being killed, what is killed is really the Muslim in the Hindu, the inauthentic part that resists incorporation and assimilation. It is this dead body, circulated privately and in the media, that is brought home as part of the Hindu nation. Hence, sacrifice in the Gujarat pogrom was an erotic procedure allowing the symbolic inversion of the imperatives of reproduction, which are invoked in nationalist imaginings through the idea of aggregate population.

Through the sacrificial mechanism, the discontinuity of life is transformed into the continuity of death (Bataille 1986 [1957]: 11–25, esp. 12–13). From the womb of the Hindu Mother, having become a Muslim against her will, the Muslim is made to return to the state of flesh, into the womb, in order to be incorporated anew as part of the Hindu national body. In the expiatory death of the intimate Muslim other, the victim is digested and freed from what is inauthentic (the Muslim-ness of that body). As in the symbolism of Indian mortuary rites, which allow a proper recycling of the dead to become the source of progeny and sustenance, dead Muslims are recycled as part of the Hindu national body (Parry 1985: 627).

With the waning of a ritual order, and under the pressure of Hindu nationalism, the complementary position of the Muslim as indicated by Pocock is lost; it can no longer occupy a redemptive position. The Muslim cannot remain outside of *hindu rashtra* and yet be internal for all practical purposes. In this context, as in other such modern nationalist formulations, ambiguity (what Pocock referred to as the "absurdity" of the system) is replaced by elimination. Ambivalent emotion is abreacted in surgical procedures that attempt somatic stabilization of the victim's identity (Appadurai 1998).[4] The Muslim's position can only be either inside or outside, not both. In 2002, in the absence of a willingness to "reconvert" or to accept subordination, the Muslim's body became the site of sacrificial possibility in an act of expiation.

The closer one analyses the nature of the phantasmagoric material circulated during the pogrom, the less it seems to have anything to do with narrow political issues as such, or with religious or cultural incompatibilities. Instead, its appeal derives from more foundational themes like sexuality, ingestion, and the affect of disgust—heterogeneous experiences that deal with bodily invasion or death. Fears expressed through phantasmagoria do not pertain or concern only Muslims but easily adhere to other groups, abject or marginal members of society, and they revolve centrally around conceptions of gender difference.

In sum, phantasmagorias are employed in order to define an absolute difference vis-à-vis Muslims that strangely fails to leave its mark in moments of coexistent calm. While such fantasies remain latent, they do not threaten the collapse of an everyday edifice that demands mutual interaction. This is partly due to the fact that mundane contact with Muslims is not incessantly structured by aggregate categories but by members of diverse communities standing in complexly stratified relations with locally specific Muslim communities.

The Gujarat pogrom and the imaginary investments that motivated and accompanied it are similar to Central European anti-Jewish pogroms of the last several centuries. For example, in 1941, in the villages of Jedwabne and Radzilow in Poland during German occupation, Catholic Polish residents murdered half of the local Jewish population (estimated at over 1,600 people). Many perpetrators alleged that their Jewish Polish neighbors were consuming Christian babies as "matzo," drinking their blood, and abducting children (Gross 2001: 79–81). Such phantasmagoric imaginaries reach deep down into the anti-Semitic bowels of European folklore and myth (cf. Rappaport 1991: 304–335; Dundes 1991: 336–378;

Hsia 1988: 1–13). The excessive nature of such imagination bespeaks the need to find something about the familiar neighbor that renders them distinct, emphasizing a difference that allows for the expenditure of rage, when in actual fact the neighbors fail to be all that unfamiliar.

As in Gujarat, there is a mimetic reversal at work: a fear of Jewish blood rituals at the very moment when Jewish neighbors were being "consumed" in a gruesome pogrom, a blood ritual of sorts. Significantly, what Catholics attributed to Jews was a transmuted form of their own central religious ritual, the Eucharist, a blood sacrifice resonating implicitly with the theme of cannibalism. The Eucharist ritual plays on the symbolism of drinking the blood of Christ (red wine) and partaking of his body (bread, wafer). What was projected onto the Jews was not something "other" but something very familiar, their own uncanny qualities: a de-symbolized version of what Catholic ritual is all about (Reik 1975 [1923]: 182–212, esp. 194–195).

The Gujarati case is more complicated because unlike in Catholic ritual, Hindu religious traditions appear more diverse and seem not to center so tightly around one specific ritual, although the VHP nonetheless invokes the language and imagery of "Vedic sacrifice" continually. Moreover, Muslims in Gujarat are internally much more heterogeneous than Polish Jews were and must first be fashioned into a unified threat, a discursive labor into which Hindu organizations invest much of their time and resources. Furthermore, the permanent political instability of neighboring Pakistan provides an ongoing affectively laden context for such labor that invokes lurking dangers and shadowy conspiracies.

The force of these invocations relates indirectly also to more local and intimate themes. One is the ongoing disappearance of the practice of animal blood sacrifice, an erasure that is not simply an empirical fact but moreover a psychological one. Today it is *shuddh* Gujaratis who, though clandestinely fascinated, have problems accounting for practices such as traditional animal blood sacrifice in the context of Shakta worship or other practices among various Vagri, Adivasi, or Dalit communities. Changes in worship styles, sometimes aided through government schemes, render temples of Mother Goddesses such as Bahuchar Mata in central Gujarat or Khodiyar in Saurashtra purely vegetarian affairs (Sheikh 2010; Tambs-Lyche 2010: 110). Such transformation implies alterations in institutional forms of memory that have become embarrassing if not incomprehensible. New affective boundaries of shame and repugnance make it difficult to even discuss the mere fact of historical change in major religious sites in Gujarat.

For an urban middle to lower-middle class, many traditional practices now adhere to communities often considered lacking in proper moral development. Their imagination is overstrewn with what in a different context has been called "carnival debris" (Stallybrass and White 1986: 171–190), which emerges in fantasies, dreams, reveries, stereotypes, and hysterical symptoms. In areas of west Ahmedabad, middle-class Gujaratis show great consternation about ritual and worship forms of "backward" communities, and they express their indignity in no uncertain terms. Bharat's collapse in the presence of a raw chicken was no singular instance, but a concrete individual expression of a larger development, which remains difficult to capture ethnographically in the detailed manner it deserves. Cultural transformations of this nature have a larger historical trajectory, whose development Elias (1976 [1939]) has investigated for Europe. Transformations—what he calls socio- and psychogenesis—are based on ongoing forms of sublimation where new cultural forms emerge out of old ones with momentous effects in modifying forms of behavior and reorganizing affective experience.

One result of these transformations in Gujarat is a deeply psychological relationship to Muslim meat eating, animal sacrifice, and the phantasmic associations that this aggregate figure now has to bear. While Hindutva organizations have not caused these larger developments, they skillfully manipulate existing prejudices and resentments by channeling them onto specific targets. They do this by establishing a symbolic relay between intimate and aggregate registers, such as vegetarian and pollution themes, with national threat.

Evocations of blood, slaughter, and dietary stigma give evidence to the quality of violent identification, based on the collapse of social or cultural distance. The stereotypes form a phantasmagoria that is uncannily beckoning from those parts of a newfound Hindu self that cannot be fully assimilated. Hence, in the figure of the Muslim, a heterogeneous element is made to return that is intimately in touch with material that has increasingly been rendered absent and even unspeakable today. It is, in other words, uncanny. Experiences of the uncanny are distinctive in their instability despite their momentous effects once they emerge (Freud 1919: 227–268).

It is here, in the need to exert control over a boundary, that the pogrom became informed by a decisive sacrificial logic.[5] Sacrifice articulates the uncertainty that the figure of the Muslim has come to represent by allowing the simultaneous collapse and refashioning of a boundary. Similar to the affect of disgust, which draws close to a revolting object, the ritual of sacrifice brings emotional ambivalence to expression directly through a procedure that destroys the victim, on the one hand, while incorporating it at the same time, on the other. In this way, the destroyed object is retained as the basis of an intimate identification.

RITUAL EFFICACY

One of the most disturbing aspects of the Gujarat pogrom is its insistence on the efficacy of this form of sacrificial expiation, despite its obvious failure over time. The object to be destroyed, the Muslim, fails to ever disappear, and the mythic Hindu unity that constitutes Hindu *rashtra* is never permanently achieved. After each pogrom or communal riot, the Muslim figure is able to signify instability or division all over again, while neighbors who happen to be Muslims remain strangely familiar; substitution has failed and countless Hindus—especially the poor—equally suffer from these endless cycles of violence.

If sacrificial cleansing is not efficacious, however, it nonetheless enables the Hindu to emerge in anger and creates, if briefly, a glimpse of the longed-for mythical unity. In Gujarat, the *krodh hindu*, turned away from the law of the father, who is associated with ahimsa, vegetarianism, and Gandhi, toward the mother, who as Goddess traditionally compelled animal blood sacrifice.[6] Today, blood sacrifice, once a ritual expressing the sovereignty of the king, has disappeared from sight, only to return unconsciously to express the sovereignty of the people, the Hindu, who rises again awoken in "anger." This identifying shift may become manifest only temporarily—for the duration of a pogrom, when it makes possible the venting of communal rage in the name of the mother, Bharat Mata. But it is also part of a long-term structural shift, meaning that we might expect a return of the logic of sacrifice and expiation in the future.[7]

SERIAL HETEROGENEITY?

Muslims in central Gujarat are caught in a sort of conceptual deadlock. For one thing, as minorities, they suffer repeated discrimination and victimization by becoming the preferred target for national and regional politicking—by the BJP and the Congress, by local politicians who both woo them for votes and make them into scapegoats during electoral campaigns. Aside from their abject status, Muslims' claims to greater collective recognition is rendered illegitimate in the eyes of many Gujaratis, who must deal with such claims from many others groups also—mainly because of Partition. For another thing, Muslims are segmented internally through cultural and social distinctions as well as religious forms and styles. If they were to attempt serious political consolidation, they would immediately confirm the looming specter of an internally fractured India, for which they, by definition, already are blamed.

The removal of the stigma of untouchability is an ongoing pedagogical task of the nation-state that promises future integration of formerly excluded categories (Chatterjee 2004: 17). If the ideology of Hindutva remains the frame for symbolic integration, as it is in Gujarat, then it is impossible to symbolically integrate Muslims; at most, we can speak of possible modes of incorporation as various modes of destructive digestion. This incorporation relegates to Muslims a location that is reminiscent of the traditional position of untouchability. Dalits and Adivasis can try to assume the identity of a respectable Hindu, arguably with very uncertain success. But it is difficult to imagine how Muslims can similarly be assimilated, as being a better Muslim today raises instead the specter of madrasa, mosque, and Shari'a—the haunting images of a global Islam.

Muslims are asked to understand their post-Partition integration into the national body as a form of benevolent tolerance, but this integration has also brought them into those dynamics that define collective subjectivization under the conditions of contemporary governmentality: the bound seriality that defines a finite, clearly demarcated community that moves towards a shared destiny, stable through time (Anderson 1999: 29–45). Occupying such an aggregate category places them in symmetrical opposition to the aggregate category "Hindu," a fact that Hindu nationalists exploit without fail for their ideological goals. Bound seriality is what makes Muslims external to Hindu *rashtra*, and at the same time suggests assimilability to the Islamic communities elsewhere by alienating them from their own unique cultural resources of a composite tradition (cf. Das 1984; Basu 1994, 2004a; Ghassem-Fachandi 2008).

Here Pocock's example, referred to above, shows its limitations. The empirical situation involves more internally differentiated subjects than he posits. For all its seductive clarity, Pocock's approach remains too formal in invoking the two ambivalent positions to traditional caste society in aggregate terms. But there are Muslim groups who are conceived of as untouchables by other Muslims and Muslim elites who will unselfconsciously refer to their Brahmin (read "noble" or "*aryan*") origins. Assimilation, imitation, and introjection between groups and individuals are rampant today as in the past. The new grammar of representation compelled by the nation form disallows such messy fractions. Instead it demands a mirage-like integrity of communal bodies that remain statistically transparent and governable by state machineries and the various calculations of capital (Anderson 1999).

The frontispiece of this book (figure 1) illustrates the contemporary Muslim impasse most exactly in displaying how the older logic of caste complementarity is being replaced by one of national seriality. "Saluting Tomorrow's India," an advertising billboard in a busy commercial center in Ahmedabad, depicts what locally goes by the name of *ekta*, oneness or unity. The iconography of the billboard reveals how difference is routinely imagined in India today within an optimistic liberal sensibility. In its well-intended egalitarian and inclusive spirit, it appears to stand in clear opposition to Hindutva ideology, which makes no allowance for Muslim integration as Muslims.

Depicted are three children: a Hindu, a Jain (possibly a Sikh), and a Muslim. They wear their respective colors—orange, white, and green—the colors of the Indian tricolor. All three are young, dynamic, indicating a bright future. All three have the same perfect skin tone—not too dark but also not too white, signifying membership in India's elite and successful classes (or rather the way these classes imagine themselves). They are boys, not girls. The equivalence established between them, without social distinction, communicates horizontality. Unlike the anachronistic Ottoman fez on older national integration posters that Shahid Amin (2004) has drawn attention to, the iconographic representation of the billboard allows only for a minute distinction to typify difference within the set: the color of the boy's headscarves.

The reduction of empirical differences elides all reference to sectarian division or social organization (class and caste distinction) and instead relegates all difference to religious markers integrated into a series.[8] The billboard disallows the messiness of the empirical—for example, the fact that Jains or Sikhs are often subsumed under "Hindu," that Gujarati Muslims are often denigrated as being "too effeminate" (read "Hindu") for a modern self-confident and global Islam. Furthermore, Dalit and Adivasi groups have their own complex relations to aggregate categories, and young women will certainly determine India's future as much as men.

That religion is the single category that remains irreducible is significant here, given the complex maze of differences and similarities that crisscross social and cultural forms in the state and, by extension, on the subcontinent. What is perhaps less obvious is that the billboard communicates the logic of contemporary consumption. In their substitutability, the three boys seem like three flavored commodities, arguably lollypops or ice cream cones. They are cute, and the spectator can choose: "I like mango, he likes lemon, and you like pistachio flavor."

Whereas unbound seriality is expressed by the fact that all three belong to the unity that is India, bound seriality is expressed by the fact that all three figures seem replaceable and interchangeable with the other. This substitutability renders each individual in the set fundamentally empty in relation to the other. The cute play on colors presents the "heterogeneity" of a middle-class imagination. Difference has become represented as a mere surface quality of a much more fundamental indistinction within the elements of the set. Yet, at the same time, each boy represents a religious section of the nation and can only stand for that section and nothing else. The fundamental indistinction underlying the surface is a product of the grammar of nationalism that internalizes the sense of a wider international world. Each of the boys could represent anybody's future anywhere. . . .

The three are depicted in a way that none could legitimately desire anything from the other—each element is whole in and of itself. Only in the spectator's gaze, presupposed by the picture's frame, is desire encouraged. Hence the boys look back at the spectator in the mode of "beguiling synecdoches for serial cornucopias of desirable commodities" (Anderson 1999: 35). My point is, while the billboard seems to celebrate difference, its configuration betrays a deep fear of it, revealing an impulse to minimize what is apprehended as divisive. Each and every community must possess itself completely. In the billboard, seriality has replaced complementarity.

The equivalence that these three faces express draws attention to the problem of communal relations and the breakdown of the logic of caste complementarity, where equality today can only be conceived horizontally, in homogeneous empty time turned towards a future in which each religious community must be completely itself yet not different from the other. Being completely oneself yet not different from the other so that one does not arouse jealousy, fear, or rejection is of course impossible, especially when difference is not limited to the level of aggregate categories. Desire traverses categories and communities perhaps more than ever before, be it in the forms of personal friendship, love, or mutual hatreds. A better solution might be to find a way to engage in the pursuit of equality without sacrificing difference in this way in the first place, a vexed problem not only haunting Gujarat or India but most other modern nation-states.

Despite the many problems with the picture Louis Dumont presents of the South Asian "homo hierarchicus," his panoptic view is a useful starting point. In caste society, he argued, each group had a being outside of itself, and thus there was an implicit recognition that each community cannot be full in itself but is dependent on the other (Dumont 1986: 460–464). Castes mingled men with gods and demons, providing differentiating and integrative continuities where other civilizations drew sharper lines. Mutual desire was kept in check through the enforcement of segmentally ordered community boundaries and by a multiplicity of ritualized behaviors between human and nonhuman groups and entities. The mutual gaze did not find resemblance in similarity but self-recognition through difference. To be sure, those lower in the hierarchy suffered more under this enforcement. Untouchables frequently bore the brunt of this system, as an expiatory category that was located beyond the pale, included only through their exclusion from recognition as an equal mem-

ber of proper society. It is no coincidence that contemporary Hindu nationalists blame the advent of Islam for the historical development of
untouchability, whose practice today though illegal is not everywhere
abolished on the ground.

Whereas the hierarchical intimacies of caste were predicated on differences, national intimacies today are predicated on similarities. Even in
attempts to emphasize cultural heterogeneity, as in the billboard above,
intimacy can only be imagined through replicable resemblance. The fear
that is being expressed here is the fear of heterogeneity, of a difference to
normative Hindu society that might force the *shuddh* bourgeois to relate
to an otherness within him- or herself. That otherness no longer seems
acceptable.

In his early investigation of the aesthetic forms of fascism, Bataille
(1997 [1933/34]: 122–146) thought together what today is often thought
apart: on the one hand, the heterogeneity of identity and cultural diversity in relation to homogeneous state and national projects, and on the
other hand, existential experiences of affective life confronted with the
unassimilability of death, eroticism, and violence. By this second form of
heterogeneity, internal to the subject, he meant those forms of expenditure characterized by nonutility that are not assimilable to homogeneous
productive society. Both forms were intimately interwoven in the violent
fabrications of the Gujarat pogrom.

The stereotypes and collective hallucinations during the pogrom—
invulnerability, sacrifice, sexual prowess, and culinary bestiality—are
obviously not part of the iconography of "Saluting Tomorrow's India."
Yet they are indirectly related. During the pogrom, the heterogeneous
elements of life were part of how the unwanted neighbor was experienced in fear but also fascination. When a lack of distinction threatens
the boundaries of communities no longer defined through an intimacy of
difference as in hierarchical complementarities, but as substitutable elements in a horizontal series, resistance can be more readily mobilized at
the boundaries of an anxious self. The negative experiences of the sacred
are now projected onto the unwanted neighbor, who becomes the site of
all those heterogeneous elements from which one has sought to inoculate
oneself. Why can the Muslim neighbor not look, behave, and feel a little
like this cute boy with the green turban that so much resembles a pistachio ice cream cone?

Hindutva ideology proposes a convergence of bound and unbound
elements. For all those who can assume the category "Hindu," the eman-
cipatory possibilities of nationalism seem affirmed on the surface. Yet
those same possibilities are denied to those who are by definition external
to that project. The strategy to deal with the Muslim presence in Gujarat
was first to subtract all heterogeneity from the *shuddh* Gujarati, then to

hallucinate the idea of the aggregate Hindu as absolutely indistinguishable from the self, and finally to "awake" to the betrayal by the unwanted neighbor, evacuating all that could not be incorporated thereafter in a violent festival, a pogrom.

For Gujarati Muslims, who cannot become Hindu, and are denied the claim of being *shuddh* Gujarati, a possible answer to Hindutva could be to subvert what their detractors so obsess about, by appropriating the unbound elements of nationalism without renouncing their various religious and social identities by finding a way to affirm radical internal heterogeneity. They could revive what is unique to India by celebrating the diversity that their own religious traditions give such magnificent evidence of. They could lay claim to the cultural heterogeneity that is associated with Indian civilization in general. If middle-class neighbors can no longer accept the Indian miracle of multiple origins, it is now up to Muslims to affirm them. The ability to resist the pressure of religious and national homogenization is what their Hindu and Muslim detractors, whether inside or across the border, are certainly most concerned about.

Postscript

ON MY FIRST RETURN TO GUJARAT after the pogrom, in 2005, I immediately took a long rickshaw ride from the railway station at the edge of the old city to the far-western parts of new Ahmedabad. I asked the middle-aged driver about the events in 2002. He politely denied any knowledge of them before hesitantly making a few observations about the pogrom. Initially he blamed the English and foreign media for overblown exaggerations, a response others later shared with me. Then he said that politicians and other men behind the scenes were solely responsible for the violence, but normal residents were largely uninvolved. Finally, he blamed extralegal actors—organizations like the VHP, the Bajrang Dal, and the RSS.

In the beginning, our discussion was relaxed, and I alternated between agreement and disagreement. I increasingly grew restless, however, and began to insist that my experiences as a resident at the time were different from what he now described. It was then that he suddenly reversed his strategy. Stopping his vehicle on the side of the road to respond more comprehensively to my annoying questions, the driver engaged in straight talk. Living in the east city, he, too, had seen it all close up. He was not going to let a foreign visitor have the last word.

His exhortations that followed were familiar to me, as he revisited idioms, tropes, and stereotypes that I had become acquainted with years earlier. Forgotten were his initial claims that the representation of violence by the media was overblown and that it was a result of the particular schemes of politicians and Hindu organizations. Now it was all about explaining to me why such a response had been absolutely necessary. Muslims were the dark blot on the promise of a better Gujarat, and by extension, of India. Convinced that his indignation was justified, he became exasperated at my skepticism.

For this man, I concluded, everything was still fresh; nothing had been relegated to the past. The compelling pressure of my address in his native tongue seemed to produce a standardized response: a chronology of paradigmatically structured claims. His response, then, was ultimately predictable (though it disappointed me). It moved from denial to detail, from the naming of actors and forces responsible to mustering intimate and personal reasons why participation was legitimate and necessary. What it lacked was an emotional disengagement with the very material that time and again was mustered to legitimate violent action when it unfolds. This paradigmatic structure suggests a failure in reckoning with the immediate past of the pogrom and is symptomatic of why the violence remains latent in Ahmedabad.

Almost every year since the pogrom in 2002 has seen small altercations such as stone throwing between residents in specific areas of the city. Most of these skirmishes never make it into the newspapers. They are part of a strange local status quo—the nooks and crannies of local communal aggregation in urban space. To allude to these episodes too directly makes one suspicious, as it disturbs the comfortable arrangement of low-intensity tension in designated urban areas, which can be manipulated whenever the need arises. It also confirms stereotypes about Dalit and Muslim communities that circulate locally. Those who talk of the violence might be accused of being instruments of some malignant anti-Gujarati plots intended to deride the state's fabulous economic development or, worse, of being anti-Hindu. What these smaller skirmishes do convey is that the city's police and other authorities are now apparently willing and perfectly able to quell all altercations quickly and effectively in the interest of larger political and economic expediencies.

As the episode with the rickshaw driver suggests, in such a continuously volatile context, *insisting* on violence often approximates *summoning* it. Hence the strategy of many a city resident to keep the compulsive logic at bay by engaging in what amounts to avoidance behavior. Nonetheless, if the logic of reaction does surface and finds expression, the onus of blame easily lies with the Muslims, because of their alleged proximity to Pakistan, their willingness to engage in terror, their insensitivity to Hindus by eating beef and slaughtering cows, their devious minds that lust after Hindu girls, and, more generally, their mental inclination to hurt Hindu neighbors.

Most other Gujaratis whom I know well had their own strategies of how to put the past behind them without reckoning with the events. Payal and her husband Hritik moved to Bombay—a safer location, they thought. Although Marathis in Gujarat, they now live as "foreigners" in Maharashtra, given the multi-ethnic atmosphere in the megalopolis. Having missed the serial bomb blasts that shook Ahmedabad in July 2008, they arrived in Mumbai in time to witness the attacks there in late November 2008.

Sejal remained in the city and seems to have found domestic peace in her marriage to a Brahmin. She thrives in writing columns for local newspapers and journals, in which she tries to bring a feminist Jain perspective to bear. Pratab returned to his wife and children in his home village in central Gujarat. He did not finish his work on Mahatma Gandhi, but he speaks, reads, and writes better Hindi than most of his village companions. He never did take much to city life anyway.

Ranjit still eats mutton but no longer eats chicken, as he together with his family have changed the lineage goddess (*kuldevi*) from Chamunda Mata to Bahucharmata. The latter's sacred vehicle (*vahan*) is the rooster. The switch occurred after the *bhuvo* of his native village, an exorcist and a worshipper of the goddess, informed him of a scandal in his family lineage: an occurrence of incest in the past. Keenly aware of the educational competition against established elites in the state, his son, visibly affected by the pressure for success by his father, plans to leave for the United States or Britain to accumulate international experience and achieve perfect diction in spoken English. In 2007 and 2008, both Ranjit and his friend Gautam were astonished, and then thrilled, that a black man was in fact running for president of the United States.

Ahmedabad, too, is changing rapidly. I returned a second time, in the winter of 2008 and stayed until early 2009. New multi-shopping complexes had been built; old ones that I used to frequent lay half abandoned. The city was filled with modern Reliance Super Markets and city residents were busy consuming. The practice of vegetarianism, while affirmed on the face of it, seemed to be less vigorously defended. The younger generation of the new middle class seemed to fancy meat, as well as discos and video games and Hollywood movies. While the interest surrounding matters of meat has not lessened, the city's edition of *The Times of India* featured prominent color spreads while I was there on how to cook a turkey for an American Christmas. If in 2001, the Shiv Sena and the Bajrang Dal had burned shops that sold Valentine's Day cards, in December 2008, no one cried foul as the city was inundated with Christmas paraphernalia.

The billboard of Mr. Shahkahari advertising the new McDonald's has been taken down, but the plastic statue of Ronald McDonald, the welcoming pale clown who always fails to be funny, remains, seated on a bench outside the entrance to the restaurant on Ashram Road. Although twice the size of the uniformed guards standing around, Ronald McDonald is usually ignored and only rarely does anyone want to sit next to him. Fancier places for young folks, especially in the new entertainment complexes mushrooming all over the city, offer sandwiches, pizzas, and burgers in all varieties. The quality of American-type fast food has improved dramatically, with the corresponding, often exorbitant, rise in prices.

Akhtar, the Muslim owner of the Nutan Tyres shop that was set on fire during the pogrom still worked in the same shop. He greeted me warmly but was not too keen on talking about the events in 2002. After all, his major clientele are his immediate Hindu neighbors—some of the same people who burned his shop. He received 12,000 rupees compensation from the Gujarat government, but his losses were over one lakh (100,000 rupees). Busy working off his debts to family members, he is still hopeful he will receive the full amount from the government. Mr. Chauhan and his son Lalu no longer live in the vicinity of Naroda Patiya, one of the sites of massacre. Salim moved to Juhapura, and Matuben left for Varodara. The former president of the Muslim butcher community and Josephbhai are still living in the city, and both are doing well.

Thin Arif has left for Dubai to find a better destiny and gain some Muslim weight, while Mohammad has become father again. His uncle Jehangir plans for retirement in his home in Varodara. All three were doing well when I last inquired. Excited that the future president of the United States might be a "Hussein," before he left Arif asked me anxiously if that possibly meant that the future president might also be of Shi'a extraction.

Bharat has achieved a full and successful *entri* into the Gujarati middle class, becoming the deputy registrar at a provincial university, where he sits in a marvelously rectangular office decorated with a life-sized picture of Swami Vivekanand and another one of his guru and former teacher from Gujarat University. His academic credentials were not enough to become a teaching professional, but in his new job he has surrounded himself with many scholars and intellectuals who represent to him that which is ultimately the great Hindu tradition (of the *mahapurusho*). He nonetheless still dreams of completing a dissertation one fine day. His income is stable now, and he is the father of two children.

Bharat has also begun to learn how to use a computer and is very serious about finally learning English properly. He rejects connecting his house to cable TV and only uses selected video material with what he considers "morally high content." Finding that most commercial Bollywood offerings lack this content, he asked me for "clean" English movies, free not of violence but of sexually explicit material, so that he can practice his English and habituate his son to the foreign language. Proud of his accomplishments, he looks confidently into his professional future. His wife has given up her plans to become a teacher. Bharat still hopes to return to Ahmedabad when a position opens there. He is sad that his many responsibilities no longer allow him the time to visit an RSS *shakha*, but he explained that politically, as a registrar, it might anyway be wiser for him to stay away from such outfits. His brother in his home village has been diagnosed with tuberculosis and direly needs Bharat's financial support.

I accompanied Bharat on his search for a better apartment in the regional town where he is now living. We visited a three-story housing complex with several rentals. His first questions to the wife of a neighboring renter were about the moral credentials of his immediate neighbors. He would accept to live only in a house that keeps strictly to a vegetarian diet, he said, and he excused himself for his severe condition of *alagi*. The woman asked, "Aren't you Darbar?" to which Bharat replied, "No, I am Rajput." Perplexed, the woman elaborated that one of the renters was a Sindhi and might sometimes indulge in eating meat outside the complex, but she assured Bharat that he would never bring the fleshy stuff home. Bharat, not satisfied with the answer, followed with a question about alcohol consumption and stressed to the puzzled woman unapologetically that his neighbors should be reasonably educated so that interaction with them would not have any adverse effects on the mental state and future inclination of his impressionable children.

Narendra Modi has become Gujarat's most celebrated chief minister since the foundation of the state. After harvesting a maximum political benefit out of the Gujarat pogrom, he now is busy proving to the country at large that a BJP-led state government can also provide good governance for economic growth. He has turned to urban infrastructural and developmental projects, which he manages as effectively as election campaigns, orchestrated pogroms, and the many legal imbroglios that have unfolded in their wake. He has weathered several attempts to implicate him directly in the pogrom and deals with annoying questions by journalists by promptly walking out of the studio. In addition to being a supremely capable organizer, he also remains a skilled orator.

Modi has been denied entry visas for the United States and for Britain, where he risks facing charges because three British citizens of Gujarati Muslim background were slain during the pogrom. Since 2002 there have been a series of extra-judicial killings by the police in Gujarat in what are locally termed "encounter killings." In one case in 2005, Gujarati policemen murdered a Muslim in police custody. The incident became known as the Sohrabuddin case. The victim's murder was followed by that of his wife, Kausar Bi, and his Hindu friend Tulsiram Prajapati. Before these murders Sohrabuddin, a petty extortionist, had been accused of a plot to assassinate Narendra Modi and it was claimed he was a Lashkar-e-Taiba terrorist. Amit Shah, minister of state for home affairs in the Modi government in 2002, has been accused of kidnapping and murder in connection with this case and is currently in police custody.

What happened to the other political protagonists of the Gujarat pogrom? Ex-minister Haren Pandya was assassinated in 2003 under mysterious circumstances. He had accused the chief minister of giving a green light to the pogrom when, at a law and order meeting on February 27, immediately after the Godhra incident, Modi allegedly told state officials and officers present that Hindus should be allowed to vent their anger. In 2010, state officers present at the meeting denied this accusation, but it was subsequently confirmed "off the record" by Sanjeev Bhatt—deputy commissioner of internal security in the State Intelligence Bureau at the time. Gordon Zadaphiya, former minister of state for home affairs, left the Modi government as part of an internal BJP rebellion and now leads a political movement opposed to the chief minister. He claims that he only followed Modi's orders during the violence. He accuses his former boss of an "authoritarian style" and alleges that Modi had no longer any interest in Hindutva or the RSS. For reasons of political expediency, Zadaphiya warned, Modi would also no longer shield or support specific rioters accused of crimes.

Maya Kodnani, a gynecologist and the former state minister for women and child development, has been charged with murder, abetment to murder, and arson. She did not initially appear for questioning in court—she "absconded" as she held a position as minister of state for higher education—but in early 2009, together with VHP leader Jaydeep Patel, she was eventually charged and arrested, then set free on bail pending trial. Both are charged for crimes in the Naroda Patiya and Naroda Gam cases.

Amidst all this and more, a senior member of the Gujarati police, R. B. Sreekumar, former additional director-general of intelligence, broke the wall of silence that surrounded the Gujarat government's actions during the pogrom. He accused the Modi government of "unconstitutional directives," including wiretapping phones of political opponents. The Gujarat police, Sreekumar explained, had a strong anti-minority bias and was completely demoralized. In his testimony to the G. T. Nanavati and Akshay Mehta Commission, he detailed the practice of police officers who take orders directly from politicians and not their superiors, the strategy to release accused perpetrators of nonbailable cases due to partisan government public prosecutors, and the faulty and incomplete filing of FIRs (First Information Reports) when Muslim victims tried to initiate legal action. Recently, the former cop published a book in Malayalam titled *The Diary of a Helpless Man*, in which he calls police officers and politicians in the Gujarat government "sophisticated sycophants."

In 2007, the weekly magazine *Tehelka* published the findings of a systematic sting operation targeting players involved in the Gujarat pogrom and uploaded to its website secretly recorded video footage of perpetrators and others bragging about their strategies and crimes. After the initial airing of the footage, many cable TV operators in Gujarat blocked it, and there has since been a noted silence about these revelations on the side of Sangh Parivar institutions.

The lines between the Congress Party and the BJP are blurred because members of both often switch sides, and there is no strong third party in Gujarat. This makes for the relative stability of the referent Hindutva, which remains a strong undercurrent, even while the ideology is more cautiously deployed publicly at present, mainly restricted to election campaigns. Meanwhile, on the national stage, the BJP has not done as well, though in Gujarat its support has been unflagging since 1995. Within the Gujarati BJP, Modi has been able to stabilize his own power despite internal opposition, indictments, alleged alienation from RSS cadres (hyped by the vernacular media), and constant pressures to reorganize the BJP leadership.

There is no closure to the events described in this book, though there is a strong desire to forget. Since 2003, India has witnessed a series of partly related bomb blasts targeting Hindu as well as Muslim religious structures and both commercial and residential areas. Muslim militant groups have claimed responsibility for most of these attacks, and although sometimes Hindu groups have also been identified, they rarely admit to anything. Most recently, in July 2008, synchronized low-intensity blasts devastatingly shook several Indian cities. Ahmedabad, too, was struck with sixteen consecutive blasts in which twenty-nine people died and about 110 were wounded. As observers pointed out, those areas of the eastern city where the BJP was strongest or that were considered "sensitive" were hit hardest. The perpetrators intended to utilize the unresolved past to incite more violence, targeting mainly those areas where Dalits and Muslims—two vulnerable segments of society—live in urban proximity to one another. The designated attackers, the so-called Indian Muhajidin, explicitly mentioned revenge for the Gujarat pogrom and retaliation against the state's chief minister as rationales for these brutal attacks.

The story goes on as of this writing, topped by a November 26, 2008, Pakistani-organized attack in Mumbai, killing 195 and wounding more than 300. A suicide mission by ten trained terrorists, this event is widely held to be India's 9/11, referred to as 26/11, lasting three horrific days. The killings were well coordinated, and the terrorists stated that the infamous ISI (Pakistan's secret service) offered logistic support. The future indeed looks bleak, with a renewed threat of war between the two sibling nations, which both pride themselves on having nuclear weapons; a revitalized Hindu nationalist rhetoric spun by chauvinistic Indian politicians; and further alienation between Hindu and Muslim citizens in India, which in turn tempts some Indian Muslims to seek succor in diverse Islamist and revivalist ideologies.

To return to the Godhra incident, which helped precipitate the pogrom explicated in this book. In 2011, a special court in Ahmedabad delivered a judgment that upheld the Gujarat government's assertion that the Godhra incident of 2002 was based on a "pre-planned conspiracy." Thirty-one of those accused have been convicted, which is unusual in India, where riot cases usually do not lead to high conviction rates. Sixty-three others, including the Maulana Hussein Umarji, initially believed to be the "mastermind" of the conspiracy, have been released without charges due to "lack of evidence." Although these formerly accused have spent up to nine years in police custody, there have been no convictions. The majority were Muslim residents of Godhra who had gathered on the street near the railway station after a rumor spread that a Muslim girl had been kidnapped by *karsevak*s. Berated as "terrorists," "traitors" and "conspirators," they have finally emerged from obscurity, although few have had anything to say; most returned home quietly to pick up their broken lives. Perhaps we will hear more about them in the future.

Who then are the thirty-one individuals that the special court did indeed sentence? It seems that none were Pakistani agents, professional killers, or members of terror organizations such as Al-Qaida or Lashkar-e-Taiba. Nor was it established that they were instructed by a central command in Lahore or Islamabad, or trained in the use of arms and the assemblage of bombs like Ajmal Kasab, the lone surviving perpetrator of the terrible Mumbai attacks in November 2008. Instead, we know only that they are individual members of a local community considered backward and largely illiterate, some having prior convictions of petty extortion or thievery, others alleged to have kept relations with co-members of their traditional community across the border. Some went so far as to prefer toothpaste imported from Pakistan.

To systematically carry out such an attack on passengers locked in a train is certainly a heinous act—a crime deserving severe punishment. But even if all charges are entirely correct, these men seem hardly capable of what they were accused: a frontal assault on Hindu society, using sophisticated methods and ingenuous designs. That accusation legitimated the unleashing of collective *pratikriya* onto uninvolved Muslims over the state's northern and central provinces. The attackers of Signal Falia, however, turn out to be versions of a familiar local menace: petty criminals, socially neglected members of Godhra's destitute slum class, some of whom spontaneously decided one night to confront *karsevak*s the next day. This is the evidence that proves the Godhra incident was a "preplanned conspiracy." The justice sentenced eleven persons to death while twenty received life imprisonment.

For the Gujarati middle class, however, these men represent a heterogeneous element that they cannot fathom or recognize as products of their own society. This society employs a detailed organization of stigma and abjection, and it organizes and condones differential and unfair access to economic and symbolic resources. The middle class happens to be the main beneficiary of the current system as surely as the Ghanchi Muslims are one of its permanent losers. The special court and Justice P. R.

Patel's verdict simply confirmed what everyone already knew, lending legal coherence to dominant beliefs and firm prejudices.

Finally, in early 2011, a special investigative team (SIT) appointed by the Supreme Court of India and headed by R. K. Raghavan leaked a report to *Tehelka* that indicts Chief Minister Narendra Modi for his alleged complicity in the pogrom. The report, based on an investigation after a complaint lodged initially by Zakia Jafri, widow of the slain Muslim politician Ahsan Jafri, accuses the chief minister of having placed two of his cabinet ministers, I. K. Jadeja and Ashok Bhatt, in the state and city police control room during the unfolding pogrom—political micromanagement of law enforcement responsibilities. Most importantly, the report upholds the charge made by the late Haren Pandya, and later confirmed off the record by Sajeev Bhatt, that in meetings with state officials on the evening of February 27, 2002, Modi gave explicit orders that Hindus should be allowed to vent their anger—an accusation of premeditation against a sitting chief minister.

In other words, a charge of conspiracy has been made against Modi. If this accusation is eventually confirmed, it means the post-Godhra pogrom was planned in exactly the same way as the Godhra conspiracy was two nights before. One charge of premeditation confronts another in mimetic congruence. Did the chief minister, and his retainers, plan to execute *pratikriya*, karmic retribution, which was invoked in his proclamation on March 1, 2002: "every act has an equal and opposite reaction"? The special investigative team appointed by the Supreme Court has severely condemned this invocation, but the victims of reaction await justice. Because the chief minister described in such exact detail, in word and image, both the threat perceived during the events of 2002 and the measures to be taken against it, he remains haunted by his own words and actions, notwithstanding his enormous political success in the state.

Notes

INTRODUCTION

1. Estimates of the number of victims of the Gujarat pogrom vary. While the official count is 790 Muslims, 254 Hindus, and 223 missing victims, the numbers circulating elsewhere range frequently between 1,500 and 2,500. While 100,000 Muslims were displaced in relief camps, the official number of Hindus is 40,000 (cf. also G. Shah 2006: 77). Variations are partly due to government manipulation, but also it is difficult to identify the religious identities of those killed. Muslim organizations in central Gujarat sometimes claim a higher number.

2. The recurrent nature of violence in Ahmedabad confronts a scholar with a set of difficult questions. When does one begin to consider violent altercations a Hindu-Muslim clash in the common sense? What makes a violent episode modern? How are historical episodes connected to one another? What constitutes a riot versus a communal clash versus a pogrom? The difficulties of these questions are enhanced by the fact that sources are not always reliable or available. One can easily gauge this when comparing the timelines chosen by four competent scholars for their respective investigations and, thus, their diverse approaches to the history of violence in Ahmedabad: Howard Spodek (1989: 766) traces endemic violence to the 1940s, Ashutosh Varshney (2002: 220) defines the period from the 1920s to 1969 as largely peaceful (while leaving open the question of what preceded that period), Ornit Shani (2007: 133–188) focuses on the emergence of ethno-Hinduism from the 1980s onward, and Megha Kumar (2009: 80–227) begins with 1969 violence and works towards the present. There were violent altercations in the city before the twentieth century, but their relationship to events immediately before and after Independence remains relatively unexplored. This is partly due to the fact that historians fear such investigations could play into the hands of Hindu nationalists who insist on the historical continuity of Hindu-Muslim violence.

3. Yagnik and Sheth (2005: 253) mention 1940–1941 as the beginning date.

4. Interview with Hannah Arendt by Günter Gaus on October 28, 1964, on the West German television program *Zur Person* on Zweites Deutsches Fernsehen (ZDF). The famous postwar interview has been published in "Was bleibt? Es bleibt die Muttersprache. Ein Gespräch mit Günter Gaus," in *Gespräche mit Hannah*

Arendt, ed. Adelbert Reif (Munich 1976), 21. It was translated and published in English as "What Remains? The Language Remains: A Conversation with Günter Gaus," in *The Portable Hannah Arendt,* ed. Peter Baehr (New York: Penguin, 2003), 3–24, esp. 11–12.

5. For a comparative perspective on how the question of violence has been discussed in the context of ritual, everyday life, and ethnic conflict in Sri Lanka, see Obeyesekere (1975), Kapferer (1988: 86–87, 101; 1997: 185–220), Spencer (1990a), Tambiah (1992: 1–4, 95–101), and Daniel (1996).

6. Veena Das (1983, 1990, 1995) has written separately on both sacrifice and violent events. She proposes the rhetorical transformation of murder into "beatific sacrificial death" in the context of Partition and the relation between the figure of the effeminate Hindu, the marauding Muslim, and the martyr Sikh. While informed by her work, my analysis differs in that Das seeks to understand the forging of violent community identification against the "narcotic" effects of nonviolence, whereas I am interested in how a community can simultaneously stress identification with nonviolence in the very moment when it allows for its reversal—the legitimate meting out of violence—without canceling this identification.

7. I am following the lead here of the sociologist Norbert Elias (1976 [1939]: 36–42), who explicates the psychogenesis of these forms of personhood and national differentiations in the context of state formation in France and Germany. Such a longer historical view of these processes in India or South Asia does not, to my knowledge, exist.

CHAPTER 1 "Why Do you Leave?"

1. Ayodhya, an important pilgrimage center since the eighteenth century, is situated in eastern Uttar Pradesh (UP). The unused mosque was built on the site of a Hindu temple that was allegedly destroyed by the Muslim king Babar. The site was chosen by the Sangh Parivar, an umbrella of cultural and nationalist Hindu organizations, as the "authentic" birthplace of Ram, an incarnation of the god Vishnu. Many Gujaratis claim that the karsevaks (activists for temple construction) who destroyed the mosque in 1992 mainly came from Gujarat. For an interesting ethnographic account of the early agitation in Ayodhya, see van der Veer (1987: 283–301). On the Ramjanmabhumi conflict, which saw the political rise of the Bharatiya Janata Party in the 1980s, see Nandy et al. (1995) and van der Veer (1996 [1994]); on Hindu majoritarianism and the decline of Congress, see Ludden (2006 [1996]); on the role of television, see Rajagopal (2001). On Hindu nationalism in general, see Jaffrelot (1996 [1993]), Hansen (1999), and Bhatt (2001); in relation to the Mother Goddess, see McKean (1998 [1996]: 250–279); on the Rashtriya Swayamsevak Sangh, see Andersen and Damle (1987).

2. For descriptions of the provocations in the days preceding the Godhra incident, compare "Bajrang Dal activists on Sabarmati Express beat up Muslims, force them to shout, 'Jai Shree Ram,'" in *Jan Morcha,* February 25, 2002. The article is reprinted in *Communalism Combat* (March–April 2002): 12, as well

as in *Varadarajan* (2002): 63–64. For an investigation into the events surrounding Godhra, compare also the documentary movie *Godhra Tak: The Terror Trail* (2003), directed by Shubhradeep Chakravorty.

3. Jyoti Punwani, "Godhra revisited," *Hindu*, April 15, 2002, http://www.hinduonnet.com/2002/04/15/stories/2002041500161000.htm, accessed June 15, 2010.

4. This was a case of phatic communication. Another translation might be "It's good, isn't it?" or "It's ok, isn't it?" On what he termed "phatic communion," see the classic formulations by Malinowski (1923: 315).

5. In Gujarat, the Vagri community is, without fail, referred to in a depreciative manner by members of other communities, but usually not as untouchables (Randeria 1989: 182). In the GED, *vaghri* is translated as "man of Vaghri caste; [fig.] dirty, rude, and mannerless" and the corresponding *vagharan* as "woman of Vaghri caste; wife of a Vaghri; [fig.] slovenly woman, slut." Pocock (1973: 30, and glossary) mentions the *vaghari* as hunters and fowlers and their association with filthiness. According to Werth (1996: 57–60), who completed ethnographic research among Vagri groups in Tamil Nadu and alludes to the closeness of their local dialect to Gujarati, the Vagri claim that their name derives from the term *vag* (tiger). Vagri then means "like a tiger." In Gujarati, *vagh* means "a ferocious man," besides "tiger." It also denotes "a mortgage" and "a slave girl; a maid servant" (TMGED). Others claim the name Vagri comes from the Gujarati term *vaghur* (net). The Sanskrit word *vagura* means "net or trap for animals," and the Marathi *vaghri* were "living by snaring birds and beasts" (Werth 1996: 58).

6. Compare, for example, the comments of Hindutva ideologue Keka Shastree on the participation of the Vagri community in the pogrom in Sheela Bhatt, "It had to be done, VHP leader says of riots," Rediff.com, March 12, 2002, http://www.rediff.com/news/2002/mar/12train.htm, accessed 12 March 2005.

7. *Dharav* means "gratification"; *dharavavu*, "to satisfy, gratify" and "to satisfy (with food)." The noncausative verb *dharvu* denotes "to catch, hold, arrest" but also "to present, produce before somebody." In *bhog dharvo*, it translates into "to offer a sacrifice" and "to place a victim before a God." In *nauvegh dharvu*, it denotes "to place a dish before an idol for acceptance." Finally, the causative *dharavavu* comes to mean, "to make an offering," "to be under an obligation or a moral debt," "to owe to" (cf. TMGED, GED). Native Gujarati speakers described the use of the causative in this context to mean literally "to make God to be satisfied."

8. There are many reasons for this. First of all, women violently stripped in front of a crowd are considered "raped" in India, not least by the victim herself. Such sexual humiliation would, without hesitation, be described by all those involved as a form of sexual crime. Only when it comes to legal proceedings do the people involved apply a more narrow definition, all too often invoked for the benefit of the accused. Furthermore, many Muslim women were brutally killed and their bodies burned leaving no evidence of rape after the crimes were committed. Forms of sexual torture, as in inserting iron rods in women's vaginas, do not fall under the legal provisions for rape (HRW-2, 2003: 23). Finally, over the last nine years, Hindu organizations and local politicians and women's help

and fact-finding groups exerted systematic pressure on law enforcement regarding the obfuscation and destruction of evidence of mass rape of Muslim women during the pogrom. The sinister success of these attempts can be gauged by the disjuncture created between accounts of activist groups at the time and the disavowal or denial of these facts by many residents. For a detailed and evenhanded analysis of sexual violence against women in the context of Hindu nationalism in Ahmedabad, see Kumar (2009). For an investigation of the failure to prosecute rape cases see HRW-2 (2003: 22–25).

9. Note that Bharat did not think the women were shamed because there were instances of mass rape of Muslim women during the Gujarat pogrom. He never mentioned instances of mass rape of Muslim women.

10. For an interesting though brief discussion of the production of sublimity and techniques of levitation through veiling practices in Mediterranean traditions see Hauschild (2008: 37–42). See Heath (2008) and Borneman (2008: 13–14) on the relation of projection to Muslim veiling.

Chapter 2 Word and Image

1. There were two investigative commissions dealing with the Godhra incident: the Nanavati Commission of Inquiry headed by Justices G. T. Nanavati and K. G. Shah instated in March 2002 (Justice Shah passed away in 2008 and was replaced by Justice Akshay H. Mehta) and the Banerjee Commission headed by former Supreme Court justice U. C. Banerjee instated in September 2004. While the former insisted that the coach was set on fire by a mob, the latter came to the conclusion that the fire was an accident. Although the Special Investigative Team (SIT) of the Gujarat police soon had to rescind its claim that the Pakistani Inter-Services Intelligence (ISI) and the Student Islamic Movement of India (SIMI) were involved in the Godhra incident, it maintained that the incident was a "conspiracy"—planned and executed by local Muslims in Godhra. On February 22, 2011, a special court in Ahmedabad delivered a judgment that upheld the charge of conspiracy. Of the ninety-four persons arrested on charges, sixty-three were released, including the by-now famous Maulana Hussein Umarji, who had been for years derided as the main culprit in the Gujarati media. The rest were charged and sentenced. Defense lawyers of the accused have pointed to the fact that the prosecution's case rested on very few witness accounts and only one single "confession." Most vital depositions were taken long after the Godhra incident was complete and thus became inextricably embroiled with the Gujarat pogrom and its political reverberations. The immense pressures exerted by political and other interests hindered proper law-enforcement and legal procedures (cf. Anupama Katakam, "Guilty verdict," *Frontline Magazine* 28 (6), March 12–25, 2011, http://www.frontlineonnet.com/fl2806/stories/20110325280603100.htm, accessed March 12, 2011). On the failures and twists of legal and investigative processes in general, see HRW-2, 2003. On the judicial process and the two investigative commissions, see also Bunsha (2006: 159–161).

2. "Godhrano banav ekaj komni ek tarafi himsanu trasvadi krutya: Modi," *Sandesh*, February 28, 2002, p. 1.

3. The term *hullad* is used recurrently in expressions such as "Hulladia Hanuman," the name given to makeshift temples erected in the honor of the deity Hanuman on the spot of destroyed or desecrated Muslim shrines. The term *tofani* can also be used tenderly for children who misbehave.

4. Cf. *Sandesh*, March 2, 2002, p. 5.

5. *Times of India*, March 1, 2002, p. 3.

6. In the public imaginary of Gujaratis, the town of Godhra has long been associated with communal violence and Partition. For preliminary thoughts on the history of violence in Godhra, see Punwani (2002b), Hardiman (2003), and Bunsha (2006: 140–142).

7. "Godhravasio kahe chhe a to varshthi chalto sarhad ni anderno antakvad chhe." *Sandesh*, February 28, 2002, p. 7.

8. Modi's rhetoric was sustained in the following weeks, especially by the Gujarat home minister, Gordhan Zadaphiya, who repeatedly asserted the "anti-national character" of Muslim residents of Godhra, who, according to this politician, were solely responsible for the incident. Cf. *Indian Express*, April 30, 2002.

9. *Times of India* (Delhi edition), March 2, 2002, p. 1. This formulation mirrors Rajiv Gandhi's infamous quote "When a tree falls, the earth shakes," which he uttered in the context of the 1984 anti-Sikh pogrom in Delhi after Indira Gandhi had been assassinated by her own Sikh bodyguards. In the case of Modi's infamous "reaction theory," however, only *after* the organized violence is in full swing does a ritualistic logic of action and reaction emerge by labeling it a legitimate *pratikriya* (reaction, remedy). This language is derived from the *Sangh Parivar*'s obscure insistence on Vedic ritualism and science. The reach into the Vedic is as common a feature of Narendra Modi's political rhetoric as is the affirmation of scientific rationality. The ritualistic dimensions are largely overlooked by commentators and in investigative reports. In consequence, most have interpreted Modi's reaction theory as invocation of Newton's third law of motion, the basis for classical mechanics. In the context of the discourse of Vedic revival, however, sacrificial mechanics do not oppose Western science. On the contrary, both are seen as complementary and supporting one another in their truth claims. What remains certain is that a language deploying terms such as *pratikriya* was understood as an invocation not only of Western science but also of what is considered "ancient" and "Vedic," a ritual mechanism that cannot be stopped once set in motion. *Pratikriya* posed a formidable answer to what is conceived of as *jihad*. For a good example of the contemporary use of reactive action in the context of *karma*, see the popular booklet *Theory of Karma* by Hirabhai Thakkar (2001 [1996]: 7–80, esp. p. 14).

10. On revenge in the form of sacrificial counteraction in ancient Brahminic thought, see Malamoud (1998 [1989]: 156–168).

11. On account of the temporal delay in mobilization for "spontaneous anger," the Gujarati writer and activist Joseph Macwan (2002) pointedly asked, "After the inhuman carnage at Godhra, Gujarat remained peaceful for almost 24 hours. What was it that happened to trigger the subsequent carnage?"

12. The expression *karvu j pade*, initially used in March 2002 by Keka Shastree, an eminent local scholar and one of the founders of the VHP, circulated widely. It was used in an interview with Rediff.com reporter Sushri Sheela Bhatt,

then also by other Gujaratis to refer to the inevitability of reaction violence. I heard the expression used in urban as well as rural settings. The interview can be viewed at Rediff.com, March 12, 2002, http://www.rediff.com/news/2002/mar/12train.htm. Parts of the interview are also available in CCT 2002, vol. 1, 288. Breman, too, mentions its use (2003: 328).

13. For other media analyses, see these fact-finding reports: RW 2002; TSS 2002; CCT 2002; GG 2003; HRW-1 2002: 34. See also Varadarajan 2002: 271–304; Chattarji 2004; Bunsha 2006: 203–214; Lobo and Das 2006: 139–163. None of these analyses concern themselves significantly with language use. RW and CCT mention the excessive screening of "patriotic" movies such as *Gadar* but do not attempt to interpret such uses. My own analysis is most indebted to James T. Siegel's insightful reading of Indonesian vernacular newspapers (1998: 90–119).

14. During the time of this fieldwork, *Gujarat Samachar* and *Sandesh* were the two largest vernacular papers in Gujarat, both known to be politically close to the BJP. *Gujarat Samachar* was a vehicle for mass dissemination of stereotypes about Muslims already during the 1969 violence (Kumar 2009: 94). In 2002, it had a circulation of 8.10 *lakhs* (1 *lakh* = 100,000). *Sandesh* had a combined circulation of 7.05 *lakhs* in 2002 and produced five different editions in Gujarat. Its circulation extends to Bombay due to that city's large Gujarati population. *Times of India*, one of the largest English-language newspapers in South Asia, had a combined circulation of 61 *lakhs* in 2002. As a national newspaper, it produces many local versions that reflect variations in ideas of newsworthiness in India.

15. "Relvena dabbamathi 10 thi 15 Hindu yuvatione khechi kadhine uthavi jatu darmjhanuni tolu," *Sandesh*, February 28, 2002, p. 1.

16. *Sandesh*, February 28, 2002, p. 1.

17. "Aththi das mahilaone tolu jhupadapattima khechi gayu chhe," *Sandesh*, February 28, 2002, p. 16.

18. *Sandesh*, February 28, 2002, p. 16.

19. *Times of India*, March 3, 2002, p. 3.

20. "Arrest culprits in 24 hrs: VHP," *Times of India*, February 28, 2002, p. 3.

21. "Ram mandir to ban kar rahega, chahe balidanon ki parampara shuru karni pade."

22. *Times of India*, February 28, 2002, p. 3.

23. *Hutashan* denotes "martyr" and *hut* means "sacrificed," i.e., offered as oblation into the sacrificial fire. The term *hutashani* indicates the *holi*, the sacrificial bonfire made on the day of the Holi festival (cf. GCD, GED, GUCD, and TMGED).

24. With one exception I have chosen not to reproduce such photographic imagery here. For examples of the rather disturbing color spreads of corpses and charred bodies, see *Sandesh*, February 28, 2002, p. 7; March 2, 2002, pp. 1, 5; March 3, 2002, pp. 1, 5.

25. The front page reads, in Gujarati: "Vanthambi hinsama 200 homaya."

26. The Ahmedabad police commissioner implicitly acknowledged the libidinal quality of rumor when he complained in 2002 that during the violence, there were "educated people, 'repeatedly . . . disobeying curfew restrictions and moving out of their houses just to participate in rumor-mongering.'" The expression "educated people" means to say "Hindu middle class." Cf. *RW*, p. 19.

27. *Gadar, Ek Prem Katha,* directed by Anil Sharma (2001).

28. "Sabarmati Ekshpress parna humlama ai-es-ai sandovani?" *Sandesh,* February 28, 2002, p. 7.

29. "Hindustan na bhagla vakhate karayeli katleamna dhrashiyo yad karavya," *Sandesh,* February 28, 2002, p. 16.

30. "Talvarni anie trenna draivarne haijek karayo . . . !!" *Sandesh,* February 28, 2002, p. 2.

31. In Gujarati, "ame je kai anubhavyu chhe te kyarey bhuli shakie tem nathi."

32. The entire sentence goes, "ava drashyo ame 'gadar' filmma joya hata ne dhruji uthaya hata."

33. The movie *Gadar* and the "abducted women" are also referred to twice on page 14 of the same newspaper in a similar way. There is nothing to be added from those references, thus I omit them here.

34. "*Gadar* runs into trouble in Lucknow too," *Indian Express,* June 22, 2001; "Another attack on *Gadar* screening, 10 held," *Indian Express,* June 24, 2001; "Screening of '*Gadar*' disrupted in Ahmedabad," *The Hindu,* June 25, 2001.

35. To showcase in creative installations the god Ganesh (son of Parvati and Shiva) together with other themes like the 1999 Kargil War in 2000, *Gadar* movie scenes in 2001, or the Godhra incident in 2002, has become a tradition only recently in western India. The festival itself goes back to the popular Maharashtrian nationalist Lokmanya Tilak (1856–1920) who joined the Indian National Congress and was replaced after his death by Mahatma Gandhi. From its inception, the festival was designed to oppose the British and fuel the Independence struggle by highlighting indigenous culture and instilling national sentiment. The *mandals* responsible for the *pandals* are often in a fierce creative competition with neighboring ones (cf. "Rewind to Godhra, this Ganeshotsav," *Times of India,* September 5, 2002, p. 1). For depictions during Janmashtami 2002, compare Hiral Dave, "Godhra tableau, floats draw visitors," *Indian Express,* September 2, 2002, p. 5, and a photo without article in *Indian Express,* August 30, 2002, p. 3.

36. "VHP will display replicas of burning bogie," *Times of India,* November 13, 2002.

37. The temporal sweep back to the time of Independence (*ajhadi*) brings into play Partition and not other post-Independence events like the 1969 violence, the anti-reservation violence in the 1980s, or the aftermath of the demolition of the Babri Masjid in 1992. There is no mention of the fact that after the BJP took power in Gujarat in the mid-1990s, the number of communal clashes in Gujarat multiplied, thus increasing communal tension in the state. Instead of internal conflict, an external enemy country is inserted to which the Indian citizen can only assume a proper relation through opposition.

CHAPTER 3 The Gujarat Pogrom

1. An excellent account of the early making and unmaking of an industrial working class in Ahmedabad that remains sensitive to the civic neglect, political struggles, and the shockingly abrasive quality of social relations of production

between employers, divided workforce, and gang foremen is offered in the marvelous work of Jan Breman (2004: 11–69).

2. Anil Pathak, "'Thank God the walled city is quiet,'" *Times of India*, March 3, 2002, p. 12.

3. This account is based on several sources: CCT, HRW-1, IIJ, GG, and several copied affidavits of witnesses and survivor accounts completed by aid workers in relief camps.

4. A *mochi* is traditionally a leather worker, a cobbler.

5. This incident is also reported in the four-hour version of Rakesh Sharma's documentary *Final Solution* (2004).

6. A *gupti* is a pointed weapon traditionally concealed in a stick, or the concealed blade of a sword.

7. In a recent article, *Frontline Magazine* wrote of seventy victims at Gulbarg Society. Compare Ramakrishnan and Katakam 2010, http://www.frontlineonnet .com/fl2705/stories/20100312270503800.htm, accessed May 4, 2010.

8. See Tanika Sarkar (2002: 151–165), who takes up the obsession with mutilation in an examination of victim accounts, and Breman (2003: 270) for examples of such behavior in previous violent altercations. Martha Nussbaum (2007: 186–210) has interpreted these acts as expressions of reactive shame to a perceived Hindu male ineffectualness and emasculation, with roots in historical humiliation. In tandem with a deepened sense of disgust, the Hindu male projects all that is repulsive onto the Muslim woman, and by performing intercourse with sharp weapons, he can possess and kill her without the risk of contamination.

9. Affidavit (rendered anonymous), Shah-e-Alam relief camp, 2002. These affidavits were given to me in relief camps by human rights activists, most of whom were Hindus. I have selected accounts for citation based on my own experience as well as a close reading and comparison of written reports. The accounts cited support the most plausible stories, but I have not been able to independently verify their contents.

10. Affidavit (rendered anonymous), Shah-e-Alam relief camp, 2002.

11. Affidavit (rendered anonymous), Shah-e-Alam relief camp, 2002.

12. In some reports, the number has now lessened to 83 (cf. TE 2003: 123). *Frontline Magazine* speaks of 110. Compare Ramakrishnan and Katakam 2010.

CHAPTER 4 The Lack of Muslim Vulnerability

1. *Daya* (compassion, pity, mercy) also means "tenderness of the heart, tenderhearted," and *nirdaya* is used to signify "mercilessness" and "cruelty." In Gujarat, the term *jivdaya*, "compassion for all life," is often used synonymously for *ahimsa* (cf. TMGED).

2. The opposite of *shakahari* (vegetarian) is *masahari* (flesh-eater), a term that can amount to an insult especially for upper-caste Gujaratis. Thus, irrespective of whether meat is in fact eaten and irrespective of the abundant use of the term *shakahari*, the term *masahari* is avoided and often replaced by the euphemism "cosmopolitan."

3. Many Hindu Sindhi residents in Kachchh as well as in central Gujarat have come as immigrants after the creation of Pakistan and effectively experience suspicion and prejudice to this day (Kothari 2007: 146–177). Sindhi immigrants frequently compensate for this by internalizing a strong identification with Hindu nationalism and, according to Ibrahim (2009: 40), with Gujarati *asmita*, forms of regional pride.

4. This practice has its roots in Gujarati fasting traditions, which included eating only white food like rice, milk, *ghi*, and sugar on certain days (cf. Enthoven 1989 [1914]: 9).

5. Historically, Abubaqr is the name of the first of the four caliphs after the prophet Mohammad's death, part of the group known to Sunnis as the Rashidun. He was the legitimate head of all, since he was the first ruler even before the Umayyad Dynasty began.

6. This particular recording has made it big: I discovered a row of DVD versions in London's East End in 2008. The seller, a Bengali Muslim, told me about its popularity among local British South Asian Muslims, not least because Rashmibhai Zaveri, a Jain, performs rather poorly in the lecture.

7. An indirect reference to the practice of bribing doctors who examine the health of animals to be slaughtered.

8. Chilies and other hot spices are used in a common torture technique during criminal interrogations. I thank Cabeiri Robinson for this insight.

9. The depiction of the man with the stick as "ugly" seems to allude to a common stereotype that imagines members of lower castes or tribal groups as "dark skinned" people who work menial jobs in Muslim slaughterhouses.

10. Another revolting object par excellence is excrement. Although coprophagia is common among animals and is sometimes found in young children, toilet training and socialization generally rids humans of such scatological curiosity. According to the psychoanalyst Sándor Ferenczi (1927: 326), there remains a coprophilic tendency in the unconscious, however, a wish to swallow that which is disgusting, while spitting and vomiting are reaction formations against this tendency.

11. Phenomenologically, hearing is the one sense over which we have the least control and that has the weakest sense of intentionality and directionality.

12. Aurel Kolnai (2007 [1929]: 7–65), to whom these observations are greatly indebted, wrote several profound essays on the phenomenology of disgust, one in the late 1920s and one in the early 1970s (cf. Smith and Korsmeyer 2004: vii–viii, 93–109). Comparing disgust to fear and hatred, he explained, "*Ekel setzt sozusagen ex definitione eine—unterdrückte—Lust an seinem Erreger voraus*" (Kolnai 2007 [1929]: 20; "Disgust is predicated by definition on a—repressed—desire for what excites it" [my translation]). The ambivalence of disgust invites the subject to ingest and touch the irritating substance while simultaneously repelling him or her from doing so. In contradistinction to early psychoanalytic interpretation, Kolnai inferred that it is not an internalized authority (like education or culture) but the invitation (*Einladung*) itself that actualizes the deterrence (*Abschreckung*). In other words, without the defense of repulsion (*Abwehrreaktion*), there is the danger that the disgusting object would be assumed, ingested, touched. The

disgusting object is avoided because it positions the subject in close contact to both death and life in one single moment. This sudden proximity to death and life—Georges Bataille (1992 [1949]: 57) called this "intimacy"—is predicated on the essential kinship between the aging human body and all rotting organic matter, which though swollen full of teaming life nonetheless signifies fatality. Kolnai speaks of *todhaftes Leben,* a life not exactly threatened by, but attached to, death (or a death-like life). In other words, the disgusting matter confronts the human with the grimace of death (*Todesfratze*), reminding us of our own affinity (*Todesaffinität*), submission (*Todesunterworfenheit*), and secret longing for death (*Todeslust*). Disgust confronts consciousness with a sense of death (*Todessinn*) in everything that lives and the minuscule creeping of life that arises in everything that is dead (Kolnai 2007 [1929]: 52–53).

13. For a comprehensive literary and philosophical study on disgust, see Menninghaus (1999); for a psychoanalytic approach on abjection, see Kristeva (1982: 1–89); for an attempt to integrate disgust, shame, and the law, see Nussbaum (2004); for reflections on the experience of disgust as renewal of life, see Bataille (1986 [1957]: 55–62).

Chapter 5 Vibrant Vegetarian Gujarat

1. Although Modi is referring to a wedding feast, *chappan bhoga* is also part of the Vaishnava feast cycle—one of the many food festivals at Mount Govardhan in Braj (Uttar Pradesh), organized by the Pushti Marga *sampradaya* (cf. Toomey 1992: 139).

2. "Speech delivered by Hon. Chief Minister of Gujarat, Shri Narendra Modi on the 2nd October 2003," at http://www.gujaratindia.com/Media/Speeches/Porbandar.pdf (accessed August 4, 2004).

3. According to Simoons (1979: 472), Gujarat at some point had the largest number of *panjrapoles* in India. Mainly financed by the Jain community, these traditional animal homes are perhaps the most prominent expression of ahimsa in practice. Besides *panjrapoles* there are also *goshalas* (homes specifically for cattle) or the government-run *gosadans* (cow shelters). See also Lodrick (1981).

4. While organizations such as the Gauraksha Samiti (cow protection society) are VHP outlets, the Ahimsa Devi Trust has received financial help from the VHP only after its founder Gitaben Rambhiya was stabbed to death by two Muslim butchers in 1993 for interfering with their trade. Thus martyred, two memorials were erected for her as the "Goddess of Nonviolence," one in West Ahmedabad and one in the old city.

5. See http://pib.nic.in:80/archieve/lreleng/lyr2001/rapr2001/r04042001.html, accessed June 6, 2009.

6. In 2003, Pandya was assassinated while jogging in a popular park in the new city. He had been the right-hand man of Modi's predecessor, C. M. Keshubhai Patel, who was first home minister and ultimately revenue minister. After Pandya's murder, his father, Vithalbhai Pandya, openly accused Narendra Modi of plotting his son's assassination and called the act a "political murder" in con-

tradistinction to the official line of "Islamic terrorism." Allegedly, once Modi took office as chief minister, he had sidelined the popular rival politician. Vithalbhai Pandya claimed that his son had been a serious political threat to Modi's unencumbered power within the BJP and the wider Sangh Parivar network of Hindu organizations. In fact, Haren Pandya, who was identified taking part in anti-Muslim street violence during the 2002 pogrom, offered a deposition to an independent citizen's investigative tribunal, in which he accused Narendra Modi of orchestrating the pogrom. See Hartosh Singh Bal and Mahesh Langa, "Who killed Haren Pandya?" Telhelka.com, March 12, 2005, http://www.tehelka.com/story_main11.asp?filename=ts031205Who_Killed.asp, accessed June 6, 2009.

7. "Drive against illegal slaughterhouses in cities," *Times of India*, February 7, 2002, p. 1; and "Gauvanshni befam katal: kanun karta kasaiona hath lamba chhe," *Sandesh*, February 9, 2002, p. 3.

8. "Juna vadajma muton shop same ugr virodh," *Sandesh*, February 15, 2002, p. 6.

9. Cf. "Gau matanu jaherma katleamthi hahakar: polis golibarma 1 nu mot," *Sandesh*, February 24, 2002, p. 1; "Police fire kills one at Bharuch slaughter spot," *Times of India*, February 24, 2002, p. 1.

10. "Cabinet nod for Ahimsa University,"*Asian Age*, August 29, 2002, p. 11; and "Gujarat will show the way: Modi," *Indian Express*, August 29, 2002, p. 3.

11. Garlic, onions, and mushrooms, as well as nightshades like tomatoes and eggplant, are not permissible to members of Jain communities, and foodstuff including them are often considered "nonveg."

12. Many local Hanuman temples in Ahmedabad, known for their communalist leanings, were openly selling *trishuls* (tridents—symbol of the god Shiva or the Mother Goddess) and swords as well as country-made revolvers during the days of violence. Some of these revolvers were of such poor quality that they were almost as dangerous to the shooter as to the target.

13. The relation and competition between Gujarati Patels and those groups that have successfully managed to claim Kshatriya or Rajput status are linked in important ways to the political developments of the state (cf. Shah 1975).

14. During the Second World War, Germans referred to French enemy soldiers pejoratively as *Knoblauchfresser* (garlic eaters), which is also part of a classic anti-Semitic stereotype. Today, if at all, it is mostly Turks or other *Ausländer* (foreigners) who receive such designations. In a seminal study, Norbert Elias (1939 [1966]) has investigated the momentous transformations in the regulation of affect in central Europe (mainly in France and Germany) and in relation to diets, table manners, forms of speech and comportment through time. Elias delineates the socio- and psychogenesis of increased shame and repugnance developing gradually from a courtly nucleus with its aristocratic notions and practices to bourgeois forms with the formation of the modern state. Such detailed and illuminating work unfortunately does not yet exist for South Asia.

15. Until the Mandal Commission recommendations, the previous 31 percent quota had been divided between 7 percent for scheduled castes, 14 percent for scheduled tribes, and 10 percent for other backward classes. The commission

suggested that the latter category be increased to 28 percent (Sheth and Menon 1986: 16).

16. The term "culture" here should not be understood in a relativist sense. The term *sanskruti* denotes "civilization" and "social progress" as well as "culture" (cf. GED). Furthermore, the estimation that the orientation of Hindu nationalist organizations such as the RSS and its many related branches and institutions ("outliers") was merely "cultural" is as old as the RSS itself (Andersen and Damle 1987: 36–37). While the organization became increasingly involved in politics after Independence, this notion remains present even today.

17. Bharat's success in using "edukashun" for upward mobility is not being replicated widely, as the quality of government schools is abysmal. Contrary to the usual development rhetoric, rural Gujarat ranks in the bottom 25 percent of all Indian provinces in reading and writing. Among Indian children generally, in the fifth grade, for example, 40 percent cannot read at that level and 70 percent cannot even subtract (see Pratham Mumbai Education Initiative 2008). This situation is particularly dire for the rural poor, who increasingly appreciate the importance of education but who lack access to any proper educational facilities.

18. The Anthropological Survey of India distinguishes between *karaida rajput* and *nadoda rajput* (Singh 2003: 992–995, 609–613). Whereas in the former branch, men were listed as nonvegetarians (avoiding only beef and pork), women were listed vegetarian (ibid.: 609). By contrast, the *nadoda rajput* are listed as simply vegetarian (ibid.: 992). The Jadavs are *karaida* of the *nadoda rajput* branch. Most established Rajput groups question their claim to Kshatriya status (Tambs-Lyche 1992: 21). According to Shah (1975: 10), they have only recently formed an endogamous group; they used to exchange women with Rajput groups in Rajasthan. If we can assume that the exchange was asymmetrical (hypergamy), as northern Rajput groups are generally considered "more noble," this would explain the volatility of status.

19. As Tambs-Lyche (1997: 231) characterized this logic in a previous context, "one must eat like demons" in order to fight them.

20. Early scholars and anthropologists—from William Robertson Smith (1889) to Émile Durkheim (1912) to Mary Douglas (1966)—have consistently shown that what is poisonous and impure in one context has magical potentiality (i.e., power) in the next.

21. The Kshatriya (warrior, king) is one of the four estates of ancient Indian society.

22. Note that the term *musalman* is a common term for "Muslim" used in Northern India. It should not be confused with the same word used for prisoners of concentration camps in the work of Primo Levi, or by extension, Giorgio Agamben.

CHAPTER 6 Ahimsa, Gandhi, and the Angry Hindu

1. Sadar Vallabhai Patel (1875–1950) was a freedom fighter and the most prominent Gujarati after Mahatma Gandhi (1869–1948). He is hailed as being

responsible for unifying the princely states into the Indian union. Ravishankar Maharaj (1884–1984), often referred to as the "silent servant," was also a freedom fighter and follower of Vinoba Bhave, famous for his cow-protection agitation and *bhudan yagna* (literally, the sacrifice of land to the poor). Following Gandhi's model, Ravishankar Maharaj is said to have moved around freely and alone during communal violence, visiting homes of all communities in order to still the passions. He inaugurated the state of Gujarat in 1960.

2. This chapter cannot deal with the longue durée of the transformations of ahimsa. Such a digression would lead us far astray from the concrete ways Gujaratis understand and employ *himsa* and ahimsa today. Such a history, which I sketch below, would necessarily draw from philological and Indological literature, and it would do the important work of tracking the structural transformation of the status of the victim in ritual sacrifice from ancient times to the present (cf. Ghassem-Fachandi 2006: 47–91). The oldest formulations of ahimsa did not emerge in opposition to violence but as a ritual technology to make the violence of Vedic sacrifice secure and controllable. The sacrifier, the patron of the sacrifice, used substitute victims to absolve himself from the need to offer himself in sacrifice. The violence perpetrated on the substitute victim needed to be symbolically undone in order to counter the reciprocal shadow of violence that it risked fomenting. The magic formulas used were mostly incantations in verse, and it is in these that we find the oldest articulations of ahimsa (Schmidt 1968: 625–655).

With the emergence of renunciation and the Upanishadic and Shramanic critique of sacrificial violence, ahimsa became an ethical pronouncement, a doctrine of nonviolence. For the renouncer sacrifice became internalized into the body and instead of a victim, the desire for the world was offered up (burnt in corporeal sacrifice). Scholars have argued that even then the doctrine did not translate automatically into vegetarian practices or opposition to animal sacrifice (Alsdorf 1962: 559–625, Heesterman 1966: 147–149). There was a pronounced division of labor between renouncers and commoners, monks and laypersons, which displaced all responsibility for the reciprocal shadow of violence onto a worldly man, who carried out *seva* (service) for the otherworldly man.

After renunciatory values were reabsorbed into the world of caste, ahimsa became part of the rationalization of the complementary distinctions between castes and communities on the basis of their relationship towards the polluting and contaminating effects of violent labor (Doniger and Smith 1991: xv–xliv). Only with the breakdown of caste complementarity, Vaishnava conversion, and modern national ideas of Hindu culture did ahimsa come into its own. The universalizing impulse of ahimsa, which Alsdorf (1962: 573) and Schmidt (1968) already identified in the ancient doctrine, could now unfold itself fully. This book argues that with Hindutva, ahimsa appears in the context of disgust, anger, and national identification, which fundamentally transforms the relation of a violent subject to the object of nonviolence.

3. The opposition to ahimsa and the claim to Hindu cowardice reaches further back in the Hindu revivalism in the last decades of the nineteenth and the first decades of the twentieth centuries (cf. Andersen and Damle 1987: 28–30).

4. For example, whereas *bhay* means fear, *abhaya* (nonfear) means also security, peace, confidence, and nonviolence; *mrta* means death, but *amrta* (nondeath)

means immortal, imperishable, not subject to decay, continuity of life, vitality; *dvaita* means duality, and *advaita* means nonduality, the term used for Vedanta monist thought; *vidya* means knowledge, but *avidya* (nonknowledge) also means ignorance; *droha* means hostile, but *adroha* means benevolence, "absence of a stern or nonfriendly attitude," nonanger (Oguibénine 2003 [1994]: 65–67; Gonda 1959: 95–117).

5. See interview by Kalyani Giri with the RSS chief in "RSS Chief Speaks Out," *Hinduism Today*, January/February/March 2002, http://www.hinduismtoday .com/archives/2002/1-3/32-33_sudarsh.shtml (accessed September 9, 2008).

6. The understanding of ahimsa as the expression of cowardice reappears when the RSS Supremo, in a discussion with Jain Acharya Mahapragyaji at Koba, distinguishes between "nonviolence and timidity." The former was properly possessed only by what he calls "fearless people," while the latter was a form of cowardice, supplementing a perpetrator's strength. In a bizarre illustration, Sudarshan cited a recent scandalous occurrence on a Mumbai commuter train where a minor had been raped while a silent, stoic crowd looked passively on. He continued that what is a religion for a saint was impractical for a layperson. Cf. "Perpetrators of crime will not fear unless taught a lesson," *Asian Age*, August 30, 2002, p. 9.

7. The German concept *Ohnmacht* denotes powerlessness but also carries the sense of palsy, swoon, or fainting as in nausea (*in Ohnmacht fallen, ohnmächtig werden*).

8. "Eve-teasing," an intrusive sexually charged behavior by men toward women, is often brought together with nonvegetarian consumption as well as alcohol consumption.

9. The usual version of this more or less unsubstantiated story is that Mountbatten was pro-India in the Kashmir question due to his wife's closeness with Nehru.

10. The portrayal of Gandhi as ineffectual and castrated is a recurrent theme in the deeply psychological relationship between the mahatma and his target audience even during his lifetime. See, e.g., the Home Department report on Gandhi's visit to the Punjab in 1924, which describes negative notions of the mahatma as a "spent force" and an "extinct volcano" among British colonial subjects (Andersen and Damle 1987: 29).

11. Cf. Manubehn Gandhi (1949). For an interesting discussion on Gandhi's maternalism, see Erikson (1969: 403–407).

12. On the other hand, Vinay Lal (2000) in an interesting article does suggest such a reading. Lal interprets Gandhi's experiments of sleeping naked with his nieces at the end of his life, which caused much uproar, in the context of his desire to regain control over Hindu-Muslim violence. According to this author, it was a last desperate attempt to regain the populist power he felt he had lost.

13. The volume appeared on the Gujarati book market sometime in August 2002. I read, discussed, and translated the following text together with Professor Raymondbhai Parmar, former teacher of the St. Xavier's College in the city. In the translation, much of the tonality and imagery is lost, which I will amend by offering some of the insights, including those of Professor Parmar, about the text in my commentary afterwards.

14. The significant sentence reads in Gujarati: "*a nam sanket kare chhe ke atla saikao pachhi aje hu samagr ane sampurn ekamna rupe, Hindu rupe, astitvama avyo chhu.*" An alternative translation of this sentence could be: "This name suggests that after so many centuries I have arrived in existence (*astitvama avvyo chhu*) in a perfectly united form, a Hindu form."

15. One crore equals 10 million; 90 crore Hindus is 900 million people.

16. This is a very common Gujarati saying: *ap bhala to jag bhala* (If you are good to the world, the world is good to you).

17. This sentence poses some difficulties for translation. The original reads: "*nihsandeh marama mara nautik temaj adhyatmik adarsh ni chetna chhe.*" Four possible alternatives to the translation in the text are: (1) Undoubtedly, in that manner, my spiritual faculty of knowledge mirrors my morality. (2) Certainly, in me, my morality is alive by way of spiritual ideals. (3) Without doubt, my morality is within me in the manner of spiritual ideals (of the faculty) of knowledge. (4) More elegantly: Most certainly, within me, my morality is mirrored by my spiritual knowledge.

18. *Dharm nirpekshvadiyo* refers to those secularists whose idea of secularism excludes any religion. There are usually three different forms of secularism referred to in Gujarat: *sarva dharma sambhav* (equal status to all religions), *bim sampradayik* (literally, without sect, without sectarianism), and *dharma nirpekshta* (without any religion at all).

19. The sentence reads: "*bhai, me tane dasvani na padi hati, fufado marvani na padi na hati.*" The verb "to hiss" (*fufado marva*) is constructed in Gujarati by a combination of the verb *marvu* (strike, kill, throw) and the noun *fufado* (hiss of a serpent). The sentence is a reference to a widely known tale about a serpent and a *sadhu* (world renouncer) from traditional Gujarati folklore.

CHAPTER 7 Split City Body

1. A note of caution is in order. My descriptions are mainly based on the time between 1999 and 2003, and then again in 2005, the main temporal frame of ethnographic field research on the ground. The city is changing very rapidly, especially in the western areas, and so are its ways to use space. On the diverse conceptualizations and use of public city space in Calcutta, see Kaviraj (1997: 83–113); on the ambiguity of pleasure and danger in the bazaar, see Chakrabarty (2002: 65–79); on the suburbanization of a new emergent bourgeois citizen in relation to heterogeneous populations, see Chatterjee (2004: 131–147); and on the conceptual and material transformation of Delhi's inner city, see Hosagrahar (2006: 47–81). For theoretical conceptions on space that have informed this chapter, see Simmel (1983 [1903]: 221–242; 1984 [1909]: 7–11; 1992 [1908]: 687–790, esp. 764–771; 2008 [1903]: 319–333). Simmel does not present a unified theory of space, and his work includes many moments that seem in tension with one another. This tension is ultimately productive because it compels reflection and fixes attention on spatial experience.

2. This transformation facilitated the indigenous elite's leaders to establish their own hegemony in the city (Raychaudhuri 2001: 678).

3. A second Ellis bridge was built in 1892 (Gillion 1968: 129).

4. These include Sardar Vallabhai Patel, Mahatma Gandhi, Jawaharlal Nehru, Indira Gandhi, Subhash Chandra Bose. Only the memory of Sadar Vallabhai Patel seems to have escaped this ambivalence, as most residents still hold him in high esteem. Muslim communities, however, which make up approximately 12 percent of the city's population, see him as an antagonistic figure who betrayed a more inclusive Gandhian ethos by insisting on the rebuilding of the Somnath temple in Saurashtra in 1955. For an interesting scholarly work on the historiography of the temple, see Romila Thapar (2005).

5. A *pol* is a dense neighborhood space, constituted by narrow lanes, barred from view by walls and gates. Traditionally, *pol* residents were members of one single caste community or of castes of similar social status. Recently, pol names have been mounted at their entrances allowing visitors a better orientation in the inner city. While the inner city of Ahmedabad is characterized by *pols*, the surrounding areas are characterized by *puras* (suburbs). Due to the large expansion, most *puras* today are within the city limits proper.

6. ISKCON stands for International Society for Krishna Consciousness.

7. With the growth of the mill industry, the emerging working class initially was composed mainly of Dheds and Vankars (untouchable groups, that is Dalits), Muslim communities, and Vagris (Raychaudhuri 1997: 136–137).

8. For example, in the *Setu City Map*, a comprehensive booklet, they are indicated as "police chowki" with the abbreviation PC, as distinct from the city police stations, abbreviated as PS. Cf. Ahmedabad/Gandhinagar Setu City Map, 1998, Setu Publications, Ahmedabad.

9. How the police are part of the conflict, and not outside of it, was brought home by Ahmedabad's police commissioner during the pogrom when on March 10, 2002, he explained: "These people also, they somehow get carried away by the overall sentiment. That's the whole trouble. The police is equally influenced by the overall general sentiments." *Star News*, March 10, 2002, printed in GG (2002: 115).

10. The monkey-faced Hanuman, an important divinity in India and character in the Ramayan epic, is traditionally invoked in the struggle against evil. The god and the values associated with him, such as martial strength and asceticism, became integral to RSS activities early on (Andersen and Damle 1987: 35).

11. Note that this is so despite the fact that Muslim priority would be historically correct in many cases as Muslim shrines in the rural countryside, often of significant age, were founded in what were then unsettled frontier lands. For a comparative perspective in Bengal, see Eaton (1993).

12. Kaviraj, by attesting that the civic does not equate with the public, describes this practice as a lower-class one in Calcutta. However, this was is not the case in Ahmedabad, where I have frequently seen and participated in this practice (1997).

13. In rural areas, such ritual acts are common, too, but usually the remainders are buried outside the village compound, or poignantly, within the confines of a neighboring village, thus displacing the evil.

14. The use of the word *tatvo* for element is no coincidence. The etymology of the word for ghost, *bhut*, indeed implies "element." A *bhut* is "gone by, past,

elapsed; . . . anyone of the five elements, animal, being, evil spirit, demon, ghost" (GED).

15. The GED simply abbreviates the meaning of *vahem* to "doubt, suspicion, superstition, misapprehension" but elides the important contradictory semantic oscillation between "doubting" and "credulous," "deep thought" and "whim," "a fancy" and "a misapprehension."

16. It is interesting to note in this context, that the *chudel*, a particularly fearsome female ghost, is described as having its feet and head turned in the wrong direction.

17. Practices such as *utar* are part of a living local folklore and documented in colonial as well as later village ethnographies in India (e.g., Enthoven 1989 [1914]: 107; Opler 1958: 557; Dumont 1986: 451–452), but less frequently in studies on urban South Asia. Perhaps more significant is the fact that the cross as a sign and symbol, far from being simply "Christian," was and still is part of many magical practices or conceptions in a wide geographic expanse. The crossroads, too, is a common site of and for magical and spiritual power (e.g., in German superstitions at *Kreuzwege* and *Wegkreuzungen*—crossways and road crossings). The Greek goddess Hecate received food offerings at crossroads and haunted them at night. The modern Western rejection of such understandings, usually considered "superstitions" of a rural populace, is predicated on the systematic attempts by the Catholic Church to eradicate heathen and syncretistic practices, or alternatively, to replace them with a Christian symbology. In Europe, this process has been going on since at least the thirteenth century (cf. Harmening 2005: 265–266, 444–445). From contemporary folklore and ethnographic studies in Europe, however, one can gauge how imperfect this eradication has been. Many illuminating examples can be found in the recent work of the German anthropologist Thomas Hauschild (2002) in Ripacandida, Italy. In this mesmerizing and incredibly detailed ethnography, Hauschild describes contemporary shamanistic practices in the context of Catholic saint worship, magic, and healing practices. A shortened version of this work is currently being translated into English. For an interesting preliminary attempt to define what constitutes superstition as against faith or belief, see Steiner (1999 [1944]: 223–229).

Chapter 8 Heterogeneity and the Nation

1. Jan Breman's (2003) excellent firsthand account of the 1992 pogrom in Surat provides a description of violence in situ. He turns to expressions such as "volcanic vomit," (275), "massive eruption" (275), "communal orgy" (277), a "once and for all" attitude (281), the "discharge of pent-up rage" (284), and the call for a "final solution" (305) to invoke the quasi-ritual quality of the violence he observed (310). In some respects, his descriptive exposition comes eerily close to my own observations in a different Gujarati city ten years later.

2. Ashutosh Varshney (2002: 35), dismissing processes of identification altogether, assumes that the single most important factor responsible for communal violence is the failure of civic institutions to unite opposed groups in common cause. Implicit in this suggestion is that civic institutions automatically can pro-

duce a form of sociality that is conducive to peace. I am not convinced by this analysis. In a society where the face of caste and community is changing rapidly, religious identifications are not fixed statuses but dynamic processes of becoming inclusive of interiorizing attributes and externalizing others. Identificatory processes redefine relationships to other communities and, hence, cannot be ignored in analysis. Furthermore, everyday civic interactions are frequently structured by cautious calibrations, silences, and gaps in between polite exchanges in the service of avoidance. Distinguishing everyday civic engagements from associational engagements, or even intracommunal from intra-ethnic, does little to clarify such complex communicative practices. As hierarchies can freeze violence into social stratification, so can civic interaction delay, displace, or condense the expression of opposition into specific actors as well as into specific spaces.

3. Varshney (2002: 71) argues that the goal of Hindu nationalism was only a "political" and not a "cultural" unity because Hinduism had no correct form and knew no heresy. While true on the surface, it seems somewhat bewildering that Varshney fails to mention that the Hindu nationalist project of political unity of all Hindus is explicitly expressed in cultural and religious terms and is committed to forms of Sanskritization, tribal conversion, and religious reconversion to Hinduism, reminiscent of other aggressively proselytizing religious traditions such as Islam and Christianity. One might instead distinguish between the many "Hindu traditions," which taken individually might be "tolerant" or not (depending on one's point of departure and how one defines the term), and the practices of Hindu nationalist organizations. As we have seen, part of the process of identification selectively instrumentalizes these traditions to express an ideology that compels the Hindu to identify with his essence, the *tatva* of Hindu, Hindutva, against competing claims over the nation. That essence unifies all those who are included in the label "Hindu" but externalizes those that stand outside of it, who can only become part of the category through submission or elimination.

4. Arjun Appadurai (1998: 905–925), in a highly suggestive contribution to the study of symbolic forms of violent acts, has argued that many proceed as if they attempted to create a kind of certainty of the identity of the victim through vivisection. He interprets this "vivisectionist violence" as a form of inspection in an advanced age of globalization, a desire that strives to concretize and clarify through perverse surgical procedures. What is rendered increasingly unstable and precarious is sought in somatic stabilization.

5. René Girard's (1977) insights on ritual and mimesis are much less useful than their popularity in academic writing might suggest. His functionalist and overly formalist assumptions become problematic when applied to concrete ritual and violent phenomena—including those implying states of emergency and sacrificial violence. The work is weakened in part because it does not argue with those authors who have written widely about violence, ritual, and sacrifice (but instead with authors such as Claude Lévi-Strauss who had no use for the concept of sacrifice and never worked on violence either). In addition, with the exception of Freud, Girard is not particularly generous to those authors from whom he has taken many of his insights: Sir James Frazer, Georges Bataille, E. Evans-Pritchard, Henry Hubert, and Marcel Mauss. I have three major reservations, informed by

the events in Gujarat: First, Girard overemphasizes the anarchist state of what he terms "mimetic crisis" (or "sacrificial crises"), where revenge and chaotic violence threaten society's disintegration. This "crisis" often has to be orchestrated, an important fact that he misses or conveniently disregards. An emphasis on orchestrations would seriously disturb the formalist picture he draws.

Second, he insists on the arbitrary nature of the surrogate victim, an individual selected as scapegoat towards whom to channel aggression. In the sphere of contemporary institutionalized ritual, a mimetic crisis does not usually precede sacrifice. It is true that violent phenomena, which are frequently assimilated to the logic of sacrifice (such as pogrom or genocide) are often preceded by many other kinds of crises, such as category confusion, collapse of ethnic distinctions, violent unanimity, an atmosphere of exception, processes of identification, and national disintegration. But they are not necessarily marked by an all-against-all dynamic that can be transformed into a scapegoating mechanism (all-against-one mechanism). Girard needs to assume an arbitrarily chosen and innocent victim because he is not trying to understand violent or ritual phenomena alone or in their own right. Instead he affirms the ultimate scapegoat that redeems the group: the mysteries of Jesus Christ. In other words, the victim needs to be pure and innocent in order to be redemptive. Most Muslims in Gujarat are innocent of involvement in the Godhra incident, and the large majority have nothing to do with terrorism, but they are as little arbitrarily chosen as were Jews during European pogroms. The choice of the victim is everywhere preceded by a history of discrimination and stereotyping that is vital to engage and understand. The idea of "innocence" in the sense of which Girard is talking is problematic. The scapegoating of Muslims allows the temporary emergence of the unified category of the "Hindu" awoken in anger. It is noticeable how Girard evades confronting the large literature on scapegoating in the context of anti-Semitism.

Third, he argues that the elimination of the scapegoat successfully reconstructs the group's solidarity and so, after the killing, he assumes that the group is indeed redeemed. Thus he affirms that the mechanics of the rite were in fact efficacious, which I find bewildering. Freud already pointed out that guilt and repression, or forms of denial, structure the phase after the killing—a point Girard apparently ignores. Finally, even after the later invention of judicial institutions and the symbolic labor of retributive discourses, sacrificial violence and scapegoat mechanisms readily continue. All in all Girard's work, while insightful on a formal level, is quite misleading for an empirical analysis of sacrificial violence in concrete historical contexts.

6. The application of ahimsa in the context of violence is not a distortion of an ancient tradition but a much more momentous process. Bruce Kapferer (1988: 19) has rightly stressed the strong religious undercurrent of nationalisms, which in the case of Sinhalese nationalism asserts and incorporates Buddhism. But while Kapferer posits a sharp distinction between Sinhalese Buddhism of nationalist practice and Buddhism, or Buddhist ideas, outside of nationalist import, ahimsa and violence are more continuously related within Indian religious traditions. Thus the nation form does not "distort" a prior unsullied religious tradition but reframes its diverse contents within an entirely novel form of temporality: the

simultaneity and homogeneity of diverse segments of a "Hindu tradition" now moving through empty homogeneous time. The rhythm of national time enlivens older semantic possibilities of the concept, such as a pre-ethical Vedic ahimsa, referred to by scholars as "ritual ahimsa theory" (Alsdorf 1962: 559–625; Schmidt 1968: 625–655), an axiological Shramanic ahimsa, or a vegetarian Vaishnavaite ahimsa, a contemporary Jain ahimsa, next to a Gandhian ahimsa. The temporality of the nation allows for the totalization of an ethic under the new category "Hindu," which before had been inflected through the principle of complementarity of caste, sect, and community. When ahimsa becomes that which, according to Schmidt (1968), it always sought to be—a value with a universal claim—it demands most stringently the transformation into its opposite. The nation form and its unique form of temporality facilitate an unfettered unfolding of this gestalt.

7. Stanley Tambiah (1996) and Paul Brass (2003) both offer general explanations for collective violence, the former in terms of crowd behavior, the latter in terms of an institutionalized riot system. My own focus is more on understanding the general complicity of those not directly involved in the violence, and is much in agreement with Sudhir Kakar's (1995, esp. 111–182) psychoanalytically informed approach, sensitive to questions of mimesis, ingestion, and identification.

8. Two brief examples must suffice to elucidate why the billboard's content remains contrived. First, what do we make of a Vohra, a member of a Gujarati Muslim community, who spontaneously relates his status to me by referring to the Nagar Brahmins from whom his ancestors supposedly converted? The Nagar Brahmins are light-skinned and one of the most respectable communities in contemporary Gujarat. On the historical origins of the two branches of Vohra and other Gujarati Muslim merchant communities as conceived by scholars, see Lokhandwalla (1955: 117–135), Engineer (n.d.: 1–49), and Misra (1985: 15–53, 122–125). The second example comes from the opposite pole of the local spectrum: the Sidi Jamat, a Muslim community mainly of East African origin that entered Gujarat centuries ago and are often referred to as "Habshi" (Basu 1994: 43–60). The Sidi community, partly registered as a scheduled tribe today, is frequently considered "untouchable" by other Muslim communities. Sidis work at Muslim shrines as ritual clowns, possessed dancers, who propitiate female and male ancestor-saints (2004: 233–253). A few Sidi groups have adopted Hindu divinities as clan gods (Naik and Pandya 1993: 93), and a large majority live in abject poverty. It is highly unlikely that the Sidis, with dark skin and "African features," could ever represent the aggregate Muslim, or even better, the aggregate Hindu. This is despite the fact that as creative ritual bricoleurs and given their complex historical origins, they in every way epitomize internal Muslim heterogeneity in Gujarat.

Abbreviations

Dictionaries

ASD—*Ankur Smart Dictionary*, comp. N. T. Varma (Ahmedabad: Ankur Prakashan, 2001).

GCD—*Gala's Concise Dictionary: English-English-Gujarati*, deluxe ed., comp. L. R. Gala (Dantali: Navneet Publications, 2000).

GED—*Gujarati-English Dictionary (Gujarati-Angreji Kosh)*, comp. Pandurang Ganesh Deshpande (Ahmedabad: University Book Production Board, 1974).

GUCD—*Gala's Universal Combined Dictionary*, comp. L. R. Gala (Ahmedabad: Navneet House, 2001).

TAD—*Trilingual Administrative Dictionary (English-Gujarati-Hindi)*, comp. N. B. Vyas (Gandhinagar: Patel Printing Press, 1988).

TMGED—*The Modern Gujarati-English Dictionary*, comp. B. N. Mehta and B. B. Mehta (Gandhinagar: n.p., 1989 [1925]).

Fact Finding Reports

CCT—Concerned Citizen's Tribunal, *Crime against humanity: An inquiry into the carnage in Gujarat*, 2 vols. (Mumbai: Anil Dharkar, 2002).

DG—Jyoti Punwani, *Dateline Godhra* (Mumbai: Nirbhay Bano Andolan, 2002).

GG—Javed Anand and Teesta Setalvad, eds., "Genocide Gujarat," *Communalism Combat* (Mumbai) year 8, nos. 77–78 (March–April 2002).

HRW-1—Human Rights Watch, "'We have no orders to save you': State participation and complicity in communal violence in Gujarat," *Human Rights Watch Report* 14, no. 3 (C), April 2002.

HRW-2—Human Rights Watch, "Compounding injustice: The government's failure to redress massacres in Gujarat," *Human Rights Watch Report* 15, no. 4 (C), July 2003.

IIJ—International Initiative for Justice, *Threatened existence: A feminist analysis of the genocide in Gujarat*, December 2003, http://www.onlinevolunteers.org/gujarat/reports/iijg/2003/fullreport.pdf.

NCI—*Report by Commission of Inquiry Consisting of Mr. Justice G. T. Nanavati and Mr. Justice Akshay H. Mehta*, part 1, September 18, 2008.

PUCL—People's Union for Civil Liberties and Vadodara Shanti Abhiyan, *Violence in Vadodara: A report* (Bajwada, Vadodara: Bharti Printers, 2002).

QET—Quami Ekta Trust, Communalism Combat, Dakshin Gujarat Adivasi Sangh, Vikas Adhyayan Kendra, SAMVAD, INSAF, IFIE, SAHRWARU, VOTE, and People's Union for Human Rights, *Saffron on the rampage: Gujarat's Muslims pay for the Lashkar's deeds* (Mumbai: Sabrang Communications, 2000).

RCR—Commission of Inquiry, Mr. Justice P. Jaganmohan Reddy, *Inquiry into the communal disturbances at Ahmedabad and other places in Gujarat on and after 18th September 1969* (Ahmedabad: Government of Gujarat, 1970).

RW—Aakar Patel, Dileep Padgaonkar, B. G. Verghese, *Rights and wrongs: Ordeal by fire in the killing fields of Gujarat*, Editors Guild Fact Finding Mission Report, New Delhi, May 3, 2002, http://www.sabrang.com/gujarat/statement/report.htm (accessed July 8, 2004).

TSS—Syeda Hameed, Ruth Manorama, Malini Ghose, et al., *The survivors speak: How has the Gujarat massacre affected minority women? Fact finding by a women's panel* (New Delhi: Citizen's Initiative, Ahmedabad, 2002).

Glossary of Indian Terms

abhaya—free from fear, fearlessness

adivasi—groups designated as "scheduled tribe;" often used in the sense of "aborigines"

ahimsa—nonviolence, harmlessness, non-injury

akasmat—accident, coincidence, incident

andhshraddha—form of false worship, superstition, blind faith

asmita—pride, identity, self-consciousness, realization

atak—surname, family name, stoppage, obstruction, hindrance

avarna—without varna; outcaste, "scheduled caste," low caste, untouchable

bakri—female goat

bakri-id—Muslim festival celebrating the Abrahamic sacrifice

bandh—closure, standstill, strike, stop

bhedbhav—discrimination, distinction, difference

bidi—Indian-made cigarettes rolled in leaves

burkho—form of female Muslim veil covering face and body

bhai—brother; as suffix to a proper name it communicates courteousness and respect

bhakti—devotional worship

bhul—mistake, defect, negligence

bhutpret—evil spirit, ghost, demon

bhuvo—medium-worshipper of the goddess

Brahma—god of the Hindu pantheon

Brahmin—priest

brahmachari—traditionally, one who observes the rules of the first stage of life; someone who remains celibate

chali—buildings with rooms organized in rows

dalit—outcaste, untouchable, "scheduled caste," Harijan

Dargah—Muslim shrine, tomb of a Pir (saintly man)

dharma—duty, law, right, justice, order; proper and appropriate, living moral law

darshan—visual exchange with a deity or religious preceptor

guna—innate quality or property, nature, attribute; the primary constitutive qualities of this worldly existence

halal—Muslim ritual slaughter in which animal is bled

halka—light, cheap, of inferior quality

himsa—violence, killing, destruction, hurt

hom—offering oblation by pouring ghee (clarified butter) into the sacrificial fire

Hindutva—Hinduness; the essence of Hindu

hullad—tumult, disturbance, riot

humlo—attack, assault

jati—caste or sub-caste, community, tribe

jhatko—Hindu ritual slaughter performed by a single stroke

jivdaya—compassion for all life, pity, mercy

kasai—butcher; also pejorative for heartless person, cutthroat, murderer

karsevak—volunteer for temple construction

khatki—butcher

khanipini—eating and drinking

kom—community; group of people belonging to the same caste, religion, nation, tribe

komvad—communal violence; communalism

kuldevi—lineage goddess that defines descent

krodh—anger, wrath, ire

kurta—Indian chemises usually worn by men

laj—modesty, shame, decorum, deference, honor; female veiling practice

maryada—boundary, decency, modesty, limitation

namaz—Muslim prayer

pakka (paku) —ripe, mature, made durable, cooked in ghee (or other products of the cow) and hence not liable to become polluted; complete, firm, perfect

patel (also *patidar*) —agricultural caste; the term is a common surname and also used in the sense of "headman"

pan—a preparation of betel-leaf and areca nut

panwala—shop for pan and cigarettes

pishach—ghost, evil spirit, demon

pol—traditional residential arrangement in the old city

prabhav—strength, majesty, prowess, luster

pratikriya—reaction, remedy, counteraction

prasad—blessing, favor, food remainders of the gods

puja—Hindu worship ritual

pura—suburbs of Ahmedabad city

rajput—warrior, prince; appeal to kshatriya status

rashstra—nation, country, state

rajkaran—politics, administration; the cause and purpose of rule

ramsevaks—devotees of Lord Ram

samaj—community, society

sambandh—connection, state of relatedness, relations

sampurn—perfect, finished, whole, complete

sampradaya—tradition, sect, branch, persuasion, practice

sanskruti—culture, civilization, progress

Sangh Parivar—family of organizations associated with the RSS such as the VHP, Bajrang Dal, BJP, and many more

savarna—belonging to one of the four estates of Hindu society; today used mainly to denote forward classes and the conglomeration of upper castes

sadhu—Hindu ascetic, world renouncer

sanyasi—world renouncer; one who has been initiated into the fourth stage of life

seva—service without selfish motive; worship, attendance

shakha—local divisions in which members of the RSS meet for physical exercises and ideological training

shakahari—vegetarian

shuddh—pure, proper, unadulterated, conscious

swayamsevako—volunteers, usually in the context of the RSS

topi—Muslim cap

trishul—weapon in the form of a trident; symbol of god Shiva

ujliyat loko—forward castes, high class; *lit.* "the radiant people"

upvas—fast; strict abstention from certain foods

utar—ford, threshold; offerings to ghosts in order to expiate an evil; remainders of small exorcism rituals

wada—industrial settlements

vagri—low caste community; term often used pejoratively

vaniya—member of the merchant communities consisting of Hindu Vaishnava and Jaina

vahan—animal vehicle of a god or goddess

valan—mental inclination; curve, verse in poem in which meter changes

varna—*lit.*, color; the four estates of Hindu society: Brahmin (priest), Kshatriya (warrior, king), Vaishya (commoner), and Shudra (artisan, servant)

vyaktitva—personality, individuality

vyasan—habit, bad habit, addiction

vrat—vow, religious observance, fast

References

GUJARATI VERNACULAR NEWSPAPERS

Sandesh
Gujarat Samachar
Western Times

ENGLISH LANGUAGE NEWSPAPERS

Asian Age
The Times of India
Indian Express
Frontline Magazine

VIDEO MATERIAL, DOCUMENTARIES, AND MOVIES

Videotaped Public Debate
Is non-vegetarian food permitted or prohibited for a human being?
Videotape of public debate between Dr. Zakir Naik of the Mumbai
Islamic Research Foundation (IRF) and Rashmibhai Zaveri of the
Indian Vegetarian Congress, Patkar Hall, Mumbai. May 9, 1999.

Documentaries
Final solution. Directed by Rakesh Sharma. 2004.
Godhra tak: The terror trail. Directed by Shubhradeep Chakra-
vorty. 2003.

Feature Film
Gadar: Ek prem katha. Directed by Anil Sharma. 2001.

PUBLISHED WORKS

Aggarwal, Gopinath. 1991. *Vegetarian or non vegetarian: Choose yourself.* 5th ed. New Delhi: Jain Book Agency.

Alsdorf, Ludwig. 1962. Beiträge zur Geschichte von Vegetarismus und Rinderverehrung in Indien. In *Abhandlungen der Akademie der Wissenschaften und der Literatur: Geistes- und Sozialwissenschaftlichen Klasse.* Wiesbaden: Franz Steiner Verlag.

Alter, Joseph. 1992. *The wrestler's body: Identity and ideology in north India.* Berkeley: University of California Press.

———. 1997. Seminal truth: A modern science of male seminal celibacy in north India. *Medical Anthropology Quarterly* 11 (3): 275–298.

———. 2000. *Gandhi's body: Sex, diet, and the politics of nationalism.* Philadelphia: University of Pennsylvania Press.

Amin, Shahid. 2004. On representing the Musalman. In *Sarai Reader 04: Crisis/ Media,* ed. Sarai Editorial Collective. Delhi: CSDS.

Anderson, Benedict. 1991. *Imagined communities: Reflections on the origin and spread of nationalism.* London: Verso.

———. 1999. *The spectre of comparisons: Nationalism, southeast Asia, and the world.* London: Verso.

Andersen, Walter K., and Shridhar D. Damle. 1987. *The brotherhood in saffron: The Rashtriya Swayamsevak Sangh and Hindu revivalism.* New Delhi: Vistaar Publications.

Appadurai, Arjun. 1998. Dead certainty: Ethnic violence in the era of globalization. *Public Culture* 10 (2): 905–925.

Arendt, Hannah. 1958. *The human condition.* Chicago: University of Chicago Press.

———. 1970. *On violence.* New York: Harvest.

———. 1976. Was bleibt? Es bleibt die Muttersprache: Ein Gespräch mit Günter Gaus. In *Gespräche mit Hannah Arendt,* ed. A. Reif. Munich: Serie Piper.

———. 2002 [1967]. *Vita activa oder Vom tätigen Leben.* Munich: Piper Verlag.

———. 2003 [1976]. What remains? The language remains: A conversation with Günter Gaus. In *The portable Hannah Arendt,* ed. P. Baehr. New York: Penguin.

Babb, Lawrence. 2004. *Alchemies of violence: Myths of identity and the life of trade in western India.* New Delhi: Sage Publications.

Barthes, Roland. 1982 [1980]. *Camera lucida: Reflections on photography.* New York: Hill and Wang.

Basham, A. L. 1954. *The wonder that was India: A survey of the culture of Indian sub-continent before the coming of Muslims.* New York: Grove Press.

Basu, Amrita. 1998. Reflections on community conflicts and the state in India. In *Community conflicts and the state in India,* ed. A. Basu and A. Kohli. New York: Oxford University Press.

Basu, Helene. 1994. *Habshi-Sklaven, Sidi Fakire: Muslimische Heiligenverehrung im westlichen Indien* ed. G. Pfeffer. Berlin: Das Arabische Buch.

———. 2004a. Ritual communication: The case of the Sidi in Gujarat. In *Lived Islam in South Asia: Adaptation, accommodation and conflict,* ed. I. Ahmad and H. Reifeld. Delhi: Social Science Press.

———. 2004b. *Von Barden und Königen: Ethnologische Studien zur Göttin und zum Gedächtnis in Kacch (Indien)*. Frankfurt am Main: Peter Lang Verlag.

Bataille, Georges. 1986 [1957]. *Erotism: Death and sensuality*. San Francisco: City Lights Books.

———. 1991 [1967]. *Theory of religion*. New York: Zone Books.

———. 1992 [1949]. *The accursed share: An essay on general economy*. Vol. 1. New York: Zone Books.

———. 1997 [1933/1934]. The psychological structure of fascism. In *Bataille: A critical reader*, ed. F. Botting and S. Wilson. Oxford: Wiley-Blackwell.

Baxi, Upendra. 2002. The second Gujarat catastrophe. *Economic and Political Weekly* 37 (34): 3519–3531.

Bayly, Susan. 2001 [1999]. *Caste, society and politics in India from the eighteenth century to the modern age*. Cambridge: Cambridge University Press.

Bhatt, Chetan. 2001. *Hindu nationalism: Origins, ideologies and modern myths*. Oxford: Berg Press.

Biardeau, Madeleine. 1989 [1981]. *Hinduism: The anthropology of a civilization*. New Delhi: Oxford University Press.

———. 2003 [1994]. Ancient brahmanism, or impossible non-violence. In *Violence/non-violence: Some Hindu perspectives*, ed. D. Vidal, G. Tarabout, and E. Meyer. New Delhi: Manohar.

Bloch, Maurice. 1992. *Prey into hunter: The politics of religious experience*. Cambridge: Cambridge University Press.

Bondurant, Joan. 1988 [1958]. *Conquest of violence: The Gandhian philosophy of conflict*. Princeton, NJ: Princeton University Press.

Borneman, John. 2009. Veiling and women's intelligibility. *Cardozo Law Review* 30 (6): 2745–2760.

Borneman, John, and Abdellah Hammoudi. 2009. The fieldwork encounter, experience, and the making of truth: An introduction. In *Being there: The fieldwork encounter and the making of truth*, ed. J. Borneman and A. Hammoudi. Berkeley: University of California Press.

Bourdieu, Pierre. 1991. *Language and symbolic power*. Cambridge, MA: Harvard University Press.

Brass, Paul. 2003. *The production of Hindu-Muslim violence in contemporary India*. Seattle: University of Washington Press.

Breman, Jan. 2003. *The labouring poor in India: Patterns of exploitation, subordination, and exclusion*. New Delhi: Oxford University Press.

———. 2004. *The making and unmaking of an industrial working class: Sliding down the labour hierarchy in Ahmedabad, India*. New Delhi: Oxford University Press.

Briggs, Geo. 1920. *The religious life of India—The Chamars*. Calcutta: Association Press.

Bryant, Edwin. 2006. Strategies of Vedic subversion: The emergence of vegetarianism in post-Vedic India. In *A communion of subjects: Animals in religion, science and ethics*, ed. P. Waldau and K. Patton. New York: Columbia University Press.

Bunsha, Dionne. 2006. *Scarred: Experiments with violence in Gujarat*. London: Penguin Books.

Chaitanya, Krishna, ed. 2003. *Fascism in India: Faces, fangs and facts*. New Delhi: Manak Publications.

Chakrabarty, Dipesh. 2002. *Habitations of modernity: Essays in the wake of subaltern studies*. Chicago: University of Chicago Press.

Chandra, Sudhir. 1996. Of communal consciousness and communal violence: Impressions from post-riot Surat. In *Politics of violence: From Ayodhya to Behrampada*, ed. J. McGuire, P. Reeves, and H. Brasted. New Delhi: Sage Publications.

Chattarji, Subarno. 2004. Media representations of the Kargil War and the Gujarat riots. In *Sarai Reader 04: Crisis/Media*, ed. Sarai Editorial Collective. Delhi: CSDS.

Chatterjee, Partha. 2004. *The Politics of the governed: Reflections of popular politics in most of the world*. New York: Columbia University Press.

Clémentin-Ojha, Catherine. 2003 [1994]. The initiation of the devi: Violence and non-violence in a Vaishnavite tale. In *Violence/non-violence: Some Hindu perspectives*, ed. D. Vidal, G. Tarabout, and E. Meyer. New Delhi: Manohar.

Dalton, Dennis, ed. 1996. *Mahatma Gandhi: Selected political writings*. Indianapolis: Hackett Publishing Company.

Daniel, Valentine. 1996. *Charred lullabies: Chapters in an anthropography of violence*. Princeton, NJ: Princeton University Press.

Das, Veena. 1983. Language of sacrifice. *Man* 18 (3): 445–462.

———. 1984. For a folk-theology and theological anthropology of Islam. *Contributions to Indian Sociology* (8): 85–99.

———, ed. 1990. *Mirrors of violence: Communities, riots and survivors in South-Asia*. Delhi: Oxford University Press.

———. 1995. *Critical events; An anthropological perspective on contemporary India*. Delhi: Oxford University Press.

———. 2007. *Life and words: Violence and the descent into the ordinary*. Berkeley: University of California Press.

Davis, Natalie Zemon. 1973. The rites of violence: Religious riots in sixteenth-century France. *Past and Present* (59): 51–91.

Davis, Richard. 2006 [1996]. The iconography of Rama's chariot. In *Making India Hindu: Religion, community, and the politics of democracy in India*, ed. D. Ludden. New Delhi: Oxford University Press.

Daya, Dalpatram. 1849. *Bhut Nibandh: An essay, descriptive of the demonology and other popular superstitions of Guzerat*, trans. Alexander Kinloch Forbes. Bombay: Bombay Print.

Doniger, Wendy, and Brian Smith. 1991. *The laws of Manu*. New Delhi: Penguin Classics.

Douglas, Mary. 2002 [1966]. *Purity and danger: An analysis of the concepts of pollution and taboo*. London: Routledge.

Dumont, Louis. 1980. *Homo hierarchicus: The caste system and its implications*. Chicago: Chicago University Press.

———. 1986. *A South Indian subcaste: Social organization and the religion of the Pramalai Kallar*. Oxford: Oxford University Press.

Dundes, Alan, ed. 1991. *The blood libel legend: A casebook in anti-Semitic folklore*. Madison: University of Wisconsin Press.

Durkheim, Émile. 1995 [1912]. *The elementary forms of religious life*, trans. K. Fields. New York: Free Press.

Eaton, Richard. 1993. *The rise of Islam and the Bengal frontier*. Berkeley: University of California Press.

Edalji, Dosábhai. 1986 [1894]. *A history of Gujarat: From the earliest period to the present times*. New Delhi: Asian Educational Services.

Eghigian, Greg, and Mathew Berg, eds. 2002. *Sacrifice and national belonging in twentieth-century Germany*. College Station: Texas A&M University Press.

Elias, Norbert. 1976 [1939]. *Über den Prozeß der Zivilisation: Soziogenetische und psychogenetische Untersuchungen*. 2 vols. Frankfurt am Main: Suhrkamp.

Engineer, Asghar-Ali. 2006. The Gujarat carnage: Causes and consequences. In *Communal violence and minorities: Gujarat society in ferment*, ed. L. Lobo and B. Das. New Delhi: Rawat Publications.

———. n.d. *Bohras and their struggle for reforms*. Bombay: Institute of Islamic Studies.

Engineer, Asghar-Ali, and Pradeep Nayak, eds. 1993. *Communalisation of politics and 10th Lok Sabha elections*. Delhi: Ajanta Publications.

Enthoven, R. E. 1989 [1914]. *Folklore Notes*. Vol. 1, *Gujarat: Compiled from materials collected by A.M.T. Jackson (Indian Civil Service)*. Bombay: British India Press.

Erikson, Erik. 1969. *Gandhi's truth: On the origins of militant nonviolence*. New York: Norton.

Evans-Pritchard, E. E. 1956. *Nuer religion*. London: Oxford University Press.

Feldman, Allen. 1991. *Formations of violence: The narrative of the body and political terror in Northern Ireland*. Chicago: University of Chicago Press.

———. 2002. Strange fruit: The South African truth commission and the demonic economies of violence. In *Beyond rationalism: Rethinking magic, witchcraft and sorcery*, ed. B. Kapferer. New York: Berghahn Press.

Ferenczi, Sándor. 1927. *Further contributions to the theory and technique of psychoanalysis*. New York: Boni and Liverlight.

Forbes, Alexander. 1924 [1878]. *Râs Mâla: Hindoo annals of the province of Goozerat in Western India*. 2 vols. New Delhi: Low Price Publications.

Frazer, James. 1960 [1890]. *The golden bough*. Vol. 1. London: Macmillan and Co.

Freud, Sigmund. 1919. Das Unheimliche. In *Gesammelte Werke XII*. Frankfurt am Main: Fischer Verlag.

———. 1931. Die Verneinung. In *Theoretische Schriften (1911–1925)*. Vienna: Druck der Vernay.

———. 1974 [1929/1930]. Das Unbehagen in der Kultur. In *Sigmund Freud: Kulturtheoretische Schriften*. Frankfurt am Main: Fischer Verlag.

———. 1996 [1900]. *Die Traumdeutung*. Frankfurt am Main: Fischer Taschenbuch Verlag.

Fuller, Chris. 1992. *The camphor flame*. Princeton, NJ: Princeton University Press.

Gandhi, Manubehn. 1949. *Bapu—My mother*. Ahmedabad: Navjivan Publishing House.

Gandhi, Mohandas K. 1927. *An autobiography: The story of my experiments with truth*. Ahmedabad: Navjivan Trust.

———. 1987 [1921]. My meaning of Sanatana Hinduism. In *The essence of Hinduism*. ed. V. B. Kher. Ahmedabad: Navjivan Trust.

———. 1996. *Mahatma Gandhi: Selected Political Writings*, ed. D. Dalton. Indianapolis: Hackett Publishing.

Gazetteer of India. 1984. *Gujarat state, Ahmadabad district*. Ahmedabad: Government of Gujarat.

Geertz, Clifford. 1973. Thick description: Toward an interpretive theory of culture. In *The interpretation of culture*. New York: Basic Books.

Geyer, Michael. 2002. "There is a land where everything is pure. Its name is the land of death": Some observations on catastrophic nationalism. In *Sacrifice and national belonging in twentieth-century Germany*, ed. G. Eghigian and M. Berg. College Station: Texas A&M University Press.

Ghassem-Fachandi, Parvis. 2006. Sacrifice, ahimsa, and vegetarianism: Pogrom at the deep end of non-violence. PhD diss., Cornell University.

———. 2008. Muslimische heilige in Gujarat: Sufismus, synkretismus und praxis im westlichen Indien. In *KulturEN*, ed. R. Krüger. Berlin: ECA.

———, ed. 2009. *Violence: Ethnographic encounters*. Oxford: Berg Press.

Gillion, Kenneth. 1968. *Ahmedabad: A study in Indian urban history*. Canberra: Australian National University.

Girard, René. 1977. *Violence and the sacred*, trans. P. Gregory. Baltimore: Johns Hopkins University Press.

Gonda, Jan. 1959. Why are ahimsa and similar concepts often expressed in a negative form? In *Four studies in the language of the Veda*. The Hague: Mouton & Co Publishers.

Goody, Jack. 1982. *Cooking, cuisine and class: A study in comparative sociology*. Cambridge: Cambridge University Press.

Gross, Jan. 2001. *Neighbors: The destruction of the Jewish community in Jedwabne, Poland*. Princeton, NJ: Princeton University Press.

Grunberger, Béla, and Pierre Dessuant. 2000 [1997]. *Narzißmus, Christentum, Antisemitismus: Eine psychoanalytische Untersuchung*, trans. M. Looser. Stuttgart: Klett Cotta.

Guha, Ranajit. 1999 [1983]. *Elementary aspects of peasant insurgency in colonial India*. Delhi: Oxford University Press.

Gupta, Charu. 2002 [2001]. *Sexuality, obscenity, community: Women, Muslims, and the Hindu public in colonial India*. New York: Palgrave.

Hacker, Paul. 1957. Religiöse Toleranz und Intoleranz im Hinduismus. *Saeculum* 8: 167–179.

———. 1983. Inklusivismus. In *Inklusivismus: Eine indische Denkform*, ed. G. Oberhammer. Vienna: Institut für Indologie der Universitat Wien.

Hansen, Thomas Blom. 1999. *The saffron wave: Democracy and Hindu nationalism in modern India*. Princeton, NJ: Princeton University Press.

———. 2008. The political theology of violence in contemporary India. *South Asia Multidisciplinary Academic Journal*. Special issue no. 2: "Outraged communities": Comparative perspectives on the politicization of emotions in South Asia.

Hardiman, David. 1988. Class base of Swaminarayan sect. *Economic and Political Weekly* 23 (37): 1907–1912.

———. 1995 [1987]. *The coming of the devi: Adivasi assertion in Western India.* New Delhi: Oxford University Press.

———. 2003. Passing blame on Godhra Muslims. In *Fascism in India: Faces, fangs and facts,* ed. C. Krishna. New Delhi: Manak Publications.

Harmening, Dieter. 2005. *Wörterbuch des Aberglaubens.* Stuttgart: Philip Reclam.

Hauschild, Thomas. 2002. *Magie und Macht in Italien: Über Frauenzauber, Kirche und Politik.* Gifkendorf: Merlin Verlag.

———. 2008. *Ritual und Gewalt: Ethnologische Studien an Europäischen und Mediterranen Gesellschaften.* Frankfurt am Main: Suhrkamp.

Heath, Jennifer, ed. 2008. *The veil: Women writers on its history, lore, and politics.* Berkeley: University of California Press.

Heesterman, J. C. 1966. Review of Ludwig Alsdorf: Beiträge zur Geschichte von Vegetarismus und Rinderverehrung in Indien. *Indo-Iranian Journal* 9 (2): 147–149.

———. 1984. Non-violence and sacrifice. *Indologica Taurinensia* 12:119–127.

———. 1993. *The broken world of sacrifice.* Chicago: University of Chicago Press.

Heidegger, Martin. 1954. Bauen, wohnen, denken. In *Vorträge und Aufsätze.* Stuttgart: Verlag Günther Neske.

Herzfeld, Michael. 1992. *The social production of indifference: Exploring the symbolic roots of Western bureaucracy.* Chicago: University of Chicago Press.

Hosagrahar, Jyot. 2006. *Indigenous modernities: Negotiating architecture, urbanism, and colonialism.* London: Routledge.

Hsia, Po-chia. 1988. *The myth of ritual murder: Jews and magic in reformation Germany.* New Haven, CT: Yale University Press.

Hubert, Henri, and Marcel Mauss. 1964 [1899]. *Sacrifice: Its nature and functions.* Chicago: Chicago University Press.

Ibrahim, Farhana. 2009. *Settlers, saints and sovereigns: An ethnography of state formation in Western India.* London: Routledge.

Iyer, Krishna, P. B. Sawant, Suresh Hosbet, K. G. Annabiran, Aruna Roy, K. S. Subramanian, Ghanshyam Shah, and Tanika Sarkar. 2003. State complicity. In *Fascism in India: Faces, fangs and facts,* ed. C. Krishna. New Delhi: Manak Publication.

Jaffrelot, Christophe. 1996 [1993]. *The Hindu nationalist movement in India.* New York: Columbia University Press.

———. 2003 [1994]. Opposing Gandhi: Hindu nationalism and political violence. In *Violence/non-violence: Some Hindu perspectives,* ed. D. Vidal, G. Tarabout, and E. Meyer. New Delhi: Manohar.

Jha, Dwijendra Narayan. 2002. *The myth of the holy cow.* New York: Verso.

Kakar, Sudhir. 1978. *The inner world: A psychoanalytic study of childhood and society in India.* New Delhi: Oxford University Press.

———. 1990a. *Intimate relations: Exploring Indian sexuality.* Chicago: Chicago University Press.

———. 1990b. Some unconscious aspects of ethnic violence in India. In *Mirrors of violence,* ed. V. Das. Oxford: Oxford University Press.

———. 1995. *The colours of violence.* New Delhi: Viking Penguin India.

Kapferer, Bruce. 1988. *Legends of people: Myths of state.* Washington: Smithsonian Institution Press.

————. 1997. *The feast of the sorcerer: Practices of consciousness and power.* Chicago: Chicago University Press.

Kaviraj, Sudipta. 1997. Filth and the public sphere: Concepts and practices about space in Calcutta. *Public Culture* 10 (1): 83–113.

Khilnani, Sunil. 1997. *The idea of India.* New Delhi: Penguin Books.

Kolnai, Aurel. 1974 [1929]. Der Ekel. *Jahrbuch für Philosophie und phänomenologische Forschung* 10:515–569.

————. 2007 [1929]. *Ekel, Hochmut, Haß: Zur Phänomenologie feindlicher Gefühle.* Frankfurt am Main: Suhrkamp Taschenbuch.

Kothari, Rita. 2007. *The burden of refuge: The Sindhi Hindus of Gujarat.* Chennai: Orient Longman Private Limited.

Kristeva, Julia. 1982. *Powers of horror: An essay on abjection.* New York: Columbia University Press.

Kumar, Megha. 2009. Communal riots, sexual violence, and Hindu nationalism in post-independence Gujarat (1969–2002). PhD diss., University of Oxford.

Lal, Vinay. 2000. Nakedness, nonviolence, and brahmacharya: Gandhi's experiments in celibate sexuality. *Journal of the History of Sexuality* 9 (1/2): 105–136.

Lefort, Claude. 1986. The political forms of modern society: Bureaucracy, democracy, totalitarianism. In *The political forms of modern society: Bureaucracy, democracy, totalitarianism,* ed. J. Thompson. Cambridge, MA: MIT Press.

Liechty, Mark. 2005. Carnal economies: The commodification of food and sex in Kathmandu. *Cultural Anthropology* 20 (1): 1–38.

Lobo, Lancy, and Biswaroop Das, eds. 2006. *Communal violence and minorities: Gujarat society in ferment.* New Delhi: Rawat Publications.

Lodrick, Deryck. 1981. *Sacred cows, sacred places: Origins and survival of animal homes in India.* Berkeley: University of California Press.

Lokhandwalla. 1955. The Bohras: A Muslim community of Gujarat. *Studia Islamica* (3): 117–135.

Ludden, David, ed. 2006 [1996]. *Contesting the nation: Religion, community and the politics of democracy in India.* Philadelphia: University of Pennsylvania Press.

Lukács, Georg. 1973. *Der junge Hegel: Über die Beziehungen von Dialektik und Ökonomie.* Vol. 1. Frankfurt am Main: Suhrkamp Taschenbuch Wissenschaft.

Macwan, Joseph. 2002. This "unique" land. *Seminar Magazine* no. 513, May. Society under siege: A symposium on the breakdown of civil society in Gujarat. http://www.india-seminar.com/semframe.html (accessed June 1, 2011).

Majumdar, M. R. 1965. *Cultural history of Gujarat.* Bombay: Popular Prakashan.

Makawana, Kishor, ed. 2002. Gusso kem avyo. Ek krodh Hindu. In *Godhra Hatyakand, Kalam no Dharma ane Adharma.* Kishor Rajkot: Pravin Prakashan.

Malamoud, Charles. 1998 [1989]. *Cooking the world: Ritual and thought in ancient India.* Delhi: Oxford University Press.

Malinowski, Bronislaw. 1923. The problem of meaning in primitive languages. In *The Meaning of meaning: A study of influence of language upon thought and of the science of symbolism,* ed. C. K. Ogden and I. A. Richards. New York: Harcourt, Brace and World.

Mallison, Françoise. 1974. La Secte Krichnaîte des Svami-Narayani au Gujarat. *Journal Asiatique* 262 (3/4): 435–471.

Marcuse, Herbert. 2007 [1947]. Feindanalysen: Über die Deutschen. In *Nachgelassene Schriften*, ed. P.-E. Jansen. Hannover: Zu Klampen Verlag.

Marvin, Carolyn, and David Ingle. 1999. *Blood sacrifice and the nation: Totem rituals and the American flag.* Cambridge: Cambridge University Press.

McKean, Lise. 1998 [1996]. Bharat Mata: Mother India and her militant matriots. In *Devi goddesses of India*, ed. J. S. Hawley and D. M. Wulff. New Delhi: Motilal Banarsidass Publishers.

Mehta, Nalin, and Mona Mehta, eds. 2010. *Gujarat beyond Gandhi: Identity, conflict and society.* New Delhi: Routledge.

Mendelsohn, Oliver, and Marika Vicziany. 1998. *The untouchables: Subordination, poverty and the state in modern India.* New York: Cambridge University Press.

Menninghaus, Winfried. 2002 [1999]. *Ekel: Theorie und Geschichte einer starken Empfindung.* Frankfurt am Main: Suhrkamp.

Misra, Satish. 1985. *Muslim communities in Gujarat: Preliminary studies in their history and social organization.* New Delhi: Munshiram Manoharlal Publishers.

Naik, T. B., and G. P. Pandya. 1993. *The Sidis of Gujarat: A socio-economic study and a development plan.* Ahmedabad: Navajivan Mudranalaya.

Nandy, Ashis. 1998a [1980]. At the edge of psychology. In *Exiled at home.* Delhi: Oxford University Press.

———. 1998b [1989]. The intimate enemy: Loss and recovery of self under colonialism. In *Exiled at home.* Delhi: Oxford University Press.

———. 2003 [2002]. Obituary of a culture. In *Fascism in India: Faces, fangs and facts*, ed. K. Chaitanya. New Delhi: Manak Publications.

Nandy, Ashis, Shikha Trivedy, Shail Mayaram, and Achut Yagnik. 1995. *Creating a nationality: The Ramjanmabhumi movement and the fear of the self.* Delhi: Oxford University Press.

Nussbaum, Martha. 2004. *Hiding from humanity: Disgust, shame, and the law.* Princeton, NJ: Princeton University Press.

———. 2007. *The clash within: Democracy, religious violence, and India's future.* Cambridge, MA: Belknap Press.

Obeyesekere, Gananath. 1975. Sorcery, premeditated murder and the canalization of aggression in Sri Lanke. *Ethnology* 14 (1): 1–23.

O'Flaherty, Wendy Doniger. 1973. *Siva: The erotic ascetic.* Oxford: Oxford University Press.

———. 1976. *The origins of evil in Hindu mythology.* Berkeley: University of California Press.

———, ed. 1990 [1988]. *Textual sources for the study of Hinduism.* Chicago: University of Chicago Press.

Oguibénine, Boris. 2003 [1994]. On the rhetoric of violence. In *Violence/nonviolence: Some Hindu perspectives*, ed. D. Vidal, G. Tarabout, and E. Meyer. New Delhi: Manohar.

Opler, Morris. 1958. Spirit possession in rural area of Northern India. In *Reader in comparative religion: An anthropological approach*, ed. W. Lessa and E. Vogt. New York: Row, Peterson and Company.

Osella, Caroline, and Filippo Osella. 2008. Special Issue—Food: Memory, pleasure and politics. *South Asia: Journal of South Asian Studies* 31 (1).

Pandey, Gyanendra. 1990. *The construction of communalism in colonial North India*. New Delhi: Oxford University Press.

———. 1991. In defense of the fragment: Writing about Hindu-Muslim riots in India today. *Representations* 26 (11/12): 559–572.

———. 2006. *Routine violence: Nations, fragments, histories*. Stanford, CA: Stanford University Press.

Parikh, C. D. 1998. *Welfare of the other backward classes in Gujarat state*. Ahmedabad: Navbharat Sahitya Mandir.

Parry, Jonathan. 1985. Death and digestion: The symbolism of food and eating in in North Indian Mortuary Rites. *Man, New Series* 20 (4): 612–630.

Patel, Sujata. 2002. Urbanization, development and communalization of society in Gujarat. In *The other Gujarat*, ed. T. Shinoda. Mumbai: Popular Prakashan.

Patterson, Orlando. 1998. *Rituals of blood: Consequences of slavery in two American centuries*. New York: Basic Civitas.

Pinch, William. 2000. Killing ascetics in Indian history. *Political and Legal Anthropology Review (Polar)* 23 (2): 134–140.

Pocock, David. 1972a. Foreword. In *Mauss, A General Theory of Magic [1902]*. London: Routledge.

———. 1972b. *Kanbi and Patidar: A study of the Patidar community of Gujarat*. Oxford: Clarendon Press.

———. 1973. *Mind, body and wealth: A study of belief and practice in an Indian village*. Oxford: Basil Blackwell.

Prakash, Gyan. 1999. *Another reason: Science and imagination of modern India*. Princeton, NJ: Princeton University Press.

Punwani, Jyoti. 2002a. The carnage at Godhra. In *Gujarat: The making of a tragedy*, ed. S. Varadarajan. New Delhi: Penguin.

———. 2002b. *Dateline Godhra*. Mumbai: Nirbhay Bano Andolan.

Punwani, Ram. 2006. Hindutva's foot soldiers: Dalits, Adivasis? In *Communal violence and minorities: Gujarat society in ferment*, ed. L. Lobo and B. Das. New Delhi: Rawat Publications.

Rajagopal, Arvind. 1999. Thinking through emerging markets: Brand logics and the cultural forms of political society in India. *Social Text* 17 (3): 131–149.

———. 2001. *Politics after television: Hindu nationalisms and the reshaping of the public in India*. Cambridge: Cambridge University Press.

Ramakrishnan, Venkitesh, and Anupama Katakam. 2010. Probing questions. *Frontline Magazine* 27 (5). http://www.hinduonnet.com/fline/fl2705/stories/20100312270503800.htm (accessed June 1, 2011).

Randeria, Shalini. 1989. Carrion and corpses: Conflict in categorizing untouchability in Gujarat. *European Journal of Sociology* 30 (2): 171–191.

Rappaport, Ernest. 1991. The ritual murder accusation: The persistence of doubt and the repetition compulsion. In *The blood-libel legend: A casebook in anti-Semitic folklore*, ed. A. Dundes. Madison: University of Wisconsin Press.

Raychaudhuri, Siddhartha. 1997. Indian elites, urban space, and the restructuring of Ahmedabad city, 1890–1947. PhD diss., University of Cambridge.

———. 2001. Colonialism, indigenous elites and the transformation of cities in the non-Western world: Ahmedabad (Western India), 1890–1947. *Modern Asian Studies* 35 (3): 677–726.

Reik, Theodor. 1975 [1923]. *Der eigene und der fremde Gott: Zur Psychoanalyse der religiösen Entwicklung*. Frankfurt am Main: Suhrkamp Taschenbuch.

Rolland, Roman. 1923. *Mahatma Gandhi*, trans. E. Roniger. Munich: Rotapfel-Verlag.

Sanghavi, Nagindas. 2010. From Navnirman to anti-Mandal riots: The political trajectory of Gujarat (1974–1985). *South Asian History and Culture* 1 (4): 480–493.

Sarkar, Sumit. 1983. *Modern India, 1885–1947*. New Delhi: Macmillan India.

Sarkar, Tanika. 2002. Semiotics of terror: Muslim children and women in Hindu rashtra. In *Fascism in India: Faces, fangs and facts*, ed. K. Chaitanya. New Delhi: Manak Publications.

Savarkar, Vinayak-Damodar. 2005 [1928]. *Hindutva: Who is a Hindu?* New Delhi: Hindi Sahitya Sadan.

Schmidt, Hanns-Peter. 1968. The Origin of Ahimsa. In *Mélanges d'Indianisme a la Mémoire de Louis Renou, Publications de L'Institut de Civilisation Indienne, serie In-8 Fascicule 28*. Paris: Editions E. de Bocard.

Setalvad, Teesta. 2005. Godhra: Crime against humanity. In *Religious politics and communal violence*, ed. S. Wilkinson. New Delhi: Oxford University Press.

Shah, A. M. 2002a. *Exploring India's rural past: A Gujarat village in the early nineteenth century*. Oxford: Oxford University Press.

———. 2002b. For a more humane society. *Seminar Magazine*, no. 513, May. Society under siege: A symposium on the breakdown of civil society in Gujarat. http://www.india-seminar.com/semframe.html (accessed June 1, 2011).

Shah, A. M., and R. G. Shroff. 1958. The Vahivancha Barots of Gujarat: A case of genealogists and mythographers. *Journal of American Folklore* 71 (281): 246–276.

Shah, Ghanshyam. 1975. *Caste association and political process in Gujarat: A study of the Gujarat Kshatriya Sabha*. Bombay: Popular Prakashan.

———. 1993. Tenth Lok Sabha elections and the BJP's victory in Gujarat. In *Communalisation of politics and tenth Lok Sabha elections*, ed. A. A. Engineer and P. Nayak. Delhi: Ajanta Publications.

———. 2002. Direct action in India: A study of Gujarat and Bihar Agitations. In *Social movements and the state*, ed. G. Shah. New Delhi: Sage.

———. 2003a. BJP's rise to power in Gujarat. In *Fascism in India: Faces, fangs and facts*, ed. K. Chaitanya. New Delhi: Manak Publications.

———. 2003b. Caste, Hindutva and hideousness. In *Fascism in India: Faces, fangs and facts*, ed. K. Chaitanya. New Delhi: Manak Publications.

———. 2006. Communalization and participation of Dalits in Gujarat 2002 riots. In *Communal violence and minorities: Gujarat society in ferment*, ed. L. Lobo and B. Das. New Delhi: Rawat Publications.

Shani, Ornit. 2007. *Communalism, caste and Hindu nationalism: The violence in Gujarat*. New York: Cambridge University Press.

Sheikh, Samira. 2010a. *Forging a region: Sultans, traders, and pilgrims in Gujarat, 1200–1500*. New Delhi: Oxford University Press.

———. 2010b. The Lives of Bahuchara Mata. In *The idea of Gujarat: History, ethnography and text*, ed. E. Simpson and A. Kapadia. Hyderabad: Orient Blackswan.

Sheth, Pravin. 1998. *Political development in Gujarat*. Ahmedabad: Karnavati Publications.

Sheth, Pravin, and Ramesh Menon. 1986. *Caste and communal time bomb*. Ahmedabad: Hetvarsha Prakashan.

Siegel, James. 1998. *A new criminal type in Jakarta: Counter-revolution today*. Durham: Duke University Press.

———. 2006. *Naming the witch*. Stanford, CA: Stanford University Press.

Simmel, Georg. 1972 [1918]. Vom Wesen des historischen Verstehens. In *Verstehende Soziologie: Grundzüge und Entwicklungstendenzen*, ed. W. Bühl. Munich: Nymphenburger Verlagshandlung GmbH.

———. 1983 [1903]. Soziologie des Raumes. In *Schriften zur Soziologie: Eine Auswahl*. Frankfurt am Main: Suhrkamp.

———. 1984 [1909]. Brücke und Tür. In *Das Individuum und die Freiheit*. Berlin: Wagenbach.

———. 1989 [1900]. *Philosophie des Geldes*. Frankfurt am Main: Suhrkamp.

———. 1992 [1908] *Soziologie: Untersuchungen über die Formen der Vergesellschaftung*. Vol. 2. Frankfurt am Main: Suhrkamp.

———. 2008 [1903]. Die Großstädte und das Geistesleben. In *Individualismus der modernen Zeit und andere soziologische Abhandlungen*, ed. O. Rammstedt. Frankfurt am Main: Suhrkamp.

Simoons, Frederick. 1979. Questions in the sacred cow controversy. *Current Anthropology* 20 (3): 467–493.

Simpson, Edward. 2008. Why Bhatiyas are not "Banias" and why this matters: Economic success and religious worldview among a mercantile community of western India. In *Divines richesse: Religion et économie en monde marchand indien*, ed. P. Lachaier and C. Clémentin-Ojha. Paris: École française d'Extrême-Orient.

Simpson, Edward, and Aparna Kapadia, eds. 2010. *The idea of Gujarat: History, ethnography and text*. Hyderabad: Orient Blackswan.

Singh, K. S. 2003. People of India: Gujarat. In *The anthropological survey of India*, ed. R. B. Lal, P.B.S.V. Padmanabham, G. Krishnan, and M. A. Mohidden. Mumbai: Popular Prakashan.

Smith, Barry, and Carolyn Korsmeyer, eds. 2004. *On disgust*. Chicago: Open Court.

Smith, Brian. 1990. Eaters, food, and social hierarchy in ancient India: A dietary guide to a revolution of values. *Journal of the American Academy of Religion* no. 2: 177–205.

Smith, William Robertson. 1889. *Religion of the Semites*. London: Adam and Charles Black.

Spencer, Jonathan. 1990a. Collective violence and everyday practice in Sri Lanka. *Modern Asian Studies* 24 (3): 603–623.

———. 1990b. Writing within: Anthropology, nationalism, and culture in Sri Lanka. *Current Anthropology* 31 (3): 283–300.

———. 2007. *Anthropology, politics and the state: Democracy and violence in South Asia*. Cambridge: Cambridge University Press.

Spodek, Howard. 1971. On the origins of Gandhi's political methodology: The heritage of Kathiawad and Gujarat. *Journal of Asian Studies* 30 (2): 361–372.

———. 1989. From Gandhi to violence: Ahmedabad's 1985 riots in historical perspective. *Modern Asian Studies* 23 (4): 765–795.

Staal, Frits. 1983. The Agnicayana project. In *Agni: The Vedic ritual of the fire altar*, ed. F. Staal. Berkeley, CA: Asian Humanities Press.

Stallybrass, Peter, and Allon White. 1986. *The politics and poetics of transgression*. Ithaca, NY: Cornell University Press.

Steiner, Franz Baermann. 1999 [1944]. How to define superstition. In *Taboo, truth, and religion*, ed. J. Adler and R. Fardon. New York: Berghahn Books.

Tambiah, Stanley Jeyaraja. 1992. *Buddhism betrayed? Religion, politics, and violence in Sri Lanka*. Chicago: University of Chicago Press.

———. 1996. *Leveling crowds: Ethnonationalist conflicts and collective violence in South Asia*. Berkeley: University of California Press.

Tambs-Lyche, Harald. 1992. *Power and devotion: Religion and society in Saurashtra*. Bergen: University of Bergen.

———. 1997. *Power, profit, poetry: Traditional society in Kathiawar, Western India*. New Delhi: Manohar.

———. 2004. *The good country: Individual, situation, and society in Saurashtra*. Delhi: Manohar Publishers.

———. 2010. Reflections on caste in Gujarat. In *The idea of Gujarat: History, ethnography and text*, ed. E. Simpson and A. Kapadia. Hyderabad: Orient Blackswan.

Taussig, Michael. 1997. *The magic of the state*. London: Routledge.

Taylor, Christopher. 2002. The cultural face of terror in Rwandan genocide of 1994. In *Annihilating difference: The anthropology of genocide*, ed. A. L. Hinton. Berkeley: University of California Press.

Thakkar, Hirabhai. 2001 [1996]. *Theory of karma*. Ahmedabad: Kusum Prakashan.

Thappar, Romila. 2005. *Somnatha: The many voices of a history*. London: Verso.

Toomey, Paul. 1992. Mountain of food, mountain of love: Ritual inversion in the Annakuta feast at Mount Govardhan. In *Gastronomic ideas and experiences of Hindus and Buddhists*, ed. R. S. Khare. Albany: State University of New York Press.

van der Veer, Peter. 1987. "God must be liberated!": A Hindu liberation movement in Ayodhya. *Modern Asian Studies* 21 (2): 283–301.

———. 1996 [1994]. *Religious nationalism: Hindus and Muslims in India*. New Delhi: Oxford University Press.

———. 1997. Victim's tale: Memory and forgetting in the story of violence. In *Violence, identity, and self-determination*, ed. H. D. Vries and S. Weber. Stanford, CA: Stanford University Press.

Varadarajan, Siddharth, ed. 2002. *Gujarat: The making of a tragedy.* New Delhi: Penguin Books.

Varshney, Ashutosh. 2002. *Ethnic conflict and civic life: Hindus and Muslims in India.* New Haven: Yale University Press.

Vidal, Denis, Gilles Tarabout, and Eric Meyer, eds. 2003 [1994]. *Violence/nonviolence: Some Hindu perspectives.* New Delhi: Manohar.

Weber, Samuel. 2000 [1982]. *The Legend of Freud.* Stanford: Stanford University Press.

Werth, Lukas. 1996. *Von Göttinnen und ihren Menschen: Die Vagri, Vaganten Südindiens,* ed. G. Pfeffer. Berlin: Das Arabische Buch.

Westphal-Hellbusch, Sigrid und Heinz Westphal. 1976a. *Hinduistische Viehzüchter im nord-westlichen Indien.* Vol. 1, *Die Rabari: Forschungen zur Ethnologie und Sozialpsychologie, Band 8,* ed. H. Thurnwald. Berlin: Duncker & Humblot.

———. 1976b. *Hinduistische Viehzüchter im nord-westlichen Indien.* Vol. 2. *Die Bharvad und die Charan: Forschungen zur Ethnologie und Sozialpsychologie, Band 9,* ed. H. Thurnwald. Berlin: Duncker & Humblot.

Williams, Raymond Brady. 2001. *An introduction to Swaminarayan Hinduism.* Cambridge: Cambridge University Press.

Yagnik, Achyut, and Suchitra Sheth. 2005. *The shaping of modern Gujarat: Plurality, Hindutva and beyond.* New Delhi: Penguin Books.

Zavos, John. 2000. *The emergence of Hindu nationalism in India.* Oxford: Oxford University Press.

Žižek, Slavoj. 1993. *Tarrying with the negative.* Durham, NC: Duke University Press.

Index